Principles of Transversality in Globalization and Education

David R. Cole · Joff P. N. Bradley

Editors

Principles of Transversality in Globalization and Education

 Springer

Editors
David R. Cole
School of Education
Western Sydney University
Penrith, NSW
Australia

Joff P. N. Bradley
Teikyo University
Tokyo
Japan

ISBN 978-981-13-0582-5   ISBN 978-981-13-0583-2   (eBook)
https://doi.org/10.1007/978-981-13-0583-2

Library of Congress Control Number: 2018942932

This Springer imprint is published by the registered company Springer Nature Singapore Pte Ltd.
The registered company address is: 152 Beach Road, #21-01/04 Gateway East, Singapore 189721, Singapore

Foreword

The Challenge for Transversality in Education Today

This volume, *Principles of Transversality in Globalization and Education*, presents a challenge to think transversality in a way that is both responsible and liberating; it gives us a transversality for popular emancipation and not for subordination to profit. The stakes of the essays collected within are clear; we might identify two incompatible definitions of this term. While one approach implements a new flexibility, but subordinated to the profit motive and marketable skills, the other promises a radical rethinking of education across the globe. The authors present compelling new theory and practice of liberation, focused around the second option, as well as delimiting our contemporary challenges in education and globalization through practical examples of transversality.

Our moment might seem to be one in which transversality is a broadly accepted method and goal, rather than a subversive or novel proposition. In business management literature, it is now common to call for an end to isolated departments of production and circulation. Institutional silos are considered inefficient, wasteful, and slow; rather, the pressures of a global economy require networks of communication and integration, with the potential for contingent interactions and frequent points of collaboration between groups and individuals with diverse competencies. Management consultants have become experts at reorganization measures around problem-solving, aimed at matters of general import. These consultants invoke transversality as the name for this new form of immanent, networked institutional structure; one in which different departments are not opaque to one another, but rather are capable of diverse and supple modes of interaction.

This new thinking on organization mirrors a transformation in the expected character of the labor force. Rather than training toward a particular specialized skill, labor in the new millennium must be prepared to constantly adapt to new markets and new technologies. Labor is no longer geared toward a fixed outcome or role in the process of production; rather, service and manufacture are intertwined. Different forms of knowledge and the ability to disseminate information are themselves assets or products to be sold or purchased. The leading edge of the economy, as embodied by firms such as Google, Apple, Microsoft, and Amazon, then, appears to act according to an understanding of transversality; their core competencies are dispersed and embedded, rather than localized, fixed, or dependent on a particular resource or purpose. These firms seem to function according to a radical pragmatism; they do business in a zone of potentiality rather than reliance on norms. From this viewpoint, the global marketplace that came into being with the end of the Cold War made way for transversal commerce; commodities can be made anywhere and circulated to anyone, for any purpose.

Education may have lagged behind business, to some degree. However, many thought leaders advocate a transformation toward global education networks, following methods and best practices employed by successful businesses. Some authors have advised a great restructuring, to overcome excessive specialization and old disciplinary barriers. It is believed that universities and other educational institutions could be reorganized to require collaboration across disciplines, organized around problems. In this new framework, flexibility would be placed above permanence; training and learning would draw from multiple sites of research and reflection. From a managerial perspective, then, transversality could be the name for the abolition of inefficient and inaccessible zones of impractical research, and their replacement by webs of interaction aimed at immediate problem-solving. In the contribution collected here, Janell Watson (Chap. 2) offers us a vivid description of this mode of transversality and its limitations.

At first glance, this form of transversality might appear liberating. But, many of us might pause; we might become increasingly suspicious. After all, this reorganization does not take place under conditions of widespread democratic empowerment. To the contrary, the theorists of collaboration and flexibility speak from a position of privilege and with the assurance of the elite. The dissolution of old protocols of research and learning, then, might threaten a liquidation of centuries of our intellectual heritage; the call to collaboration in order to solve general problems seems to carry with it presumptions about what constitutes a "problem" and who might justifiably benefit from its solution. From this viewpoint, we might be tempted to unmask the apparent egalitarianism and potentiality of transversality as another name for neoliberalism; the gutting of any assurances of stability in favor of low-cost contingent labor and the replacement of disinterested inquiry by research geared toward that which is most quickly made profitable.

But what if the concept of transversality were something else entirely than what goes by that name in managerial discourse? Maybe its principles are not best understood as a form of managerial restructuring toward the goal of efficiency; maybe it is something freely created from the experience of humans before their disciplining by the workplace. Further, maybe transversality is an aspect inherent to the nature of learning itself, rather than a new buzzword to describe a process of adaptation to the market. Félix Guattari, the first author to speak of transversality in the context of education, believed this.

According to Guattari, transversality undoes vertical hierarchies or pyramids, in which power is concentrated at the top and by which those placed lower in the hierarchy are increasingly less autonomous. Naturally, then, this counters the presumption that education is a process of the transmission of knowledge from some people who know and understand the means of knowing, toward others who are initially ignorant and lack the means to overcome this ignorance. Further, it conflicts with the belief that some cultures or nations are most advanced in their economic and social understanding, while others remain mired in traditions and tasked with catching up to those ahead of them. For these reasons, Guattari's transversality is very different from the most widespread understandings of contemporary globalization and education reform, which share his interest in the decentralized, the contingent, and the pragmatic, but maintain the priority of the nation-states of core economies and the privileges of the wealthy.

Guattari's insistence on transversality was aimed at the creation of new collectivities that would avoid alienation into hierarchies of obedience or the subordination of creativity to commodification. In his elaboration, a non-alienating education would require a network of reflexivity in which participants would work and think together. Moreover, this network—contrary to the neoliberal formulation—would avoid organizing the horizon of its inquiries around that which is marketable or which can be sold. And further, a transversal collective of education needs to establish consistency and functionality, avoiding a tendency to dissolve into inaction, lethargy, or chaos. The transversal acts against the commercialization of learning, as well as against the unthinking replication of past activity. Rather than accountability to profit, transversality has a different type of responsibility. As Guattari developed it, the understanding of the intertwined interactions of all the elements of our situation requires an ecological point of view. A true education, then—one in which we learn about our place in the world, what we know about it, and how to act in it—requires not just cross-cultural communication but understanding of the natural world and its potential and activity beyond human consciousness or practice.

This form of transversality, then, is not widespread, but rather might seem to be quite marginal, something in short supply. The drive toward flexibility in service of profit mirrors some transversal principles, in that it calls for collaboration, but it obscures and destroys the possibility for a broader and more consistent thinking or acting along transversal lines. It is heartening, then, to find a volume that provides such a rich resource on not only the conceptual underpinnings of transversality but a record of varied and provocative experiments, around the world today. We find a series of striking cases that help us to reflect on Guattari's own activities—in France, Italy, Brazil, and elsewhere—but also on original experiences that emulate or invite comparison with his discoveries.

I think the experience of the Zapatistas, in Chiapas, perhaps makes most clear the incompatibility between Guattari's transversality and the neoliberal application of the same term (Chap. 10). Management consultants and education reformers today call for efficiency, speed, and disruption. Their mindset calls for just-in-time production; the needs of the future cannot be known in advance, so students and teachers must be entirely flexible, adapting to immediate needs. Traditional skills, from this perspective, are not worthwhile; we must all become digital natives, entirely at home with the newest tools and without nostalgia for what came before. In their essay, included in this volume, Mark LeVine and Brian Reynolds show that the Zapatistas constitute a stubborn obstacle to all of this. While they make use of contemporary communications technology, they do so according to their own needs and desires, rather than those of the market. They refuse to be hurried by the expectations of core economic powers. They decide, collectively, the tools and the knowledge that is best suited to their existence and creativity, and their continuing interaction with the ecology that sustains them and with which they communicate. This is a transversality that we can learn from, and that impedes our exploitation.

Principles of Transversality in Globalization and Education is a vital contribution to discussion of the philosophy of education today, particularly with regard to transnational comparison and experience. Contributors help us learn from events in North America, Hong Kong, Japan, Australia, Iran, and elsewhere. It will be of great use to anyone reflecting on the role of the university, the social conditions of education, and the interaction between technology and the classroom. We can hope to discover in its pages a transversality worthy of the name, and the reader will no doubt link the experiences here to his or her own life and work.

Fort Worth, TX, USA   Andrew Ryder
                                                     John V. Roach Honors College
                                                        Texas Christian University

Preface

This book comes as a follow up to the 2016 edited volume, *Super Dimensions in Globalization and Education*, edited by David R. Cole and Christine Woodrow, and also published by Springer. In this volume, a connection was established between globalization and education through the so-called super dimensions, which were an extension and combination of superdiversity and supercomplexity. Rather than a developmental or solely empirical approach to understanding how globalization works in specific educational contexts, the super dimensions offer a theorized account of what globalization does in and through education. However, even though this theorization was satisfying and to an extent gives educationalists a rigorous new framework to work with, there was a question of the agency and hence any activism that might result from recognizing and understanding the super dimensions in education. Hence, a second volume was proposed that puts to work Guattari's notion of transversality that precisely moves the argument on from recognizing and working with the super dimensions to doing something about them. Guattari's ideas are complex, yet we face a complex situation, and anything more straightforward would be easily swallowed up, regurgitated, and repackaged as the latest in learning enhancement. That is the opposite aim to the editors and the authors in this book.

All chapters in this book have been double-blind reviewed and separately reviewed by both the editors. David R. Cole would like to thank Prof. Michele Simons at Western Sydney University for giving him dedicated time to complete this important text, and Joff P. N. Bradley would like to thank his students at Teikyo University for acting as his transversal experimental subjects.

Penrith, Australia

Tokyo, Japan

David R. Cole

Joff P. N. Bradley

'Guattari's notion of 'transversality' that dates from 1964 that famously emphasises a micro-physics of desire in a material semiology that predates the discourse on globalization. Now for the first time in educational theory Cole and Bradley's collection spells out Principles of Transversality in Globalization and Education in lucid and imaginative terms.'

—Michael A. Peters, *Professor, University of Waikato*

'Editors Cole and Bradley have assembled a ground breaking collection of essays by international luminaries on the ways in which Guattarian transversality remaps educational theory and practice that will become a touchstone for a new generation of critical educators.'

—Gary Genosko, *University of Ontario Institute of Technology*

'An important collection of essays that not only illustrate the brilliance of Felix Guattari's mind and the importance of his work (independent of his better known collaborator Gilles Deleuze), but also make an important contribution to the study of global education trends and practices. A valuable text for both students and researchers.'

—Ian Buchanan, *Founding Editor of Deleuze and Guattari Studies*

'This collection of essay is essential reading for anyone interested in the philosophy of education: drawing on some of the most exciting theoretical ventures of the twenty-first century these thoughtful essays provide new ways of thinking about what transversality might mean in challenging learning environments. To think, teach and learn through the concept of the transversal is to be open to new imaginations of the globe, the self and—most importantly—the generation of relations.'

—Claire Colebrook, *Professor of English, Penn State University*

'This boundary-crossing collection of essays illuminates, explores and in some way also explodes the notion of transversality, from a range of thematic and inter-disciplinary angles. Systematic in its meta-methodological approach, this is a brilliantly timed intervention on what education is capable of becoming. An inspiring read.'

—Rosi Braidotti, *Distinguished University Professor, Utrecht University*

Contents

1   **Principles of Transversality in Globalization and Education**   1
David R. Cole and Joff P. N. Bradley

Part I   Universities, Transversality and the Future

2   **The Transversal Campus: Open Black Box?**   19
Janell Watson

3   **Wild Studios: Art, Philosophy, and the Transversal University** . . .   31
Gray Kochhar-Lindgren and Kanta Kochhar-Lindgren

4   **A Transversal University? Criticality, Creativity and Catatonia
in the Globalised Pursuit of Higher Education Excellence**   47
Christian Beighton

Part II   Transversality, Education and Becoming

5   **On Philosophical and Institutional "Blinkers": SOAS and
Transversal Worldviews**   67
Joff P. N. Bradley

6   **The Incorporeal Universe of Childhood in the Tactical
Pedagogies of Félix Guattari and Tanigawa Gan**   83
Toshiya Ueno

7   **Towards a Pedagogy of Immanence: Transversal Revolts Under
Neoliberal Capitalism**   97
Hans Skott-Myhre, Veronica Pacini-Ketchabaw and Luke Kalfleish

**Part III   Transversal Movements Across International Educative
             Borders**

**8   Transversality, Constraint and Desire in Australian and Iranian
      Classrooms** 117
      David R. Cole and Mehri Mirzaei Rafe

**9   Transversal Resettlement Transitions: Young Refugees
      Navigating Resettlement in Greater Western Sydney** 131
      Mohamed Moustakim and Karin Mackay

**10 Fugitive Pedagogy: Guattari's Ecosophy in the Mural Discourse
      of the Zapatistas** 149
      Mark LeVine and Bryan Reynolds

**Part IV   Further Issues in Transversality, Education and
            Globalization**

**11 *Alice's Adventures*: Reconfiguring Solidarity in Early Childhood
      Education and Care Through Data Events** 175
      Susan Naomi Nordstrom, Camilla Eline Andersen, Jayne Osgood,
      Ann-Hege Lorvik-Waterhouse, Ann Merete Otterstad
      and Maybritt Jensen

**12 The Ontological Plurality of Digital Voice: A Schizoanalysis of
      Rate My Professors and *Rate My Teachers*** 195
      Eve Mayes

13 Schizoanalysis, Counselling Praxis and a Sandbox Dirge 211
      Jeff Smith and Scott Kouri

14 *Afterword: Zhibo*, Existential Territory, *Inter-Media-Mundia* 227
      Joff P. N. Bradley and David R. Cole

Index 245

Chapter 1
Principles of Transversality in Globalization and Education

David R. Cole and Joff P. N. Bradley

Abstract This chapter sets out the principles of transversality in globalization and education that underpin the contributions in this book. These principles are derived from the *oeuvre* of the French theorist and activist, Félix Guattari. For too long, Guattari has been overshadowed by his co-author, Gilles Deleuze, with whom he wrote four major works, as well as publishing at least a dozen or more on his own or with other authors. Furthermore, Guattari did not lead the life of an isolated scholar, or reclusive academic. Indeed, he traveled extensively to Brazil, Japan, Poland, and Mexico, for example, and made it plain that he wanted his theories to work practically and in real situations, to really make a difference. There is then a political, social, and applied edge to Guattari's transversality that makes it absolutely relevant to the many ways in which globalization impinges upon and can negatively transform educational practice today. Even though Guattari was writing between the 1960s and 1990s, it is the conviction of this book that the principles that can be derived from his concept of transversality are timely, critical, and in need of extensive exploration and elaboration in order to make inroads into the unfolding, contemporary global educational landscape. In sum, it is argued in this chapter that Guattari's transversality could be included in the central theoretical architecture of the field of globalization studies in education, due to the crucial link to activism which it provides.

Keywords Transversality · Globalization · Education · Guattari

Introduction

As soon as one enters an official place of learning such as an early learning center, school, college, training center, or university, vertical lines of power relationships

D. R. Cole (✉)
Western Sydney University, Penrith 2750, Australia
e-mail: david.cole@westernsydney.edu.au

J. P. N. Bradley
Teikyo University, Tokyo, Japan

© Springer Nature Singapore Pte Ltd. 2018
D. R. Cole and J. P. N. Bradley (eds.), *Principles of Transversality in Globalization and Education*, https://doi.org/10.1007/978-981-13-0583-2_1

1

are immediately apparent. These lines of power have been defined in advance by pre-designated roles from the top down and the organization that keeps the institute functioning. Further, these vertical lines of power are re-enforced through educational policy documents, curricula structures, learnt knowledge, examinations, social mores, and the very habits, beliefs, and unconscious thoughts about the vertical educative dimension. One may argue that this dimension has been eroded by access to instantaneous information, smart phones, and the preference for 'street-smarts' to make money over formal knowledge; however, one cannot deny that the vertical dimension in education still exists. Perpendicular to the vertical dimension in education is the horizontal dimension of peer groups, friendship, ad hoc gatherings, camaraderie, community work, and other lateral connections that, for example, inquiry-based learning, group work, or play can encourage in teaching and learning situations. Cole has argued elsewhere that these two often clashing dimensions can be addressed in education through the construction of a two-role model of affect (Cole, 2011) and effective communication between these dimensions. In this book, the dimension of transversality from Guattari (2015) is introduced in the analysis of education throughout the chapters, and this new direction acts as a non-vertical and non-horizontal plane through which the forces of globalization can be mapped and redirected.

Globalization assails and transforms education multi-dimensionally through the current dominance of global capitalism as a one-world system (Cole & Woodrow, 2016). Teaching and learning in the context of global capitalism are procedures to reroute and work with capital, which flows through educative situations as: 'edu-debt' (Cole, 2013), qualifications to apply for jobs, learning products which are sold to educational providers, such as the latest in ICT teaching and learning innovation, and educative fads in the field such as 'managerial leadership,' 'financial literacy,' and 'collaborative teamwork' that primarily serve the corporatization and monetary standardization of the world. It is against this backdrop that we pit Guattari's 'transversality,' which can be defined for the purposes of this book as:

> … a dimension opposite and complementary to the structures that generate pyramidal hierarchisation … this dimension can only be seen clearly in certain groups which, intentionally or otherwise, try to explore the meaning of their praxis and establish themselves as subject groups. (Guattari, 1984, p. 23)

The transversality of and in groups is importantly not reducible to its membership or purpose, nor is it a mechanism by which some new form of social capital is concentrated, but, rather, is an expression of the 'extractions' from the heterogeneous levels at which it operates and the interchanges and inquiries that it enables: in effect, the transverse group both 'hears and is heard' (Guattari, 1984, p. 14). Guattari (1984, 2015) describes how such groups are frequently created in institutional lacunae and interstices, and often in response to uncertainties or ambiguities in policy or practice. Unlike working parties, consultation panels, or other organizational forms with circumscribed remits, limited time frames, and predetermined roles and responsibilities, the transversal subject group is self-directing and reflexive: 'Transversality' as such involves continued inquiry into one's own role and those of others in the group, as well as that of the overall directions being taken by the 'subject group' that is no longer subjugated. In contrast to other kinds of collectivities which do not question their own existence, the transverse group 'keeps asking whether it is right, whether it should be totally transforming itself, correcting its aim, and so on' (Guattari, 1984, p. 39). Guattari (1984, 2015) cautions against the tendency to create new hierarchies and elites to replace established 'group phantasies,' and also warns of the dangers of falling back into lateral associations in which the main purpose of the group is the mutual reinforcement of 'togetherness' or some kind of 'faux' ideal collegiality (cf. Biesta, 2011). As such, the formation of group subjects through transversality runs throughout this book as a combinational and moving material process and works against the subjugation under capital in and as part of globalized educational units. To explicate and make these subject groups function effectively in the context of globalization and education, one may formulate four basic principles for transversality in globalization and education that guide the unfolding empirical and theoretical nature of this book, and that are taken up by different authors in their own ways.

Principle One: Capitalism Uncovered

Since the 1990s and through creative deployment of the concepts from Deleuze and Guattari (1984, 1988) there has been a concerted, growing, and well-researched effort to oppose the takeover of education by the forces of globalization, as pertaining to the processes of capitalism (e.g., Carlin & Wallin, 2014). This collective of thinkers and ideas has complemented the incursion of critical theorists *contra* capitalist norms inspired by Marx (1887) and, for example, draws on resources from the Italian autonomists, continental philosophy, and relevant scientific, social, informational, cultural, and cognitive theories to disavow the hold of capital on reality. These entwined research and thought processes are part of a combined research project to uncover the many ways in which capitalism has taken over and redefined collective practices such as education, and has left in its wake a hollowed out and alienating experience, serving principally to make money (Marazzi, 2011). As an additional, post-psychoanalytic approach to liberatory anti-capitalist educational thinkers such as Paulo Freire (1970), the application of Guattari's transversality to the takeover of education by capitalism, acts as a thoroughgoing 'detection device'; it is a 'probe-head' to the many, complex ways in which teaching and learning are now an integral part of the circuits of economic power and their consequent psychic controls. For example, educational theory and practice via Guattari would rethink Freire's (1970) challenge of liberating education in relation to the emergence of economic formations via the subjective power of 'love' and thus avoid the analytic failure being perpetrated by those capitalist forces that have resituated the globalized problem of the social squarely upon the object of education, its structures, and its organization (Guattari, 2009b). Rather than seeking out new ways of altering the role of the teacher and lecturer or the attitudes of students, i.e., in treating the problems caused by globalization *in* education *as* educational/psychological/personal, one could argue that the task for this book in the arena of globalization and education, and that deploys Guattari's transversality purposefully, involves the explicit elucidation of how the social functions in order to bring about discernible changes in the first place (Guattari, 2009a, b).

For example, students may be alienated by the impersonal and clearly unfair ways in which capitalism redirects resources socially, in terms of those at the top of the pile going to elite private schools and progressing to even more elite, well-resourced universities, and who become integral to the next capitalized rulers of that society. Instead of taking a straightforward, Marxian approach to alienation based on the intersubjectivity of humans (Marx, 1887), Guattarian transversality identifies alien-ation as a 'system attribute,' and as a more literal, 'alien'-ation, that has been built into the very machines in and through history, via group and collective subjuga-tion, and through and by which we now function as a 'machine-whole' society. This is why it is not enough to simply establish oneself in a fixed political position in terms of standing up to and opposing the ways in which capitalism works to dis-criminate, subjugate, and empty relations of their essence and fixity (e.g., McLaren, 1998). Guattarian transversality looks to continuously open up new dimensions to the effects of capitalism on education as elsewhere, a process that Cole has called 'super dimensions' in terms of the multifarious paths through which globalization impinges upon and transforms educational practice in a complex, often context-inspired, and in many ways personal, affective manner (Cole & Woodrow, 2016). The Guattarian approach to uncovering capitalism in these processes is to draw maps of changing, entwined practices (Guattari, 2011, 2013), which in this book are represented by the different globalized educational topics under investigation in each chapter. In terms of the axioms that underpin this writing, the Guattarian perspective reveals a particular mode of subjectivity, which is best suited to carrying out and performing such a research project.

Principle Two: Only Our (Multiple)Sel(ves) Remain

One could state that the continual searching, checking, and acting upon capitalist influence by globalization in education is in itself an exhausting and probably not too obviously rewarding activity. Guattari himself traveled extensively (e.g., Guattari & Rolnik, 2008) and sought out evidence of this capitalist influence, what he termed as 'Integrated World Capitalism' (IWC) in different parts of the world. His studies included inquiry into colonization theory, and the rights of indigenous populations under globalization, as well as attending to gender, class, poverty, and other equity and cultural issues usually addressed in the sociology of education (e.g., Urry, 2000) such as access to knowledge in a mobile society. The difference that Guattari and transversality make in this field is that his model is not a straightforward, squared, simply liberatory, or critical approach to these problems. In consequence, transver-sality requires a new angle on data, theory, and practice, and it is cartographic in order to enact this continually new approach and cannot be caught in oscillatory or moralistic dualisms between good and bad, right and wrong, left and right. Rather, Guattari accepts and promulgates the social as and through 'the phylum' or technological lineage and 'the machinic'; in effect, he reversed Latour's interpretation of Tarde (Latour, 2002), and instead of dissolving 'the social' amidst the chaos and flux of how things come together and function (both human and non-human), he interprets the social as the fundamental problematic to be addressed (e.g., Guattari, 2011, 2013). In this light, he came up with a malleable and multiple notion of the self that reflected and augmented his political activism and militancy, often in the light of overwhelming capitalist odds, and, for example, 'the pathology of reason' (Guattari, 2009b, p. 288), which is unable to respond cartographically.

However, there is no straightforward going back to a pre-capitalist, healed, animist self in Guattari, which is completely filled with immanence, in touch with and moved by the natural forces of the world. Rather, this book, under the influence of Guattari's transversality, could be figured as the fight for liberation from what assails us through the combined ways in which globalization seizes and redirects social and educational matters (Buroway et al., 2000) in everyday practice. The social is not an ideal problematic for Guattari, but is crisscrossed by combinatory, machinic, and natural forces; as a result, the Guattarian 'social' is somewhat strange, contingent, unlikely, and surprising. The multiple selves that inhere as relating to the social are not spontaneously turned into ideal functioning communities through the application of Guattari's transversality, or define any sense of human exceptionalism (Haraway, 2016). Rather, their potential for movement, combination, synthesis, and political militancy may be realized through transversality as enhanced and subtle movements, combinations, synthesizes, and political militancies. Educational systems and innovations that have deployed strategies and tactics taken from Guattari and other collaborators at the La Borde clinic in France such as Fernand Oury, who was the creator of the 'institutional pedagogy' movement, show definite gains, educational autonomy, and an increase in what may be called 'community inquiry', seen, for example, on a large scale in Finland (MoE, Finland, 2009), whose education system was inspired by Célestin Freinet's Modern School Movement, and which influenced both Guattari and Oury. An important aspect of these positive educational offshoots and forerunners of Guattari's experimental procedure of transversality is a concern for writing, and a mode of writing that importantly deals with the multiple ways in which we are conditioned, herded, and drained of imagination in the current moment. This is explained in the next section through semiotics.

Principle Three: *We Are Deluded by Semiotics*[1]

There are colossal monuments to the current state of globalization, such as the Hamad International Airport in Doha. This enormous construction, funded by the fossil fuel revenue of Qatar, is a shiny and clean, hyper-commercial, high-tech 'hub' for international travelers and business. At its heart, there is a gigantic screen, which transmits on a loop, a depiction of an ideal family, all with a light skin color, but Middle Eastern and elegant in appearance, and who enjoy the benefits of a privileged lifestyle, such as a luxury car, house, foreign holidays, and an elite, agreeable education for their children in a friendly, well-resourced international school. In this one, continuous, soft-focused narrative, all the varied aspects of Integrated World Capitalism (IWC) come together according to Guattari (Guattari, 2009a). Chaos and change have been arrested and replaced by the stasis of an ideal, prosperous, capitalized life; this is a uniform semiotic regime at its most pernicious and decisive. Poverty, philosophy, nature, and anti-capitalism have been extinguished and banished in this non-place. Capital is flowing everywhere through its nexus, creating meanings, imaginings, images, and tips on how (and how not) to lead one's life; Guattari (1996a, b) counters this with the only possible response, an 'a-signifying' semiotics, which is a theory of meaning-making devoid of signification, and that therefore 'flows' between nodules of analysis, such as the zenith of fossil capitalism in Doha, or the high-tech education system of South Korea, which is orchestrated by Samsung, and some have tied into helping to produce one of the highest suicide rates in the world (Berardi, 2014).

Guattari was influenced in the 1970s by abstractions in socio-linguistics (e.g., Hjelmslev, 1953) that looked to explain how signs and symbols circulate and move in society, and anticipated much of the discourse and semiotic analysis work in globalization and education studies to come (Hodge & Kress, 1988). This has attended to the ways in which global, business-related linguistic matters, usually mediated by the profit code and transmitted in English, have taken over local and unique methods of speaking and thinking. In the current situation, with constant pressure from international learning companies to use their textbooks, methods, and digital products (Hogan, Sellar & Lingard, 2015), Guattari's a-signifying semiotics and the way that it has been applied (Genosko, 2008) act as an escape route from the global commercial dogfight for a market share in educational businesses, and the resultant homogenization that this implies. The point here is to retain a plane, consistently called 'the transversal' throughout this book, that enables and performs on the level of avoiding and defying the commercialization of the learning process. The manipulation of Guattari's a-signifying semiotics in education points to the fact that language learning is not just about picking up linguistic cues, becoming communicably competent, or functioning on a linguistic level in social situations in a target language (Cole & Bradley, 2014), but includes the incorporation of signs and symbols on a deep, unconscious level, that act as 'order words' and that perform

---

[1] Semiotics is one of the key drivers for Guattari's theoretical analysis of capitalism, and, in particular, how one may be deceived by the practice.

'incorporeal transformations' (Deleuze & Guattari, 1988, pp. 75–110), which means that things/words and actions get mixed up and redistributed according to specific power dimensions. The dominant power of globalization worldwide is encapsulated by and through capitalism, which is therefore the focus of the Guattarian transversal synthesis, and which Guattari consistently attended to in terms of an ecological unraveling of the ways in which capitalism assails and deludes us through semiotics.

Principle Four: *The Move to Eco-Revolution*

The Anthropocene had not been named during the period when Guattari was writing, but the ecological effects of human activity were apparent, and Guattari was a pioneer in terms of understanding the ways in which humans and nature interacted, and the ramifications of this interaction (Guattari, 1996b). Deleuze and Guattari (1984, 1988) are often attributed with attending to the dualisms that have been forced upon us by and through Western metaphysics such as the mind/body, culture/nature, or good/evil by constructing a viable 'middle' to these potentially alienating opposites. In contrast, the monist line out of Deleuze and Guattari, that was inspired by Spinoza, and the notion of nature as a machine, was strategically investigated by Guattari in terms of understanding how social change can be enacted while accounting for the chaotic forces of nature and the machinic becomings that could be said to drift through us like flux (Guattari, 2009b). Theorists such as Jane Bennet (2010) have mobilized concepts from Guattari such as the 'material vagabond,' 'affect,' and 'the assemblage,' to enable on her terms a 'political ecology' that 'recasts the self in the light of its intrinsically polluted nature and in so doing recasts what counts as self-interest' (Bennett, 2010, p. 115). Bennett's 'vital materialism' owes much to Guattari's ecologically driven, transversal formulations, in that social change on these terms is now dependent on the realization of the full environmental impact of human activity. In this book, and expressed as a new dimension in thought, social change combined with environmental care is encapsulated in and by the term 'transversality.' This singular realization is manifest not only as protest against the vast anthropological, environmental disaster that is underwritten by economic progress, but by the timescale in which we now sit.

There is an urgency to Guattari's writings from the 1960s to his death in the early 1990s that shows that he understood how economic progress and environmental catastrophe for humans were on a collision course (e.g., 1996b). It was not perhaps until the Nobel Prize-winning chemist, Paul Crutzen, popularized the term the Anthropocene as a wakeup call to the amount of CO_2 that human activity was putting into the atmosphere (2002) that the environmental impacts movement went from a fringe-dwelling lobby group to a mainstream aspect of any political party with a social or environmental agenda. Yet still, any move to a greener future has to directly contend with the stark realism of economic exchange, and the global politics that backs it up. In the main, populations do not want to or cannot pay for increased energy bills. Coal-fired power stations continue to be built to produce baseload energy. Oil reserves are being exploited without any signs of slowing up (Newell & Paterson, 2010). In sum, the authors of this book believe that Guattari's transversality has the power to work on every level from the micro to the global, to help change the direction of the current eco-catastrophic situation, and one of the most likely vehicles for social change is one connected to the environmental movement *through and in education* as theory, policy, and practice. Perhaps it will come too late, but at least by collectively aiming at the transversal connections between globalization and education (in its most literal sense)—this publication can push for ecological movement in a new, transversal direction.

The Chapters of the Book

The fourteen chapters of the book have been designed to establish a connection between the four principles in transversality, globalization, and education, as listed above, and empirical studies in the field that enable a relation between the principles and the real and practical world of educational action. As such, transversality is both a basis for action and participation, and further research and reflection; further, this book itself works transversally to make maps of what education is and what it will become given the impingement of the forces of globalization. We believe that these aims are in keeping with the beliefs of Guattari himself, whose ethico-aesthetic paradigm consistently linked high-end, experimental theorization with practical applications on spheres of social and cultural production, such as in education. We do not buy into the notion of theory being for its own sake, or praxis devoid of theory. Rather, it is suggested that through transversality, the rush to apply theory to practice can be avoided, and praxis can be rethought through theory. In sum, the chapters of this book are as much for practitioners as for educational theorists; they are for anyone interested in moving the field along, and not becoming stuck in continual redesignations of global yesterdays. Transversality is not the only way to wed theory to practice in education, and vice versa, but it is an important route to enabling consistent activism in the face of an increasingly homogenized capitalist shutdown of alternative modes of thought. Each chapter deals with the principles above in its own way, reconfiguring transversality depending upon the specific work that they want the chapter to achieve.

Part I: *Universities, Transversality, and the Future*

The first section of the book involves the future of higher education, and, in particular, universities. The three chapters offered in this section take different approaches to understanding how transversality works in the context of globalization and education. In the first instance, Janell Watson notices the correspondence between trendy university administrators, and their designation of new higher education learning spaces as being 'transversal,' and the transversality of Guattari (2015), which he worked out at the La Borde institute. Of course, after the recognition of the same name designation, that is where the similarities between Guattari's transversality and the transversal classrooms of the new learning spaces effectively end. Guattari's transversality is steeped in radical educational and psychological experimentation, and in political militancy to anything which might try and curb such experimentation. In contrast, the transversal design of new learning spaces in universities is backgrounded by attending to learning outcomes, enhanced pedagogic performance, the profit motive, and the full integration of ICT with teaching and learning. One of the exciting aspects of Watson's chapter is that she takes on this difference between Guattari and new collaborative learning space design in terms of applying the cybernetic notion of black boxes to these problematics; i.e., we can understand inputs and outputs of both systems, but there will always be a part of the learning process which is internal to a black box and therefore out of sight. Watson concludes by stating that universities are now dominated by assessment and control, and that the experience of real transversality in the radical mode of Guattari is an increasingly rare and privileged event.

It is precisely this rare and privileged event which Gray Kochhar-Lindgren and Kanta Kochhar-Lindgren describe in Chap. 3. This exciting work imagines and depicts from their own experimental practice and experience: 'Wild Studios'. In contrast to educational theory which accepts the status quo, this chapter takes us on an incredible journey through the possibility of an open, transversal, arts-based practice for universities, which is not co-opted by global capitalism and its demands. This chapter shows how Guattari's transversality could be purposefully deployed to challenge the norms and everyday working of the university as it is currently conceived and enacted. This is truly a conception of the future of the university, and what it could become if a theorist such as Guattari is redesignated to be at the heart of its rationale and functioning, and transversal arts practice takes a central role in what a university does. The last chapter in this section attends to the rhetoric and often false claims that now are proposed as headlines for the activities of universities. Christian Beighton approaches these statements through a new synthesis of Guattari's transversality and Deleuze's (1994) ontological difference as theorized in *Difference and Repetition*. Beighton argues that globalization contains the trends of prosumption, liquefaction, and 'dividualisation,' which are manifest in the functioning of higher education today. This chapter proposes that the new onto-transversal synthesis provides a link between the critique of what universities now say they do, the realities of the forces of globalization, and how they work in higher education today.

Part II: *Transversality, Education, and Becoming*

Section II extends the transversal analysis of universities into powerful, concrete trends in education and becoming. Joff PN Bradley outlines how transversality works in the context of a report about racism at the School of Oriental and African Studies. While the report sketches the continuing legacies of colonialization and racism in the UK, it also paints an uncompromising picture of 'white privilege' and how it still operates in the academy. Bradley suggests that the mobilization of Guattari's transversality in this context is more than an equalizing or philosophical underpinning to social justice and/or anti-colonialization, but could be used for a new philosophy of education, which is fundamentally future-orientated and interdisciplinary. Bradley contrasts Guattari's transversality axioms with the ideas of the American–Korean philosopher, Hwa Yol Jung, whose transversal phenomenology presents a means to extend transversality into a new transversal curriculum. Through this new transversal curriculum, Bradley believes that theorists and practitioners can challenge the status quo in terms of how globalization currently works in and through education. Bradley takes us on a sophisticated, alternative, transversal journey by confronting and questioning what globalization looks like, as it seizes and manipulates learning subjects and objects in education. In the next chapter, Toshiya Ueno extends Bradley's analysis by looking at the question of childhood in the context of transversality and the Japanese theorist and activist, Tanigawa Gan. Gan was a post-war Japanese intellectual who became an activist to try and maintain the 'poetry of life' through the establishment of micro-group circles. Ueno looks at what Guattari takes from childhood, and how the spontaneous, lateral, joy-filled days of childhood are potentially drained of this particular energy, as the adult responsibilities of modern life are indicted into children through pedagogy as work. As such, Ueno argues that Guattari and Gan present a means to avoid the stifling seriousness of adult life in learning, as they are continually seeking the life principle manifest in childhood and frequently lost by the adult. Ueno argues that the transference of the energies of childhood into pedagogy through notions such as transversality and the circle groups is a tactical means to explore a new mode of becoming, which defies and subverts the monotonous and repetitive conditioning of globalization.

This section finishes with Hans Skott-Myhre, Veronica Pacini-Ketchabaw, and Lucas Kalfleish's, Towards a Pedagogy of Immanence: Transversal Revolts under Neo-Liberal Capitalism. The authors suggest that by strategically examining a UNESCO report that deploys the term transversality in a framework for emerging markets, Guattari's use of the term can be separated out and act as a guide to working other than the dictates of neoliberal capitalism in the current moment. Through careful theorization of Guattari's transversality in relation to the effects of neoliberalism on the unconscious and pedagogy, this hopeful chapter looks to return to Guattari in order to steer a way out of the dismal ideology of relating everything to the market. The authors offer two fully theorized provocations to exemplify and stimulate thought with respect to how transversality works with respect to pedagogy and the unconscious. They suggest that defiance of neoliberal norms starts in early childhood and needs to carry on throughout one's educational life.

Part III: *Transversal Movements Across International Educative Borders*

Globalization, as the name suggests, is an international process that does not respect international borders. In the first chapter, David R. Cole and Mehri Mirzaei Rafe contrast the educational systems in Australia and Iran using transversality. Interestingly, Iran has, to an extent, been sheltered from the last 40 years of globalization, due to the sanctions imposed on it since the 1979 Islamic Revolution. In contrast, Australia is fully in the grip of globalization, being connected to global markets through numerous mechanisms. The Iranian educational system has undergone Islamic reform since 1979, whereas the Australian system has made reforms according to neoliberal agendas enshrined in and by free market economics. Cole and Mirzaei Rafe show how Guattari's transversality is a vital concept in this context, by foregrounding the notions of desire and constraint in this comparative analysis of two systems. This chapter shows how the deployment of transversality can open up international educational study to the benefit of the analyst, educationalist, and activist. In the second chapter of this section, Mohamed Moustakim and Karin Mackay examine the transversal stories of migrant youth resettling in Western Sydney, Australia. Transversality operates here both to open up and allow for the complicated stories of the migrants to become pertinent to the theorization of their educational progress, and as a research paradigm in terms of interpreting and working with these stories. This chapter charts a year-long research program, through and in which the researchers and migrants shared their stories through art, discourse, and online means, and in the process, enhanced their sense of community and collective becoming. Moustakim and Mackay became fully involved with the migrants' stories in a transversal manner, which represents a redistribution and realignment of the lines of power and has the potential to challenge our notions of resettlement, research, learning, and migration.

Lastly in this section, Mark LeVine and Bryan Reynolds relate a fascinating research project that investigated the pedagogy of the Zapatista movement in Mexico. LeVine and Reynolds argue that the murals of the Zapatistas are a living representation of Guattari's educational principles, and through careful theorization, proceed to explain why. The Zapatista movement has been fighting for the autonomy and the rights of the indigenous Mayan peoples of Chiapas for 30 years, and this fight has been against the homogenizing Mexican state system. The state system has tried to impose on the Mayan peoples an education system that encourages the primacy of the Spanish language and universal knowledges that take no account of the particulars of the environment and culture where the Mayan peoples live. In contrast, the Zapatista murals depict a slow education that respects the traditions of the past, and urges the children to take care of the particular landscape where the Mayans have lived for thousands of years before Spanish colonialization. The murals are strategically placed where the children go back and forth in their villages, and the authors argue that this presents the youth with a transversal, semiotic system in defiance of the norms of current global capitalism as funneled through and lived in Mexico. This chapter represents a major theorization of an indigenous-led educational system that continues to defy the universal dictates of a state organized system backed by capital. In this context, Guattari stands out as a theorist still capable of mobilizing such a philosophy.

Part IV: *Further Issues in Transversality, Education, and Globalization*

The fourth section of this book begins with a chapter called: *Alice's Adventures*: Reconfiguring Solidarity in Early Childhood Education and Care through Data Events by Susan Naomi Nordstrom, Camilla Eline Andersen, Jayne Osgood, Ann-Hege Lorvik-Waterhouse and Ann Merete Otterstad. Instead of reporting on a research project, the team uses transversality to create and theorize a data event. Through the excitement and chaos of the research event, transversality can be deployed to open up the ways in which *Alice in Wonderland* interacts with concepts in early childhood education such as care and solidarity. Further, in the face of the multiple pressures of globalization on early childhood education (ECE), and governmental responses to neoliberal ideology, these sorts of data events act as a means to disrupt and question the certainties and assumptions inherent within ECE. This chapter blends transversality as a strategic method for data events and analysis with poststructural feminism, which questions the subject of research, and includes the researchers as active players in the game of analysis. The next chapter by Eve Mayes, named: The ontological plurality of digital voice: A schizoanalysis of Rate My Professors and Rate My Teachers, examines the recent phenomena of students rating the performance of their teachers through online surveys. In contrast to taking a conventional critique of this phenomenon, Mayes uses Guattari's transversality to reconstruct the act of rating one's professor as a plural digital voice. This chapter shows how careful research and retheorization of the rating of a professor's teaching work can refigure this activity as a digital voice and/or *intercesseur*—a French word that is often translated as 'mediator,' but that may be better translated as intersection/intercession. The digital voice demonstrates how the flows of energies work in the context of rating a professor's work online, and avoids the temptation to either ignore the activity as an inevitable aspect of postmodern educational functioning, or to judgmentally critique the rating system as an incursion and intrusion on 'real' intellectual pedagogy. Transversality acts in this chapter to creatively remake the rating of university work as something unexpected and new.

The last chapter of the book, by Jeff Smith and Scott Kouri, deals with counselling through transversal pedagogy and is named: Schizoanalysis, Counselling Praxis and a Sandbox Dirge. Smith and Kouri argue that many of the dualisms may be collapsed in the practice of contemporary counselling by strategically deploying Guattarian concepts that refigure the subject of counselling, and the act of interviewing and dialogue, with a view to deal with the solving of the problems created by contemporary capitalism. This chapter includes entertaining accounts of counselling interactions that demonstrate the ways in which patients are part of and exacerbate the capitalist system, and how counselling tends to extend these tendencies, rather than provide any answers, or move in an opposite direction. Transversality, which is strategically aligned with schizoanalysis in this chapter, is able to open up more fruitful modes of interpreting and working with the concerns of counselling, precisely because it is an open mode of unconscious pedagogy and analysis, and does not lock up interpretation in terms of the self, language, or, indeed, explanation. This chapter represents a new mode of opening up and working with the subject and shows how counselling may be reinvented as a transversal, pedagogic practice. The afterword of this book is a warning. New, online streaming services make it possible for students to broadcast themselves on a 24 hour basis. Bradley and Cole chart the exploits of one student, who we give the pseudonym Subject R, and who uses the online streaming service, Zhibo, to broadcast herself to an audience of 10,000 back home in China while she studies in Japan. Subject R's subjectivity is captured and to an extent controlled by her online presence, her schedule from an unscrupulous (machinic) employer, and a fickle fanbase. In an era of the neoliberal subject, where the domination of global economics means that we all have to think about new ways to make money, students such as Subject R could become the new norm, almost as a means to survive. Bradley and Cole retheorize this situation using transversality, and even though they cannot change the behavior of Subject R, they show how it could be rethought and reimagined. This chapter demonstrates how transversality can be inserted into the becomings of the digital era, in which education is fully implicated and involved. It does not extinguish the variant ways in which subjects may be captured by the digital infosphere, but points to escape routes from the continuous world of work, training, and instrumental reason that can trap subjectivity in numerous forms of profit making.

Conclusion

This book demonstrates the versatility and applicability of Guattari's (2015) conception of transversality by applying it in different manners and to different contexts. The practice of education is multifarious and takes place in an enormous number of settings, from early childhood to university, from designed online learning environments to the adventures of going outdoors. Transversality sits in-between the subject and the object of education, between the teacher and the student, and between teaching and learning; it works between the institute and all who function within it. Transversality does not start anything, but is it not neutral, and it acts to redistribute and to rearrange what already exists. In this book, the use of transversality acts as a tactical move; it is not reactive or critical in a normative sense, but opens up the field and shows new ways forward for the future, and complementary to other approaches in the field. Transversality is political, and in a situation dominated by capitalism as an almost unassailable one-world system, offers the possibility of hope for something different. Transversality does not point to the evolution of a new economic system, but can act as a dimension for the redistribution and reinvention of wealth. The editors and authors would like to commend this volume as a serious and committed means to revolutionize education by attending to and mapping the production of flows and the flows of production transversally.

References

Bennett, J. (2010). *Vibrant matter: A political ecology of things*. Durham, NC.: Duke University Press.
Berardi, F. (2014). *Neuro-totalitarianism in Technomaya Google-colonization of experience and neuro-plastic alternative*. Los Angeles, CA: Semiotext(e).
Biesta, G. J. J. (2011). *Learning democracy in school and society: Education, lifelong learning and the politics of citizenship*. Rotterdam/Boston/Taipei: Sense Publishers.
Burawoy, G., Blum, J. A., George, S., Zsuzsa, G., & Thayer, M. (2000). *Global ethnography: Forces, connections and imaginations in a postmodern world*. Berkeley: University of California Press.
Carlin, M., & Wallin, J. (Eds.). (2014). *Deleuze & Guattari, politics and education: For a people-yet-to-come*. New York and London: Bloomsbury.
Cole, D. R. (2011). The actions of affect in Deleuze—Others using language and the language that we make …. *Educational Philosophy and Theory, 43*(6), 549–561.
Cole, D. R. (2013). Affective literacies: Deleuze, discipline and power. In I. Semetsky & D. Masny (Eds.), *Deleuze and education* (pp. 94–112). Edinburgh: Edinburgh University Press.
Cole, D. R., & Bradley, J. P. N. (2014). Japanese English learners on the edge of 'chaosmos': Félix Guattari and 'becoming-otaku'. *Linguistic and Philosophical Investigations, 13*, 83–95.
Cole, D. R., & Woodrow, C. (Eds.). (2016). *Super dimensions in globalisation and education*. Singapore: Springer.
Crutzen, P. (2002). Geology of mankind. *Nature, 415*, 23. https://doi.org/10.1038/415023a.
Deleuze, G. (1994). *Difference and repetition* (P. Patton, Trans.). New York: Columbia University Press.
Deleuze, G., & Guattari, F. (1984). *Anti-Oedipus: Capitalism & Schizophrenia* (R. Hurley, M. Seem & H.F. Lane, Trans.). London: The Athlone Press.
Deleuze, G., & Guattari, F. (1988). *A thousand plateaus: Capitalism & Schizophrenia II* (B. Massumi, Trans.). London: The Athlone Press.
Freire, P. (1970) [2010]. *Pedagogy of the oppressed*. New York, NY: Continuum.
Genosko, G. (2008). A-signifying semiotics. *The Public Journal of Semiotics, 11*(1), 22–35.
Guattari, F. (1984). *Molecular revolution: Psychiatry and politics* (R. Sheed, Trans.). Harmondsworth: Penguin Books.
Guattari, F. (1996a). Semiological subjection, semiotic enslavement. In G. Genosoko (Ed.), *The Guattari reader* (pp. 141–148). Oxford: Blackwell.
Guattari, F. (1996b). *The three ecologies*. London: Athlone Press.
Guattari, F. (2009a). *Soft subversions: Texts and interviews 1977–1985*. Semiotext(e): Los Angeles.
Guattari, F. (2009b). *Chaosophy: Texts and interviews 1972–1977*. Semiotext(e): Los Angeles.
Guattari, F. (2011). *The machinic unconscious: Essays in schizoanalysis*. Los Angeles, CA: Semiotext(e).
Guattari, F. (2013). *Schizoanalytic cartographies* (A. Goffey, Trans.). London: Bloomsbury.
Guattari, F. (2015). *Psychoanalysis and transversality: Texts and interviews 1955–1971*. (A. Hodges, Trans.). South Pasadena, CA.: Semiotext(e).
Guattari, F., & Rolnik, S. (2008). *Molecular revolution in Brazil* (K. Clapshow & B. Holmes, Trans.). Los Angeles, CA: Semiotext(e).

Haraway, D. J. (2016). *Staying with the trouble: Making Kin in the Chthulucene*. Durham, NC.: Duke University Press.

Hjelmslev, L. (1953). *Prolegomena to a theory of language*. Baltimore: Indiana University Publications in Anthropology and Linguistics.

Hodge, R., & Kress, G. (1988). *Social semiotics*. Cambridge: Polity.

Hogan, A., Sellar, S., & Lingard, B. (2015). Commercialising comparison: Pearson puts the TLC in soft capitalism. *Journal of Education Policy, 31*(3), 243–258. https://doi.org/10.1080/02680939. 2015.1112922.

Latour, B. (2002). Gabriel tarde and the end of the social. In P. Joyce (Ed.). *The social in question. New bearings in history and the social sciences* (pp. 117–132). London: Routledge.

Marazzi, C. (2011). *The violence of financial capitalism* (K. Lebedeva & J.F. McGimsey, Trans.). Los Angeles: Semiotext(e).

Marx, K. (1887) [1965]. *Capital* (Vol. 1). Moscow: Progress.

McLaren, P. (1998). Revolutionary pedagogy in post-revolutionary times: Rethinking the political economy of critical education. *Educational Theory, 48*(4), 431–462.

Newell, P., & Paterson, M. (2010). *Climate capitalism: Global warming and the transformation of the global economy*. Cambridge: Cambridge University Press.

Ministry of Education, Finland. (2009). *Finnish education system in an international comparison*. Helsinki: Ministry of Education Policy Analyses.

Urry, J. (2000). *Sociology beyond societies: Mobilities for the twenty-first century*. London: Routledge Press.

David R. Cole is an Associate Professor in Education at Western Sydney University, Australia and the leader of the Globalisation theme in the Centre for Educational Research. He has published fifteen academic books, and numerous (100+) journal articles, book chapters, conference presentations and other public output. He has been involved with thirteen major educational research projects across Australia and internationally, and is a world leading expert in the application of the philosophy of Gilles Deleuze and Félix Guattari to education. David's latest monograph is called: A Pedagogy of Cinema (2016, Sense Publishers) with Joff P.N. Bradley.

Dr. Joff P. N. Bradley is Associate Professor in the Faculty of Language Studies at Teikyo University, Tokyo, Japan. He is currently researching the teaching of critical thinking and philosophy through film in the Japanese university. With David R. Cole, he is co-author of *A Pedagogy of Cinema* (2016) and co-editor of both *Educational Philosophy and New French Thought* (2017), and with Dr. Tony See, co-editor of *Deleuze and Buddhism* (2016).

Part I
Universities, Transversality and the Future

Chapter 2
The Transversal Campus: Open Black Box?

Janell Watson

> *Being in bigger interactive spaces encourages*
> *expansive thinking, while being in a box of a room*
> *encourages box thinking.*
> —Dan Huttenlocher, founding dean and vice
> provost, Cornell Tech
> *The place of existence, for example a psychiatric*
> *hospital, carries out a radical modification of*
> *anything, of any order, that appears there.*
> —Félix Guattari, Psychoanalysis and Transversality

Abstract Many universities are creating new learning spaces designed to encourage interactions among students and faculty in an attempt to foster the kind of creative thinking demanded by today's innovation economy. These new campus spaces share several characteristics of transversality, Félix Guattari's descriptor for spatially open, socially interactive, and communal institutions, organized very differently than the spatially segregated, isolating, and hierarchical disciplinary institutions analyzed by Michel Foucault. The trend toward transversality on campus is predicated on the assumption that space itself shapes learning outcomes. To claim that a particular strategy or design will result in specific outcomes is to treat the teaching–learning process like a black box, as theorized by cybernetics, the science of command and control, and this claim shall be investigated in this chapter.

Keywords Transversality · Guattari · Classroom design
Black box theory · Cybernetics

J. Watson (✉)
Virginia Tech, Blacksburg, USA
e-mail: rjwatson@vt.edu

© Springer Nature Singapore Pte Ltd. 2018
D. R. Cole and J. P. N. Bradley (eds.), *Principles of Transversality in Globalization and Education*, https://doi.org/10.1007/978-981-13-0583-2_2

Transversality According to Corporations and Guattari

On-trend university administrators around the world boast of "learning spaces" that foster innovation by facilitating interaction among students and professors. Compared to traditional classrooms with fixed seating oriented toward a single lectern, the flexible spaces "of the new learning landscape" are "more interactive, informal, and social," designed to "maximize encounters among people, places, and ideas" (Boys, 2015, pp. 44, 96, 98). University policymakers describe these new learning spaces with terms like connected, active, interactive, collaborative, flexible, innovative, dynamic, and learner-centered (Wulsin, 2013). Huttenlocher, founding dean and vice provost of a particularly ambitious learning space project, posits a direct cause–effect relationship between spatial layout and innovative thinking when he declares that "Being in bigger interactive spaces encourages expansive thinking." He credits big spaces with generating big ideas. Conversely, he adds, "being in a box of a room encourages box thinking," suggesting that small enclosed spaces restrain ideas (quoted in Lange, 2016, Cornell Tech section, para. 3). He contrasts the new large, open, interactive learning spaces to the "box of a room" typical of traditional classrooms, faculty offices, or laboratories—cell-like boxes that output box-like thinking. Brown and Long echo the claim that spatiality shapes thinking when they write: "Learning spaces in the 21st century need to foster discovery, innovation, and scholarship, not simply contain them" (2006, p. 95). To "simply contain" academic pursuits is to enclose them in an inert architectural box. To "foster" innovative scholarly discoveries, the space itself must nurture them. Expansive spaces facilitate interactions that lead to innovation, according to the formula of the new campus design. The words of Huttenlocher, Brown, and Long succinctly express the paradigm of what I will call the transversalized classroom, a space designed to extract innovation from a heterogeneous group gathered within.

The strategy of staging interactive encounters in order to produce creative outcomes brings to mind Félix Guattari's principle of transversality, an organizational technique characterized by open communal spaces, social interaction, communication across ranks, role reversals, and work spaces that flow into living spaces. Institutional design matters. As Guattari puts it, "the place of existence, for example a psychiatric hospital, carries out a radical modification of anything, of any order, that appears there" (2015a, p. 122). The transversality practiced at La Borde, the experimental in-patient psychiatric hospital where Guattari worked all his adult life, was modeled on another mental hospital run by the militant Marxist psychiatrist François Tosquelles, as well as the open schoolrooms and non-authoritarian pedagogies of Celestin Freinet and Fernand Oury (Watson, forthcoming; Genosko, 2009, pp. 34–37; Wallin, 2013). As formulated by Guattari, transversality found its models in leftist movements.

In contrast, the new campus learning spaces are modeled on the corporate work spaces of the so-called knowledge economy, and vice versa, in a pattern of circular coevolution. Information-era companies such as Microsoft, Apple, Google, and Facebook conceptualize their headquarters as "campuses," offering their employees on-site services like restaurants, coffee shops, lounge space, lushly landscaped out-door areas, gyms, and even medical care, on the model of self-contained American universities. Design trends at universities and corporate office parks have converged (Lange, 2016). Whether for education or for business, this architectural trend favors large windows with expansive views, multi-story atriums, and few partitions. On my university campus, new laboratory spaces with glass walls allow any outside observer to view the equipment and people inside. Modular classroom furnishings can be arranged and rearranged to suit collaborative, hands-on, group activities, mimicking the interactions among engineers, architects, designers, or inventors in layouts inspired by the spaces of engineering firms, architectural studios, design workshops, high-tech startups, and hackers' basements (Raths, 2016). CEOs and university leaders alike embrace the idea that open spaces foster productive encoun-ters, based on the conviction that spontaneous human interaction sparks the kind of creativity, invention, and entrepreneurship capable of maintaining the rapid pace of constant innovation demanded by what my own university's provost calls the "innovation economy" (Boys, 2015, p. 96; Virginia Tech, 2017).

The transversality practiced on campuses, whether educational or corporate, serves the needs of information-era global capitalism. Transversality can function for better or for worse, to borrow a phrase that Guattari used more than once (see, for example, 1996, p. 193). It would be a mistake to think that transversality alone can save us. Guattari's uses of the term changed over time (Genosko, 2000, pp. 106–107). In his later writings, transversality appears as a kind of thinking that can be used in social struggles against neoliberalism, or coopted for repressive ends. For example, he declares that "Transdisciplinarity must become transversality between science, the socius, aesthetics and politics," emphasizing the need to work across not only across academic disciplines, but also and at the same time across the three ecologies—mental, social, and environmental (2015b, p. 134). He advises think-ing "transversally" to understand the interactions between the economy, technology, society, and subjectivity, in order to address the proliferation of large-scale prob-lems like urban gentrification, child labor, and environmental damage (2000, p. 43). Elsewhere, he cites examples of transversality used for nefarious purposes. He says, critically, of the first Gulf war (USA versus Iraq) that "there was a transversalist integration… of machines of mass mediatized subjectification, of intellectual and religious machines" (in Alliez & Goffey, 2011, p. 31), suggesting that state warfare takes advantage of transversality when it incorporates such domains as the media, ideas, and religion. He warns that even in Western Europe today, microfascism could suddenly emerge if "a general principle of transversality" enabled the interpenetra-tion of paranoid or fascist reterritorializations, catastrophic mass deterritorialization, and minuscule lines of flight (Guattari 2011, p. 148). Transversality can create and liberate, or it can repress and destroy.

A number of contemporary education researchers have embraced Guattari's liberatory version of transversality, which they adopt as an essential tool for imple-menting student-centered, creative, and socially enriching pedagogies (Carmichael & Litherland, 2012; Masny, 2013; Wallin, 2013; Cole & Bradley, 2014; Ringrose, 2015; Cole, 2016). These scholars show how transversality can empower learners and teachers, enabling them to follow through on their own initiatives despite constraints such as stifling administrative dictates imposed from above. Successful practitioners of transversal pedagogy manage to find "the holey spaces where room for transverse practices can be carved out" (Carmichael & Litherland, 2012, p. 102), even if they are working in ordinary educational facilities. After all, an institution's "coefficient of transversality" is not measured on the basis of its interior architecture or high-tech equipment, but on the richness of the human relationships among the people inside it. The "coefficient of transversality" determines the degree of communication among an institution's various personnel and users (Guattari, 2015a, p. 112).

Defined as thinking and acting across domains, transversality also describes the interpenetration and integration of education and business. Universities and the corporate sector, especially in the USA, must be studied transversally, given the increased pressure on universities to seek corporate funding, to cultivate public–private research partnerships, and to purchase the latest learning products from the growing education industry. Learning spaces modeled on corporate architecture reflect a shared goal of producing ideas, interns, and future employees to fuel the innovation economy. Institutions of higher education transversally connected to private businesses are, as Boys puts it in *Building Better Universities: Strategies, Spaces, Technologies*, actively forging "alternative kinds of relationships" among "learning, teaching, research, enterprise, and communities; and among learners, scholars, citizens, and employers," (2015, p. 4). Do these transversal relations between education and industry serve the greater social, subjective, and environmental good (ecosophy), or do they primarily serve corporate clients (economy)? A distinction could be made between ecosophic transversality, focused on keeping all three ecologies healthy, and corporate transversality, focused instead on economic health and profit making.

Guattari encourages academics to pursue the ecosophic goal of working for the greater social good when in *Chaosmosis* he proclaims that "intellectuals should no longer be asked to erect themselves as master thinkers or providers of moral lessons, but to work, even in the most extreme solitude, at putting into circulation tools for transversality" (1995, p. 130). Promoting ecosophic transversality necessitates an ongoing critical examination of the relationship between education and corporations. This implicates all of education, including elementary and secondary schools, but this chapter more specifically examines the ideology of innovation on university campuses in neoliberal democracies, whose public support for higher education is dwindling, prompting many universities to seek closer ties to the private sector. Cornell Tech proves to be exemplary not only in its open architecture, but also in its public–private industry partnerships. Cornell University established this New York City outpost upon winning a competition for funding from Bloomberg Philanthropies and the Applied Sciences NYC initiative, which mixed public and private resources, including acreage on Roosevelt Island provided by the city (Lange, 2016; Chen, 2017).

In the era of innovation, transversality can either incite molecular revolution or serve the needs of what Deleuze called "the society of control." Transversal design trends on control-era campuses manifest a displacement of the disciplinary apparatuses of industrial capitalism in favor of a corporate transversality adapted to the demands of the innovation economy. Just as the box-like spaces of earlier classrooms served disciplinary society, so the expansive spaces of the innovation university serve the knowledge economy. In order to better understand the appeal of transversal design to control society, I turn to cybernetics, the science of command and control.

Transversal Design and Cybernetics

In describing disciplinarity and transversality, Foucault and Guattari (respectively) argue that institutions remodel the subjectivities and social relations within them. "As students know well, the effects of institutional organization inform upon potential behaviours and becomings," writes Wallin (2013, p. 35). At the same time, students' "behaviors and becomings" in turn affect the institution, forming a cybernetic feedback loop. In designing institutional space, planners and architects must work with future users in mind, imagining their "potential audience, the observer/occupants of a space or building" (Gage, 2007, p. 1332). Design teams must try to predict future user behavior in order to improve the design. Designing—or redesigning—an institution in order to effectuate changes in its users thus raises the cybernetic questions of circular causality and of control. Glanville, an architect and cyberneticist, explains that the designer may retain greater control by limiting the future user's options or may give up some of this control so as to open up unforeseen possibilities for users to use the design in innovative ways (2007, p. 1195). In other words, one can sacrifice control to enable innovation, or sacrifice innovation in order to remain in control.

Disciplinary spatiality (Foucault, 1979, 2003) can be conceptualized as an implementation of what Glanville calls a "restrictive control" which inhibits or disenables (2007, p. 1180). Boxlike, constraining architectural structures, such as monastic or prison cells, proliferate in disciplinary institutions, which spatially partition individuals by enclosing them within physical or virtual walls, according to a system of hierarchical classification. Categories like rank, role, or expertise determine a person's place within an institution's gridded social hierarchy, which assigns certain types of people to specific spaces. Foucault calls this spatialized classificatory apparatus *quadrillage*. Sometimes translated as "spatial partitioning," *quadrillage* in French refers to the little squares formed by horizontal and vertical gridlines, as inscribed on graph paper, a map, a pastry crust, or a grilled steak (2003, pp. 44–45). Among his examples of *quadrillage*, Foucault includes schools which place each student in a seat at a desk inside a classroom, assigned based on age classifications. To place each person in their own designated space is to control them by isolating and classifying them. When people are spatially and categorically boxed, transversality—the degree of interactivity among those within the institution—remains minimal. Restrictive control is built into disciplinary design.

Control over its future users and uses is relinquished by transversal design. La Borde gave up control over patients' actions by liberating them from their rooms and wards in which traditional mental hospitals confined them, severely limiting opportunities for movement or interaction. La Borde loosened its grip on control mechanisms, in the hopes that unexpected encounters would create new social connections that could lead to therapeutic breakthroughs. All members of staff, from housekeepers to doctors, were encouraged to join in daily activities alongside the patients. Everyone, including the patients themselves, participated in the therapeutic work of nurturing intersubjective interaction and self-expression (Guattari 2009, pp. 176–194; Guattari, 2015a, pp. 102–120; Goffey, 2016; Watson, forthcoming).

From the perspective of institutional design, to create a space that facilitates new relationships among users, the architect must create "a construct that can be reconstructed in different ways at different times by other observers" (Gage, 2007, pp. 1332–1333). The exact nature of this reconstruction by users cannot be controlled by design. Despite the innovation designer's best efforts, the users of the space may not interact at all, or they may interact without producing any new ideas, or they may do something else entirely. It is futile, warns Glanville, to try to control the uncontrollable actions of users (2007, p. 1195). However, as Deleuze famously argues, advanced capitalism has developed less obvious, more diffuse means of control, such as electronic modes of surveillance and enforcement, about which more in a moment (1992, p. 7).

In the early years of cybernetics, the engineers of command and control concerned themselves primarily with clear-cut, directly controllable systems, like heating regulated by a thermostat or automated telephone switchboards (Glanville, 2007, p. 1186). Disciplinary *quadrillage*, which limits possible interactions, can be understood as a first-order cybernetic system which aims at full control. In contrast, second-order cybernetics tolerates the ambiguities and uncertainties inherent in social systems. Designers of transversal space expect users to constantly reconfigure and reconstruct, in unpredictable ways that can lead to novelty. Krippendorff defines second-order cybernetics as the participation "in systems under continuous reconstruction by its constituents," underlining the agency of the user (2007, p. 1391).

Unpredictable users can be thought of as black boxes within an institution's carefully orchestrated spaces (Gage, 2007, p. 1332). The cybernetic theory of black boxes provides a tool for studying an institutional system, despite the unknowns and uncertainties within it. Rather than worrying about understanding a complicated mechanism or process, the "observer" can "black box" it and instead focus on inputs and outputs. In the case of education, the observer may be a researcher, administrator, policymaker, or even a planning committee. All systems include elements that an observer, even an expert, does not or cannot know. Even if the observer does not comprehend what is happening inside the black box, she can develop a working description of it, based on observing the relationship between inputs and outputs. To cite an example from everyday life, I can start my car even if its starter mechanics remain a black box to me, because I have observed that turning the key in the ignition (input) turns over the motor (output). I create a working idea of what the black-boxed mechanism does, because input and output behave predictably. However, the observed input–output correlation remains only "a functional description that has worked in the past. That it will continue to do so is a pure article of faith: the black box's regularity is an assumption" (Glanville, 1982, p. 2). There are many assumptions involved in predicting the output of a system as complicated as education.

Any university administrator who claims that a particular strategy or design will result in a specific outcome treats the educational institution and its users as black boxs (Braster, Grosvenor, & del Mar del Pozo Andres, 2011). A number of education scholars have criticized policymakers for overly simplifying the learning process by focusing on select inputs and outputs, while treating classroom practice as a black box (Black and Wiliam, 2010; Murray, 2011; Braster et al., 2011). For example, a school district may impose a testing program (input) with the aim of motivating better teaching (desired output), without examining the many other components of teaching and learning. They in effect black box the classroom's users—teachers and students. In *Inside the Black Box of Classroom Practice: Change without Reform in American Education*, Cuban (2013) describes actual classroom practice as a black box "where inputs (e.g., money spent per pupil, facilities, teacher qualifications) go into a box called 'schools' or 'classrooms' and outputs emerge (e.g., test scores, skilled and knowledgeable high school graduates) with no clue as to how that transformation occurred" (p. 13). Cuban here identifies the black box as that which actually happens in the classroom, the input as policies or resources, and the output as test scores or graduates. He accuses policymakers of neglecting to look inside the black box, about which they have "no clue," as they focus instead on their own inputs (new resources or policies) and then claim any positive outcome (improved test scores, successful graduates) as their own successes (2013, pp. 11–13). Cuban is cautioning against assuming simplistic cause–effect relationships between inputs and outputs when considering a system as complex as a classroom full of teachers and learners.

The model critiqued by Cuban situates the observer outside the black box full of unpredictable human interactions. People are, to borrow from pioneering cyberneticist Ashby, the blackest of black boxes, with "far too many variables for a study in every detail to be practical," making any user an "incompletely observable box" (Ashby, 1956, p. 113). The observer experiments with the system by varying the inputs into the box. Foucault and Guattari argue that institutions transform their users by subjecting them to a process of subjectivation. This process occurs deep inside a black box, the mysterious mechanism at work inside the institution. They black box subjectivation. The observer–experimenter (educator, hospital administrator, educator) inputs a particular organizational strategy (such as disciplinarity or transversality) in order to output certain modes of thinking and acting (such as docile bodies or subject groups capable of creating novelty).

Foucault, for example, describes inputs (*quadrillage*) and outputs (docile bodies), which can be observed without fully understanding the subjectivation process that happens in between. Disciplinary *quadrillage* encloses students in boxy rooms, forcing them to sit still in chairs aligned on a fixed grid. Knowledge flows one way, from the master teacher to the subordinated student, with the aim of producing docile employees willing to unquestioningly accept their assigned place within the hierarchies of industrial production (Guattari, 2015a, pp. 93–100). Instead of trying to explain the unobservable internal workings of the black box of subjectivation, Foucault instead focuses on the input of spatial classification and the output of docility.

However, it is not clear exactly how the black-boxed subjectivation process translates box-like architecture into bodies capable of withstanding the boredom of the repetitive tasks programmed by Taylorization.

Transversality counters that if confinement in a small space (input) encourages inside-the-box thinking (output), then opening the space (new input) will expand thinking (new output). The university classroom design team inputs expansive glass-walled architecture into the cybernetic black box of subjectivation and claims to output expansive thinking. If disciplinarity outputs obedient workers, then transversality outputs thinkers capable of initiating change, according to the innovation paradigm. Subjectivation can remain in the black box as long as inputting disciplinary space or transversal space consistently outputs docile labor or entrepreneurial subjectivity, respectively. Knowledge economy employers want inventors, not workers (which they have replaced with robots or exploited populations deprived of basic rights). Knowledge workers sell their cognitive and social skills—their subjectivities rather than their hands or muscles—hence Guattari's declaration that subjectivity itself is "the number one objective of capitalist society, of contemporary society" (in Alliez & Goffey, 2011, p. 40).

I have been describing the version of black box theory proffered by first-order cybernetics, which places the observer–experimenter outside the system. Externalizing the observer presumes that she maintains an omniscient view of inputs and outputs. She thus occupies a "power relationship" with the observed. The policy-makers portrayed by Cuban (2013) assume the outside observer's position of power over the observed—the teachers and students in the classroom. However, second-order cybernetics suggests that this externality is illusory, instead positing that the system always includes the observer, which together form an observer-black box system. The observer cannot escape the box. Furthermore, according to the second-order model, the observed also observes the observer. The output from the box becomes the input into the observer, who in turn inputs this output back into the box, creating a feedback loop (Glanville, 2004, pp. 1380–1382). Viewed according to this more sophisticated model, observation goes two ways, which puts observer and observed on much more equal footing.

Second-order cybernetics goes even further, allowing for multiple observers positioned in various relationships to different boxes. Multiplying observers, and allowing them to observe one another, raises the transversality coefficient of cybernetic modeling. The multiplication of observers, at all levels within the system, characterizes both transversality and second-order cybernetics. Guattari insists that transversalizing a group or institution is an ongoing process that involves not only the gaze of the analyst (therapist, researcher, or theorist), but also the return gazes of those under observation. Transversality implies recognizing all participants as active observers, according agency to even the lowliest staff or least advanced students. Everyone's observations enter the feedback loop. Savvy educational experimenters not only seek feedback from all involved, but also acknowledge their own participation inside the black box. They remain aware that they can only see inputs and outputs, without fully knowing the details of the transformation process at work within the psychic spaces of the institution. Transversality is not an institutional structure, but rather operates within an ongoing process that Guattari called "institutional analysis," which entails continuous self-assessment, rather than policy directives from above (2009, pp. 37–38). Transversality could be defined as "the cybernetic interaction and feedback involved with living organisms and social structures," to borrow the words of Guattari himself, who avidly followed cybernetic thought (1995, p. 124).

Guattari learned firsthand at La Borde that transversality requires constant readjustment, self-monitoring, and experimentation, since human groups easily fall back into alienating hierarchical patterns of repressive control. Transversality, never given, must always be "conquered through a pragmatics of existence," he insists (2015a, p. 112). Ethico-political transversality requires combining creative singularity with social mutation but, Guattari warns, holding these elements together is not easy (1995, pp. 132–134). A transversal group within an institution is a subject group which "endeavors to control its own behavior," to set its own goals, and to examine its own practices, explain Carmichael and Litherland. They add that "the transverse subject group is self-directing and reflexive: transversality involves continued inquiry into one's own role and those of others, as well as that of the directions being taken" (Carmichael & Litherland, 2012, pp. 96–97). Control comes from within. Autopoietic cybernetic systems operate with autonomy (Glanville, 2007, pp. 1184, 1192). A subject group of teachers and students engaged in creating knowledge together, working on a project they initiated, motivated by their own goals, operating autonomously, can create an autopoietic classroom, self-sustaining and self-directed, independently of external control (Cole & Bradley, 2014, p. 84). Such collective creative endeavors resist external control, but "universities and the capitalist system that supports them necessarily tolerates academic innovation and divergence as long as its inevitable troublesomeness is outweighed by its apparent or potential usefulness" (Carmichael & Litherland, 2012, p. 108). The system risks autonomous creation in the hopes of fostering innovative breakthroughs that will bring glory and research dollars.

I now turn to another observer–participant in the university-corporation feedback loop, and that is the vendors of educational support products. Unlike the La Borde Clinic, which operated in an old chateau on a limited budget, many universities are devoting serious capital resources to create the transversalized learning spaces in vogue today. In the USA, a consortium called Educause provides studies of open, innovative classroom design, which often includes expensive technology products. Its researchers come from many different fields, roles, and ranks, often working collaboratively. Here is a description of an Educause project, an assessment tool for rating learning spaces:

> Planning, design, and support of learning spaces is a collaborative and communal undertaking between instructors, learners, administrators, technologists, facilities personnel, and planners. Only by working across the institution can we sustain a campus environment that treats learning spaces holistically and provides an ecosystem to sustain and promote productive instructor and student interactions. (Brown et al., 2017, p. 5)

At first glance, their efforts seem exemplarily inclusive, given that their collaboration includes "instructors, learners, administrators, technologists, facilities personnel, and planners." However, it is concerning that actual teaching faculty and students are far outnumbered by the administrators, support staff, and paid consultants. Educause membership comprises nearly 2000 universities, but also 348 corporations catering to the higher education marketplace (Educause, 2017). The report quoted just above lists among its coauthors Shirley Dugdale of Dugdale Strategy, a consultancy specializing in university spatial configuration. Transversalized universities and corporate interests converge, collectively contributing to an economy that is widening the wealth gap between the global elite and the vast majority of humanity.

Conclusion

Both university and corporate campuses provide protective sanctuary for privileged students and well-paid high-tech employees, while those on the outside struggle. This amounts to a reverse confinement. Rather than enclosing marginal populations or young people deemed in need of discipline in cell-like boxes, as in the disciplinary era, the new glass-walled campuses of universities and technology corporations cocoon the elite in comfortable enclaves offering enhanced ecologies: social (recreational spaces of encounter), mental (care provided by university clinics or good corporate health insurance), and environmental (filtered air and well-tended green spaces). Despite the ease of circulation, interactive teamwork, expansive exterior views, and healthy ecologies, these transversalized campuses exhibit key features of what Deleuze described as societies of control (1992). Throughout these campuses, data-collecting technology constantly monitors and assesses students and employees, tracking their activities and evaluating their output of innovative ideas.

Control society has morphed into assessment society. Offices of assessment are proliferating on university campuses across the USA. They evaluate programs and "outcomes" at all levels, with the support of outside, for-profit vendors. For example, the Student Success Collaborative Campus platform provides analytics meant to help student advisors predict the academic success of their advisees. Academic Analytics is a commercial provider of data for measuring faculty research output. University admissions officers rely on predictive analytics products to predict the future success of applicants. Helping students succeed is certainly a noble cause, but it does nothing to help those who, for whatever reason, will not earn university degrees and who will thus be excluded from well-remunerated positions on corporate campuses. Meanwhile, in the USA, the self-appointed leader of the so-called free world, disciplinary techniques still reign supreme outside of these cozy campuses, which shelter the privileged from the police brutality and disproportionate incarceration rates that afflict minorities and the poor. Campuses today offer assessment for all, transversality for the few, and precarity for the rest.

References

Alliez, E., & Goffey, A. (Eds.). (2011). *The Guattari effect*. London: New York: Bloomsbury Academic.

Ashby, W. R. (1956). *An introduction to cybernetics*. New York: J. Wiley. Retrieved from http://archive.org/details/introductiontocy00ashb.

Black, P., & Wiliam, D. (2010). Inside the black box: Raising standards through classroom assessment. *Phi Delta Kappan, 92*(1), 81–90. https://doi.org/10.1177/003172171009200119.

Boys, J. (2015). *Building better universities: Strategies, spaces, technologies*. New York: Routledge. Retrieved from http://ebookcentral.proquest.com.ezproxy.lib.vt.edu/lib/vt/detail.action?docID=1843473.

Braster, S., Grosvenor, I., & del Mar del Pozo Andres, M. (2011). *The black box of schooling: A cultural history of the classroom*. Brussels: Peter Lang.

Brown, M., Cevetello, J., Dugdale, S., Finkelstein, A., Holeton, R., Long, P., & Meyers, C. (2017). Learning Space Rating System: Version 2. Educause. https://www.educause.edu/~/media/files/educause/eli/initiatives/lsrsv2.pdf?la=en.

Brown, M., & Long, P. (2006). Trends in learning space design. In D. G. Oblinger (Ed.), *Learning spaces* (p. 9.1–9.11). Educause. Retrieved from https://www.educause.edu/research-and-publications/books/learning-spaces.

Carmichael, P., & Litherland, K. (2012). Transversality and innovation: Prospects for technology-enhanced learning in times of crisis. In D. R. Cole (Ed.), *Surviving economic crises through education* (pp. 95–114). New York: Peter Lang.

Chen, D. W. (2017, March 22). Where halls of ivy meet silicon dreams, a new city rises. *The New York Times*. Retrieved from https://www.nytimes.com/2017/03/22/nyregion/nyc-cornell-columbia-nyu-campuses.html.

Cole, D. R. (2016). Unearthing the forces of globalisation in educational research through Guattari's cartographic method. In D. R. Cole & C. Woodrow (Eds.), *Super dimensions in globalisation and education* (pp. 145–161). Singapore: Springer.

Cole, D. R., & Bradley, J. P. N. (2014). Japanese English learners on the edge of 'chaosmos': Félix Guattari and 'becoming-Otaku'. *Linguistic and Philosophical Investigations, 13*, 83–95.

Cuban, L. (2013). *Inside the black box of classroom practice: Change without reform in American education*. Cambridge, Massachusetts: Harvard Education Press.

Deleuze, G. (1992). Postscript on the societies of control. *October, 59*, 3–7.

Educause. (2007). About EDUCAUSE. Retrieved June 27, 2017, from https://www.educause.edu/about.

Foucault, M. (1979). *Discipline & punish: The birth of the prison* (A. Sheridan, Trans.). New York: Vintage Books.

Foucault, M. (2003). *Abnormal: Lectures at the Collège de France, 1974–1975* (G. Burchell, Trans.) London: Verso.

Gage, S. (2007). How to design a black and white box. *Kybernetes: The International Journal of Cybernetics, Systems and Management Sciences, 36*(9–10), 1329–1339.

Genosko, G. (2000). The life and work of Félix Guattari: From transversality to ecosophy. *The three ecologies* (pp. 106–159). London: Continuum.

Genosko, G. (2009). *Felix Guattari: A critical introduction*. London: Pluto Press.

Glanville, R. (1982). Inside every white box there are two black boxes trying to get out. *Behavioral Science, 27*(1), 1–11. https://doi.org/10.1002/bs.3830270102.

Glanville, R. (2004). The purpose of second-order cybernetics. *Kybernetes, 33*(9/10), 1379–1386. https://doi.org/10.1108/03684920410556016.

Glanville, R. (2007). Try again. Fail again. Fail better: The cybernetics in design and the design in cybernetics. *Kybernetes: The International Journal of Cybernetics, Systems and Management Sciences, 36*(9–10), 1173–1206.

Goffey, A. (2016). Guattari and transversality: Institutions, analysis and experimentation. *Radical Philosophy, 195* (online, https://www.radicalphilosophy.com/article/guattari-and-transversality).

Guattari, F. (1995). *Chaosmosis: An ethico-aesthetic paradigm*. (J. Pefanis, Trans.). Bloomington: Indiana University Press.

Guattari, F. (1996). *The Guattari reader*. (G. Genosko, Ed.). Oxford, UK: Wiley-Blackwell.

Guattari, F. (2000). *The three ecologies* (I. Pindar and P. Sutton, Trans.). London: Continuum.

Guattari, F. (2009). *Soft subversions: Texts and interviews 1977–1985* (S. Lotringer, Ed., C. Wiener & E. Wittman, Trans.). Los Angeles: Cambridge; Massachusetts: Semiotext.

Guattari, F. (2011). *Lignes de fuite: Pour un autre mode de possible*. La Tour d'Aigues, France: Aube.

Guattari, F. (2015a). *Psychoanalysis and transversality: Texts and interviews 1955–1971* (A. Hodges, Trans.). South Pasadena, CA: Semiotext(e).

Guattari, F. (2015b). Transdisciplinarity must become transversality. *Theory, Culture & Society, 32*(5–6), 131–137. https://doi.org/10.1177/0263276415597045.

Krippendorff, K. (2007). The cybernetics of design and the design of cybernetics. *Kybernetes: The International Journal of Cybernetics, Systems and Management Sciences, 36*(9–10), 1381–1392.

Lange, A. (2016, August 4). The innovation campus: Building better ideas. *New York Times*. Retrieved from https://www.nytimes.com/2016/08/07/education/edlife/innovation-campus-entrepreneurship-engineering-arts.html.

Masny, D. (Ed.). (2013). *Cartographies of becoming in education: A Deleuze-Guattari perspective*. Rotterdam: Springer Science & Business Media.

Murray, J. (2011). Cybernetic principles of learning. In N. M. Seel (Ed.), *Encyclopedia of the sciences of learning* (pp. 901–904). Springer Science & Business Media.

Raths, D. (2016, June 8). Designing learning spaces for innovation. *Campus Technology*. Retrieved from https://campustechnology.com/articles/2016/06/08/designing-learning-spaces-for-innovation.aspx.

Ringrose, J. (2015). Schizo-Feminist educational research cartographies. *Deleuze Studies, 9*(3), 393–409. https://doi.org/10.3366/dls.2015.0194.

Virginia Tech. (2017). Division of advancement expands its presence in National Capital Region. May 9. Retrieved May 13, 2017, from https://vtnews.vt.edu/articles/2017/05/advancement-ncr.html.

Wallin, J. (2013). Get out from behind the lectern: Counter-cartographies of the transversal institution. In D. Masny (Ed.), *Cartographies of becoming in education: A Deleuze-Guattari perspective* (pp. 34–52). Rotterdam: Springer Science & Business Media.

Watson, J. (forthcoming). Living with madness: Experimental asylums in poststructuralist France. *Cultural Critique*.

Wulsin, L. R. Jr. (2013). Classroom design literature review. Prepared for the special committee on classroom design, Professor Mung Chiang, Chair, Princeton University. https://www.princeton.edu/provost/space-programming-plannin/SCCD_Final_Report_Appendix_B.pdf.

Janell Watson is Professor of French at Virginia Tech, USA. She is the author of *Literature and Material Culture from Balzac to Proust* (Cambridge University Press, 1999) and *Guattari's Diagrammatic Thought* (Continuum, 2009), as well as numerous articles on critical theory and culture. She is Editor of *the minnesota review: a journal of creative and critical writing* (published by Duke University Press).

Chapter 3
Wild Studios: Art, Philosophy, and the Transversal University

Gray Kochhar-Lindgren and Kanta Kochhar-Lindgren

The sovereign clouds came clustering. The conch

Of loyal conjuration trumped. The wind

Of green blooms turning crisped the motley hue

To clearing opalescence. Then the sea

And heaven rolled as one and from the two

Came fresh transfigurings of freshest blue.

—Wallace Stevens, "Sea Surface Full of Clouds" (Collected Poems, p. 98)

Abstract "Wild Studios" argues that an enactment of transversal art and philosophy—which re-configures modes of activity that move across questions, disciplines, and sites of learning—will enable the contemporary university to more continuously reinvent itself. This transversality that drives within and beyond institutional boundaries toward more conceptual precision, fliexible materialities, and social power will generate greater capacities for the university to transfigure the most pressing issues of our time.

Keywords Art · Philosophy · Architecture · University · Studio · Guattari

G. Kochhar-Lindgren (✉)
University of Hong Kong, Hong Kong SAR, China
e-mail: gklindgren@hku.hk

K. Kochhar-Lindgren
Folded Paper Dance & Theatre, Hong Kong SAR, China
e-mail: foldedpaperdance@gmail.com

© Springer Nature Singapore Pte Ltd. 2018   31
D. R. Cole and J. P. N. Bradley (eds.), *Principles of Transversality in Globalization and Education*, https://doi.org/10.1007/978-981-13-0583-2_3

Transfiguring Blue: Entering the Wild Studio

In *The Three Ecologies*, Félix Guattari is writing to change the logic by which we live. As he emphasizes, this new "ecosophical logic…resembles the manner in which an artist may be led to alter his work after the intrusion of some accidental detail, an event-incident that suddenly makes his initial project bifurcate, makes it drift [*dériver*] far from its previous path, however certain it had once appeared to be" (2008, p. 35). This chapter therefore presents a logic of the event, a non-transcendent ordering of a juncture of chance and intentions, a movement drifting toward a rhizomatic multiplication of possibilities. How might this logic of (non)place, convergences, divergences, and unexpected encounters play across the ecosystem of the contemporary global university?

Wild studios are transversal crisscrossings of the usual borders within a university that provide performative stages for dynamically cultivating our practices of engagement in the world. These studios surface in diverse locations: tucked away as a lean-to in a quiet clearing in the woods, in a digital experiment with projecting onto a mapped surface of a house, down the stairs in a basement, outside in the garage, or reclaimed from an abandoned industrial building along the edges of a city, and the chaos inside and outside our doors, windows, laboratories, classrooms, cities, and planet. The studio is an experimental space of opening.

In 1862, Henry David Thoreau began his famous essay "Walking" with the following thought on behalf of wildness:

> I wish to speak a word for Nature, for absolute freedom and wildness, as contrasted with a freedom and culture merely civil—to regard man as an inhabitant, or a part and parcel of Nature, rather than a member of society. I wish to make an extreme statement, if so I may make an emphatic one, for there are enough champions of civilization… (p. 1)

The binaries are too simple and would be too easy to deconstruct, but the "extreme statement" that speaks on behalf of wildness stands as a marker of a possible path for the university in an age when the cybernetic posthuman emerges within and alongside the Anthropocene. We live along a threshold between those forms of life that are the *regulae* of the contemporary neoliberal university that runs *as if* of its own accord toward the quantification of all quality and the dominance of a certain vision of technocapitalism. To work in the university is to work in this context. Nevertheless, there can always be found fissures, pockets, and seams where something else is occurring, an elsewhere opening toward the unforeseen. How can we activate a pedagogy that might tip current university structures toward these transversal pathways of art, philosophy, and science (although we will have the most to say about the first two)?

Studios are places of messiness and ordering, of dissolving and coagulating, of cutting, shredding, and of gluing things to a surface. From first goes and rough cuts through rehearsals to refinements and the opening curtain of the show. From crash-and-burns to works of beauty or of profound ugliness. What if the university were imagined as an enactment of such workplaces, often modularized and portable, that are built across the "normalized" pathways of learning, research, and credentialization where movements could occur that might create a torque in the university as, a being-coming-upon by surprise (Cole & Bradley, 2016)? Dreams and things might change places, morph. The moon might rise through the 3D printers; blue might tinge the genomic readouts or the equations of econometrics; projective video mapping might transform the classroom into a mutable site for discovery; and dancing might blur the boundaries between image, concept, and materiality. These interstitial structures enable the movement of transversality, the pragmatic and conceptual practices of modulated cutting-across, and an essential aspect of reconfiguring the dated structures of the university and its relations with its locales.

The transversal can be accomplished by all human activity, and, in relation to the university "the three domains—art, science, and philosophy—each enter into a singular struggle with chaos. Each unfurls a map over what is wild and treacherous to trace a territory. Different forms of thought are created from chaos as a result" (Bradley, 2014, p. 105). There is, in each of these distinctively creative domains, a different relation to language, but in this context we are giving preferential treatment to the movements of art and philosophy since we want to stitch alternative patterns along the edges of the university in which science usually commands an allegiance as the only representative of the rational, and, more importantly, because our own work springs most directly out of the performativity of philosophy and art. The wild is felt most intimately and turbulently, after all, when it is closest to the ancestrally nomadic home (Cole & Woodrow, 2016).

While both art and philosophy usually have a formal disciplinary place within the university—although this arrangement differs in various areas of the world—neither of them as transversal activities can be contained by their departmental boundaries. As Deleuze and Guattari make clear:

> Art is not chaos but a composition of chaos that yields the vision or sensation, so that it constitutes, as Joyce says, a *chasmos*, a composed chaos—neither foreseen nor preconceived. Art transforms chaotic variability [the formlessness of the dynamic sublime] into *chaoid* variety…Art struggles with chaos but it does so in order to render it sensory. (1994, pp. 204–05)

The university, like art and philosophy, can be understood as a "composition of chaos" in which a set of translational operators called "disciplines" or "methods" all act, necessarily and often with enormous benefit, to partially and provisionally domesticate the wild.

In today's educational climate, the wild tends to be ever more eclipsed, while the spaces of domestication become more rigidly embedded in the global society of surveillance, command, and control. And, yet, wild studios sit, often invisibly, along the edges of committee meetings and departmental politics, of the funding crises for research, the anxiety of the job search or of promotion, and the obfuscations of global rankings. Even in the deepest tangles of the bureaucracy of the university *chaosmosis* is in motion and possibilities whisper quietly when the minutes of a meeting are riffled by a slight gust of wind.

There is, of course, a long history of pedagogical models that have sought to re-situate art, philosophy, and the sciences in a more dynamic relationship to each other and the university's outside, including—among many other possible examples—Jane Addams's Hull House; John Dewey's University of Chicago Laboratory School; Ranbindranath Tagore's project at Santiniketan; Highlander Research and Education Center (formerly the Highlander Folk School); Black Mountain College in the mountains of North Carolina; and Arcosanti in the Arizona Desert. Other projects have sought to re-valorize campus-community relations across disciplines, such as *Imagining America* which engages artists and scholars in public life; the SARAI Programme at the Centre for the Study of Developing Societies (CSDS, Delhi, India) which acts as a research platform for media, urban life, and the public domain; and the Transdisciplinary Research Undergraduate Exchange between the University of Hong Kong's Common Core and Utrecht University's Humanities Honours programme.[1] We ask: What binds them together, internally and externally? How might they form an archival legacy for a more creative assemblage that will keep the university in motion beyond itself?

Wild studios become a set of transactional movements that fire the synapses of an emerging nervous system of the university, one that extends digitally and physically beyond what used to be considered—at least in contexts we are most familiar with—the "campus." Our own current investigations into how we might construct pop-up spaces for the wild grow from an experience of the unfolding of a campus into a studio of the streets where thinking, feeling, and making are constantly changing places. The city—for us Lugano, Philadelphia, New York, Seattle, Hong Kong, Kochi—is what *catalyzes* transversality as we make our modest efforts to confront the contradictions, beauty, pain, and possibilities that urban space, already globalized and planetarized, demands of philosophy, art, and the university. The street breathes stories in and out. The street is an event of politics, economics, ecology, and the internal questions that drive such questions across traditionally established fields. The university is never self-contained; it breaks out and the studio is where people gather to keep an eye out for what needs to happen.

An Evolving Studio: Traveling Architectures

One of our most recent experiments with wild studios has been *Traveling Architectures*, a multidisciplinary collaborative research and design performance platform

---

[1]There is an immense history of educational experiments and the ones we have mentioned are just a handful of examples. See, for instance: Jane Addams's Hull House: Jackson (2001), more info at: http://www.hullhousemuseum.org/. John Dewey's University of Chicago Laboratory School: Rudd and Attwood (2014). Hein (2004). Rabindranath Tagore's Santiniketan School and the Visva-Bharati University: Mukherjee (2016). Highlander Research and Education Center (formerly the Highlander Folk School); Glen (2015). Black Mountain College: Díaz (2014). Arcosanti: Soleri (1987) *Imagining America*: http://imaginingamerica.org/. SARAI Programme at the Centre for the Study of Developing Societies (CSDS, Delhi, India) http://sarai.net/. Transdisciplinary Undergraduate Research Exchange between the University of Hong Kong's Common Core and Utrecht University's Humanities Honours programme: https://commoncore.hku.hk/2016/10/transdisciplinary-undergraduate-research-exchange-2017/.

that created transportable installations—of performance, objects, and workshops—that were adaptable to diverse community sites. In one of our initial projects, running from January to June 2017 and funded by Design Trust (an initiative of Hong Kong Ambassadors of Design), we formed a team of an artistic director and choreographer, a landscape architect, a documentary filmmaker, and a lighting designer in order to engage in a research laboratory, workshop series, and interactive exhibit culminating in a multimedia performance.[2]

The research structure of the project necessitated a mixture of the use of iterative design and performance investigations as well as the inclusion of critical ethnographies and cultural studies analysis with a focus on how memory, performative architectures, biography, and multiple art forms, including new media, can catalyze in the imagining of new futures. The most crucial fulcrum point in this project was to identify how engaging with the materialities in their known and unknown forms began to transform these questions into harbingers, then instantiations, of different transversal relationships between object, disciplines, people, and places: a wild studio on the move.

Pai Dongs in Hong Kong

Grounding the project were the *pai dongs*, hawkers' stalls, served as the central figure around which the other examples of everyday design culture such as lighting, textiles, and cinema were arrayed (Fig. 3.1).

We first tracked the history of the folding and unfolding facades of the everyday design culture of Hong Kong's street merchants. The *pai dong*, as well as the *dai pai dong* (food stalls), had a tremendous upsurge after WWII as refugees from mainland China fled to Hong Kong and set up street stalls, movable and often temporary shops, in order to sell their wares and food across numerous Hong Kong neighborhoods.

By the 1960s, the *pai dong* had become an emblem of what was considered unique about Hong Kong both as a cultural reservoir and cultural trigger. In the late 1970s, partially as a response to the increasing urban development, the Hong Kong government began seeking ways to regulate—to moderate the wildness—of the *pai dong* culture. Nevertheless, this culture continues to persist and its vestiges of portability of everyday work sites have also lent themselves to material, social, and conceptual metamorphoses including new contemporary artistic versions by Hong Kong artists Kacey Wong, Michael Leung, and many others.[3]

In our project, we developed a series of emergent forms that not only reflect the histories of the *pai dong* design cultures, but also began to open out to new

---

[2]For more on Design Trust and *Traveling Architectures*, for which Kanta Kochhar-Lindgren was the initiator and artistic director, see http://designtrust.hk/grant-recipients/traveling-architectures/ ; https://www.facebook.com/travelingarchitectures/; and http://www.foldedpaperdanceandtheatre.com/traveling-architectures/.

[3]For additional artistic projects on the *pai dong*, see https://www.facebook.com/events/386499124738004/.

Fig. 3.1 Pai Dongs in Hong Kong. Gwyn Edwards, photographer. Courtesy of Folded Paper Dance and Theatre

spaces of interaction between communities and between art forms. What kinds of performative architectures are possible and what can we discover as we experiment with the *pai dong* as a movable form across various scales? *Traveling Architectures* captures one example of what we mean by wild studios as "pedagogical experiments that cut across registers." The project activated spatial materiality that recalibrates perception, thought, and sociability, that can engage broad-based audiences interested in "building as we go" across geographies, inter-arts, and material fabrication in ways that can also track patterns of labor, migration, and everyday design. All studios require provisional borders and frames to be in place. Elizabeth Grosz writes that "[t]he frame is what establishes territory out of the chaos of the earth" (2008, p. 11) and each project in a studio creates a chaosmatic provisional framing. We want to learn how to balance between the territory and the chaos where art, philosophy, and the university are an "extension of the architectural imperative to organize the space of the earth" (2008, p. 10).

This type of "organization," however, attends to the contact points with chaos and remains wary of the tendency toward embedding an essentialism whose purpose is to capture the wild. Wild studios are many sets of interlocking, shifting spaces, folding, and unfolding, carrying and transforming the exigencies of our multiply manifold lives. What are the implications, more specifically, of folding and refolding the buildings, projects, texts, and politics that we inhabit for our vision of wild studios that traverse the university?

Miniature Houses on Wheels

A miniature house on wheels is one of the traveling architectural forms that emerged from our collaborations as a kind of happy accident. Made from PVC sheets, the structure sits on a 5-foot wood frame with wheels, an analogy of the most basic form of the *pai dong*: its rectilinear shape. It also can unfold so that the house becomes a wall that can be used as a projective surface as well as completely unfold so that it lays flat, the support in the middle can be removed, and the accordion side frame dropped all the way down. At its most compact, each house is $15'' \times 15'' \times 15''$. Materially, the miniature buildings refract our earlier claim that "studios are places of messiness and ordering, of dissolving and coagulating, of cutting, shredding, and of gluing things to a surface." This materiality also provoked myriad cross-cultural, cross-temporal associations through its irregular surfaces and shifting frames (Fig. 3.2).

In the final *Traveling Architectures Multi-Media Performance*, we engaged with the moving miniature buildings in several ways, most significantly by using video mapping to project archival footage inside the buildings. Here, the quality of the rough-hewn traveling architectural form both contradicted and highlighted projections which we knew could disappear at any moment in a way that the buildings could not. Grosz writes: "[a]rchitectural framing produces the very possibility of the screen, the screen functioning as a plane for virtual projection, a hybrid of wall, window, and mirror" (2008, p. 17).

As a result, the moving image inside the moving building on wheels shifted time and space, putting a wedge into the perceptual dimensions of the performative so that the angle of this scalar composition required new thinking, even if only for the blink of an eye.

This particular studio-on-the-move represents, as one example, all those structures that we want to gesture toward when we articulate the wild studio in relation to the university, both of which require transversal research, collaboration, and intensities of conceptual, material, and imaginative expressiveness (Fig. 3.3).

The Transversality of Ecosophical Chaosmosis

Félix Guattari has called this wildness, this movement of movement, by different names: *chaosmosis*, *heterogenesis*, and *ecosophy*. Each of these names indicates a singularization of making and thinking, both of which are material and both of which are conceptual. (Spinoza, the lens-grinder, is the *genius loci* of all studios.) The operational manner, which is not quite a "method," of art and philosophy as transversal movements that face the wild is that of what the Situationists called a *dérive*, a movement that wanders, loops unexpectedly, and returns to cross its previous paths before once again taking its leave rather than the straight lines of classical logic, algorithms, and instrumental rationality. *Dérive* is the name for that which, in any way, disrupts the normalizing routines of the university, opening as a slit for the wild

Fig. 3.2 Miniature house on wheels. Wing Hong Tung, photographer. Courtesy of Folded Paper Dance and Theatre

to flow back through the orderliness of programs, tenure clocks, impact factors, and organizational charts. [4]

---

[4]The introduction to the Situationists on *Ubuweb* tells us that: "When the Situationist International was first formed, it had a predominantly artistic focus; emphasis was placed on concepts like unitary urbanism and psychogeography. Gradually, however, that focus shifted more toward

Fig. 3.3 Video projections inside the buildings on wheels. Courtesy of Folded Paper Dance and Theatre

This happy accident of the emergence of the three miniature buildings on wheels informs our work on wild studios. To more often enter this space of the wild, we are developing methods for tilting the frames. We need to develop a pluralism for geo-spatialities along with a philosophical-artistic *praxis* that retools how we actually give dimensions to our work in the university. This teaching operates as the creation of reflective-projective projects that illuminate a question, a different articulation of politics, work, and community; and an engendering of interstitial spaces enfolded along the axis of the chaosmotic processes of the earth (Fig. 3.4).[5]

revolutionary and political theory. The Situationist International reached the apex of its creative output and influence in 1967 and 1968, with the former marking the publication of the two most significant texts of the Situationist movement, *The Society of the Spectacle* by Guy Debord and *The Revolution of Everyday Life* by Raoul Vaneigem. The expressed writing and political theory of the two aforementioned texts, along with other Situationist publications, proved greatly influential in shaping the ideas behind the May 1968 insurrections in France; quotes, phrases, and slogans from Situationist texts and publications were ubiquitous on posters and graffiti throughout France during the uprisings." (http://www.ubu.com/film/si.html).

[5]We have explored additional aspects of this reconceptualization in Kochhar-Lindgren (2016); Kochhar-Lindgren (2014); and Kochhar-Lindgren (2017).

Fig. 3.4 Wild Studios drawing, folding/unfolding. Ng Lai Ching Daisy, Artist. Courtesy of Folded Paper Dance and Theatre

Art ~ Philosophy ~ University: Wild Studios and the Redistribution of the Sensible

Archimedes needed only a place to stand and a lever in order to move the world. Art and philosophy often require even less, only the thinnest of surfaces on which to draw, dance, and scribble as the originary thrust of the art–philosophy moment erupts into the world as a scratch that becomes ever more complex with the pages of the book, the yarns of the tapestry, or the metals of a sculpture which turns, like a whirling Janus, in different directions at the same time. Art and philosophy are an ancient magic carpet, the results of the arabesque of a tapestry worn toward translucence by the vicissitudes of history. The carpet, its insignia woven into its very fabric, is a platform for creating the possibilities of the university, possibilities that unfold simultaneously in all directions and across all dimensions, from the subterranean to the heights, and take all the forms between the straight line and the dimensional spiral of a labyrinth. Without them—as well as the inventiveness of the sciences—the university merely drones along as a utilitarian profit machine that absorbs its inventiveness until it eventually implodes from its own dull heaviness into the instrumentalized mediocrity of a pervasive audit culture. Ozymandias in the desert.

Change, however, is always possible for the university as concept, activity, and as a place where wildness waits in the wings to appear, take shape, and do its work. Thinking and making are always twists, torques of transversality, and this always creates turbulence. This dynamism, unless it becomes a completely dissipative chaos, keeps the expressive platforms of art and philosophy in motion along the edges of commodification and codification as they rework the interweavings of the dead, memory, fashions, methods, materials, and conceptualities that shape a university of learning that moves forward, backwards, and to the sides as it spirals through the world in a form of creative turbulence. The magic carpet curls at the front edge and hurtles beyond the edge of the last galaxy. "The brain," as Emily Dickinson reminds us, "is wider than the sky" (1924/2000, CXXVI). And the brain is a sociopoetic assemblage. Philosophy and art—which synaptically, sensorially, historically, and digitally perform transdisciplinary contact points with *all the other disciplines* that currently abide within the house of learning—are powerful transversal affiliations that will transform, at different rates of speed in different sites, the relational networks of the university-to-come.

In *Schizoanalytic Cartograpies*, Guattari reminds us that *all* models of collective and individual subjectification are, "in a certain fashion," *all* valid. "This is solely to the extent that their principles of intelligibility give up any universalist pretention and admit that they have no other mission than to contribute to the cartography of existential Territories, implying sensible, cognitive, affective, aesthetic, etc. Universes, for clearly delimited areas and periods of time" (2013, p. 3). Philosophy and art, like the sciences, create cartographies for lived universes of alternative possible futures that come-and-go over time. Wild studios are where individualities, collectivities, and assemblages are constructed. And, while we are all attuned to the necessary cautions about "universals," we do want to claim that the need to remain open to the mutability of the wild is a universal necessity, for human existence and its infinite others. Without exposure to chaos, there is no learning. These changes about the "most dazzling transversals" and are the "*Universes of virtuality*, the best furnished with line of processuality" (Guattari, 2013, p. 5). The virtual is the capacity to extend, in unpredictable ways, beyond a current border, boundary, restriction, or constraint.[6]

Speaking of "analytic cartographies [that] extend beyond the existential Territories to which they are assigned," Guattari argues that "in painting or literature, the concrete performance of these cartographies requires that they evolve and innovate, that they open up new futures, without their authors having prior recourse to assured theoretical principles or to the authority of a group, a school or an academy…Work in progress!" (2008, p. 27). Painting, literature, dance, theater, and philosophy—as *concrete performances*—are always works in progress, unfolding along their experimental edges that sinuously join and unform forms of knowledge and expression as demonstrated in this chapter through Wild Studios.

Each act, concrete and singular, creates pathways for "new futures" that we cannot see ahead of time. These are "analytic" in a general sense—that is, they loosen and reorganize into a more comprehensive understanding—and transversal: they do not stay put, but travel across and through the university like a series of diffracted waves. They must, however, find gardens, benches, classrooms, theaters, stairways, and corridors where moments of formalization can take shape. The time and space of the university must be punctuated by articulation, but articulation depends on spaces, punctuation, and the inventiveness of language.

---

[6]From a larger temporal perspective, Guattari explains that we are all working in the space of the "three zones of historical fracture": the age of European Christianity, the age of capitalistic deterritorialization of knowledge and techniques, and the age of planetary computerization. We are compressing all of these, for the moment, into the concept of the "university."

The Parasitical Redistribution of the Sensible

Everything lives off of everything else. The university as it stands today is a system of credentialization constructed as a curricular organization of required and elective credits, majors, minors, assessments, grades, and degrees. The university curriculum necessarily entails structural pathways and flows and a central question for those of us inside, or alongside, the university is how we can stay cognizant of wildness even as we construct sequences of prerequisites and graduation requirements. Michel Serres, in *The Parasite*, has explored what he calls—following Lucretius and many others—a *disequilibrium* created by a "cantilever" that throws things, however slightly, off balance and therefore creates movements. "The parasite has a relation with the relation and not with the station. And it puts the relation in the form of a cantilever" (2007, p. 33).

Archimedes, again. If we are to move things along and create performative channels for curricular, epistemological, and social change, then we must stand to one side, a tiny lever in hand. We never have relations with the "things as such, and, undoubtedly, never to subjects as such... *And that is the meaning of the prefix para- in the word parasite: it is on the side, next to, shifted; it is not on the thing, but on its relation.* It has relations, as they say, and makes a system of them. It is always mediate and never immediate" (2007, p. 38).

These "relays" and "stations" operate through a series of switching points where knowledge, people, places, and systems crossover and change places in acts of learning that occur along a manifesting edge. These switching points can be anything: a text, a painting, a gesture, a building, a conversation, a bike rack. It is where translations occur in-between. The milieu of the host and the guest, which require one another, creates "quasi-objects" and "quasi-subjects" whose only essence is the mutability of changing places. These switching points, translational operators, have differential temporalities that are sometimes instantaneous and sometimes take a lifetime of practice.

The wild breaks the boundaries of bureaucracy, enabling the possibility of a space for creative university administration, the task of which is to provide the platforms for contact between knowledge generation, enhanced liveability, and the unforeseen. The wild, which is not a thing-object-being, is the freedom of the manifestation of manifesting *natura naturans*, which art and philosophy as transversal forces of reconfiguration constantly enact. The university is caught in many ways between the *uni-* and the *poly-*, but it must work assiduously to hold itself in this space of ambiguity and tension in order to avoid the double dangers of either attempting to close its borders to the unruliness of contingency or to dissipate into formlessness. Currently, the most dangerous delusion of the neoliberal fetishized image of the university is its wish to exterminate the wild and replace it with an algorithm of absolute predictability that translates, to many decimal points, all qualities into the precise measurability of quantity as a literal or metaphorical profit. Listening for the wild keeps the doors open, the windows cracked, and the streets alive with a deep salsa beat.

What does it take to keep a university alive? To let parts of it die, decompose, and become food for future generations and to realize that everything lives off of everything else, however, distant or close-at-hand. The university must learn the art of the parasite, how to ride along on the backs of other animals and how to give its body for the good of the other. A curriculum can never completely map the infinite number of ecosophical micro-operators in any one experience, but it can provide the opportunities for the ecstatic experience that is learning: image, text, test tube, task, topic, laboratory, particle accelerator, dance, cadaver, painting, poem. Learning is always metamorphic, though at different speeds and scales, and the discovery is not of a pre-established object in the world but of an *encounter* that constitutes an event out of which precipitates objects of knowledge. Teaching is learning the practice of providing catalytic platforms for this encounter. Made things are real things and the real reveals itself to making under whatever name this making carries: art, philosophy, science, the university.

As we reshape, redistribute and *throw-ahead-of-ourselves* the university, we will clear new ground, water, and air for the experience of learning, discovery, invention, and a reciprocity of the differentiated commons. There will be, in Jacques Rancière's terms, a "redistribution of the sensible":

> I call the distribution of the sensible the system of self-evident facts of sense perception that simultaneously discloses the existence of something in common and the delimitations that define the respective parts and positions within it. A distribution of the sensible therefore establishes at one and the same time something common that is shared and exclusive parts. This apportionment of parts and positions is based on a distribution of spaces, times, and forms of activity that determines the very manner in which something in common lends itself to participation in what way various individuals are a part in this distribution. (2004, p. 7)

This requires the construction of new studios for a university that can learn to live rhizomatically along the edges. This "redistribution of the sensible" will create a new aesthetic of, in, and across the university, not as a "pure" form of art or of thought—those are always mirages—but as a formation of the entirety of our sensibility. We treat the classroom as the studio; the studio as the classroom; and theaters, maker spaces, and the city as both. All are porous spaces filled with kinetically potential energy: all await the unexpected, which teaching and learning delight in triggering.

Working the *Trans-*: Art, Philosophy, and the University

Art and philosophy offer extraordinary resources to be drawn from—we need to know as much as possible about the archives, theories, and styles of these studios—but the act of making as the act of making exposes, exposits another seam in our experience. And we need to share this off-balance balancing act, this living-with-ambiguity, with our students as we become collaboratively philosophical artists across a variety of domains of knowledge. We teach them to work the balance beam, the tightrope. We walk with them, leap with them, let them fall, provide a net when necessary. We teach them to build their own studio work.

This movement of the wild entails *practicing*, over and over again, the structuration of the *trans-* that opens up the potentialities of transferral, translation, transformation, and transversality: A movement that cannot be captured as any sort of completely determinate form of knowing (which is always a phantasmatic lure). This *trans-* immediately unsettles. As an operator for the hope of new futures, it is always at risk, threatened by myriad forms of naming, control, disciplining, fear, and the regulations that are part of the law of the university that drives experience toward false measurability or attempts to create a policy environment without the space of play that is structurally necessary for creative change to occur. Systems must have buffers, be porous to differences, and the *trans-* is itself only by exposing itself to fundamental risks.

The process of transversality demonstrated by philosophy and art is what Guattari has named, as one name among others, *heterogenesis*:

> processes of continuous resingularization. Individuals must become more united and increasingly different...By means of these transversal tools, subjectivity is able to install itself simultaneously in the realms of the environment, in the major social and institutional assemblages, and symmetrically in the landscapes and fantasies of the most intimate spheres of the individual. The reconquest of a degree of creative autonomy in one particular domain encourages conquests in other domains—the catalyst for a gradual reforging and renewal of humanity's confidence in itself starting at the most miniscule level. (2008, p. 45)

This happens, but it is not always trackable, certainly not countable or rankable. Instead, making and thinking spread across domains from the intimate to the collective—and these are not only *epistemological but also affective* domains—in a paradoxical process that singularizes and draws us differentially into the commonality of heterogenesis.

Philosophy and art, which are finite works that touch the edges of infinity, "could be understood as the lever that Archimedes sought, highly efficient multipliers of possibility that creates and gives access to our largest capacities" (Robinson, 2016, p. 259). The *chaosmosis* of art and philosophy exerts powerful transversal levers of experimental procedures that are not determinable beforehand, of innovative practices for catalyzing the movement of new machines of learning.

Philosophy and art are telekinetic and telepathic twins, differentiable but inseparable. They always have been and always will be. One is the lining of the other's sleeve; one is each side of the magic carpet and the fringe marks the leading edge (which also moves toward what we call the "past," but this is a dimension of time which also always precedes us to greet us ahead of time). "Artistic practices [as well as philosophy] are 'ways of doing and making' that intervene in the general distribution of ways of doing and making as well as in the relationship they maintain to modes of being and forms of visibility" (Rancière, 2004, p. 8). Studios are sites where the materialities of discovery, imagination, and history converge and the invisible becomes visible.

Endless Conclusion

The university is in motion with the *uni-* and the *poly-* doing a nonstop tango. Nothing stands still: the curriculum flows through us. *Panta rhei*: the river, its banks, our foot, our consciousness, and all of that. The subject, the object, the context, and the milieu are all changing. The task is not to pin the flow permanently into place—except for a short duration that may last the lifetime of the universe and for provisional purposes of testing the machinery of a material concept—but to learn to swim, to float, to be carried along, to be carried down in a deep dive, and then to bob back to the surface for as long as we are able. This is the learning of teaching, the way that universities might exhibit in the face of the deep resistance of habit, tradition, and the obsessive neoliberal drive toward the normativization of "profit" and the evacuation of singularity as the *telos* of the university.

The labors of teaching and learning in the university that acknowledges the wild activates the transformations, translations, and turbulences of a set of mutually constitutive registers that bring forth skeins of the new university with its scintillating possibilities of futurity: that is, the stitching together of bodies, conceptualities, and architectures as *events*. This perpetual and singularizing dynamic of heterogenetic ecosophy generates new forms of disciplined and composed chaos in which we work ourselves to the bone for the sake of thinking that makes and a making that thinks. The university will flourish if these currents are (re)iterated in the transversal movements within and beyond in wild studios where philosophy and art activate the twists that torque, wavelike, and blue, along the edges of that institution we call, still, the university.

References

Bradley, J. P. N. (2014). Zigzagged: Ripped to bits, torn to shreds. *Dialogos, 14*(2), 83–106.

Cole, D. R., & Bradley, J. P. N. (2016). *A pedagogy of cinema*. Rotterdam: Sense Publishers.

Cole, D. R., & Woodrow, C. (Eds.). (2016). *Super dimensions in globalisation and education*. Singapore: Springer.

Deleuze, G., & Guattari, F. (1994). *What is philosophy?* (H. Tomlinson & G. Burchell, Trans.). New York: Columbia University Press.

Díaz, E. (2014). *The experimenters: Chance and design at black mountain college*. Chicago: University of Chicago Press. Also at: http://www.blackmountaincollege.org/.

Dickinson, E. (1924). *The complete poems of Emily Dickinson*. Boston: Little, Brown; Bartleby.com, 2000. www.bartleby.com/113/. (July 24, 2017).

Glen, J. M. (2015). *Highlander: No Ordinary School 1932—1962*. Lexington: University Press of Kentucky. Also at: http://highlandercenter.org/.

Grosz, E. (2008). *Chaos, territory, art: Deleuze and the framing of the earth*. New York: Columbia University Press.

Guattari, F. (2008). *The three ecologies* (I. Pindar & P. Sutton, Trans.). London: Continuum.

Guattari, F. (2013). *Schizoanalytic cartographies* (A. Goffey, Trans.). London: Bloomsbury Academic.

Hein, G. (2004). John Dewey and museum education. *Curator the Museum Educator, 47*(4), 413–427.

Jackson, S. (2001). *Lines of activity: Performance, historiography, hull-house domesticity*. Ann Arbor: University of Michigan Press.

Kochhar-Lindgren, G. (2017). Hong Kong's laboratory of liberal learning: Design- thinking, *Phronēsis*, and the Common Core. In D. Araya & P. Marber (Eds.), *The evolution of the liberal arts in a global age* (pp. 126–134). New York: Routledge.

Kochhar-Lindgren, K. (2016). Participatory Choreographies, our future cities, and the place of creative learning in international arts exchanges. In P. Blessinger & L. Watts (Eds.), *Creative learning in higher education: international perspectives and approaches* (pp. 93–104). New York: Routledge.

Kochhar-Lindgren, K. (2014). The turbulence project: Touching cities, visual tactility, and windows. *Performance Research International, 19*(5), 13–22.

Mukherjee, H. B. (2016). *Education for fullness: A study of the educational thought and experiment of Rabindranath Tagore*. New York: Routledge.

Rancière, J. (2004). *The politics of aesthetics* G Rockhill (Ed. & Trans.). London: Bloomsbury.

Robinson, M. (2016). *The givenness of things: Essays*. London: Virago Press.

Rudd, A. G., & Attwood, A. (2014). Dewey lab school at the university of Chicago (Vol. 2). In D.C. Phillips (Ed.), *Encyclopedia of educational theory and philosophy* (pp. 455–458). Thousand Oaks, CA: Sage.

Serres, M. (2007). *The parasite*. Minneapolis, MN: University of Minnesota Press.

Soleri, P. (1987). *Arcosanti: An urban laboratory?* Santa Monica: VTI Press. Also at: https://arcosanti.org/.

Stevens, W. (1990). *The collected poems of Wallace Stevens*. New York: Vintage.

Thoreau, H. D. (1862, June) Walking. *The Atlantic*. https://www.theatlantic.com/magazine/archive/1862/06/walking/304674/.

Gray Kochhar-Lindgren Professor & Director of the Common Core at the University of Hong Kong (https://commoncore.hku.hk/), Kochhar-Lindgren holds a Ph.D. in Interdisciplinary Studies from Emory University and has also taught in the United States, Switzerland, Germany, and, most recently, as a Visiting Professor at the Institute of Cultural Analysis at the University of Utrecht. As an administrator, he was the inaugural Director of the Discovery Core and the inaugural holder of the Associate Vice Chancellorship for Undergraduate Learning at the University of Washington-Bothell. In 2009–10, Kochhar-Lindgren served a Fulbright Scholar based at HKU, teaching in both philosophy and comparative literature and consulting across the city on the system-wide curricular change in Hong Kong's tertiary institutions. Having recently launched GLADE (Global Liberal Arts Design Experiments), an international network of General Education programmes, Kochhar-Lindgren writes, reads, and develops projects on the contemporary global university and on the relationships between philosophy, aesthetics, and urban life.

Kanta Kochhar-Lindgren, Ph.D. Founding Director of *Folded Paper Dance and Theatre*, focuses her collaborative endeavors on building cross-cultural networks and new forms of dance, theatre, and community laboratories. Recent projects include *Traveling Architectures* (2017 Hong Kong), *Water in Kerala: Art, Performance, Science* (2015 in Kochi and Kollam, India), and *Pier Windows* (2014 Hong Kong). She has recently served as a Fulbright-Nehru Scholar in India, is the author of two books and many articles; is a former editor of *Theatre Topics*; and has taught a range of Theatre, Dance, and Performance Studies courses at the University of Washington-Bothell, Macalester College, and the Hong Kong University of Science and Technology.

Chapter 4
A Transversal University? Criticality, Creativity and Catatonia in the Globalised Pursuit of Higher Education Excellence

Christian Beighton

Abstract This chapter uses the concept of transversality to analyse developments in the increasingly globalised delivery of higher education (HE). Writing from the perspective of higher education provision in England, I first discuss the use of the term by Félix Guattari, before drawing on Gilles Deleuze's use of the concept in connection with learning as an apprenticeship in signs. This analysis allows me to use a Deleuzo–Guattarian transversal ontology to critique drives for excellence, social mobility and student choice in higher education. I highlight connections between these increasingly ubiquitous demands and wider global trends of prosumption, liquefaction and dividualisation. Referring to the nature of this transversality in this connection, I stress the differential operation of transversal practices which emphasise productive forms of criticality and creativity in HE. Transversality therefore provides an impetus and a model for higher learning as a creative, rather than repetitive, process.

Keywords Higher education · Transversality · Ontology · Prosumption Liquefaction · Dividualisaiton

Introduction

In October 2017, Conservative politician Chris Heaton-Harris wrote to universities in England asking for details of their teaching of politics. It was subsequently claimed that he was carrying out "research" for a book about the politically volatile issue of Britain's leaving the European Union ("Brexit") (BBC, 2017). The intervention has been described as an unwarranted McCarthyite interference with freedom of speech, reminding us that the right to criticality in higher education institutions (HEIs) can never be taken for granted. With this in mind, this chapter argues that criticality is under threat from discourses which place it at the services of globalisation and its

C. Beighton (✉)
Canterbury Christ Church University, Canterbury, UK
e-mail: Christian.beighton@canterbury.ac.uk

© Springer Nature Singapore Pte Ltd. 2018
D. R. Cole and J. P. N. Bradley (eds.), *Principles of Transversality in Globalization and Education*, https://doi.org/10.1007/978-981-13-0583-2_4

correlate, reproduction. This threat undermines one of the academy's core democratic missions of ensuring basic freedoms, but, like globalisation itself, my analysis is multiple. Drawing on the work of Felix Guattari and Gilles Deleuze, I put transversality at the heart of super-complex developments in the increasingly globalised delivery of higher education. Focusing on the way drives for excellence, social mobility and student choice in HE are linked to globalisation, this context and its implications are analysed from the perspective of three demands which accompany the globalisation of the academy: the requirement for teaching excellence, the facilitation of mobility and the promotion of choice. These three demands are analysed as the effects of three specific features of globalised service delivery: prosumption, liquefaction and dividualisation. While all three, I argue, explicitly require the homogenisation of education, the value of transversality lies in the fact that these developments are a function of practices which also emphasise productive forms of creative criticality in HE. Transversality thus provides both a critique of and an impetus for higher learning as a fundamentally creative operation rather than repetitive academic mimesis.

Transversality

Despite experience which highlights the "dynamic, diverse and difficult" nature in which markets are actually formed as entities, much work on higher education views the latter as "simple, static, unwanted, practices", (Komljenovic & Robertson, 2016, p. 2). Diversification, to be sure, lies at the heart of the globalised pursuit of capital, but as Cole (2014, p. 71) suggests, the task is to ask what *kind* of diversification is in train: is proliferation merely the catatonic repetition of the same, or a production of the new? The concept of transversality owes its existence to this question.[1]

Developed by Félix Guattari in his work on institutional psychoanalysis (Guattari, 1974; see also Deleuze, 2002; Fourquet, 2007), transversality has its roots in Guattari's challenge to Freudian concepts of subjective unity in the sense that they undermine the ways in which the self comes back together in Freud. It is thus important as an affirmation of difference which provides a means overcoming the tired dualism of private versus public subconscious (Dosse, 2007) built on Freudian subjectivity. Such a priori explanations reduce complex experience to a repetitive set of drives, repressions and fantasies, defining the subject as an entity unaffected by changing relations in space and time. Deleuze (1925–1995) describes such dualism as a form of absolute narcissism. Reliant on an indiscriminate use of the death drive to explain phenomena, he criticises the way in which psychoanalysts wheel out such explanations to interpret even the most disparate social phenomena (Deleuze, 2007).

---

[1]Bosteels (1998, p. 156) attributes the original importation of the concept into philosophy to Jean Paul Sartre's critique of Husserl before its adoption by Guattari in 1964. While both thinkers use the term to rethink the relation between individual and group consciousness, a key difference lies in the way Sartre insists on the prevalence of action in the present rather than Guattari's focus on the dynamism and future orientation of a subject evolving over and within time (see, for example, Schrag, 2000).

Instead, transversal connections allow a subject as group to escape such a reified definition, connecting instead with its own possibilities of non-sense and its own outside. Identity itself becomes a territory defined by habit and its "passing places" (Sarnel, 2007, p. 99), and the brain itself operates "across fields, bringing them together in new ways" (Murphie, 2010, p. 28).

Transversal relations also aim to explain how is it possible for things to exist in a flow of time which changes them and thus refer to a wider understanding of the interconnections which embody social change. Guattari is keen to repeatedly refer to the creative potential of an immanent constructivist process which operates outside of hierarchical or even horizontal ontological relations (Guattari, 1974). Transversality is thus a dimension of pragmatic action which develops reciprocally and diagonally between entities instead of reverting to relationships of similarity, analogy or sameness:

> If we are to understand the interactions between ecosystems, the mechanosphere, and the social and individual universes of reference, we have to learn to think 'transversally'. (Guattari, 1989, p. 135)

To enable this, time, understood as an equally dynamic multiplicity is also always becoming other, allows transversal links between series which operate in the joint medium of difference which is determined in new series where creativity can actually happen. The transversal subject is an anti-self, a fundamentally creative multiplicity (Deleuze, 2002, p. 277) or "revolutionary side-step" (Massumi, 1992, p. 106).

I want to suggest that the importance of transversality for higher education can be seen in the way Deleuze puts the concept to work to think differently about the role of signs in Marcel Proust's canonical *In Search of Lost Time* (Deleuze, 2007). His immediate aim is to use the concept to analyse stylistic relationships in prose (Deleuze, 2007, pp. 201–202; see also Deleuze & Guattari, 2004a, pp. 42–43), but he also links such transversality to learning. Transversality is one of the central tropes from the very first volume of Proust's narrative: the Guermantes way and the Méséglise way are, in fact, connected in the same unsuspected way that characters are transversal: Swann and Odette, Gilberte and Albertine, Saint-Loup and Morel all evolve and (dis)connect through the network of their differences.[2] It is because these transversal relations between the characters are revealed throughout Proust's narrative, particularly in its final chapter (Proust, 1990), that the novel recounts an apprenticeship in the signs and their heterogeneity. Learning in such conditions must be dynamic and collective, rather than linear and didactic (Deleuze, 2007, pp. 31–32). As we will see below, this view of learning presents a clear challenge to homogenising trends in the globalisation of HE. Deleuze's critique, however, coming as it does from an analysis of the functioning of signs in a literary work, does not fall into the criticism of the global tendency to homogenise which literature has already amply pointed out

---

[2] See, for example, Proust (1988, p. 400), where transversality is a "secondary and artificial" line used to describe the way a character changes over time as the narrator comes to relate to and understand their complexity better. This leitmotif drives the journey of (self)-revelation around which the novel, its characters, and notably its topography, are all structured (see, for example, Sheerin, 2009, pp. 133–134).

(see Appadurai, 1990). To see why his analysis is both original and instructive in this regard, we need to see the role played by transversality in his critique.

Deleuze's analysis draws philosophical conclusions about the nature of thought which sit at the heart of *Difference and Repetition* (Deleuze, 1968, 1994), arguably Deleuze's most important work. As a concept, transversality functions, as so often in Deleuze's work, as both a commentary on another thinker and as an explication of crucial aspects of Deleuze's own philosophy: it is itself a transversal concept which explicates itself in and through the connections he develops with others' thoughts. It is by definition metaphysical insofar as it postulates dynamism in the structure of relations between philosophical concepts and ideas (Williams, 2005). For Proust/Deleuze, things are defined by relations which change, fragmenting our sense of their identity. Since transversality provides a way to think of things without reducing them to essences, it offers a point of view on how we function as thinking subjects. Transversality is therefore more than a way of describing the famously shifting, often aberrant, relationships at the heart of Proust's plot. It is also intended to flesh out the mechanics of Deleuze's own ontology in action. Deleuze is showing the mechanics of the most profound levels of being and inviting us to think through our own relation with the world with these concepts. Deleuze is, in fact, explicit on this score: the status of things is defined by the way in which we as subjects are positioned not above or outside noumenal reality but beside or contiguous to it. Our relations with the world are thus not hierarchical, linear or even, properly speaking, subjective: they are instead transversal (Deleuze, 2007, p. 194; see also Deleuze, 2002, p. 278).

Transversality is thus a key feature of Deleuze's wider ontology. Relations, for Deleuze, do not serve to identify the things they relate, but rather create spaces where further relations can take place and are thus differential rather than simply different. These relations are often aberrant, since by definition they concern that which has not yet occurred and reveal for us the virtual within the shifting Heraclitean world growling beneath us. Such a world view puts intense pressure on any systems' practices or attitudes that assert that things must be dealt with in themselves. In particular, transversality undermines the desire for hierarchy and serves, therefore, the double purpose of grounding both a critical regard for being and a creative existence. Transversality, then, is inseparable from the potential for change which exists when affects collide, creating sense, constructing spaces of possibility and forming bridges between new ways of being. And because Deleuze's affirmation of such change is ontological, his transversal world is a material one, where our actual experiences are formed, informed and reformed by affective collisions which ensure that everything is always already other.

As Deleuze tries to show in his analysis of Proust, these ontological considerations cry out to be implicated in the concrete ways in which we think about and do other things. His insistence on transversality offers lessons for higher education, especially the latter's own preoccupation with criticality and creativity. For Deleuze, criticality and creativity, rather than the subordinates of predefined forms of rationality, exist in diagonal relation to it. This is to say that, for Deleuze, we do not employ existing forms of reason or rational categories either to critique or to create. Instead, it is by the development of networks of transversal relations, and especially the interstices they make possible between the individual and the social, that thought takes flight. The concept of transversality shows therefore that a conflation of critique and rationality cannot function, I point I will return to below.

It also shows that there is nothing inevitable in any given picture of higher education practices. If we agree with Deleuze that transversality defines the relational nature of things in this way, it allows us to describe higher education developments as a spatial rather than purely temporal phenomenon. This spatialisation allows, first, a superposition of outcomes, a key feature of properly complex systems. Second, it highlights the fact that particular actualisations are only one among many possibilities whose conditions of existence imply the equally powerful reality of other possibilities waiting for their own actualisation (see, for example, Deleuze, 1985). The encroachment of global issues into the local world of higher education is a case in point and thus demands a change in point of view, a shift which lies precisely at the heart of transversality. To look at this shift, I want to discuss how three connected trends intersect with three related effects: local concerns for teaching excellence, mobility and choice are implicated in more complex global trends of prosumption, liquefaction and dividualisation. To show how these transversal intersections work, I want to first sketch out some of the fundamental features of globalisation in HE.

Globalisation and Higher Education

It seems clear that HE is simultaneously a subject and a producer of globalising effects: while universities are certainly subjected to the development of a more globalised knowledge economy, universities themselves are instrumental in the development of the cognitive capital at its heart. English-speaking universities, particularly elite institutions based in the UK, are certainly keen to welcome the substantial (economic) benefits of a globalised higher education system. Many of them express pride in a reputation which attracts funding and students from across the world, as well as growing revenue, increased status and a related boost in capacity in, for example, research (see, for example, Browne, 2010; BIS, 2016).

These are all pursued by globalised universities whose funding is under threat as market forces increasingly occupy political concerns, particularly the democratisation of higher education. The twin development of more democratised, more globalised provision has already changed the UK higher education landscape since the 1990s, where a previously elite system has shifted towards the provision of higher education for a much wider and diverse "non-traditional" student cohort (Barnett, 2011; Wingate, 2015). More diverse institutions, qualifications and higher education practices reflect this democratisation and the increase in the variety of learning needs and motivations which it implies (Tapp, 2015).

This diversity has been described as a bewildering dimension of the accelerated changes of a super-complex global economy (Cole & Woodrow, 2016; see also Appadurai, 1990). When global tendencies take on local forms, they inflect wider trends and complexify outcomes in conjunction with (g)local conditions. Analysis of this complexity within complexity, however, indicates a persistent tendency towards homogenisation of provision (see, for example, Beighton, 2017). This is because super-complexity, and the emergent processes it entails, has themselves become the focus of the globalised production of knowledge. The promotion of creativity has become a bio-political goal at the dynamic heart of higher education treated as a "factory of knowledge" efficiently processing cognitive capital (Raunig, 2010, 2013). Critics such as George Ritzer have long bemoaned the quasi-vitalistic logic and practices of mass production/consumption (Ritzer, 2013, 2014). For Ritzer, a fundamental irrationality results from these attempts to guarantee the predictable, cost-effective distribution of mass-produced consumer goods. These include the bland repetition of "nothing" products which replaces the sense of value and meaning which more individual, localised production offers (Ritzer, 2003). Efficiency and profitability are no longer means but ends in "the bureaucratic arm of the unipolar capitalist system", a unipolarity which has a greater interest in catatonia than either creation or critique. Whether such unipolarity serves the needs of a higher education system tasked with the production of original knowledge is at best debateable. These views have proven prescient as globalisation's impacts have included widespread austerity and increased consumption of learning, both of which continue to dominate the goals, practices and identities of the academic world of the "corporate university" (Ritzer, 2013). But they are also a recognisable feature of globalised capital, using prefabricated systems of signification to ensure the general transferability of content, expressions, opinions and affects which all too often prove vacuous, trivial or both (see, for example, Bosteels, 1998, p. 167).

Although it is tempting to see higher education as the passive recipient of these changes, the transversality of the relations between these trends would predict that the greatest challenge of globalisation comes from the fact that we cannot simply observe it from the outside. Its complexity does not allow simple cause–effect relationships to be identified, and a certain vocabulary associated with transversality is needed to describe the relations it maintains. We can take this vocabulary from Deleuze's own philosophy: if relations are transversal, this means that they are *implicated* in the development of experience, as they are *complicated* and *explicated* by the unfolding of the series of events which form globalisation.[3] It is thus only by playing out or dramatising concepts—*a fortiori* transversality—in specific cases that we can actualise them. Transversality is a tool, or a brick, whose function is defined by its use, and is therefore not limited by meaning or interpretation but actualised by use. Like a brick, it can be used to destroy or to build, and it is thus an example of Deleuze's belief that critical destruction and creative generation rely on the same transversal conditions. But what can a concept like transversality accomplish? Can a "parauniversity" (Rolfe, 2013) exist as a minor, molecular entity in transversal relation to its molar counterpart in the form of the globalised academy? What practices,

---

[3]It is worth pointing out that this perspective is set out in Deleuze's early work on Spinoza and thus forms part of his fundamental metaphysics that "what is expressed has no existence outside its expression" (Deleuze, 1990a, p. 40; see also Deleuze, 2007, pp. 55–58).

if any, might undermine the normalisation heralded by globalisation's demand for hierarchy, reproducibility and dividualisation in the McAdemy?

Among the many possible responses to this question, I want to discuss here the role of two features of higher education which continue to distinguish HE from other education sectors. Criticality on one hand and creativity on the other together define HE's specific role as challenger of received wisdom and generator of new knowledge. Often presented as formulaic correlates to accepted ways of thinking, criticality and creativity are powerful vectors of transversal practice in HE. The question is how far they are allowed to play this role, and how far they have become the instrument of "paranoiac engineers" of the homogenised masses, organised aggregates and fixed statistical formations (Deleuze & Guattari, 2004a, p. 308; see also Deleuze, 2002, p. 277).

Higher Education: A Transversal Assemblage of Concepts

Higher education does not have to be destroyed through globalization. On the contrary, transversality suggests that apparently isolated developments in the field are in fact connected in an evolving discursive assemblage with reciprocal, material effects—not a foregone conclusion based on some immaterial, globalising telos. For instance, as I show below, transversality—or its lack—can be seen in a tripartite conceptual framework of excellence/prosumption, mobility/liquefaction and choice/dividualisation which maps the relationships between the assemblage of concepts at play. It situates university teaching's discourse of excellence in relation with fundamental shifts in what the academy is for and how it might develop in the near future. A look at each of these features in turn will provide a diagram of trends in higher education today.

Excellence and Prosumption in HE

The discourse of excellence in UK HE has never been stronger: excellent education, we are told, unlocks opportunity and empowers children from all backgrounds to "shape their own destiny": regardless of social or geographical background, ability and need, a "world class education" is needed so that young people can "reach their full potential" and "succeed in adult life"—and thus contribute to Britain's competitive status (DFE, 2016, p. 5). Higher education is targeted as a key driver for this successful, high-tech, high-skill knowledge economy. This drive for excellence in HE reflects a common preoccupation with quality of customer experience triggered by increases in competition and the development of an affective economy in experiences, feelings and desires.

However ephemeral, such excellence must of course be subject to measurement and the regular display of its own efficacy. English universities have traditionally been assessed by a "Research Excellence Framework" (REF), a regular exercise in peer review to assess the quality (i.e. excellence) of research output. The REF is now accompanied by a "Teaching Excellence Framework" (TEF) and is soon to be followed by a "Knowledge Exchange Framework" (KEF) to measure the impact of research beyond the research community itself. The new "Teaching Excellence Framework" (TEF), for example, is in place since 2016 with the aim of to "recognising excellent teaching" and "[providing] information to help prospective students choose where to study" (HEFCE, 2017).[4] It is described as "the lens through which any other reform to quality processes would be viewed" so that provision remains "world class" (BIS, 2016, p. 4). TEF accompanies the liberalisation of the mechanisms which grant university status and degree-awarding powers to new institutions, all in the pursuit of excellence. However, an existing body of recent literature already questions the ability of such changes to enhance quality when austerity, globalisation and consumption increasingly dominate the goals, practices and identities of the academic world and the corporate university in particular (Rolfe, 2013; Holmwood, 2014; Keep, 2014; Beighton, 2016b; Brunila & Siivonen, 2016). Competing with discourses of creativity in student assessment (e.g. QAA, 2014), would a TEF guarantee excellence or academic poverty? One answer to this question lies in the way these HE frameworks demonstrate the continued McDonaldisation of higher education. McDonaldisation is more than a simply derogatory attack on the incursion of profit-making practices in public bodies. For Ritzer (2013), it defines a set of processes which can be summarised under the heading of rationalisation. Its four defining features (increased efficiency; greater predictability; higher calculability; and more control across the learning landscape), for Ritzer not only signal McDonaldisation in HE and the wider economy but also introduce its fundamentally irrational effects. Practices which are promoted with the intention of increasing rationalisation actually lead to less efficiency, predictability, calculability and control, for example, when they incur very high costs in terms of the health and environmental damage they provoke. Specific examples from higher education might include the marketing of programmes as "professional" when their content boils down to a training in compliance; the dehumanization implied by assessment techniques which reduce potentially meaningful learning to the empty repetition of received wisdom; and the homogenisation of knowledge in technology-based products and services in ways which facilitate its distribution but undermine its relevance and authenticity—the "propaganda of progress" (Virilio, 2012, p. 47; see also Cole & Gannon, 2017).

Such effects, however irrational, are nonetheless an example of how a discourse of excellence implicates the increasingly important phenomenon of prosumption (see, for example, Cova & Dalli, 2009; Ramaswamy, 2011; Coll, 2013; Eden, 2015; Zajc, 2015, Beighton, 2016a). Prosumption happens when a consumer simultaneously produces the object of consumption, rather than passively consuming it (Ritzer, 2014). Prosumerism, here, is not a "thing" but a continuum of processes, each involving a more or less "balanced" mix of consumption and prosumption. There are no

---

[4]Note that in the UK, higher education policy is devolved to individual countries (Scotland, Northern Ireland and Wales) who "are also able to take part if they wish to" (HEFCE, 2017).

purely consumerist or purely productivist activities, and prosumption itself is an ever-expanding, hybrid affair in tune with globalisation's super-complex dynamic.

This prosumerism is marketed in education as personalisation, but provides only a veneer of distinctiveness. Moreover, as costs rise, they are offset by more and more (unpaid) customer input into production and distribution processes. When this work involves the production of cognitive capital (knowledge creation) and affective capital (student experiences), we can see the importance of prosumption in HE contexts (see, for example, Masika & Jones, 2016). Globalisation is implicated in this shift, with the expansion of the tech-driven interactive media market, for example, which situates the HE student as co-creator of learning spaces and experiences (Beer & Burrows, 2010; Swist & Kuswara, 2016).

We prosume in more material ways when we assemble our own furniture or self-checkout at the supermarket. Our prosumption is increasingly digital when we buy books, self-diagnose health care and, of course, consume higher education online by or self-registering for a degree before deploying our own material, financial and cognitive resources to "personalise" course content or feed back to providers on how to better develop or manage provision. HE prosumerism adapts itself to different institutions, raising efficiency by putting learners to work as unpaid consumers–consultants who create value for the organisation through, for example, product design, presentation, packaging and the day-to-day business of maintaining the supply chain. Prosumersim thus develops horizontally between sectors, reproducing its practices, assumptions and language as a discursive assemblage; it is rarely transversal because its cost-effectiveness depends on its ability to self-replicate. Prosumption in HE, far from providing an opportunity for creative participation, builds on the market's existing tendency to extend the culture of surveillance and commodification of emergent forms of marketable but essentially empty knowledge (Alvesson, 2013; Ritzer, 2014; Beighton, 2016c).

Mobility and Liquefaction in HE

Such horizontal self-replication and emptiness point to a shift of focus from production to channels of distribution and are facilitated by a second parameter which links mobility to a liquefaction of learning processes. Going beyond existing accounts of liquid modernity (e.g. Bauman, 2012), the academy is following the precedents of "fast capital" by focusing its energy on channels, speed and logistics in education rather than on education productivity per se. I have argued elsewhere that such circularity in learning implies liquefaction as the focus shifts from the commodification of learning onto liquefied subjects which flow as "solutions" through the learning sector's "pipelines" and "channels", "influenced" by the need to constantly "move on" (Beighton, 2015b, 2016d).

This liquefaction means that the already marginalised risk losing further agency because they lack the resources to use higher education to invest in cognitive capital, thereby becoming further objectified and powerless. This discourse is powerful because it taps into a growing preoccupation with speed as "[o]ther education systems—from Shanghai and Singapore to Poland and Germany—are improving even faster than we are (DFE, 2016, p. 6). This focus continues, regardless of any perverse outcomes on the quality for learners and learning as the speed of change underpins coercion through the threat of being left behind (cf. Virilio, 2012 *inter alia*; Masschelein & Simons, 2015; Beighton, 2016d). It is a case of "more this and more that" as knowledge and enquiry become saleable commodities to the point where the modern university has "lost its way" (Badley, 2016, p. 635) as the emphasis on mobility treats learning as an essentially circular transactional exercise.

The transversal connections required by creative thought and practice are lost in this circularity, particularly in the discourse of investment in (consuming) education. Investment, it is believed, will reap dividends, since "[i]nvesting in our education system is an investment in the future of our nation" (DFE, 2016, p. 3). Admittedly investment, even circular, may benefit some—although critics have long argued that the rhetoric of lifelong learning misrepresents complex, bifurcating marketplace realities by portraying them as simple, linear pathways. The expectation that one will invest in one's own cognitive capital implies a treadmill of disadvantage whose benefits to individuals are hard to discern. The focus on further investment, employment, consumption, and just keeps the flow flowing.

Choice and Dividualisation in HE

Equally troubling from the point of view of a transversal subject is the view that such an investment involves higher education "choices", a third feature of a tendency in globalisation towards subjectivation. Greater choice, facilitated by better information for HE students and wider choice of providers, is held to improve quality (BIS, 2015) through individual empowerment. It signals an intensification in the processes by which learning subjects are created (Lazzarato, 2012; D'Hoest & Lewis, 2015; Ecclestone & Brunila, 2015). Far from empowering them, however, critics argue that participants in higher education are constructed in the image of a machinic discourse of reproduction. They are impoverished and repositioned as the raw material of investment capital and called on to engage in subjectivating processes of financial flow referred to as "new opportunities" (BIS, 2015, p. 18).

This works through processes of what Deleuze calls "dividualisation" (Deleuze, 1990b). Dividualisation is a fundamentally ambiguous, vital concept which cannot be judged as good or bad: determined as a concept by dividedness at the heart of being, it is simultaneously productive and destructive. It is, therefore, encouraged and exploited by globalisation because it can be managed to produce compliant "dissemblages" (Raunig, 2016), creating subjects who are "demarcated as a flow in the financial capitalist setup" (Cole & Gannon, 2017, p. 79). When this happens, an individual is constrained to the half-life of "dividualism" rather than one of participation and agency, echoing the criticism, above, of any attempt to reduce the complex social relations to a single signifier or repetitive self-perpetuation. Essentially, the dividualised subject becomes little more than a quantum of information to fuel the sector's increasing liquid obsession with flows of excellence. It is a synonym not for quality but rather for the cultivation and farming of data and its deployment for the purposes of bio-political control (see, for example, Genosko & Bryx, 2005; Coll, 2013; Lazzarato, 2014).

This "dividualisation" of the HE learner can also be seen in the operation of institutional discourse. Transversality, among other actions, reminds us that discourse, *a fortiori* language, does not exist in isolation from its material effects and affects. "Order words" exist not to simply direct and instruct, but to establish channels of communication between sovereign subjects and directions for the flow between them (Deleuze & Guattari 1976, 2004b). This facilitates the liquefaction of learning, as we have already seen, resulting in a pedagogy of channels which is harder to disrupt than words themselves, since the educator operates as a channel of cognitive quanta flows rather than a vector of critical autonomy. The result is overtly non-transversal, as learning is equated with the passive consumption of the cognitive capital being disseminated and the learner themselves as a feature of the system. The marketisation of this model of education may well claim to deliver transformative learning, but in reality it typifies the approach of "self-help" literature and its focus on the individual's ability to cope, their resilience and ability to integrate. Seeking out problems only in order to justify existing *solutions*, educators are seen as "enlightened person[s] doing something to the underdeveloped or incompetent" (Matheson & Matheson, 2000, p. 199). Effectively this means vehicling a "therapy" model which offers solutions to the various psycho-social deficits from which HE students are presumed to suffer, be it a lack of "confidence", poor "communication skills" or insufficient "criticality" (see, for example, Ecclestone & Brunila, 2015).

Criticality, Creativity and Catatonia: A Transversal University?

References to criticality are perhaps the most significant here. From its roots in a critique of the limitations of Freudian psychoanalysis, transversality has become a fundamental part of a wider critique of the complexity of psycho-socio-economic relations and their reciprocal connections. From the point of view of HE, this can best be seen in the perennial importance of criticality which has been described as "closely aligned with the 'higher' in higher education" (Danvers, 2016, p. 282). Often considered the practice of scepticism towards truisms (Burbules & Berk, 1999), it has also been described in terms of being rather than doing: "[c]ritical persons" Barnett says, "are more than just critical thinkers" because they are "able critically to engage with the world and with themselves as well as with knowledge" (Barnett, 1997, p. 1). This focus on critical engagement highlights the continuing tension between a vocational higher education system and a more democratic one allied to a tolerant liberal culture (Badley, 2016). But criticality has more often been seen as a basic element of formal learning and the assessment of the basic truth value of statements (Ennis, 1962). As the "educational cognate" of "student rationality", criticality is the "basic epistemic aim of education itself" (Siegel, 2005, p. 358), and a fundamentally logical activity.

However, if criticality does no more than serve rationality, the relation between the two raises an important and topical question for globalised higher education. If critique and rationality are synonymous and repetitive rather than transversal and productive, critique risks falling into the dreary mantra of overly rational criticism rather than the development of new ideas. Critique must for this reason be more than a mechanistic search for defects and implies the creativity of imagining things differently. This is perhaps why some also argue that "critical thinking is creative thinking" because it involves questioning, imagining, connecting, interpreting and applying ideas (Gray & Malins, 2004, p. 38; see also Inglis & Aers, 2008).

Conflating criticality, creativity and rationality, however, is unhelpful, and risks asserting the primacy of reason through the back door because creativity is not performed. On this view, and contra Guattari, critique and creation can exist, but only within a given conceptual framework of rational categories of thought. The hierarchy which results is explicitly non-transversal: it imposes illegitimate boundaries on the way we think as if thought were to be both prescribed and proscribed, a priori, by reason. For it is criticality itself which is guilty of treating things as mere objects to be reflected upon by a sovereign subject. The failure of this type of objectivism to reach any meaningful conclusion about the world is precisely what makes learning so disappointing for Proust's narrator/learner and, by extension, us (Deleuze, 2007, p. 43).

Transversality reminds us that criticality in HE concerns the possibility of thought itself, not the relative validity of individual ideas, because it creates a dimension whereby this thought is possible. The attempt to legislate on possible experience is instructive today because it prefigures closely the kind of homogenisation of learning being carried out in higher education, thus providing a warning. The description of the limits of experience can seem censorious, reflecting a desire for order rather than a more complex empirical reality. This approach to the way we deal with the world is Kantian in its assertion that reason transcends other faculties. In the *Critique of Pure Reason* (1797/2007), Kant limits experience to the boundaries imposed by the basic fact of our subjective finitude, our essentially rational nature and its ability to conceptualise and thus represent things in time and space. Kant's legacy for critical thinking in higher education lies in the view that judgments about our experience of the world, be they critical, creative or otherwise, are by their very nature defined by the concepts and categories which make this experience possible. His argument rests on the establishment of a sovereign subject guided by an inner faculty of judgment, awareness of itself and a series of related moral obligations (Hampson, 1968, pp. 197–198). But this sovereignty can be criticised as a narcissistic obsession with history which invites a kind of postmodern, ironic cynicism. Hence, we regard knowledge with "a detached spectatorialism" whose "excess of (self) awareness" replaces engagement and involvement; this is a view of criticality which risks inspiring an essentially catatonic subject increasingly distanced from a world in which it no longer believes.

This catatonia ignores the way in which these developments are part of a shifting, multiple frameworks of change in more globalised HE systems, practices and attitudes—the emerging irrational post-neoliberal order described by Strom and Martin (2017). While seemingly hierarchical in nature, relations between these systems, practices and attitudes are developing in transversal ways. To understand why this matters, it is helpful to remember that, for Deleuze, while criticality and creativity are different, the conditions of their possibility are the same:

> The conditions of a true critique and a true creation are the same: the destruction of an image of thought which presupposes itself and the genesis of the act of thinking in thought itself. (Deleuze, 1994, p. 139)

For Deleuze, criticality and creativity happen in the same moment, when "something in the world forces us to think" (ibid.: see also Deleuze, 1985, 2005); hence, the belief that thought is somehow given or regulated by subjective consciousness is overturned by a practice of criticality and creativity, which re-establishes thought as a living, dynamic engagement with things. Thought is consequently transversal and does not have a rational, predetermined "image" in the natural search for truth (Deleuze, 2007, pp. 115–116). Such a tendency to posit an image of thought, he argues, relies on the rationalistic view that it suffices for thought to abstract itself from the outside influences which divert it from its natural path. But the truths which result from this process are abstract, because they arbitrarily take thought for granted, and lacking the encounters which force thought to think in the first place (Deleuze, 2007, p. 177).

Thought, on the contrary, can only take place when boundaries break down as a result of a violent encounter with signs (Deleuze, 2007, p. 32). When thought is shocked into rethinking itself by such an encounter, relations literally create transversal spaces for the new to emerge. It is not simply that this novelty has no preset destination, good, bad or otherwise; in fact, Deleuze argues, it is the function of such artistic endeavour to make us (re)discover time itself (Deleuze, 2007, p. 41 and p. 107). The objective truths of voluntary thought and intelligence break down, just as their subjective counterpart is undermined by this encounter with profound otherness (Deleuze, 2007, pp. 46–48). Rather than creating some personal museum of dead ideas, transversal thought goes beyond: taking a witch's flight, barking like a dog, or developing like flies in Brownian motion! A new point of view is developed which envelops subject and object, a nomadic distribution of thought as complication, experimentation and co-development (Deleuze, 2007, pp. 54–63; see also Deleuze and Guattari, 1976, 2004b; Deleuze, 1962, 1983).

This argument is especially pertinent as the discourse of higher education increasingly embraces ideas for which Deleuze is well known. In particular, criteria for success at level 8 stress the importance of creativity in student writing (QAA, 2014), an aspect of Deleuze's thought which grounds his approach to philosophy as the creation of concepts and to art and life itself (cf. Deleuze, 1993, 1997; Deleuze & Guattari, 1976, 2004b). If criticality in such writing is to do more than reproduce given world views (the inevitable impact of globalisation in the learning economy for example), then criticality excludes creativity and falls into the catatonia of what

Guattari calls an "an ever-watchful intra-psychic death drive" (Guattari, 1989, p. 142) If, on the other hand, thinking can operate according to the claims of transversality, then criticality and creativity are united in the same affirming gesture of affective engagement with the things that (literally) matter. This analysis is less utopian than it might seem and has already influenced work on critical thinking, where the latter, far from being a fixed notion, involves "multifarious capillaries of associations and action". It provides a useful description of the conditions of higher education, especially research, whose goal is to seek out and engage with what we don't know (see Mazzei & McCoy, 2010).

If we are to encourage such transversality, HE can, for example, be more awake to the ways in which so-called high-tech colludes in the commodification of knowledge by establishing distribution channels which, for all their rhetoric, rarely do more than assist the flow of learning quanta, the predictability of capital begetting capital (Cole, 2014, p. 81) Academic writing is just one area where this benefit from transversality can be felt. We can stop limiting our teaching to the reproduction of given forms and simplistic false problems, insisting on connections between disparate ideas rather than recounting existing ones. A transversal intellect emerges in such practices because knowledge is fabricated by moving across dichotomies rather than reproducing them (Raunig, 2016, p. 19).

Conclusion: A Transversal University?

In this chapter, I have tried to show how drives towards globalisation in HE exemplify the development of transversal connections. It creates the links between demands for teaching excellence, mobility and choice on one hand and wider global trends of prosumption, liquefaction and dividualisation on the other. But the very existence of these developments implies globalisation's "complex, overlapping, disjunctive order" (Appadurai, 1990, p. 296) where diversity, disparity and therefore the possibility of creative pedagogies and creative learning are produced. Transversality is the principle of n + 1 articulations at the core of both theory and practice (Bosteels, 1998, p. 158). It is concerned with becoming and the future, not the past (Deleuze, 2007, p. 10), undermining hierarchies, superegos and molar aggregates in the form of a concatenating flow that partial objects produce and cut again, reproducing and cutting at the same time (Deleuze & Guattari, 2004a, p. 89). I have argued elsewhere that engagement with this form of virtuality implies practices of improvisation, chance and error whose flows are the opposite of the nihilism of McDonaldisation (Beighton, 2015a). Higher education which engages with these transversal flows will be more creative while demanding a greater ability among students and teachers to diagnose the catatonia of banality which, sadly, the marketised globalisation of higher education often seems to require. If this critical and clinical moment has always been fundamental, it is precisely because a lack of transversality in thought is a sure sign of a lack of learning.

References

Alvesson, M. (2013). *The triumph of emptiness: Consumption, higher education and work organization*. Oxford: Oxford University Press.

Appadurai, A. (1990). Disjuncture and difference in the global cultural economy. *Theory Culture & Society, 7*, 295–310.

Badley, G. (2016). The pragmatic university: A feasible utopia? *Studies in Higher Education, 41*(4), 631–641.

Barnett, R. (1997). *Higher education: A critical business*. Buckingham: Society for Research into Higher Education and Open University Press.

Barnett, P. E. (2011). Discussions across difference: Addressing the affective dimensions of teaching diverse students about diversity. *Teaching in Higher Education, 16*(6), 669–679.

Bauman, Z. (2012). *Liquid modernity* (2nd ed.). Cambridge UK: Polity Press.

Beer, D., & Burrows, R. (2010). Consumption, prosumption and participatory web cultures: An introduction. *Journal of Consumer Culture, 10*(3), 3–12.

Beighton, C. (2015a). *Deleuze and lifelong learning: Creativity, events and ethics*. London: Palgrave Macmillan.

Beighton, C. (2015b). Closed circuit? Flow, influence and the liquid management of learning and skills. *Discourse: Studies in the Cultural Politics of Education, 38*(4), 603–618.

Beighton, C. (2016a). Groundhog day? Nietzsche, Deleuze and the eternal return of prosumption in lifelong learning. *Journal of Consumer Culture, 0*(0), 1–18.

Beighton, C. (2016b). *Expansive learning in professional contexts: A materialist perspective*. London: Palgrave Macmillan.

Beighton, C. (2016c). Payback time? Discourses of lack, debt and the moral regulation of teacher education. *Discourse: Studies in the Cultural Politics of Education, 37*(1), 30–42.

Beighton, C. (2016d). Moving on: Speed, flow and the liquefaction of lifelong learning. In E. A. Panitsides & J. P. Talbot (Eds.), *Lifelong learning: Concepts Benefits and Challenges* (pp. 1–16). New York: Nova.

Beighton, C. (2017). Telling Ghost stories with the voice of an Ogre. Deleuze, identity, and disruptive Pedagogies. *Issues in Teacher Education, 26*(3), 111–127.

BIS. (2015). *Fulfilling our Potential: Teaching Excellence, Social Mobility and Student Choice*. Retrieved April 12, 2016 from www.parliament.uk/bis.

BIS. (2016). *The Teaching Excellence Framework: Assessing quality in Higher Education, Third Report of Session 2015–16*. Retrieved April 12, 2016 from www.parliament.uk/bis.

Bosteels, B. (1998). From text to territory: Félix Guattari's cartogrpahies of the unconscious. In E. Kaufman & K. Heller (Eds.), *Deleuze and Guattari: New mappings in politics, philosophy, and culture* (pp. 145–174). Minneapolis: University of Minnesota Press.

British Broadcasting Corporation. (2017). *Tory MP Under Fire Over 'Sinister' Brexit Demand to Universities*. Retrieved October 26, 2017 from http://www.bbc.co.uk/news/uk-politics-41735839.

Browne, R. (2010). *Securing a Sustainable Future for Higher Education: An Independent Review of Higher Education Funding and Student Finance*. Retrieved July 25, 2013 from http:// www.bis.gov.uk/assets/biscore/corporate/docs/s/10-1208-securing-sustainable-higher-education-browne-report.pdf.

Brunila, K., & Siivonen, P. (2016). Preoccupied with the self: Towards self-responsible, enterprising, flexible and self-centred subjectivity in education. *Discourse: Studies in the Cultural Politics of Education, 37*(1), 56–69.

Burbules, N.C., & Berk, R., (1999). Critical thinking and critical pedagogy: Relations, differences, and limits. In T.S. Popkewitz & L. Fendler (Eds.), *Critical Theories in Education*. New York: Routledge. Retrieved November 13, 2017 from http://faculty.education.illinois.edu/burbules/papers/critical.html.

Cole, D.R. (2014). Inter-collapse...educational nomadology for a future generation. In M. Carlin & J. Wallin (Eds.), *Deleuze and Guattari, Politics and Education: For a People-yet-to-Come* (pp. 49–76). London: Bloomsbury.

Cole, D. R., & Gannon, S. (2017). Teacher-education-desiring-machines. *Issues in Teacher Education, 26*(3), 78–95.

Cole, D. R., & Woodrow, C. (Eds.). (2016). *Super dimensions in globalisation and education.* Singapore: Springer.

Coll, S. (2013). Consumption as biopower: Governing bodies with loyalty cards. *Journal of Consumer Culture, 13*(3), 201–210.

Cova, B., & Dalli, D. (2009). Working consumers: The next step in marketing theory? *Marketing Theory, 9*(3), 315–339.

Danvers, E. C. (2016). Criticality's affective entanglements: Rethinking emotion and critical thinking in higher education. *Gender and Education, 28*(2), 282–297.

Deleuze, G. (1962). *Nietzsche et la Philosophie* (5th ed.). Paris: PUF.

Deleuze, G. (1968). *Différence et Répétition*. PUF.

Deleuze, G. (1983). *Nietzsche and Philosophy* (H. Tomlinson, Trans.). London: Althone Press.

Deleuze, G. (1985). *Cinema 2: L'Image-Temps,* Paris: Minuit.

Deleuze, G. (1990a) *Expressionism in Philosphy*: *Spinoza* (M. Joughin, Trans.). New York: Zone Books.

Deleuze, G. (1990b). *Pourparlers* 1972–1990. Paris: Minuit.

Deleuze, G. (1993). *Critique et Clinique.* Paris: Minuit.

Deleuze, G. (1994). *Difference and Repetition* (P. Patton, Trans.). New York: Columbia University Press.

Deleuze, G. (1995). Negotiations. (M. Joughin, Trans.). New York: Columbia University Press.

Deleuze, G. (1997). *Essays critical and clinical* (D. Smith & M. A. Greco Trans.). (1997). Minneapolis: University of Minnesota Press.

Deleuze, G. (2002). Trois Problemes de Groupe. In D. Lapoujade (Ed.), *L'Ile Déserte: Textes et Entretiens 1953–1974.* Paris: Minuit.

Deleuze, G. (2005). *Cinema 2: The Time Image* (H. Tomlinson and B. Habberjam, Trans.). London: Continuum.

Deleuze, G. (2007). *Proust et les Signes*, Paris: PUF.

Deleuze, G. & Guattari, F. (1976). *Mille Plateaux*. Paris: Editions de Minuit.

Deleuze, G. & Guattari, F. (2004a). *Anti Oedipus* (R. Hurley, M. Seem, H.R. Lane, Trans.). London: Continuum.

Deleuze, G. & Guattari, F. (2004b). *A Thousand Plateaus* (B. Massumi, Trans.). London: Continuum.

Department for Education (DFE) (2016). *Educational Excellence Everywhere.* Retrieved October 29, 2017 from www.gov.uk/government/publications.

D'Hoest, F., & Lewis, T. E. (2015). Exhausting the fatigue university: In search of a biopolitics of research. *Ethics and Education, 10*(1), 49–60.

Dosse, F. (2007). *Gilles Deleuze, Félix Guattari – Biographie Croisée.* Paris: La Découverte.

Ecclestone, K., & Brunila, K. (2015). Governing emotionally vulnerable subjects and 'therapisation' of social justice. *Pedagogy, Culture & Society, 23*(4), 485–506.

Eden, S. (2015). Blurring the boundaries: Prosumption, circularity and online sustainable consumption through Freecycle. *Journal of Consumer Culture, 0*(0) 1–21.

Ennis, R. H. (1962). A concept of critical thinking. *Harvard Educational Review, 32,* 81–111.

Fourquet, F. (2007). La Subjectivité Mondiale: une Intuition de Félix Guattari in le Portique: Philosophie et Sciences Humaines: Gilles Deleuze et Félix Guattari: territoires et devenirs. 20, 33–50.

Genosko, G., & Bryx, A. (2005). After Informatic striation: The resignification of disc numbers in contemporary Inuit popular culture. In I. Buchanan & G. Lambert (Eds.), *Deleuze and Space* (pp. 109–125). Edinburgh: Edinburgh University Press.

Gray, C., & Malins, J. (2004). *Visualizing research: A guide to the research process in art and design. Aldershot.* Hants: Ashgate.

Guattari, F. (1974). *Psychanalyse et Transversalité*. Paris: Maspero.

Guattari, F. (1989). *The Three Ecologies* (C. Turner. Trans.). New Formations 8, 131–147.

Hampson, N. (1968). *The enlightenment: An evaluation of its assumptions, attitudes and values*. London: Penguin.

HEFCE (Higher Education Funding Council for England). (2017). "About the TEF". Retrieved November 15, 2017 from http://www.hefce.ac.uk/lt/tef/whatistef/.

Holmwood, J. (2014). From social rights to the market: Neoliberalism and the knowledge economy. *International Journal of Lifelong Education, 33*(1), 62–76.

Inglis, F., & Aers, L. (2008). *Key concepts in education*. London: Sage.

Kant, I. (1797/2007). *Critique of Pure Reason* (N. K. Smith, Trans.). Basingstoke: Macmillan Education Press.

Keep, E. (2014). *What does skills policy look like now the money has run out?*. Oxford and London: ESRC Centre on Skills Knowledge and Organisational Performance and Association of Colleges.

Komljenovic, J., & Robertson, S. L. (2016). The dynamics of 'marketmaking' in higher education. *Journal of Education Policy, 3*(2), 127–143.

Lazzarato, M. (2012). *The Making of the Indebted Man* (J.D. Jordan. Trans.). Los Angeles: Semiotext(e).

Lazzarato, M. (2014). *Signs and Machines: Capitalism and the Production of subjectivity.* (J.D. Jordan. Trans.). Los Angeles: Semiotext(e).

Masika, R., & Jones, J. (2016). Building student belonging and engagement: Insights into higher education students' experiences of participating and learning together. *Teaching in Higher Education, 21*(2), 138–150.

Masschelein, J., & Simons, M. (2015). Education in times of fast learning: the future of the school. *Ethics and Education, 10*(1), 84–95.

Massumi, B. (1992). *A user's guide to capitalism and schizophrenia: Deviations from Deleuze and Guattari*. Boston: Swerve/ MIT press.

Matheson, C., & Matheson, D. (Eds.). (2000). *Educational Issues in the learning age*. New York: Continuum.

Mazzei, L., & McCoy, K. (2010). Thinking with Deleuze in qualitative research. *International Journal of Qualitative Studies in Education, 23*(5), 503–509.

Murphie, A. (2010). Deleuze, Guattari, and Neuroscience. In P. Gaffney (Ed.), *Deleuze, science and the force of the virtual* (pp. 330–367). Minneapolis: University of Minnesota Press.

Proust, M. (1988). *Du Cote de chez Swann*. Paris: Gallimard.

Proust, M. (1990). *Le Temps Retrouvé*. Paris: Gallimard.

Quality Assurance Agency for Great Britain. (2014). *UK Quality Code for Higher Education Part A: Setting and Maintaining Academic Standards PART A The Frameworks for Higher Education Qualifications of UK Degree-Awarding Bodies*. Retrieved October 9, 2015 from http://www.qaa.ac.uk/en/Publications/Documents/qualifications-frameworks.pdf.

Ramaswamy, V. (2011). It's about human experiences… and beyond, to co-creation. *Industrial Marketing Management, 40*, 195–196.

Raunig, G. (2010). *A Thousand Machines* (A. Derieg. Trans.). Los Angeles: Semiotext(e).

Raunig, G. (2013). *Factories of Knowledge, Industries of Creativity* (A. Derieg. Trans.). Los Angeles: Semiotext(e).

Raunig, G. (2016). *Dividuum: Machinic Capitalism and Molecular Revolution* (A. Derieg. Trans.). Los Angeles: Semiotext(e).

Ritzer, G. (2003). The globalisation of nothing. *SAIS Review, 2*(2), 189–200.

Ritzer, G. (2013). *The McDonaldization of Society*, 20th Anniversary ed. London: Sage.

Ritzer, G. (2014). Prosumption: Evolution, revolution, or eternal return of the same? *Journal of Consumer Culture, 14*, 3–24.

Rolfe, G. (2013). *The University in dissent: Scholarship in the Corporate University*. London: Routledge.

Sarnel, R. (2007). « Lieux de passages et transversalités: Pour une dynamique deleuzienne ». In le Portique: Philosophie et Sciences Humaines: Gilles Deleuze et Félix Guattari: territoires et devenirs, 20, 99–110.

Schrag, C. (2000). *Transversal rationality in American continental philosophy: A reader*. Bloomington: Indiana University Press.

Sheerin, D. (2009). *Deleuze and Ricoeur: Disavowed affinities and the narrative self*. New York: Continuum International.

Siegel, H. (2005). Philosophy of education, epistemological issues. In D.M. Borchert (Ed.), *Encyclopedia of philosophy. Vol. 7: Oakeshott—Presupposition*, 2nd ed (pp. 358–360). Detroit, MI: Sage.

Strom, K., & Martin, A. (2017). Thinking with theory in an era of Trump. *Issues in Teacher Education, 26*(3), 3–22.

Swist, T., & Kuswara, A. (2016). Place-making in higher education: Co-creating engagement and knowledge practices in the networked age. *Higher Education Research and Development, 35*(1), 100–114.

Tapp, J. (2015). Framing the curriculum for participation: A Bernsteinian perspective on academic literacies. *Teaching in Higher Education, 20*(7), 711–722.

Virilio, P. (2012). *The Administration of Fear* (A. Hodges, Trans.). Los Angeles, CA: Semiotext(e).

Williams, J. (2005). *The transversal thought of Gilles Deleuze: Encounters and influences*. Manchester: Clinamen.

Wingate, U. (2015). *Academic literacy and student diversity*. Bristol: Multilingual Matters.

Zajc, M. (2015). Social media, prosumption, and dispositives: New mechanisms of the construction of subjectivity. *Journal of Consumer Culture, 15*(1), 28–47.

Christian Beighton is Senior Lecturer in Post-Compulsory Education and Training at Canterbury Christ Church University, based in the School of Teacher Education. He has held a wide variety of roles in HE, FE and private settings in the UK and abroad since a first teaching post in 1991. His research interests include creativity, policy, and practice in professional and lifelong learning settings, as well as research into teacher education and higher education practices. He is a fellow of the UK's Higher Education Academy and an Honorary Firearms Instructor with Kent Police.

Part II
Transversality, Education and Becoming

Part II
Transversality, Education and Becoming

Chapter 5
On Philosophical and Institutional "Blinkers": SOAS and Transversal Worldviews

Joff P. N. Bradley

Abstract In the wake of the report "Degrees of Racism" on the attitudes of Black and minority ethnic students attending the School of Oriental and African Studies (SOAS) in London—(BME Attainment Gap project, 2016)—and the resultant verdict of the students' union at the university on the realities and prospects of a "decolonized education," this chapter, with the concept of transversality operating at its core, reflects not only on the possibility of writing contra "epistemic violence" via a transversal curriculum but also how one might compose a philosophy of education consistent with such a task. Transversality is pitched as a tool to critique non-inclusive curricula. The chapter aims to set out "lines of flight" for what can be termed a transversal geophilosophy of education, whose aim is to connect the practical problems of a transversal curriculum and the abstract philosophy of education that springs from it. We shall make the case that transversality cannot be thought of as anything other than *outlandish*—so from precept to precedent, the very premise of transversality is transformatory and radical, which is to say, it grasps the matter at the root of itself.

Keywords Guattari · Hwa Yol Jung · Schizoanalysis · Geophilosophy · Asia

Introduction

We must learn to think "transversally". (Guattari, 2000, p. 29)

In the wake of the report "Degrees of Racism" on the attitudes of Black and minority ethnic students attending the School of Oriental and African Studies (SOAS) in London—(BME Attainment Gap project, 2016)—and the resultant verdict of the students' union at the university, this chapter reflects not only on how to write a transversal curriculum but also how to compose a philosophy of education consistent with such a task, with the concept of transversality operating at its core. While

J. P. N. Bradley (✉)
Teikyo University, Tokyo, Japan
e-mail: joff@main.teikyo-u.ac.jp

© Springer Nature Singapore Pte Ltd. 2018
D. R. Cole and J. P. N. Bradley (eds.), *Principles of Transversality in Globalization and Education*, https://doi.org/10.1007/978-981-13-0583-2_5

predictably the furore in the British press overshadowed important observations on underachievement in the non-white student demographic, with reports and headlines predominantly and predictably concentrating on attitudes to the "whiteness" issue—for example, comments on complaints among students that "60-year-old white men" are "potentially racist" (Times, January 15, 2017),[1] that the canon of Western philosophy—from Plato, Descartes to Kant—ought to be "decolonized" (Observer)[2] from its white, European heritance, and whether "universities should eschew Western philosophers"[3] altogether, for the writer of this chapter what the reaction did precipitate was a reflection on the nature of transversality itself. While we may quickly dismiss the view as *ad hominem* that the problem at root is the color of the professor's skin rather than the truth value of the thoughts and beliefs conveyed, what is timely and thought-provoking about the report is that it raised the issue of how to write an "academically robust and relevant"[4] transversal curriculum on intellectual history which is and does indeed provide an encompassing syllabus which can function to represent a vibrant, non-Anglo-Saxon world of thought, and can thereby appeal to a broad student demographic.

Outlining the principles of transversal and schizoanalytic thought or what I call a transversal geophilosophy of education, I make the case that such a geophilosophy of education provides an ecosophical dimension to transversality which not only critiques the excesses of globalization, but invokes the notion of "worlds to come"—that is to say, something beyond globalization. While a distinction can be made between transversality as an experimental means of institutional analysis (Guattari) and transversality as a philosophical problematic or heuristic (phenomenology), the point to be made is that the concept has the potential to relay between both contexts.[5] The SOAS case is highlighted because it demonstrates a concrete case of how transversality explains both the perception of institutional inertia (failed dialogue between students, teachers, and administrators) and how curriculum reform might be assisted by a transversal methodology, which is to say, how the student-directed adjustment of both "institutional blinkers" and "philosophical blinkers" at both the macro- and micro-level may improve the educational experience at SOAS and contribute *ecosophically* to the world outside (e.g., improve race relations, make society fairer, contribute to the critique of colonialism, ask questions of what might lie beyond the status quo of representative democracy, global capitalism).

---

[1]Griffiths, S. & Henry, J. (January 15 2017). "Old white dons 'unable to teach black students'." https://www.thetimes.co.uk/article/old-white-dons-unable-to-teach-black-students-320hl9flf.

[2]Malik, K. (19 February 2017). "Are SOAS students right to 'decolonise' their minds from western philosophers?" https://www.theguardian.com/education/2017/feb/19/soas-philosopy-decolonise-our-minds-enlightenment-white-european-kenan-malik.

[3]BBC2's Newsnight. (9 January 2017).

[4]SOAS statement on Degrees of Racism report for students' union, https://www.soas.ac.uk/news/newsitem117787.html.

[5]It is important to note that while Deleuze and Guattari are usually considered anti-phenomenologists, it would be a mistake to think that their work is not heavily influenced by phenomenology. Indeed, both writers recognized their indebtedness to Sartre.

While the issues of institutional racism, mental health issues, student support, complaint procedures, degree attainment of Black and ethnic minority undergraduates at SOAS (and at other less-privileged institutions) are clearly pressing and much work needs to be done to address and resolve these issues, this chapter hones in on the political discussion and ramifications which emerged in the report's aftermath. The report by and large urged curriculum reform and a response to the institutional factors contributing to the ethnicity (under)-attainment gap, for example, "unconscious bias," in reading lists (underrepresentation of Black scholarship and female authorship), "exclusion by design," racialized object of study and priority of white perspective to the exclusion of scholarship outside of Europe and North America. In sum, it provoked important questions regarding the erasure of non-Eurocentric perspectives, experiences, and marginalized voices at an educational institution which was founded in 1916 during the height of the British Empire with the remit to instill cultural and linguistic know-how to administrators, managers, military officers, missionaries, doctors, and teachers, etc., who were bound for the colonies.

To set about the task of exploring the underlying principles of what a transversal curriculum may look like, following Guattari, a *schizoanalysis* of transversal philosophy is undertaken, incorporating an array of thinkers from European and non-European sources and adopting concepts from Europe and elsewhere. The point is to put transversality to work, to make philosophy itself a "tool of transversality" through a "pragmatics of existence" as Guattari calls it, that is to say to make it function in accord with ecosophical principles—or in other words, to connect such tools with wider considerations pertaining to environmental, mental, and social ecologies (Guattari, 2000).

Many of the demands of the SOAS student report are consistent with the *oeuvre* of Korean-American philosopher Hwa Yol Jung (Jung, 2002, 2009, 2010, 2011; Chŏng & Pak, 2009). What can be taken from both Jung's work and the report's findings is the sense that the current dominant *Weltanschauung* is incomplete. The search for a new worldview we shall call geophilosophy. Geophilosophy is concerned with articulating a world philosophy, with creating worlds contrary to globalization, worlds which refuse to compromise with the status quo and the defense of "natural" globalized privilege (Cole, Dolphijn, & Bradley, 2016). In Jung's work, geophilosophy is perceived as a *worlding* doctrine, expressing a *mondialization* rather than globalization (contra the Americanization of the world). Resonating with Guattari's affirmation of utopia late in his life (2016), it invokes another possible world, beyond the realities of the *dehumanization* of the world at present. It refuses any unthinking substitution of mondialization for humanization. Hwa Yol Jung is offering a critique of the goals of the Enlightenment, Renaissance, and humanism, which are construed by him as espousing philosophies which unconsciously defend racial privilege. His work is part of an ongoing dialogue of how to proceed. He is writing a philosophical curriculum of sorts which is consistent with the goals of the SOAS report. Although the goal in a transversal curriculum is to convey worlds through affirming differing voices, beliefs, and philosophies, where difference is affirmed across multifarious paradigms and intellectual legacies, a caveat must be added that the project is not to forge a new totality or universality out of the old—to merely exchange or substitute one binary code for another—West–East, East–West—but to think *transversally* and *ecosophically* across paradigms. Behind the "Degrees of Racism" report is a desire to think across borders, beyond individuality and community—to radicalize the curriculum—to set in train intellectual transformation. In itself, the report is not transversal but the demands if enacted are tantamount to making the curriculum so. In this light, the debates at SOAS, which claims for itself the mantle of "the first post-colonial university," can be read as a microcosm of larger debates about globalization and the Americanization of the world.

Working with Transversal Epistemologies

In the political and philosophical thought of Hwa Yol Jung, we find a phenomenology which is purposefully transdisciplinary and *radically* transversal. Throughout Jung's extensive *oeuvre* which dates back several decades from his doctoral thesis on Jacques Maritain (1960) to his *Transversal rationality and intercultural texts* (2011), Jung seeks to enjoin and crisscross Oriental and Occidental philosophies in an innovative, transversal, and ecological manner. This has important ramifications for the construction of a geophilosophical pedagogy as it contains not only East–West, but North–South, and with all manner of strange conceptual contraptions, zigzags and experimental theoretical concoctions. It is this aspect of Jung's transversal rationality (Jung, 2011) and phenomenology which I not only wish to explore but to extend and critique by combining it with Guattari's ecosophy, schizoanalysis, and ethico-aesthetic paradigm (Guattari, 1995).

A geophilosophical pedagogy makes forays and relays across and beyond boundaries, disciplines, schools, and paradigms—so as to think seriously about the current social and ecological crises afflicting the world. This in sum informs a transversal curriculum and the principles of a new practico-theoretical schizoanalytic model of transversal geophilosophy of education, whose purpose is to think of the transversal as an ethical and ecological antidote and challenge to planetary capitalism. Paraphrasing Guattari let us modify different "coefficients of unconscious transversality" at multiple levels of critique so as to bring about "a structural redefinition" of the notion of transversality and therefore to vivify concepts and reorient ecological practice (Guattari, Deleuze, & Hodges, 2015, p. 113). To reiterate, the point is that transversality goes hand in hand with ecological concerns and this is what should be at the heart of the aforementioned "Degrees of Racism" report.

In the second edition of *The Cambridge Dictionary of Philosophy*, the Korean-American philosopher Hwa Yol Jung defines the concept of transversality, according to his phenomenological, existential, and hermeneutical viewpoint. Using Deleuze and Guattari, and drawing on Calvin Schrag's extensive work (Schrag, 1992, 2016), Jung explains the concepts of geophilosophy and transversality and suggests the possibility of a "post-national politics of cosmopolitan world democracy" (Schrag, 2016, p. 43)—a vision which is consistent with the student demands at SOAS. Jung describes the concept, citing a constellation of thinkers; he explains the concept firstly via Heideggerian phenomenology and then via Merleau-Ponty and Sartre to argue that the concept is a replacement for the "Eurocentric formulation of truth as universal" (Audi, 1999, p. 928).

Transversality is propounded as a philosophical antidote and rebuttal to the pseudo-universality of the Western concept of truth. Transversality is articulated as a means to decenter Western truth claims so as to understand truth as "polycentric and correlative." Here, for example, and in terms of a decolonized education and curriculum, it would address the voices, beliefs, and philosophies perceived as excluded from the canon of a particular discipline. If thinkers such as Hegel, Kant, or Hume considered Africa, Asia, and other regions as deprived of "viable philosophical or epistemological traditions" (Abdi, 2007, p. 252), what emerges from the SOAS students' union report and the philosophy of Hwa Yol Jung is a demand to contest such colonial philosophies and epistemological traditions of the West, from the perspective of worldviews and ecologies excluded from this canon. This amounts to a perspectival deconstruction of dominant epistemic and epistemological locations of learning. In *Decolonizing Philosophies of Education* (2007, p. 5), Abdi contends that the problems are not only philosophical and epistemological but "onto-existentially debilitating," which we can read from Foucault's view as a matter of power/knowledge. Abdi (2007) writes that it is timely to "establish new decolonizing trajectories that affirm the onto-epistemological and philos-pedagogical liberations that can reconstruct the learning structures that re-affirm the right identity and intentions for all those who aspire to benefit from them" (p. 11). For Abdi, writing from the perspective of the epistemologically colonized is a question of thinking the possibility of "re-enfranchising suppressed epistemes and ways of knowing" (Abdi, 2012, p. 11).

With respect to epistemology, transversality is a means to both transcend Eurocentric prejudices (which Jung largely sees stemming from the master thinker of identity *par excellence*, Hegel) and to contest Western notions of universality. In contrast, truth is posited as particular, contextual, and correlative—and transversally expressed—neither absolute nor relativistic, nor a simple choice between totality or fragmentation, Enlightenment or postmodern chaos. Referring to Schrag, who argues for the transversal logos of communicative rationality as a means to refute the universal (read: Western) logos, Jung describes transversality as "the new hinge" enabling philosophy to "swing across" disciplinary and cultural boundaries. As he says of Schrag (Drummond, Embree, & Behnke, 2010, p. 562):

> It is a way of weaving different texts, of composing intertexts. By transmuting universality into transversality, he opens up a new horizon in order to deconstruct what might be called modern man's white mythology, which has masqueraded as Eurocentrism, sexism, and even speciesism.

The sense of thinking other than this form of logocentrism is also found in Édouard Glissant's work. Jung derives from this Martinican philosopher a notion of transversal relationality which is without "universalist transcendence" (Glissant, 1981, p. 190). Glissant's concept of *tout-monde* (all-world or world total) is synonymous with a creolizing, unpredictable, turbulent "*chaos-monde*" relating immanently to itself—a world in which people hold a "right to opacity" instead of succumbing to a global will to transparency. As Glissant (2009, p. 94): "Chaos-monde is neither fusion nor confusion: it acknowledges neither the uniform blend—a ravenous integration or muddled nothingness." If thinking about the "One" is not thinking about "All" or "Many," the move thereby escapes claims of surreptitiously sneaking in another form of universality. I read this sense of *chaos-monde* as sharing profound affinities with the concepts of the new earth and "people to come" in Deleuze and Guattari's *What is Philosophy?* (1994). In their last book, they write that what can be extracted from the chaos inhering in art, philosophy, and science is a shadow of the "people to come"—a concept derived from Paul Klee (Deleuze & Guattari, 1994, p. 218). What is summoned forth is a "mass-people, world-people, brain-people, chaos-people" (p. 218). Glissant conceives this sense of identity, following Deleuze and Guattari, as nomadic, fluid, but also inclusive and accommodating. Finding a kindred sense of meaning in the rhizome (Deleuze's "ethic of flow") and his "*poetique de la relation*," Glissant writes (2009, p. 11) that the rhizome challenges "a totalitarian root," adding that rhizomatic thought is the chief principle of his theory "in which each and every identity is extended through a relationship with the Other."

For Jung, transversality is one of philosophy's "most inventive modes" (Chŏng, 2014, p. 171). Echoing Charles Taylor, his argument is that transversality invokes a "global imaginary" (Taylor, 2007) and worldview. For our purposes, this sense of the global imaginary is pivotal if we are to grasp how global history and global nature have seemingly permeated each other and have been flattened into a one-dimensional planetary process. Picking up this emphasis, Michel Serres also notes the blurring of distinctions and dichotomies (Serres in Jung, 2011, p. 229):

> At stake is the Earth in its totality, and humanity, collectively. Global history enters nature, global nature enters history: this is something utterly new in philosophy.

Transversality is this diagonal movement. From multiple beliefs and practices, habits of thought and attitudes, prejudices and assessments, transversality is perceived as heuristic in explaining "a multiplex phenomenon of converging and diverging configurations" (Stapleton, 1994, p. 67). It seeks to escape hegemonic models as well as inert seriality. And it is here that the demands of the SOAS students can be heard prominently. Guattari explains (1984, p. 18):

> Transversality is a dimension that tries to overcome both the impasse of pure verticality and that of mere horizontality; it tends to be achieved when there is a maximum communication among the different levels and, above all, in different meanings.

Addressing issues across cultures, philosophies, and religious traditions through a transdisciplinary methodology, Jung does so in terms of transversal vectors and transpositional, lateral movements—in the sense of an *in-between* or *interbeing*. It is this sense of interbeing that equally affirms transversal movement. As the take on transversality is posited as a potential rival to "outmoded Eurocentric ideas of univer-sality" in Western modernity or the "all-encompassing world of cultural sameness" in Glissant (1999, p. 97), transversality as an epistemology suggests the emergence of the "middle" or "third" term—a new way of facilitating "lateral border crossings" which are at once intercultural, "interspeciesistic," interdisciplinary, and intersensorial—a kind of *included middle*. To summarize, the third term is consistent with the concepts of *intermundia* or *interworld,* with the notion of the "poetics of relation" (Glissant, 2009) and the metaphor of the rhizome as a new space for the repressed and ignored.

Introducing Transversal Logos and "Interbeing"

In his definition of postmodernity for the *Encyclopedia of Phenomenology* (Drummond et al., 2010, pp. 558–559), Jung grants the figure of the rhizome the characteristic of "lateral, subterranean, and profuse growth" with neither beginning nor end. Rhizomatic becoming can be construed as "transversal alliances of heterogeneous terms whose plural, symbiotic and machinic functionings (or technics) constitute an open-ended 'unity'" (Protevi, 2006, p. 417). Moreover, the rhizome is consistent with transversal philosophy and the principles of interbeing because, as Jung says, it "cherishes the transversal movement of the rhizome" (Drummond et al., 2010, p. 558). Put otherwise, interbeing, the concept derived from the order of Tiep Hien in the Vietnamese Buddhism of Thich Nhat Hanh (Nhat & Eppsteiner, 1987), affirms the transversal movement of the rhizome. Rhizomatics pertains to connectedness, multiplicity, heterogeneity, alterity, and marginality. As we have seen, for Schrag (2004, p. 76) the transversal logos offers a rival claim to the universality of the logos. For him, it operates as the "lynch-pin for the philosophy of the new millennium." Transversality is again a "diagonal" crossing, resolving the "deadlock" between "the Scylla of a hegemonic unification" ("vacuous universalism") and "the Charybdis of a chaotic pluralism" ("anarchic historicism"). Put another way, it "cuts and reaches across ethnocentric universalism" through a praxis of intercritique (Dosse, 1999, p. 345) and as such affirms hybridity and creolization. In the crisscrossing of boundaries and deconstruction of the myths of universality, transversality is presented as the interdisciplinary and cross-cultural *beginning* for a pedagogy of geophilosophy. Such coordinates and principles could be adopted in curriculum reforms at institutions such as SOAS to better reflect the histories and cultures of the student demographic (Cole & Bradley, 2014).

For Jung, transversality is fundamentally geophilosophical in import as it is intimately bound with the *Great Chain of Ecological Interbeing*. Indeed, this Asian philosophical and ecological aspect, for Jung, will govern the very future of philosophy. A transversal geophilosophy then offers an ecological "topology of Interbeing." The emphasis on transversal and dialogical phenomenology then is on interbeing relations, which Jung derives from an array of thinkers and philosophies from the West such as Merleau-Ponty, Heidegger, and Sartre, but also figures from the East or South such as Glissant, Thich Nhat Hanh, Nishida Kitaro and through Sinism (Daoism, Buddhism, Confucianism) and Maoist dialectical materialism. On this point, Jung writes (Chŏng, 2014, pp. 154–155): "What Being is to the West from Heraclitus to Heidegger, Interbeing is to East Asia from Confucius to Wang Yangming,

Watsuji Tetsurō, and Mao Zedong." And again (in Cataldi, 2007, p. 246) Jung says: "It may be said that the East is to silence, what the West is to talk. The East is spatial, whereas the West is temporal." In sum, Jung derives from the philosophy of interbeing an ecosophy and relational ontology which he claims is the basis for a new ethics and politics. Transversal geophilosophy is thus positioned as *ultima philosophia* or global philosophy, whose remit is to save the earth from destroying itself. This again as I have argued is consistent with the SOAS campaign to decolonize the curriculum. Geophilosophy, whence aligned with Guattari's ethico-aesthetic paradigm, may coalesce heterogeneous elements "within a single embrace" (1994, p. 85) into a non-doctrinal mode and open form of pedagogy.

One of the most significant contributions of Jung's transversal geophilosophy is his attempt to *reOrient* future philosophy—which is to say to use the notion of the transversal as a relay between and in-between different schools of thought. Indeed, this is timely as in Deleuze and Guattari's work there is little mention of geophilosophical ideas in the non-Western world. We can agree with Jung then on the importance of this aspect and take up the gauntlet to reOrient geophilosophy.

As the aim of transversality "is to build bridges that would promote and facilitate cross-cultural, cross-speciesistic, cross-disciplinary exchanges as well as globalization toward the creation of planetary thinking" as Jung says (2011, p. xvi), the *telos* of transversality is posited as the creation of planetary or global thinking. This accent on the planetary has clear Deleuzian overtones, especially so because in *Desert Islands* (Deleuze, Lapoujade, & Taormina, 2004, p. 157), Deleuze, in comments regarding the definition of the planetary by Kostas Alexos, spells out the non-unitary dimension to the concept:

> Planetary thought is not unifying: it implies hidden depths in space, an extension of deep universes, incommensurate distances and proximities, non-exact numbers, an essential opening of our system, a whole fiction-philosophy.

It is clear that Jung also affirms Foucault's vision of a philosophy of the future and the end of an era of a certain form of Western thought. Indeed, speaking in 1978, Foucault famously tells a Zen master in Japan: "The crisis of Western thought is identical to the end of imperialism. ... Thus, if philosophy of the future exists, it must be born outside of Europe or due to of meetings and impacts between Europe and non-Europe" (Mickey, 2016, p. 210). This again can be seen to be expressed in the demands of the students at SOAS. Indeed, Jung expressed the hope in his essay 'Transversality and Geophilosophy in the Age of Globalization' (2002, p. 85) that Asian concepts and influences would transform philosophical practice in the West and beyond. Crucial for the movement of the logic in this chapter is Jung's description of globalization as "a movement to create a new world" (2010, p. 88)—one less European or Euro-American, and more tri-continental (Asian, African, and Latin American)—a kind of transcontinental philosophy. This view again is consistent with the SOAS students' views in the "Degrees of Racism" report as this perspective is clearly concerned with the plurality of cultures and is thus an axiom of a pedagogy of geophilosophy. From his transversalist perspective, Jung (2002, p. 14) argues that globalization, in striving to decenter Western hegemony and to empower "the nonWest" to participate fully in "worldmaking," must perform acts of hybridization or imbrication. However, while this focus is part and parcel of a transversal trajectory for a geophilosophy of education, without a fundamental critique of the worst excesses of globalization under Integrated World Capitalism (IWC), the goal of participation for all seems politically impotent. This aspect will be underscored below using Deleuze and Guattari's concept of schizoanalysis.

The World as "Metamodelization"

A schizoanalysis of transversal geophilosophy critiques globalization or IWC, seeing in it not only a system of economics but also as a modelization of "behavior, sensibility, perception, memory, social relations, sexual relations, imaginary phantoms, etc." (Guattari & Rolnik, 2008, p. 39)—a point which has clear ramifications for a geophilosophy of education and indeed for the "Degrees of Racism" report, which itself picked up on the "unconscious bias" at the institutional level at SOAS. To grapple with the production of IWC *qua* modelization, we must construct/deconstruct transversality with the "tool box of modelization" itself (Guattari, 1996, p. 192). Transversality is thus consistent with Deleuze and Guattari's vision of what theory *can do*. It can be used as a precise theoretical tool to decolonize the curriculum. In the dialogue *Intellectuals and Power*, Deleuze makes the point with Foucault that "true" theory does not totalize, it rather multiplies. Theory is praxis. It is a "box of tools," disconnected from the linguistics of signs and the signified. Consequently, it must be practical in its functioning. As Deleuze says (Foucault, Bouchard, & Simon, 1980, p. 208):

> A theory does not totalize; it is an instrument for multiplication and it also multiplies itself. It is in the nature of power to totalize and it is your position. And one I fully agree with, that theory is by nature opposed to power.

For Guattari, transversality functions to overcome certain impasses. For example, it strives for maximum communication between different levels and different directions. Transversal communication operates between "heterogeneous populations" (Deleuze & Guattari, 1987, p. 239). Again, the need for better communication was something that came out in the "Degrees of Racism" report. Responding to this point, a transversal geophilosophy then cannot merely interpret the *unworld* or vile world of globalization but must therefore work to change it for the better. By way of schizoanalysis, it must offer an ecosophical alternative. The point to be made is that we can better understand the interpretation of the concept of transversality if we draw upon Guattari's notion of "metamodelization" (Watson, 2011). In this light, transversality is perceived as the intellectual pursuit of creating or constituting networks and rhizomes, with the aim of escaping "the systems of modelization" in which we are "entangled" and "which are in the process of completely polluting us, head and heart" (Guattari, 1996, p. 132). In this way, those writing the SOAS students' union report demanded a non-racist, non-sexist, non-anti-Semitic vision of the world.

A Note on Mondialization

One of the aspects of transversality is to rethink the notion of *mondialization* so as to posit the creation of worlds or a "becoming-worldly" of the world. In this way, transversal geophilosophy is manifestly utopian—as it fabulates an ontology of global relation *à venir*. Against a background of a vile, unworld (Nancy, Raffoul, & Pettigrew, 2007), or general logic of autoimmunity (Habermas, Derrida, & Borradori, 2003), it must be tasked with making worlds—a point which is consistent with the purpose of the humanities *qua* sites for the creation of *Bildung*. Importantly, as globalization leads to the "suppression of all world-forming," a transversal geophilosophy must be tasked with responding to the worldlessness of the current milieu, the desert world, or "the withering away of everything between us" (Arendt & Kohn, 2005, p. 201). As such it thus opposes the worst excesses of the world of work and reason—a world "heavy with suffering, disarray, and revolt" (Nancy and Librett, 1998, p. 9)—to regain its role as the site of "world-forming." This aspect is missing in Jung's phenomenology, but an effort is made to correct this lacuna later in this chapter. To summarize here, one of the tasks of geophilosophy is to form worlds, to be an activity of world-forming; it is to think the space in-between the *Unwelt* and *Umwelt*—respectively, the *unworld* and the immediacy of the milieu.

On being-in-the-unworld

> There is no longer any world: no longer a *mundus*, a cosmos, a composed and complete order (from) within which one might find a place, a dwelling, and the elements of an orientation. Or, again, there is no longer the "down here" of a world one could pass through toward a beyond or outside of this world. There is no longer any Spirit of the world, nor is there any history before whose tribunal one could stand. In other words, there is no longer any sense of the world. (Nancy, 1998, p. 4)

In her definition of Nancy's sense of justice, Marie-Eve Morin explains that justice is given with the world but on the condition of a demand "to create a world tirelessly" (Gratton & Morin, 2015, p. 133). This demand acts as a precautionary principle to stem the world from collapsing into the *general equivalence* of the unworld, which is to say a general equivalence of catastrophe (Nancy & Mandell, 2015). Such a general equivalence produces the "global injustice" (Nancy et al., 2007, p. 54) of a hermetic unworld, an "earth without sky" (Nancy et al., 2007, p. 34). For Nancy, globalization produces something both squalid and "unworldly," what Heidegger calls Unworlding (*Entweltlichung*) or Unworldliness (*Weltfremdheit*)—or what Agamben calls the "outside" of being (2004). This unworld of contemporary civilization is productive of a "destructive jouissance" (Gratton & Morin, 2015, p. 10). So the struggle against the unworld of globalization (Nancy et al., 2007, p. 55) appears only in or as a plurality—neither solitary individual nor traditional group dynamics—but as a plurality of beings. From the point of view of a transversal geophilosophy to grasp the meaning of this plurality of voices and beliefs is to undertake a schizoanalysis of the unworld. In its own way, this can be understood as a philosophical expression of solidarity against domination and hierarchical power relations, the colonial legacy of the British Empire, and other forms of imperialism, as well as echoing the campaigns to decolonize knowledge production at SOAS, Cape Town University in South Africa and in India, as well the Rhodes campaign at Oxford University.

Reaching the "Intermundia"

As a point of demarcation from Jung's work, the *intermundia* or absolute deterritorialization in Deleuze and Guattari (1994) is invoked as a site of "exteriority" (Karatani & Koso, 2005) precisely in the "intercrossing" spaces outside or between discursive systems, states, or communities. This sense of exteriority is based on Japanese philosopher Kojin Karatani's notion of "transcritical space," which is taken as a crossroads at which relations with others are possible without the risk of totalitarian closure. This is therefore not just a transcendent *interbeing* but the immanent intermonde of schizos, madmen, children, and primitives—as interpreted through schizoanalysis (Deleuze & Guattari, 1983, p. 243). The point here is to explain the meaning of philosophy's new or third reterritorialization in *What is Philosophy?*—from the Greeks in the past, from the democratic State in the present, to the new people and the earth to come (Koizumi, 2018). Here a transversal geophilosophy critiques the unworld of the world to create new circuits of transversality. This is consistent with the task and commitment of this chapter, which is to treat the transversal *schizoanalytically*. In order to think fundamentally about the social and ecological problems facing humankind in the immediate and long-term future, it is stressed that transversality is a methodology to zigzag across the residual *eco-piety* in Hwa Yol Jung's deep ecology and the sometimes unthinking affirmation of militant social ecology (Bookchin, 1970, 1974). It is schizoanalysis which is sufficiently robust as a means of modelization to work across these different approaches.

Transversal Dissensus

A geophilosophy of transversality must approach the cracking points of neoliberal and globalizing forces (in educational institutions and beyond). This point is entirely in keeping with Guattari's demand to move from transdiscipinarity to transversality (Guattari, Osborne, Sandford, & Alliez, 2015). In essence, Guattari's thought can be differentiated from Jung's geophilosophy because of its focus on *dissensus*. For Guattari, the task ahead is to escape "mind-numbing and infantilising consensus." In terms of the education institution, and in the spirit of the "Decolonise Our Minds" campaign at SOAS,[6] it is students who call the group into being, who engender new modes of living and thinking, who produce transversal relations (Bradley, 2012), who pass from inertia to action, from in-itself to for-itself, and adjust both the philosophical and institutional blinkers. Thinking and teaching both transversally and schizoanalytically is experimenting with alternative bifurcatory models of thought and action—in other words, it is a method to decolonize the mind. Transversal philosophy so conceived is a theory of permanent decolonization—it is a theory of the permanent decolonization of not just education and society, but also of thought itself. Transversal philosophy is posited as a zigzagging theory of the decolonization of both society and universal reason. The confluence of Western, non-Western, tricontinental worlds is a planetary project to ward off the risk of being recolonized and reterritorialized. As it is based on the creolization of ideas, cultures, and races, this is not a will to universalize, but one to hybridize and transversalize. So another world is possible—another economy is possible, as are other media, philosophies, and art forms. It is this question of the possible which asks, if nothing else, if the possible is impossible, then purely and simply we are faced with planetary catastrophe and collapse.

This aspect of transversality conveys a utopian dimension, serving as a futural way to experiment with institutional formations of subjectivity, beyond analysand-analyst, and rhizomatic temporal relations. It is a way to think across paradigms, frozen hierarchies, and a means to forge new paths and cartographies of thought, from *aporia* to finding the right path, a new practice of *Bildung* making: in sum, to experiment with the coefficient of unconscious transversality[7], the adjustment of philosophical "blinkers" (Guattari, Deleuze, & Hodges, 2015, p. 112). The unconscious bias noted by the students at SOAS is a concrete expression of institutional inertia.

Following Guattari, it is possible to pass from the ethico-aesthetic paradigm and conceptualization of the world *qua* globalization process to a new paradigm, conceptualization and critique of the *unworld*. The aesthetic paradigm is a transversal one as it crisscrosses all levels of matter, transforming open structural systems through desire. The task of schizoanalysis is to transform the unconscious structures of blindness between disciplines and institutional structures, so as to redefine the transformatory task ahead. Transversality, *qua* vector of deterritorialization, is one such crossing. It is at once a means, a paradigm space, and methodology for the resingularization of subjectivity and for the concrete analysis of institutions and groups. A transversal geophilosophy is thus intent on exploring ecologies of the virtual to foster processual openings or "transversalist bridges." This form of schizoanalytic metamodelization is the basis for the reappropriation of the production of subjectivities. The project is to have more open, less hierarchical groups and structures—acting in accord with Derrida's rethinking of university education as "diagonal or transversal interscientific research" or "philosophical transcontinentality"

---

[6]Available at https://soasunion.org/activities/society/8801/.

[7]Guattari defines the "coefficient of transversality" as the degree of blindness of people in a given institution (hospital, school, university) (2015, p. 112).

(Derrida, 2004, p. 241). Transversality thereby charts the passage from alienated sub-jugated groups (seriality—students resigned to the exigencies of institutional racism) to subject-groups (group-in-fusion—students demanding a more encompassing, non-Eurocentric curriculum) and all the while offering the promise of bringing unheard of collective assemblages of enunciation into existence—and questioning that which sustains epistemic violence in the wider socius.

It is therefore vital to modify the "coefficients of transversality" at different edu-cational institutions. In operating transversally across different fields, we find a means to bring once hermetic or monadic disciplines together in profound, thought-provoking ways. The transversal alliances of heterogeneous terms—plural, symbi-otic, and machinic—constitute an open-ended "unity," but one not in the sense of a totalizing fusion but in difference. This move rejects the hierarchical binary opposi-tions between mind and body, man and woman, humanity and nature, Occidentalism and Orientalism. Transversality is thus not asking for a unity of perspective, a seduc-tive totality, but rather introduces a way to communicate *in-between* the segments, in another space or dimension. It is by definition transgressive in the sense that it trans-forms stratified hierarchies and genealogies. In this way, when proto-subjectivity is transmitted from one sphere to sphere, something inaugural emerges. As such, transversality redraws the map of the horizontal and vertical to prise open move-ments of becoming—a question is posed regarding intra- and inter-assemblage rela-tions. In the traversing of two discontinuous expressions of semiotic code, there is a release of new forms of subjectivization—constructions and destructions of the sub-ject. Transversality is thus ambulatory; it does not pertain to the first or second person but to a third impersonal voice (Cole & Bradley, 2014). To return to the suggestion of inclusiveness of different modes of thinking, this demands the deconstruction of Eurocentrism and the universality of Enlightenment reason. Such a challenge stems from a thinking based on a "middle" or transversal voice found in Asian philosophies for example. This intersecting middle or crossroads is for Jung, as we have seen, the basis for a new paradigm of "global thinking". He writes that transversality signifies trans(uni)versality and describes this new version of phenomenology as "a phoenix rising from the ashes of universality" (Jung, 2010, p. 90).

In constituting a move from the transdisciplinary to transversality and transindi-viduation (which is to say the constitution of intergenerational circuits, for example, between teacher and student) and in keeping with Guattari's philosophical trajec-tory, the chapter has striven to explore the key concepts in Jung's work such as transversality *qua* world philosophy, eco-piety, relational ontology, interbeing. We have argued that much can be gleaned from such a philosophy whence combined with the political thrust of Guattari's schizoanalytic, "generalized ecology." In my view, this is a gift from phenomenology to social ecology to ask if the other side can think transversally and relay back a different vision of the world. In other words: Can social ecology extricate itself from anachronistic forms of modelization as found in the SOAS example. Moreover, as we find a residual aspect of deep ecology in Jung's work, a case has been made for an ecosophy more attuned to the experimental, prag-matic, and militant spirit found in Guattari's practice and his theoretico-existential speculations rather than the deep ecology or ecosophy of Næss (2001). It is through

Guattari's "generalized ecology" and the "pragmatics of existence" that we may
begin to construct a new paradigm of processual creation, which links aesthetics in
the social and political domains.

Conclusion

> The West was built on racism... In schools and at universities we are sold a lie. It is the lie
> that the three great revolutions, of science, industry and politics are solely responsible for
> the advancement of the West... But the narrow Eurocentric parade of dead white men as the
> centre of knowledge is finally being challenged in our institutions... The knowledge that the
> establishment is so quick to defend produced the racism that has shaped the unjust world that
> we live in today... The world can only ever be as equal as the knowledge it is built upon. The
> battle to decolonize education is the first step in shaking us out of our progressive delusions
> and creating the world anew. (Kehinde Andrews, Guardian website, 18 January, 2017)[8]

Responding to the quotation above and as a way to offer a commitment beyond the
bleak diagnosis of the contemporary moment, we can say that Andrews' criticism of
Western racism (2017) and demand to "create the world anew" is consistent with and
pivotal to debates surrounding transversality, education, and globalization, because
it addresses how Eurocentric philosophies and epistemologies continue to shape the
world but also highlights how the old paradigms of knowledge are under assault from
new ways of thinking across different traditions, histories, and cultures—emerging
from the Global South, out of diasporas, and due to the vast flows of immigration
across the planet. Andrews makes the case for a democracy of knowledge so as to
radically redress the inequality in the world. He calls this a "battle to decolonize education" and he is right. Moreover, in this respect his perspective mirrors Stiegler's
war cry against stupidity and the entreaty to "battle for intelligence" in *Taking Care of
Youth and the Generations* (2010). Consequently, a transversal education according
to the experimental modelization I have endeavored to chart embraces this movement
to rid ourselves of malignant delusions (racism, imperialism, sexism, class discrimination) so as to create the not-yet and renew the world as it is, as preparatory for
creating a new common world for those yet to come.

---

[8]T. Andrews, H. Guardian website. (18 January, 2017). 'The west was built on racism. It's time we
faced that (video)'. https://www.theguardian.com/commentisfree/video/2017/jan/18/the-west-was-
built-on-racism-its-time-we-faced-that-video

References

Abdi, A. A. (2007). *Diaspora, indigenous, and minority education: Studies of migration, integration, equity, and cultural survival*. London: Routledge.

Abdi, A. A. (2012). *Decolonizing philosophies of education*. Rotterdam: Sense Publishers.

Agamben, G., & Attell, K. (2004). *The open: Man and animal*. Stanford: Stanford University Press.

Arendt, H., & Kohn, J. (2005). *The Promise of Politics*. New York: Schocken Books.

Audi, R. (1999). *The Cambridge dictionary of philosophy*. Cambridge: Cambridge University Press.

Bookchin, M. (1970). *Ecology and revolutionary thought*. New York: Times Change Press.

Bookchin, M. (1974). *Our synthetic environment*. New York: Harper & Row.

Bradley, J. P. N. (2012). Materialism and the mediating third. *Educational Philosophy and Theory, 44*(8), 892–903.

Cataldi, S. L. (2007). *Merleau-Ponty and environmental philosophy: Dwelling on the landscapes of thought*. Albany: State Univ. of New York Press.

Chŏng, H. (2014). *Prolegomena to a carnal hermeneutics*. Lanham: Lexington Books.

Chŏng, H. Y., & Pak, J. Y. (2009). *Comparative political theory and cross-cultural philosophy: Essays in honor of Hwa Yol Jung*. Lanham, Md.: Lexington Books.

Cole, D. R., & Bradley, J. P. N. (2014). Japanese English learners on the edge of 'chaosmos': Félix Guattari and 'becoming-otaku'. *Linguistic and Philosophical Investigations, 13*, 83–95.

Cole, D. R., Dolphijn, R., & Bradley, J. P. N. (2016). Fukushima: The geotrauma of a futural wave. *Trans-Humanities Journal, 9*(3), 211–233.

Deleuze, G., & Guattari, F. (1983). *Anti-Oedipus: Capitalism and schizophrenia*. Minneapolis: University of Minnesota Press.

Deleuze, G., & Guattari, F. (1987). *A thousand plateaus: Capitalism and schizophrenia*. Minneapolis: University of Minnesota Press.

Deleuze, G., & Guattari, F. (1994). *What is philosophy?*. London: Verso.

Deleuze, G., Lapoujade, D., & Taormina, M. (2004). *Desert islands and other texts: 1953–1974*. Los Angeles, CA.: Semiotext(e).

Derrida, J. (2004). *Eyes of the university: Right to philosophy 2*. Stanford, Calif: Stanford University Press.

Dosse, F. (1999). *Empire of meaning: The humanization of the social sciences*. Minneapolis: University of Minnesota Press.

Drummond, J., Embree, L., & Behnke, E. A. (2010). *Encyclopedia of Phenomenology*. Dordrecht: Springer, Netherlands.

Foucault, M., Bouchard, D. F., & Simon, S. (1980). *Language, counter-memory, practice: Selected essays and interviews*. Ithaca, NY: Cornell Univ. Press.

Glissant, E. (1981). *Le discours antillais*. Paris: Gallimard.

Glissant, E. (2009). *Poetics of relation*. Ann Arbor: University of Michigan Press.

Glissant, E., & Dash, J. M. (1999). *Caribbean discourse: Selected essays*. Charlottesville: University Press of Virginia.

Gratton, P., & Morin, M.-E. (2015). *The Nancy dictionary*. Edinburgh: Edinburgh University Press.

Guattari, F. (1984). *Molecular revolution: Psychiatry and politics*. Harmondsworth: Penguin.

Guattari, F. (1995). *Chaosmosis: An ethico-aesthetic paradigm*. Sydney: Power Publications.

Guattari, F. (1996). *Chaosophy*. New York: Semiotext(e).

Guattari, F. (2000). *The three ecologies*. London: Athlone Press.

Guattari, F. (2016). *Lines of flight: For another world of possibilities*. London: Bloomsbury Academic.

Guattari, F., Deleuze, G., & Hodges, A. (2015). *Psychoanalysis and transversality: Texts and interviews 1955–1971*. Semiotext(e): South Pasadena.

Guattari, F., Osborne, P., Sandford, S., & Alliez, É. (2015). Transdisciplinarity must become transversality. *Theory, Culture & Society, 32*, 131–137.

Guattari, F., & Rolnik, S. (2008). *Molecular revolution in Brazil*. Los Angeles, CA: Semiotext(e).

Habermas, J., Derrida, J., & Borradori, G. (2003). *Philosophy in a time of terror: Dialogues with Jürgen Habermas and Jacques Derrida*. Chicago: University of Chicago Press.

Jung, H. Y. (1960). *The foundations of Jacques Maritain's political philosophy*. Florida: University of Florida Press.

Jung, H. Y. (2002). *Comparative political culture in the age of globalization: An introductory anthology*. Lanham, MD: Lexington Books.

Jung, H. Y. (2009). *The way of ecopiety: Essays in transversal geophilosophy*. New York, NY: Global Scholarly Publications.

Jung, H. Y. (2010). And what 'Global Asia' means in an age of hyphens and hybrids. *Global Asia, 5*(4), 88–97.

Jung, H. Y. (2011). *Transversal rationality and intercultural texts: Essays in phenomenology and comparative philosophy*. Athens: Ohio University Press.

Karatani, K., & Kōso, I. (2005). *Transcritique: On Kant and Marx*. Cambridge: MIT.

Koizumi, Y. (2018). From dreaming of desert islands to reterritorialising philosophy. *Deleuze and Guattari Studies, 12*(2), 268–282. Edinburgh University Press.

Mickey, S. (2016). *Coexistentialism and the unbearable intimacy of ecological emergency*. Lanham, Maryland: Lexington Books.

Naess, A. (2001). *Ecology, community and lifestyle: Outline of an ecosophy*. Cambridge: Cambridge University Press.

Nancy, J.-L., & Librett, J. S. (1998). *The sense of the world*. Minnesota: University of Minnesota Press.

Nancy, J.-L., & Mandell, C. (2015). *After Fukushima: The equivalence of catastrophes*. New York: Fordham University Press.

Nancy, J.-L., Raffoul, F., & Pettigrew, D. (2007). *The creation of the world, or, globalization*. Albany: State University of New York Press.

Nhat, H., & Eppsteiner, F. (1987). *Interbeing: Commentaries on the Tiep Hien precepts*. Berkeley, Calif: Parallax Press.

Protevi, J. (2006). *A dictionary of continental philosophy*. New Haven: Yale University Press.

School of Oriental and African Studies Students' Union. (2016). *Degrees of Racism A report by SOAS Students' Union*. London: SOAS Press.

Schrag, C. O. (1992). *The resources of rationality: A response to the postmodern challenge*. Bloomington: Indiana University Press.

Schrag, C. O. (2016). Geophilosophy, the life-world, and the political. *Contributions to Phenomenology, 84*, 43–48.

Schrag, C. O., Matuštík, M. B., & McBride, W. L. (2002). *Calvin O. Schrag and the task of philosophy after postmodernity*. Evanston, Ill: Northwestern University Press.

Stapleton, T. J. (1994). *The Question of hermeneutics: Essays in honor of Joseph J. Kockelmans*. Dordrecht: Kluwer Academic.

Stiegler, B. (2010). *Taking care of youth and the generations*. Stanford, Calif: Stanford University Press.

Taylor, C. (2007). *Modern social imaginaries*. Durham: Duke Univ. Press.

Watson, J. (2011). *Guattari's diagrammatic thought: Writing between Lacan and Deleuze*. London: Bloomsbury Publishing.

Dr. Joff P. N. Bradley is Associate Professor in the Faculty of Language Studies at Teikyo University, Tokyo, Japan. He is currently researching the teaching of critical thinking and philosophy through film in the Japanese university. He is co-author of *A Pedagogy of Cinema* (2016) and co-editor of both *Educational Philosophy and New French Thought* (with David R. Cole, 2017) and *Deleuze and Buddhism* (with Tony See, 2016).

Chapter 6
The Incorporeal Universe of Childhood in the Tactical Pedagogies of Félix Guattari and Tanigawa Gan

Toshiya Ueno

Abstract This chapter looks to analyze the philosophy of Felix Guattari alongside the Japanese intellectual and writer, Tanigawa Gan, with a focus on pedagogy. The pedagogy that one might draw out from Guattari's writings presents a tactical means to avoid the desubjectifying and annihilatory aspects of contemporary capitalism. Similarly, the pedagogy that one may draw from the work of Tanigawa Gan is defiant and resistant to the dominant, conformist forces of contemporary capitalist life. This chapter works with Guattari and Gan as a combinatory force to hold onto what is most powerful and pertinent about childhood, and to carry it forward as pedagogy. As such, this chapter opens up a new movement in education through transversal becomings and serves as a method to understand how to work positively with subjective singularities in the world.

Keywords Tanigawa Gan · Guattari · Potential · Unlearning · Stupidity
Diagramatism · Oury · Freinet

Introduction

Félix Guattari addressed the topic of childhood in his *oeuvre* by questioning conventional educational assumptions regarding the assimilation of children into adult society. Generally, to code children into society is to interiorize or inculcate values and ethical norms into them. One could say that the behaviors or gestures, morals or common sense of children are translated into a certain form of signification through the articulation of dichotomies or dualisms: good and bad, sacred and profane, beauty and ugly, etc. Therefore, children have to learn a variety of codes or semiotizations as they grow older. Certainly, there are no longer prescribed rituals of initiation in modern society as found in premodern or primitive societies, but one could argue

T. Ueno (✉)
Wako University, Tokyo, Japan
e-mail: vyc04344@nifty.com

© Springer Nature Singapore Pte Ltd. 2018
D. R. Cole and J. P. N. Bradley (eds.), *Principles of Transversality in Globalization and Education*, https://doi.org/10.1007/978-981-13-0583-2_6

that the camp of initiation in contemporary educational formation now continues for almost 15 years (Guattari, 2011, p. 169; 2008, p. 55).

As has been well documented (Guattari, 2008), the mid-1970s signaled the beginning of the shift from material labor under Fordism to info-labor (immaterial labor) under semio-capitalism or Integrated World Capitalism (post-Fordism). It could be said that through the indoctrination of dominant capitalist modes of production and consumption semiotizations in and through education, children can lose their own incorporeal universes of values and possibilities (or potentialities) not connected to these modes. To learn coding here means to constitute the self as a person who endures forms of labor under capitalism. Education and society as a whole, from Guattari's view, act as a kind of death sentence on children (2012, p. 304). Then, one could ask, what are the universes of values and semiotics to which children have been forced to adopt? The relationship between the semiotic coding of adults and that of children is complicated. In order to deal with such complexities, Guattari insists it is more valuable to address ethnology (relational interactions with cultural others) than pedagogy (an ideal communication model in a given society), and ethology (relational fields of affects and behaviors) rather than psychology (an individual or mental sphere). If one utilizes the quadruple schematic found in *Chaosmosis* (1995), Guattarian pedagogy can be understood as a practice of transversing heterogeneous universes of values (U) and flows (F) of knowledge or desires by affording existential territories (T) to children with specific machinic phyla (Φ) of media and technologies.

In fact, Guattari often addressed the issue of education or pedagogy in his work. Indeed, Guattari himself traced the restless and careless character of his own childhood (Guattari & Lotringer, 1995, p. 7), in which one might be tempted to recognize the diagnosis of ADHD or hyperkinesis, if he had grown up in USA or Japan in recent years. Having received great inspiration from the events of May 1968 in Paris, Deleuze and Guattari (2005) paid much more attention to the universes (of incorporeal values) of childhood than previous cultural or critical theory had hitherto undertaken. Careful readers of Guattari will grasp that chaosmic experiences understood in *Chaosmosis* should not be limited to schizophrenic states, but extended to more widespread observations and analyses of varied mental problems in daily life. Guattari refused to account for the issue of childhood or infancy solely in terms of educational science or developmental psychology, especially given his own childhood, and because both disciplines presuppose a certain ideal image of "progress" and "development." Moreover, due to his involvement with delinquent neighborhood groups, his local high school (Lycée) rejected his application, forcing him to travel further to school. This proved fortuitous because there he met a teacher and crucial figure in his life, Fernand Oury, who was inspired by the youth hostel movement which Guattari subsequently joined. In the 1950s, he was also involved with the movement, which crucially encouraged Guattari into activism. In addition, it should not be downplayed that Fernand Oury was one of the disciples of Celestin Freinet who defined the autonomy of children as a principle of education in his Modern School Movement. Further, the very person who established the movement of "institutional psychiatry," Jean Oury, was younger brother of Fernand, and he was the founder of the La Borde clinic, where Guattari worked during his lifetime. What is institutional psychiatry? It is not merely the organization or installation of "hard-ware settings" for mental care, nor is it solely concerned with the administration of "software" in psychiatric hospitals. Indeed, the generic term "institutional" here indicates the tactical method to question "care" itself through interactions within relational fields. This is a kind of collective analysis of transversal rhythms, vibes, facial traits, expressions, gestures of a-signifying communications (Guattari 1995, p. 89). The institutional here is deployed through and engaged with what takes place as the singular event of collective assemblages in any given community, be it in a hospital or school. It seems to us therefore that Guattari had an implicit notion of "institutional pedagogy" in his overall project of transversality. Although there is no sustained analysis of institutional pedagogy in Guattari's writing, a certain per-spective on pedagogy can be extracted. The question arises: What kind of initiative did Guattari have in mind in terms of education and pedagogy? How is it related to his conception of "machinic unconscious" and "ecosophy" (or "chaosophy")? In response to these questions, this chapter will draw an auxiliary line to interpret Guattari's thought in detail by addressing and comparing his work with the Japanese intellectual, Tanigawa Gan.

Tanigawa Gan

Tanigawa Gan (1923–1995) was a poet, critic, and intellectual in post-war Japan, whose work as a literature critic had a great impact on the social and student move-ments in the late 1950s to the late 1960s. He was therefore more or less a con-temporary with Jean Oury's generation in France. Tanigawa fascinated Japanese youth and leftist students during this period because of his provocative charm and almost magical, but highly conceptual style of writing, in which he wrote many leg-endary slogans on cultural and social movements. In Kyushu in the south of Japan, in the mid-1950s, he organized networks of small literary groups called the "circles movement" ("circle" was a buzzword in a variety of social movements at that time in Japan) and published zines which featured amateur writers or workers' poetry. Although he was sometimes arrogant and even authoritarian in collaborative work, he remained a dissident and critical intellectual. His tactics based in local communi-ties explored the movement from the local or the native toward the universal or rather the trans-local, in which children were posited not as the target of control from the adult society, but as the reserve or resource of incorporated potential. Moreover, his notion of "circle" can be associated with small "subject groups" in the Guattarian sense. For example, Guattari eloquently stressed the significance of small tribes and groups, asking rhetorically: "Why don't groupuscules multiply infinitely instead of eating each other?" (2015, p. 368). Here self-analytical groupuscules are treated as a potential "*unit of subversion*" (italics by Guattari). Tanigawa himself respected the conception of transversality without utilizing this term. In his trans-local cultural and critical theory, it is only through digging to the underlying layers of the native or local milieu that someone could reach the universal, while the flow toward the universal conversely clarifies the roots of the native or the local in and through childhood.

Universe of Values in Childhood

The connection between Tanigawa and Guattari can be exemplified with reference to the notion of universe of values in childhood, which is frequently associated with Freinet in *Guattari's Molecular Revolution of Brazil*. Guattari says: "I've always remained interested in them, which may be a remnant of childishness, or immaturity, because generally these things stop at certain age" (Guattari, Rolnik, Clapshow, & Holmes, 2008, p. 442). So, what is crucial for potential alternative learning and teaching for Guattari with reference to Freinet lies in how to retain one's own sense of childishness. Guattari adds:

> I always trust in the people, in *childhood*, in the madness of what is most differentiated, that is, most machinic. So I didn't come, like Ivan Illich, to plead for the structures of togetherness, for returns to a bit more unity. No, I'm truly fascinated by machinic processes, and I'm thinking precisely about what they bring to these pseudosystems of territorialization and, at the same time, of undifferentiation. So, as I say, the primitives, the people, children, the insane, and so on are the bearers of the most elaborate and the most creative abstract machines. (p. 458)

Certainly, this is not an issue of infantilization in the context of contemporary global capitalism, but rather about a radical pragmatic option in life. Guattari confesses openly his love and trust in *infantility*. For him, both childhood and "craziness" are *an immanent aberrance* in all human beings. However, while in no sense does Guattari intend to celebrate or idealize a series of people such as those of primitive tribes, the insane, fools or children, a latent idea of pedagogy might be drawn from his attitude to the question of *becoming* which, of course, has nothing to do with imitation. An example of this potential form of Guattarian pedagogy is as follows: If you have disruptive, noisy children at the back of a classroom, there are ways to deal them, for instance, by excluding them or sending them to psychologists or mental counselors. But, Guattari et al. say what is more effective is to question how problematical acts retain the singularity of the class as a whole (2008, p. 69). Even adults can assume such a singularity in collective enunciations or formations. Therefore, it is not unreasonable to say that we may find a permanently latent childhood in ordinary adults, for example, when people engage in music, write poetry, or perhaps meditate on the cosmos. In a way, Guattari finds here a certain hyper-lucidity of children lingering in adults (1995, p. 84). This potential or latent infantility is envisioned through an account of the notion of the diagram or cartography. Guattari begins by addressing the relationship between thinking and drawing in *Machinic Unconscious*:

> In the first place, let us consider the embryonic writing that manifests in the draft of a child around three or four years of age. Here we can only speak of the index of 'a writing'. Nothing is played out, nothing is crystallized, everything is still possible. But taken on by the school machine this index undergoes a radical reworking. The draft loses its polyvocality. There

is a disjunction between, on the one hand, the draft - impoverished, imitative - and, on the other, a writing entirely shaped by adult expression and tyrannized by an anxiety to conform with the dominant norms. (2011, p. 161)

The word "embryonic" here is to be understood as an equivalent of the possible, of potential, and the chaosmic. Diagramatism intends to keep some layers *in-form* or *in-act* which have not yet been realized but remain virtual. According to Deleuze and Guattari (2003), the affect and activity of children inflect the cartography of ecology of mind because "a child who runs around, plays, dances, and draws cannot concentrate attention on language and writing, and will never be a good subject" (p. 180). Children *think* by drawing images and pictures. Indeed, thinking starts with combinations and is transformed by figures and diagrams. Just think about the moment when one would like to write textually by using memos, notes, figures, schema, maps, images, or flowcharts in order to make one's own image of thinking or to reach a more persuasive argument. Here the linearity of writing and thought recedes away. For example, the outliner (outline processor) of computer applications serves such a procedure of writing and thinking. In a way, conceptual thinking can be said to *be possessed* or *haunted* with and by diagrams and figures.

In his *The Natural Method of Lecture*, Freinet insists that learning has a certain temporality by which one can always realize retroactively what one does after the act. Children are aware of what they have done after accomplishing something. Freinet confirms the significance of repetition to seek and find by engaging in trial and error in any form of education (Freinet, 2015, pp. 56, 79). This view helps to inform what a plausible "institutional pedagogy" might be. Generally, the diagram is not merely a picture or drawing, but rather constitutes or assembles the scheme of habits, or in other words, a de-structuring activity in the unconscious. The diagram carries an alternative twist of signification with different semantic articulations from ordinary languages, in the sense that it tends to convey figurative, non-discursive, or a-signifying signification. There are concrete cartographies, for navigation and orientation, which search for possible territories on the one hand, while there are *speculative cartographies* on the other, which are not concerned with making fixed or concrete territories at all, but with letting users think, articulate, and organize assemblages that have never been known (Lazzarato & Jordan, 2014, p. 212). The space of education is thus envisioned as a relational field similar to sites and a community of informants in psychiatry or ethnology.

Perhaps, this vision is close to the thoughts of Fernand Deligny, a strange intellectual who loved and lived together with autistic children in an experimental woodworking studio, and whose writing ranges from philosophy through pedagogy to psychology and psychiatry (Deligny visited La Borde in 1965). It is well known that both Deleuze and Guattari were inspired by his writings and practices, especially in elaborating the notions of the line of flight, cartography, rhizome, and spider webs in reading Proust and Kafka. His concept of the Arachnean network illustrates how the paths of autistic children are instructive for understanding the relationships between subjectivity and ambience (milieu). The Arachnean network of wandering lines of autistic children, a kind of ethology and ecology of mind, reflects to what extent we are a being of the milieu (as a natural or social environment) and how subjectivity itself is a becoming ambience beyond represented locations. The *diagramatism* of wandering lines or speculative cartography invites and induces us to come toward a different deterritorialization and aberrant vectors of incorporeal universes of values. Through this procedure, one has to detach from oneself and follow other detours toward singular events. Guattari says brilliantly:

> A diagrammatic trait, as opposed to an icon, is characterized by the degree of its deterritorialization, its capacity to escape from itself in order to constitute discursive chains directly in touch with the referent. There is a distinction, for example, between a piano pupil's identificatory imitation of his teacher and the transference of a style likely to bifurcate in a singular direction. (2008, p. 40)

If pupils initially imitate the master or teacher, the emergent transference should bifurcate in infinitely different articulations. Thus is a crucial point for Guattarian pedagogy, which passes through a constant double bind: the double posture of imitating and deviating. In other words, both practices of making detours and inventing aberrations are integrative for a Guattarian institutional pedagogy. In this vector of aberration, one should think about how a posture of "unlearning" is important in education. The term "unlearning" indicates the gesture of "everyday intellectuals," of *abandoning what they have already learned* in order to fathom a different dimension within the same conceptual scheme, here figured through transversality. The knowledge, skills, methods, and concepts acquired are to be at once cast off and relinquished in order to reflect critically upon his/her own position and pedagogical achievement. To abandon something learned or studied, in this context, does not mean dismissing established forms of knowledge. Rather, it is creative, positive, and affirmative in the sense of *undoing* or *unfolding* what has been already been done and actualized. It is a process of repeating in a different way or unfolding what is bound up virtually in the nexus of thinking and events.

As Wittgenstein had already shown with language games, one can perform the rules by playing a game without knowing the rules explicitly. In other words, people can learn what they have not yet known or studied. Everybody is capable of anticipating what he/she will learn through an ability of "unlearning" by abandoning what he/she has already learnt or studied. That is the reason why Guattari's (2013) concept of metamodelization is so crucial for pedagogy. The metamodelization is inclined to open up new dimensions of thinking, because it demands the negation of models invented in previous trials. Thus, the metamodelization is a doubling and superposing of models for conceptualization and theorization in unknown cartographies, in which a model is raised and constructed precisely because it should be abandoned retroactively. The infinite refrain of making models is the very meaning of metamodelization. Therefore, the practice of metamodeling is permanently transforming itself into the series of self-modeling. Indeed, unlearning is a metamodeling inside cognition and personal intelligence via collective assemblages of enunciations. Even the self or the subjectivity as such, for Guattari, is more or less the effect of metamodelization.

What a Guattarian education demands is to propel the process of "collective re-singularization" toward artistic creativity liberated from the coding of both macro and mass levels of society. Guattari contends in *Chaosmosis* that "poetry today might have more to teach us than economic science, the human sciences and psychoanalysis combined" (1995, p. 21). This phrase definitely supports my comparative approach and analysis between Guattari and Tanigawa as reading and writing poetry or literature allows us to reflect critically, and even to radically change our ways of life. Moreover, poetry or literature's measure of values and aesthetic initiatives is crucial for a Guattarian virtual ecology. The aesthetic here has to do with the surplus or excess of potential of expressive creativity and performative events. In *The Three Ecologies*, Guattari states "there is a proverb 'the exception proves the rule', but the exception can just as easily deflect the rule, or even recreate it" (2008, p. 35). The aesthetic thus pertains to the notion of "included middle" within the exception. Unlike with Aristotle's metaphysics, it no longer functions according to the law of exclusion. The *inclusive middle* is becoming itself: a threshold or interstitial zone between A and non-A. Of course, the exception generalizes or universalizes nothing, which is always isolated and recedes from the surrounding or abruptly foregrounds and decontextualizes itself from others. There is a way of thinking and living the (singular) event as such by letting itself be based on contingency or exception. Rather the gesture to embrace and begin with the exception offers an escape from the habit of distinguishing between contingency and necessity. Generally, this attitude is very significant for artists, but the same holds true for child development and education: the exception as a singular and incipient moment in any pedagogical context. Just as art gives itself to contingency which exceeds conventional rules and habits, ecosophical pedagogy reinvents itself along with contingent events which arise without anticipation.

According to this perspective, the exchanging of roles as a mutual intercessor is very significant. In *Negotiations,* Deleuze explains about the necessary presence of the mediator or negotiator in politics and movements. He writes: "But the Left needs indirect or free mediators, a different style, if only the Left makes it possible. The Left really needs what, thanks to the Communist Party, has been debased under the ridiculous name of 'fellow travelers,' because it really needs people to think" (Deleuze, 1995, p. 128). In fact, no one can deny that Guattari himself was a kind of mediator, negotiator, and intercessor traversing between heterogeneous dimensions such as various social movements, cultural activities, psychiatric and pedagogical practices. But the question of how to present or become such a mediator in an appropriate manner in any given situation has yet to be responded to fully in this chapter. As such, we shall look to Tanigawa for a possible answer in the next section.

Tactician of Manoeuvre

It is worth addressing Tanigawa's enigmatic but radical proposal of the "tactician of manoeuvre" (工作者) mediating or traversing between different social or cultural movements. In his essay entitled "What is sprouting in the dead body of the tactician of manoeuvre" (*Kousakusha no Shitai ni Moerumono*, 2009, p. 48), Tanigawa proposed a certain breakthrough in overcoming the contradictory polarities between the language of everyday life and that of organizers of movements. In his own definition, the "tactician of manoeuvre" (工作者) is the person or agency who opts for the intellectual way of discourse in front of ordinary people and conversely opts for the folksy manner of discourse in front of professional intellectuals. This double agent or "media of hybridized monster with double heads" rejects the mere translation or enlightenment of political or conceptual discourse for people by intellectuals, and deploys a hypocrite or betrayal tactics for both sectors.[1] Needless to say, Guattari himself was definitely such a type of author, writer, and interlocutor—that is to say, a "tactician of manoeuvre" despite his failures, defeats, breakdowns, and depressions. In other words, he himself was a sort of "vanishing mediator" which combines different modules smoothly into one invisible, transversal plane. Therefore, in Tanigawa's view, the tactician of manoeuvre strives to listen to the silence in the populace and engages in creating an empty space or vacoule for "any infinite conversation by plural media which seek a solidarity and aren't afraid of an isolation" (2009, p. 58). It therefore seems possible to assimilate the figure of the tactician of manoeuvre with the figuration of the Guattarian activist or Deleuzian "mediator/intercessor." Moreover, this double agency of the tactical mediator is applicable to the sphere of education. As is well known, the exchange of roles and tasks among clients, nurses, helpers, social workers, and doctors at La Borde clinic was crucial for both medical care practices and Guattarian schizoanalysis. For example, everybody had to cook at some time at La Borde. In other words, everybody had to engage with different kinds of work, which were not always based on individual preferences. What was required for the staff at La Borde was to become the patient or the client. Guattari insisted that therapists and mental health workers had to re-invent and re-create themselves as a sort of "bodies without organs" which could embrace the non-discursive intensities of clients (1995, p. 86). The same holds true also for pedagogy in his view: becoming pupil or becoming teacher in a singular gesture from both positions.

The ideal of pedagogical practice for Guattari consists in a sort of recursive cycle of pedagogical roles in the school system, in which professors not only teach students or pupils, but students teach administrators, and administrators teach professors. Here it is possible to detect an echo with the way Guattari strived to transcend the polarity between "subjugated group" and "subject group." The former always has certain models to imitate or rely upon, while the latter is self-directed and efficacious autonomously, open to alterity and finitude of each agency in the process of becoming other. Certainly, it is easy to perceive an echo with Sartre's concept of the "practico-inert" in his argument, but the subjugated group is not simply the reified or alienated mode of the subject group. For instance, one cannot enter or experience the subject group without any expectation in the operations by the subjugated group. Some parts or partial initiatives of the subjugated group might be able to invoke the characteristics of the subject group. As one can readily conceive, both types of group

---

[1] This idea of betrayal has an affinity with arguments on the mutual betrayal between God and man by Deleuze and Guattari, (2003, p. 123).

are recognizable in the educational classroom. Both nodes should not be put into a Manichaean dichotomy, but by permanently going back and forth in-between.

Tetkku

After his withdrawal from the militant struggles of mine workers, Tanigawa founded the corporate firm called *Tetkku* ("Tech") which dealt with specially manufactured devices (a kind of cassette tape record player for hearing and speaking English) and story-telling tapes (software). He also organized the commercial circulation and English workshops across Japan by mobilizing housewives as tutorial readers. Despite his masculine style of activism and exploitation of housekeepers, to a certain extent his organization was open to new ideas found in feminism and gender politics. Along with the company, he established "the Institute of Labor Language Center" in 1966, which organized conferences and invited international intellectuals such as Noam Chomsky and Roman Jakobson. On one level, it contained expressive, aesthetic, and performative initiatives, insofar as it utilized music, theater plays, poetry, narrative and common prose as educational resources. On another, the device is a good example for representing the machinic phylum in the post-media context, for the common technology was appropriated as a "tactical media." In a sense, the experimental manner of the company could be seen as a precursor of the neoliberal entrepreneur or post-Fordist renovation (Tanigawa's own repressive attitude against the workers' union in the company was quite notorious). Moreover, his day of "Tech" (until his expulsion from managerial positions) is comparable with the days of Le Centre d'études, de recherches et de formation institutionnelles (CERFI) for Guattari in the mid-1970s.

Stupidity

In a sense, education presupposes a mode of stupidity. A stupidity (bêtise in French) is induced when it combines one intelligence with another. In fact, two different wishes and intelligences are situated in the very activity of teaching and learning. When different agencies coincide with each other, a stupidity is already enacted. We can therefore ask: In what way can stupidity be guaranteed in pedagogy? Put differently, how can we keep the elasticity or plasticity of our own behavior, ways of using language and spatial segmentations, etc., open in the field of education? Interestingly, both Guattari and Oury frequently employed the term *vacoule* in conceptualizing their experimental cure or analytical practices exercised at La Borde. Oury defined it as the "anti-group" in actualizing or empowering a given collective practice (Oury, 2015, p. 101, 2012, p. 41). Guattari took over the idea as the binding point of varied demands and desires in collective formations. The vacoule is a certain virtual loose room, or emptied place of communications, which always emerges as an "institutional vacuole" (Guattari, 2015, p. 225). By applying this view, one can see that children deploy independent or autonomic communications by inventing or creating the singular space or vacoule without the help of professionals such as educationists or psychoanalysts (Guattari and Goffey, 2016, p. 85). Such a vacuole is demanded in the process of learning when we understand the collective assemblages of pedagogy as the "umbilical point" of chaosmosis. Exchanging roles in the kitchen at La Borde or the classroom can induce each role participant to take on the position of the "partial analyzer" ("partial enunciator"). Not only just cooking meals, but also cooking itself is operated as an expressive and performative activity in this experimentation. All tools and objects can be used as instruments or parts of an installation without the contextualization of art. As the partial enunciator, all kinds of audience/viewer/readers can assume certain potentials of creativity, which resemble the position of a conductor in an orchestra, editors in publishing, or DJs in dance music (Guattari, 2015, p. 114). Just as psychoanalysis deals with transferences among humans by tracing back to a repressed memory or interpreting a past experience, Guattarian schizoanalysis tends to prompt *transferences with things* (and objects) in order to open up the new vector of potential experiences. In Guattari's words, "the analysis of the Unconscious should be recentred on the *non-human processes of subjectivation* that I call machinic, but which are more than human....." (1995, p. 71, italics for emphasis). In teaching children how non-human modes of existence are truly significant for the production of subjectivity, we can demonstrate the integrative moment for Guattarian (institutional) pedagogy.

In 1982, after his long silence in publishing and writing, Tanigawa inaugurated the new cultural movement called the "Circle of Narrative Cultures" (*monogatari bunka no kai*), which consisted of networks of small groups of parents and children who were involved in experimental and performative education. The performative workshop called "human body symphonic theater" (人体交響劇) is especially famous as a pedagogical practice and resource for literature, theater play, music, and languages. This is quite different from the conventional modern theater play, because children play not only human characters but also trees, rocks, wind, water, plants, animals, things, and other non-human beings. Tanigawa was interested in the *Jōmon period* (14,000–300 BC) of the Japanese archipelago (Holocene) especially in terms of ecological ways of living which run alongside shamanistic or animistic practices. The plots and narratives of performances were selected from widespread genres such as Japanese ancient myths, fairy tales, and stories by Kenji Miyazawa.

Now we come to the real conjuncture between Guattari and Tanigawa with respect to institutional pedagogy, as it lets children enact cosmological, affective, and vibrant matters of the living world. The performativity aided by audio and visual machines can provide children with actual occasions of becoming other, becoming animal, becoming plant, and all other ramified agencies. One imagines with the advance of technological devices and post-media tactics (Φ), for instance, that both the pedagogical perspectives of Guattari and Tanigawa would deploy non-human objective time-space as existential territories (T). Why? Because this would give pupils the computer- or machine-aided subjectivity which may afford flows of knowledge and desires (F) and also lead to the emergence of different incorporeal universes (U) through the unfolding of animal, vegetable, cosmic, and machinic becomings (Guattari, 2008, p. 26). The following quotation from *Chaosmosis* can be read as a precise conceptual explanation of Tanigawa's practice:

> Strange contraptions, you will tell me, these machines of virtuality, these blocks of mutants percepts and affects, half-object half subject, already there in sensation and outside themselves in fields of the possible. (1995, p. 92)

This should be not read as a romantic celebration of, or unification with nature, but rather envisioned as the description of an exercise in embracing the living world and nature as machinic assemblages. Certainly, this understanding of the subjectivity as ambience is not only close to the shamanistic or animistic state of mind, but also related to the maladapted mind-sets of delayed or disabled children (Tanigawa also emphasized their potential in a more open type of pedagogy).

Although in the era of bio-politics, "mental health" is concerned primarily and prevailingly as a buzz term, and this point is not concerned solely with the symptoms of autism, ADHD, depression, anorexia, and all other chaosmic states in childhood or adolescence, but rather about confirming that the affective or libidinal transference is not merely ascribed to regression toward the maternal or imaginary other. All mind-sets and affections incorporate certain chaosmic universes. Like the institutional psychiatry inaugurated by Oury, Guattarian institutional pedagogy concerns itself with the very transferences for all different kinds of things, objects, machines, non-human actors, and quasi-subjectivities. Only the gesture of diving into the dark umbilical point of chaosmosis with collective enunciations can illustrate how much normapathy is also indebted to pre- or trans-individual, polyphonic, vibrant objectivities as proto-subjectivities (1995, p. 111). The term normapathy, which both Oury and Guattari utilized in their separate works (1995, p. 72), treats the "ordinary or health" conditions of people as a certain state of mental malfunction. From this perspective, mental health can be grasped as a fragile piece of chaosmosis, even if it is often misinterpreted as stupidity in the negative sense.

Stupidity, in any educational system, neither comes from, nor is reducible to, the inferiority of intelligence or failure of knowledge. For each learning subject, in teaching and learning, there is always a bifurcation between will (motive or desire) and intelligence (knowledge or skills). Although schoolmasters tend to assimilate both moments, if students or pupils follow their own wishes and motivation, then they can realize the gap or crack in both. In this case, a stupidity gives rise to an emancipation of intelligence revolving around the pivot of double posture: *combining an autonomy of unlearning and a heteronomy of learning*. One could say that this attempt at emancipation is the self-awareness of mutual (un)learning and the equality of intelligence. What makes people stupid in a given education system is not merely a lack of instruction or knowledge, but the very belief about their putative inferiority among people or students. A stupidity is an effect of bare action or the zero degree of the practice of education, in which both teaching subject and learning subject can take over each other in a certain context. At the same time, the attempt at exchanging roles can be a driving force of pedagogy. What is at stake in the coming institutional pedagogy is to focus, articulate, interpret, and even posit a presence of stupidity immanently embedded within our everyday life. Put differently, stupidity has creative potential under certain conditions. Stupidity can be enacted, embodied, and performed in scenes of education in the broadest sense. The space for pedagogy should be envisioned as a kind of laboratory or relational field, from which the varied expressive and conceptual—sometimes political—initiatives could emerge within.

In *Difference and Repetition* (the fifth postulate of the third chapter), Deleuze (2007) insisted that stupidity or bêtise does not imply an error or "the greatest weakness of thought," but rather "the source of its highest power" in what it enforces. He also contends that bêtise is just an interaction between thought and individuation, insofar as individuation, which can neither afford a background nor a form to a thought, traverses the ego/self by constituting all cognitive and collective processes through what is not recognized, that is to say, the unknown (2007, p. 188). From a different angle, Deleuze and Guattari raised the question of stupidity in terms of the life of workers, especially its negative aspect under the capitalist formation. As they say, "although he has mastered a flow of knowledge, information, and training, he is so absorbed in capital that the reflux of organized, axiomatized stupidity coincides with him, so that, when he goes home in evening, he discovers his little desiring-machines by tinkering with the television set—O despair!" (2005, p. 236). In this way, the capitalist system requires a certain sense of stupidity in order to stabilize and sustain itself, because capitalism is always dependent on the effusion and apparatus of anti-production, which is brought into the very production of an "accursed share" at all levels of daily life. Insofar as the education system is the apparatus to let children enter into the formation of capitalist labor and ways of living, the moment of anti-production must be invoked as well. Turning back to our context, the effusion of anti-production—if not play, game, and ludus in daily life—puts the flow of capitalistic knowledge and skills in a superposition with a stupidity that is permanently demanded for integration into the capitalistic system.

In the 1970s in works such as *Molecular Revolution*, Guattari frequently criticized parental behavior which left children alone with a television set, which is now extended to other multimedia gadgets such as video games or smart phones (2012, pp. 295–299). In *Chaosmosis*, however, Guattari figures out another potential of television consumption in order to grasp the post-media tactical usage. When indulging or absorbed in TV or the net, one is located in the intersection of hypnotic effects of luminous images, personal fascination with narratives or story-telling, eventual phantasmatic participation in them, and surrounding noises. All of these constitute the absorbant, partial, and pathic subjectivity (1995, pp. 16, 25). They appear as unimportant, but can catapult one beyond stupidity toward a chaosmic zone.

Conclusion

In conclusion, it should be confirmed that the combined pedagogy of Guattari and Tanigawa involves a type of stupidity, which is not simply a lack of intelligence, but is more concerned with critiquing the sustainability of capitalism and modern society. The teachers who are accustomed to and identify themselves with disciplined matters cannot understand and even imagine the virtue or potentiality of stupidity. But something has to be invented such as a willing or tactical stupidity. The virtue of expressive cultures, for instance, including music and visual experiments, seemingly retain the potential to re-actualize the vibes, atmosphere, info-environment, and milieu that are potentially immanent in all pedagogical, relational fields. Unknown creativities and capacities emerge out from different kinds of stupidity. Our stupidity is forged from differends and dissensus as immanent aberrations in unlearning (2008, p. 33). Only the person who performs in unreason or stupidity, however, can be in tune with a certain reason, while diving into the social craziness as a chaosmic umbilical point can exhibit the potential of affective reason via stupidity beyond passive emotions. This is nothing less than the secret kernel of Guattarian and Gan's combined ecosophical pedagogy.

References

Deleuze, G. (1995). *Negotiations, 1972–1990*. New York: Columbia University Press.

Deleuze, G. (2007). *Difference and repetition*. London: Continuum.

Deleuze, G., & Guattari, F. (2005). *Anti-Oedipus: Capitalism and schizophrenia*. Minneapolis: University of Minnesota Press.

Deleuze, G., Guattari, F., & Massumi, B. (2003). *A thousand plateaus: Capitalism and schizophrenia*. London: Continuum.

Deligny, F., Burk, D., & Porter, C. (2015). *The Arachnean and other texts*. Minneapolis: Univocal.

Freinet, C. (2015). *Gengo no Shizen na Manabikata, [The Natural Method of Lecture]* (S. Minoru, Trans.). Osaka: Tarojirosha edidasu.

Gan, T. (2009). *Kousakusha no Shitai ni Moerumono, [1958] in Genten ga Sonzaisuru*. Osaka: Kodansha Bungei Bunko.

Guattari, F. (1995). *Chaosmosis: An ethico-aesthetic paradigm*. Bloomington: Indiana University Press.

Guattari, F. (2008). *The three ecologies*. Bloomsbury Academic: London; New York.

Guattari, F. (2011). *The machinic unconscious: Essays in schizoanalysis*. Semiotext(e): Los Angeles.

Guattari, F. (2012). *La Revolution Moleculaire*. Paris: Les Prairie Ordinaires.

Guattari, F. (2013). *Schizoanalytic Cartographies*. London: Bloomsbury.

Guattari, F. (2015). Ecosophical Practices and the restoration of the subjective. In G. Genosoko & J. Hetrick (Eds.), *Machinic eros: Writings on Japan* (pp. 34–45). Minneapolis: Univocal.

Guattari, F., Deleuze, G., & Hodges, A. (2015). *Psychoanalysis and transversality: Texts and interviews 1955–1971*. South Pasadena, CA: Semiotext(e).

Guattari, F., & Goffey, A. (2016). *Lines of flight: For another world of possibilities*. London: Bloomsbury.

Guattari, F., & Lotringer, S. (1995). *Chaosophy*. New York, N.Y: Semiotext(e).

Guattari, F., Rolnik, S., Clapshow, K., & Holmes, B. (2008). *Molecular revolution in Brazil*. Los Angeles, CA: Semiotext(e).

Lazzarato, M., & Jordan, J. D. (2014). *Signs and machines: Capitalism and the production of subjectivity*. Los Angeles, CA: Semiotext(e).

Oury, J. (2012). *Rencontre Avec Le Japon*. Reams: Chapms Social.

Oury, J. (2015). *Seishinigaku to Seidoseishinryoho* (Y. Miyawaki, Trans.). Tokyo: Shunjusha. Shunjusha.

Toshiya Ueno is Professor of critical theory, philosophy, and cultural studies in the Department of Transcultural Studies in Wako University, Tokyo. His research fields are critical theory, media theory, and social thought. He has published numerous books in Japanese and essays in English. His most recent project is on Guattari and ecosophy. The underground techno party is also his field as both DJ and text jockey (TJ).

Chapter 7
Towards a Pedagogy of Immanence: Transversal Revolts Under Neoliberal Capitalism

Hans Skott-Myhre, Veronica Pacini-Ketchabaw and Luke Kalfleish

Abstract In this chapter, we propose to articulate Guattari's concept of transversality as applied to education as neoliberal pedagogy under twenty-first-century capitalism. To do so, we will delineate an "adversarial relation" between definitions of transversality in the work of Guattari and the appropriation of Guattari's concept by neoliberal pedagogical imperatives. In particular, we will investigate a recent report from the United Nations Educational, Scientific, and Cultural Organization (UNESCO) that purports to set a framework for the deployment of transversality within the emerging markets of global capitalism. In contrast, we will offer two pedagogical provocations in this chapter that we suggest may open avenues to the further development of antidotes to the neoliberal appropriation of transversality in education.

Keywords Neoliberal capitalism · Immanence · Pedagogy · Affect

Introduction

> Modern power is not at all reducible to the classical alternative "repression or ideology" but implies processes of normalization, modulation, modelling, and information ... both subjection and enslavement taken to extremes, as two simultaneous parts that constantly reinforce and nourish each other. (Deleuze and Guattari, 1987, p. 458)

In this chapter, we propose to articulate Guattari's concept of transversality as applied to education as neoliberal pedagogy under twenty-first-century capitalism. To do so, we will delineate an "adversarial relation" between definitions of transversality in the work of Guattari and the appropriation of Guattari's concept by neoliberal

H. Skott-Myhre (✉)
Kennesaw State University, Kennesaw, USA
e-mail: hskottmy@kennesaw.edu

V. Pacini-Ketchabaw
University of Western Ontario, London, Canada

L. Kalfleish
University of West Georgia, Carrollton, USA

© Springer Nature Singapore Pte Ltd. 2018
D. R. Cole and J. P. N. Bradley (eds.), *Principles of Transversality in Globalization and Education*, https://doi.org/10.1007/978-981-13-0583-2_7

pedagogical imperatives. In particular, we will investigate a recent report from the United Nations Educational, Scientific, and Cultural Organization (UNESCO) that purports to set a framework for the deployment of transversality within the emerging markets of global capitalism. In contrast, we will offer two pedagogical provocations in this chapter that we suggest may open avenues to the further development of antidotes to the neoliberal appropriation of transversality in education.

The first pedagogic provocation in this chapter that shows how revolts under neoliberal capitalism could work engages "transversing" the K-12 classroom, specifically the roles of the student/teacher relation. To do this, we will take an immanent approach to learning derived from Spinoza (2000), which does not congeal toward a transcendental subject or "I", or neoliberal subject, and this is here extended in the Guattarian concept of transversality. We will argue that learning, like life itself, is an expression of non-capitalist immanence, which acts as a self-producing process that acts as an alternative to the abstract immanence and exploitation of capitalism.

One of the key legacies that Guattari (2005) derives from Spinoza's conceptual frameworks is the concept of "immanent surplus." We would argue that this reading of living force as infinite virtuality, rather than dialectical lack, is the driving of impetus in his relation to structuralism and psychoanalysis. We will suggest that the immanent relations of student/teacher encounters, read as surplus, constitute a radical alternative to the neoliberal abstractions of what constitutes teaching and learning. In exploring learning as a form of living relations (Cole, 2011a), we hope to engage the contextual entanglements of the teacher/student body as a certain kind of nervous system immanent to its own effects, to specifically maintain these living effects.

Our second provocation sets out to experiment with pedagogies of relationality that attend to the encounters of human and more than human bodies in an early childhood education classroom. As opposed to the coded relations of pedagogy under capitalism, we propose that nothing in pedagogical encounters acts as a singularly appropriate model of practice. In other words, in education here is nothing to rehearse, nothing to appropriate. What is central to the Guattarian project and profoundly applicable to our investments in education is experimentation through encounter (Guattari, 2005), which will be demonstrated below. Through reading the entanglements of human and more than human bodies in early education, we endeavor to propose pedagogy as an engagement with each of these encounters as an event that demands its own questions, its own concerns, and its own ethos.

The Unconscious of Pedagogy

At the center of our project here is the question of what is to become of pedagogy as we enter the globalized realm of, what Hardt and Negri refer to as, capitalist and corporate Empire (Hardt & Negri, 2001)? We argue that what is at stake in such a question is the social and cultural articulation of the unconscious in the writings of Deleuze and Guattari (1977). In particular, the unconscious as a site of infinite productive capacity for the proliferation of thought and action. While we will not address the unconscious directly in this writing, it is without a doubt the "ghost in the machine" for what we are proposing (Cole & Hager, 2010). For us, pedagogy read through a Guattarian lens refuses the configurations of a solely Western unconscious, or unconscious dominated by the desires of and in the West. To teach and learn transversally is neither instrumental nor constituted axiomatically. The unconscious of pedagogy, à la Guattari (2010), is not available to any form of universal signification because the unconscious for Guattari exceeds the capacities of language. Teaching and learning as a function of the unconscious of pedagogy are a matter of the production of multiplicities rather than binaries; affective transits rather than taxonomic signification; and relational pragmatics rather than abstract coding, all of which are demonstrated in this chapter.

We suggest, after Guattari, that the collective unconscious, as the center of social relations, is key to notions of transversality as founded in his material investments and extensions of the work of Sartre and Lacan (Guattari, 2005, 2010). This is, however, not the individual unconscious, the Freudian unconscious, nor the linguistically structured unconscious. Each of the proposals about the structure and function of the unconscious from Sartre, Lacan and Freud are rooted in a teleological trajectory rooted in historical family trauma. Instead, for Guattari, it is a machinic unconscious or an unconscious "turned toward the future whose screen would be none other than the possible itself" (Guattari, 2010, p. 10). This is the unconscious as sheer living capacity driven by desire as absolute productive force. Desire, for Deleuze and Guattari (1977), is not founded in lack or the *desire for*, but in living force as the *desire to*. This shift opens the unconscious as a machine of desiring production for worlds yet to come and for futures not yet imagined. We would argue that it is the future itself that is at stake in transversality and its applications within the realm of pedagogy under global capital. If we are to take Guattari seriously in his assertion that the production of future social configuration is to be found in the unconscious, then it is the unconscious itself that becomes both the vehicle and the site of production of social forms, such as pedagogy under global capitalism as explored in this chapter.

Appropriating the Unconscious

To think through the role of the unconscious under global capitalism as it applies to neoliberal pedagogy requires a transversal analysis of how capitalism and the unconscious have coevolved in the transition from industrial capitalism to the current stage of what Hardt & Negri, (2001) have termed as the "global capitalist Empire." In Guattarian (2010) terms, the machinic unconscious, as a site of production within the realms of dominance and control deployed by neoliberal global capitalism, might well be articulated as an embedded point of transit for both the extractions of desire by capital and the articulations of its alternatives. In this moment of what Marx (1993) termed the real subsumption of living labor under capitalist relations, modes of human consciousness become primary points of appropriation as the ground out of which the abstract coding of desire might be strip-mined. As Marx (1993) noted presciently in the *Grundrisse*,

> Once adopted into the production process of capital, the means of labour passes through different metamorphoses, whose culmination is the *machine*, or rather, an *automatic system of machinery* (system of machinery: the *automatic* one is merely its most complete, most

adequate form, and alone transforms machinery into a system), set in motion by an automaton, a moving power that moves itself; this automaton consisting of numerous mechanical and intellectual organs, so that the workers themselves are cast merely as its conscious linkages. (p. 693)

Marx goes on to note, that living labor becomes subsumed within this global, distributed network of machinery in such a way that the individual worker no longer finds their unity in living force, but in the unity of the machinery into which it is embedded. Marx (1993) speaks of this relation as a "confrontation" between the "mighty organism" of capitalism's global machinery and the worker (p. 693).

In our contemporary period, we would argue that the confrontation between, on the one hand, living labor as a form of consciousness rooted in unconscious desiring production and, on the other, the global machinery of capitalism has come to full fruition through accelerated globalization (Sellar & Cole, 2017). For our interests here, it is important to note that, historically, pedagogy played a dual role in the period of industrial capitalism simultaneously shaping the bodies of workers, while opening modes of resistance and rebellion in the productions of labor unions and revolutionary working class movements. The shift in capitalism into, what might be called, a virtual economy now transfers the site of confrontation into the realm of, what Negri (1996) calls, "immaterial labor" or the appropriation of our powers of intellect itself. We would argue that this capitalist appropriative expansion into the realm of our very social capacities for thought and creativity centers pedagogical relations in the schools as battlegrounds for new confrontations and revolutionary struggles.

In the opening epigraph to this chapter, Deleuze and Guattari (1987) suggest that the deployments of modern power as an apparatus of capture invest the social with a simultaneity of subjection and enslavement. That is to say, it is through the production of ourselves as modern subjects that we become ensnared in the machinery that, as Foucault (1979) points out, is both produced by us and produces us. Indeed, it is Foucault (1979) who maps, in many ways, the role that education and pedagogical practice play in profoundly instrumentalizing our subjection and enslavement.

The Real in Education

Of course, the relation of any given pedagogical imperative to the dominant social of a historical period is neither smooth nor seamless. Social configurations, like education, are rife with inherent contradictions and antagonisms. These tensions in any given social formulation simultaneously foreclose and open seismic shifts in the distribution of living force in a process of, what Guattari (2005) referred to as, "subjectification." Subjectification, as Guattari (2005) delineates, is the process by which modes of subjectivity are articulated both socially and within the interior consciousness of each of us. The production of subjectivity is profoundly impersonal and is an immanent process that draws on nascent forms of virtual subjectivity in combination with instantiated majoritarian constructs. Subjectification is an entanglement of elements in a particular historical moment, brought to a singularity of form particular to the composite capacities of a given body or bodies. Subjectivity, thus, can be indeterminate as in the nomadic subjectivity of Braidotti (1994) or highly overcoded by the dominant system of the social. Of course, this is not a distinct bifurcation. Each of these processes is mutually productive of each other as a force of mutagenic social capacity,

We would argue that it is specifically these modes of subjectification that become the processual entanglement produced by pedagogical relations in the classroom. That is to say, pedagogical practices as modes of subjectification are inherently indeterminate and relational as well as entangled and coevolutionary. They are composed of both territorializing and deterritorializing functions. Pedagogical entanglements of subjectification can function as molar lines (Deleuze & Guattari, 1987) that structure majoritarian systems of rule that range from systems of normalization, to fascizing systems that work to fully overcode living force. Conversely, education can open fields indeterminate of social and personal experimentation as molecular lines, or even lines of flight (Deleuze & Guattari, 1987), that can initiate and sustain emerging forms of worlds and peoples to come.

In the molar register, we can see that conventional practices, such as teaching or instruction, constitute forms of liminal relations through which existing forms of social configuration may echo in varying degrees of amplitude. This increase in the force of social indoctrination through repetitive habitual circulations of dominant logic extends the imperative of dominant logic through the collective enunciation of extensive variations of the same.

In this repetition of socially dominant vernacular, we have the sheer appropriation of living force through the mechanisms of deploying the capacity of the symbolic, which tends toward an infinite proliferation of signification as difference, and the inherent longing for the sign to signify what it cannot.. That is to say, capitalism, as an abstract system, encodes life so that life can be misunderstood as an infinite series of empty signs. In doing this, it defers any direct relation to what Lacan (2013) refers to as the Real. In this context, the Real could well be defined as a space of immanent production "devoid of the negativities of absences, antagonisms, gaps, lacks, splits, etc." introduced by encoding systems such as language (Johnston, 2013, para 21, online).

As an infinitely deferred Real and mad extrapolation of signification, the current regime of postmodern global capitalism extracts and overcodes the human capacity for linguistic expression, "scissioning" the reference to living form and opening a virulent form of an immanent, self-referent, *abstract, and symbolic* unconscious. Such simulacrum of unconscious process opens *a copy … of a copy … of a copy* of what Deleuze and Guattari (1977) refer to as desiring production. This apparatus of capture creates a cruel simulation of the *and … and … and* that constitutes the logic of the *living* unconscious.

Neoliberal Transversality

In terms of the topic of this volume, this process of capture by neoliberal capitalism begins to overcode the conceptual frameworks of transversality itself. Indeed, in a recent report by UNESCO on transversality in education (Yoko, 2015), we find that the relation of transversality to subjectification and the unconscious is simply absent. The possibilities of transversally opening vistas of new peoples and experimental social formations are redeployed into neoliberal vernacular. The role of affect as a transition between states and degrees of power that constitute indeterminate sites of sense for subjects to come is similarly redeployed. We can say that key elements of Guattari's transversality, founded in the Guattarian unconscious, are not so much missing as they are emptied of their genetic living capacity and used to quite different ends on behalf of the world of global capitalism.

Indeed, the Asia Pacific Educational Research Network (Yoko, 2015) promotes "transversal competencies" as the gateway for students to enter the workforce of twenty-first-century capitalism through enhanced thinking, communication, and interpersonal skills (see Table 7.1). Based on research done by UNESCO, transversality is defined as,

> Education policies and curricula [that] aim to incorporate a broad range of skills and competencies necessary for learners to successfully navigate the changing global landscape. "Transversal competencies", sometimes referred to as "21st Century skills", are broad based skills that aim to meet these challenges, such as technological advances and intercultural communication. (p. 1)

Couched in the language of equity and critical thinking, transversality becomes highly instrumentalized as a method for training young people in the skills required for work. Likewise, the following two tables (UNESCO, pp. 5–6) demonstrate the way in which the transformation of transversality as a pedagogical method for subjectification is turned toward the neoliberal objectives of the current regimes of appropriation and control.

Table 7.1 UNESCO's working definition of transversal competencies

Domains	Examples of key characteristics
Critical and innovative thinking	Creativity, entrepreneurship, resourcefulness, application skills, reflective thinking, reasoned decision-making
Interpersonal skills	Presentation and communication skills, leadership, organizational skills, teamwork, collaboration, initiative, sociability, collegiality
Intrapersonal skills	Self-discipline, enthusiasm, perseverance, self-motivation, compassion, integrity, commitment
Global citizenship	Awareness, tolerance, openness, respect for diversity, intercultural understanding, ability to resolve conflicts, civic/political participation, conflict resolution, respect for the environment
Optional domain: (example) physical and psychological health	Healthy lifestyle, healthy feeding, physical fitness, empathy, self-respect

Table 7.2 Rationale for integration of transversal competencies into education

	Economic discourse	Social discourse	Humanity discourse
Global perspective	Competitiveness	Understanding and peace	Global citizenship
National perspective	GDP growth	HDI growth	Patriotism
Personal perspective	Employability	Community/harmony	Moral formation

Of particular interest here in terms of the neoliberal imperatives that have implications for, what we might call, the "strip-mining of desire" are the inclusion of entrepreneurship as an aspect of critical thinking, as well as the innovation and deployment of sociability (see Table 7.1). The conflation of our social lives into our work lives is a hallmark of what Negri (1996) refers to as the development of *immaterial labor*. Hardt and Negri (2009) note that this redeployment of sociability as a new "job skill" is key to what they have termed the *feminization of labor*. This effort to extend labor time deeply into all of our lived experience is founded in the appropriation of our very ability as humans to be social.

In addition, there is the rather ominous determination of compassion, enthusiasm, perseverance, health, empathy, and self-respect as job skills (see Table 7.1). Finally, the flattening of economic, social, and humanity discourses into the domains of the global, national, and personal might well appear to give an equivalence to competitiveness and peace or employability and moral formation (See Table 7.2).

This instrumental use of transversality as a method for flattening and abstracting living force is, without a doubt, at singular odds with Guattari's intentions in explicating his method. If we are to take him seriously, transversality in education might invest instead in,

> Subjectification under the sign of processuality and singularization, thereby breaking with both a centering on the transcendent unity of the subject and the becoming-subject of a transcendence dialectically immanent to consciousness, accomplishing instead a transversalist enlarging of enunciation through matters of expression that are worked over by forms of praxis … generative of heterogeneity and complexity. (Alliez & Goffey 2011, p. 5)

Instead of an instrumental reading of our capacities as universal categories to be deployed within the emerging global markets and regimes or control, Guattari (2010) focuses his definition of transversality on the unique, idiosyncratic capacities of subjectification. As we have noted above, for Guattari, subjectification, or the production of ourselves within the context of the social, is a process of composition of all the elements of a historical moment and the geographical/temporal coordinates of bodies colliding in a space. In this, there is no dialectic construction that would constitute a necessity for training in the social skills a body might lack. Nor is there an assumption that there is an ideal body that exists outside the actual configuration of living bodies in their radical anomalous alterity. Instead, Guattari (2010) proposes that transversality opens a field of radical difference as an engine of infinite proliferative production that cannot be yoked to the necessities and abstract desire of any symbolic regime such as transversal competencies. In what follows, we will outline two examples of what this might look like.

First Provocation: Transversing the Classroom

The appropriation of the concept of transversality in the UNESCO report indicates an effort by neoliberal capitalism to bring its apparatuses of capture ever closer to life. In particular, we would argue that this is an effort to overcode living force in its immanent capacity for desiring production. Pedagogically, this effort to appropriate and capture the living force of the pedagogical encounter is premised in producing classroom settings where the subjectification of teachers and students is predicated on a relationship of lack. This relation which is initiated under industrial capitalism is extended and amplified in neoliberal capitalism under the conditions of real subsumption, where there is no outside to the logic of capitalist appropriation. As bleak as this seems, it is important that this process of strip-mining desire and the elimination of its alternatives, however dynamic such a process may be, is understood as subservient to or delayed in a responsive relation with the varying modes of production that such apparatuses of capture attempt to seize.

Echoing Hardt and Negri's (2009) work in exploring apparatuses of capture and resistance within global capital, it is apparent that, like other twenty-first-century institutions, schools function as sites of production and capture. These sites are constituted by desiring production, which grow and are expressed through certain social aggregates to produce common and singular modes of subjectivity. Life as desiring production within these institutions is dynamic and in surplus, and thus, it must be controlled or captured by apparatuses that function through flexibility and motion.

Foucault (1979) articulates the flexibility and dynamic quality of power in the production of control or capture in his delineations of the workings of sovereign power, disciplinary power, and bio-power. In his explication of these forms of power, he argues that none of these techniques of power function equally or in uniform ways. Instead, they exist together within social institutions encompassing one another and rupturing along their fault lines. In this sense, they are constantly dispersing and then re-accumulating around events of sudden expressions of desiring production.

For the sake of this chapter, we will include one common example of a teacher standing up to a despot principal, in order to allow cell phone use in their classroom. We argue that this rather minor and mundane conflict is saturated with sovereign and disciplinary power echoing the molar force of industrial capitalism, while simultaneously engaging modes of production and appropriation pertinent to neoliberal capital in a subtle contestation.

The sovereign relation of the industrial period is illustrated by the supervisor/overseer and embodied by the principal. Disciplinary power is being played out in a power struggle with the worker/teacher over who controls the classrooms and the behavior of the students. From one perspective, it is a simple struggle for the democratization of the classroom. However, we would argue that there remains another dimension to the terms of power being contested. On the surface, the teacher is contesting the overt hierarchical power structure of the institution so as to allow the students greater freedom of expression. However, embedded in this confrontation is the technology of the cell phone itself.

The question of the cell phone as an extension of neoliberal capitalist technology raises the issue of a subtler regime of control and discipline. From this perspective, cell phone usage could well indicate the subtle intrusion of the embedded figure of global capital into the classroom. This complicates the power relations of the classroom and the institution, entangling the teacher in complex modes of subjectification derived through and by coevolving modes of capitalist production. Caught in the intersecting fields of discipline and control, the act of the teacher becomes less a matter of resistance than it is a fleeing of one power structure to another, or a lived transition from one power structure to another.

Such an image does not undermine potential acts of resistance within schools, but rather prevents the seeking out of resistance in an ideal space, outside of another form of power. We take Foucault's work here as blueprints of varying forms of techniques and strategies to be understood, resisted, or wielded at certain times, which is dependent upon its contextualizing as a secondary response to emerging acts of resistance within the student/teacher relation. Put another way, these acts of disobedience within the classroom are conceived as affective eruptions of immanent power, which are primary to any techniques of discipline, punishment, or control. Positioning resistance as acts of primacy thus eliminates the seeking of an outside to the world of forces or power relations, opening up our capacity to seek out transversal modes of transit instead.

Affect as Transit

This immanent capacity of living force as, what Negri (1999) denotes as resistance that precedes domination, cannot be articulated in axiomatic modes of signification. It is concomitant with language, but exceeds any capacity at full explication or containment. If we think of a Guattarian pedagogy as an immanent field of liberative struggle, then such a field requires highly mobile and heterogenous modes of subjectification. We would suggest that the mechanisms for such a fluidity of transit might well be found in the Deleuzian concept of affect.

According to Deleuze (1988), affect is the embodied transition or passage from one state to another. It takes place on the fringes of discourse, which is why it escapes every attempt of the apparatuses of dominant power to seize it entirely for the sake of appropriation or exploitation. In this way, affect cannot be instrumentalized, simply because it cannot be wholly translated into discursive structures. As per Spinoza's parallelism, affection (*affectio*) is composed of the states of the mind that indicate the presence of an affecting body, which is constituted by both the nature of the affecting body as well as the affected body itself. Further, in accordance with parallelism affect (*affectus*) is the passage between these states in constant variable duration of both the mind and the body in parallel. Deleuze (1988) however is careful to remind us, vis-a-vis Spinoza, that such a definition is a constellation of ideas adjacent to the event of affect and is not the actual affect itself, which constantly flees such talking games and cannot be represented:

> It is certain that the affect implies an image or idea, and follows from the latter as from its cause. But it is not confined to the image or idea; it is of another nature, being purely transitive, and not indicative or representative, since it is experienced in a lived duration that involves the difference between two states. This is why Spinoza shows that the affect is not a *comparison of ideas*, and thereby rejects any intellectualist interpretation. (p. 49)

Affect as a lived transition or passage, as opposed to a passage between two imagined states, means that it never ceases to exist and never comes to be experienced directly, but is always an in-between-ness, similar to the atmosphere of a place, e.g., a school. To construct the student/teacher relation around such a dynamic concept as affect repositions our ideas of what a teacher and a student can be while repositioning us to seek out what it is we can do (Cole, 2011b).

In relation to our example of the teacher/principal/student/cell phone above, this may well imply a compositional rather than a confrontational approach, or as Deleuze and Guattari (1987) express it, it is about "assemblage." The question becomes: What forms of transit are opened outside the traditional configuration of such subjects, or in terms of what transversal relations might be enjoined?

Reframing the teacher/principal/student/cell phone as a heterogenous assemblage composed of a dynamic field of affect poses many possibilities for transversing the prefigured apparatuses of capture that seek to manage and contain the production of subjectivity. It is fitting that a concept as fruitful as affect can be used to resist subjects of enclosure given that it is constantly fleeing them. Such dynamism also creates avenues for us to revaluate some of our most basic presumptions about teaching, learning, and thinking within pedagogy. This is pertinent in challenging neoliberal abstract imperatives premised fully in universal signifiers, such as the UNESCO report, which reduce the rich living complexity of affectual pedagogical relationships to skill sets and qualifications for employment.

Consciousness as Transit

As Guattari (2005, 2010) has forcefully argued, it is in our apprehension of states of consciousness that challenges to the existing system of rule might be mounted. For Guattari, the relation of conscious and unconscious apperception is critical to the process of subjectification and we would argue deeply interrelated with the question of affect. We would propose that Deleuze's Spinozist accounting of affect is profoundly influential in notions of consciousness in Guattari. For Deleuze, according to Gregg and Seigworth (2010), affect theory is centered around Spinoza's infamous statement that, "no one has yet to determine what the body can do" (p. 3). The effect of this notion, per Deleuze (1988), is not to simply reverse the positioning of the Cartesian mind-over-body split, but instead, to seek out a "devaluation of consciousness in relation to thought: a discovery of the unconscious, of an unconscious of thought just as profound as the unknown of the body" (p. 19). We would propose that this is vital to our project of transversing the classroom and re-conceptualizing the student/teacher relation around affect, simply because it opens up possibilities for understanding subjectivity beyond common articulations of consciousness.

Instead of seeing the issue of mobile phones as a struggle for hierarchical primacy, arguments over appropriate technocratic pedagogical intervention, or the classroom as a laboratory for democracy, thinking affectually offers the opportunity to creatively engage with phones, bodies, human, and more than human assemblages as sheer capacity. However, such experimentation requires conscious apperception adequate to the task and, we would argue alongside Deleuze, that conventional modes of conscious awareness are woefully inadequate to the task. In short, teaching and learning within frameworks of contemporary modes of consciousness holds little capacity for anything other than reifying the existing neoliberal imperatives for pedagogy such as the UNESCO report.

Put another way, Deleuze and Spinoza articulate consciousness as the last or slowest form of thought, and that is prone to certain illusions which function as mechanisms for maintaining itself as an ideal producer of knowledge, or as its own first cause. More concretely, we would suggest that the taken-for-granted superiority of consciousness over thought as a cause of knowledge acts as a major pillar for the neoliberal enclosures that exist in the immanent field of the classroom setting discussed previously.

According to Deleuze (1988), Spinoza frames desire (conatus) as the cause of consciousness, therefore positioning it as a secondary process to the more dynamic relation of affections/affects and desire. For Spinoza, desire is the connection of the appetite of the body with consciousness, the latter acting merely as a witness of the initial passage of affect. Therefore, similar to affect, consciousness is "purely transitive" or "the awareness of the passage from these less potent totalities to more potent ones, and vice versa" and all the while remains secondary to the primary passage or lived transition of affect (p. 21).

Given this triad of desire, affect, and consciousness, we can restructure the student/teacher relationship as a transversal immanent process of production, carried through by desire from unconsciousness to consciousness. From this perspective, a relationship centered on affect must involve the unconscious components of desire in order to work toward expanding the capacities of the minds and bodies involved as passages. Therefore, we must also revaluate what it means to raise consciousness or expand its capacity because consciousness plays only a part of a larger cycle of production and thus must be approached this way given its specific function within a larger process. In terms of our example of the struggle over mobile phones, the question becomes one of how we understand the technology within the broader canvas of consciousness as a contested field of subjective production.

To engage the mundane struggles of the school as a neoliberal institution requires an understanding that states of consciousness as living force are at the heart of pedagogical imperatives, both liberatory and fascistic. In this regard, the political deployment of consciousness as a secondary passage means that the common goals of teaching, such as "expanding" consciousness, must be about opening up capacities of expression, rather than the building of ideas to know the world in their own limited way. Within the pedagogical apparatuses of control and discipline, teachers and students are trained as modern subjects built to know the world consciously in its totality. In contrast to consciously thought totality, affects are the lived transitions that escape such forms of knowing, shifting the subjects from knowers with ideas to expressions of capacities. In this mode, affects are carried by desire from the cause of the encounter of other bodies, which are carried through the striving of the unconscious, and dispersed into the echoed effects of the conscious mind as inadequate traces of what it once was, all of which occurs as a continuous cycle. We would argue that this reading of transversal passage is at extreme odds with the neoliberal version UNESCO is advocating above.

Classroom as Nervous System

If desire is the striving of what we do, then affect is the electrical charge that sparks us into motion. The sounding bell, the sharpness of a teacher's voice, and the colors of the classroom all cease to be just subtleties of a carefully crafted room, and instead become objects of affections, collisions of bodies, and producers of affects. On this microscale of objects and encounters, as well as in the macroscale of larger social and political configurations, it is easy to see infinite examples of webs of relations tiered over webs of relations. Configurations that range from micro- to macroscales most primarily register beyond our consciousness or language in many ways; thus, how we communicate with our environments is in an unspoken cause and effect of thresholds and intensities or more concretely as a "nervous system of bodies" in affective relations to other bodies.

Perceived through the neoliberal lens articulated by UNESCO, the vision of the classroom as a living nervous system might well spark anxiety and initiate discourses that advocate micromanaging every intimate detail of the classroom. However, any impulse to know or master all the possible encounters of a classroom is the fallacy of consciousness as first cause returning out of habit. Instead, then, as advocates of transversality, the goal of affective pedagogy is to expand our capacity to engage with the surplus charges of affect, or as Deleuze (1992) puts it, "What a body can do corresponds to the nature and limits of its capacity to be affected" (p. 218). Therefore, we need to rely then on a shift from *consciousness as knower* to *consciousness as passage*, and specifically, a passage toward an embodied intuition, or, what Spinoza (2000) referred to as, the "Third Kind of Knowledge" to enact transversality.

In this sense, rather than having an arsenal of ideas to encompass the totality of its relations, one must instead strive toward an embodied awareness that aims itself at an intuitive knowing beyond conscious ideas, thus treating consciousness as a passage to a greater capacity of intuitive awareness. An awareness such as this, of the mind and body in parallel, holds tightly with the image of a nervous system both within our imaginations and felt in their enacted duration, or more simply put—as a student/teacher relation that strives for its own undoing. In this, we are returning to Guattari's notion of transversality that we cited earlier. Alliez and Goffrey (2011) had noted transversality as a mode of subjectification that functions "under the sign of processuality and singularization" (p. 5). We would propose that the act of opening the classroom to the desiring processes of the unconscious through affective compositions clearly breaks,

> with both a centering on the transcendent unity of the subject and the becoming-subject of a transcendence dialectically immanent to consciousness, accomplishing instead a transversalist enlarging of enunciation through matters of expression that are worked over by forms of praxis … generative of heterogeneity and complexity. (Alliez and Goffrey, 2011, p. 5)

Second Provocation: Experiments with Pedagogies of Relationality in Early Childhood

In working toward the classroom as nervous system, we would suggest along with Guattari (2005) that one avenue for opening affective relations of the unconscious is by shifting from "a pedagogy based on static interpretation and meaning making" to "a pedagogy that is moving, emergent, breathing and intimate" (Rotas & Springgay, 2013, p. 278).

In the excerpts that follow (in italics), we describe a series of encounters and events that took place between early childhood educators, a group of young children, and non-human actors. The encounters are part of a larger ethnographic project (Pacini-Ketchabaw, Kind, & Kocher, 2017) that investigated materials as events in the early childhood classroom. In the excerpts, we emphasize the encounter and open vistas of new peoples and experimental social formations, and foreground "production, movement and affect" in encounters (Rotas & Springgay, 2013, p. 279). To that effect, the excerpts are pure enactment of transversal pedagogies that take inspiration from Deleuze and Guattari's (1987) writings on movement. In other words, we do not move from "a localizable relation going from one thing to the other and back again," but instead perceive enactment as "another way of traveling and moving: proceeding from the middle, through the middle, coming and going rather than starting and finishing" (p. 25).

Clay Forces us to Think

Clay arrives in a large, rectangular, cardboard box. Educators carefully pull it out and place sliced small slabs on the large canvas that covers half of the classroom. A group of curious children gather around the clay. Clay is quickly transformed. Rolled into various sized balls. Carried in tiny hands. Flung and thrown onto the canvas. Rolled, pinched and stretched. Jumped on. Foreheads and footprints are pressed into it.

Forms emerge: long and thin snakes, baskets that transform into nests. Eggs, large and minuscule. Lots of stories that invite the children to share ideas, to become more and more engaged with the specificities of clay.

'We need more nests!', two children exclaim. With more nests on the canvas, eggs become hatching birds, snakes become worms, worms become food for baby eggs. Birds hatch. We wonder with the children if the classroom will become a space for caring for baby birds.

New and related stories continue to emerge: Bunnies hatch from the carefully moulded eggs. Educators ponder. We stay with the trouble that this chunk of clay brought to us.

Clay forces us to think. Children become, as philosopher Haraway (2013) would say, "writers/thinkers/makers" who "remake worlds" through their clay stories. We are reminded that clay is a new participant in the classroom.

As air and clay interact, some children notice that clay becomes harder and harder to work with. Water makes clay soft and squishy again. It's not just about human bodies. The world itself is in constant transformation beyond our own doing and consciousness.

Clay slows things down in the classroom. It invites the children to follow its unexpected movements as it interacts with hands and feet, with canvas, with floor, with air. In this 'clay ecology' (Stengers, 2005), the production that is going on has a life of its own.

This clay ecology demands from us; it makes us think.

Nest Making; Making Nests

Clay exploration intensifies as clay moves the children to 'make nests'. Children 'lose themselves' in the process of shaping the clay: what the clay needs to move, how the clay responds, where to press, how to push. The focus, though, is on the nests themselves.

We simply then make nests: big nests, small nests, funny-shaped nests, and nests that do not look like nests. Each single nest comes into the world with a story, a place, a protagonist. Children share their stories and the nests bring stories to the children. Stories about the squirrels in the playground. Stories about the geese that try to find shelter in some of the children's backyards. Stories about the robins that look for shelter in winter. There are also stories about nests for dragons, nests for snakes, nests for bears, and nests for moose.

'The nests need eggs', a child announces. How to make eggs? We show the children how to make eggs by placing a piece of clay in between the palms of their hands. This is not small task for little hands! Yet, it is the excitement to make more and more eggs that keeps the children going. We count the eggs we make. We carefully decide where each single egg will be placed. Which nest will want this egg? Which egg will want this nest? It matters. The children are meticulous about placing the eggs. They are also precise about the eggs' shape and size. When they ask us (educators) to make an egg, they provide detailed instructions on what egg they exactly want.

And then there are always the 'what if...?' conversations: What if the dragon eggs hatch? What if the bunnies hatch in the classroom? What if the squirrels need more nests? What if a moose decides to hatch when we are having lunch? What if the moose eats the squirrels? And on and on and on.

After several weeks of nest and egg making, we (educators) decided to surprise the children. We met to make nests. We became fascinated with nests – as much as the children have. Our clay nests are received with great excitement. Nests of all kinds inhabit the classroom. Books about nests. Nests projected on the walls. A wasp nest that an educator brings in. And of course, many more clay nests that the children continue to make as they discuss the possibilities for each nest, for each egg, and for each piece of clay.

In our nest making inquiry, we are inspired by Ingold (2000), who reminds us that "the forms of artefacts are not supposed to have their source within the human mind, as preconceived intellectual solutions to particular design problems" (p. 340). In our inquiry, it is not the children who are always in control of what will happen in their nest making process. The children are always open to what might emerge from the assemblages that are created. Thinking with Ingold (2000) as we make nests, we might say that:

> [A nest] comes into being through the gradual unfolding of [a] field of forces set up through the active and sensuous engagement of practitioner and material. This field is neither internal to the material nor internal to the practitioner (hence external to the material); rather, it cuts across the emergent interface between them. Effectively, the form of the [nest] emerges through a pattern of skilled movement, and it is the rhythmic repetition of that movement that gives rise to the regularity of form. (Pacini-Ketchabaw, 2017, para 3, online)

Gifting a Nest

The children decide that it is time to gift the many nests that we carefully made. Together we plan with great anticipation where to go and where to place each nest.

A walk to the park delivers! The city's squirrels and a group of geese join the inquiry. After children leave a nest besides a tree, a squirrel approaches to check the nest out. Picking up the clay nest, the squirrel moves the nest to the other side of the tree. The children and the squirrels are now in a dance of communication. Paying attention to each other's movements, we become aware of each other.

A child is interested in leaving a nest high up on a tree for the squirrels. She has noticed that the squirrels assemble their nests in the forks of tall trees. "How to get there?", she asks. Another child suggests that we watch how the squirrel climbs. "Maybe," he says, "we can learn from them". We stop every time we spot a squirrel climbing. We observe. We pay attention. We slow down. The squirrels though are fast. They move up or down the trees so quickly that the children are having trouble grasping exactly how they do it.

Then there are the geese who flew into the park right at the time we were carefully placing the clay nests throughout the park. A child guests that the geese came into the park because they saw us with our nests. "They are hoping to nest in one of our nests", she says. May be. Why not? After all biologists remind us that urban geese use human-built structures during nesting season....

A few weeks after our encounter with the geese, a child announces that he was going to make eggs with clay (not nests) while the other children continue to diligently make clay nests to take to our next walk. About half an hour later, an educator sees the child sitting in a corner of the room with approximately 10 large eggs on his lap. Not knowing what was going on, the educator invites the child to join the rest of the group in nest making. Immediately, the child responds that he can't. "I'm nesting," he says.

Toward Pedagogy in Motion

From this enactment, we might note that transversal pedagogies attend to the spaces "where things pick up speed," take "a perpendicular direction... that sweeps one and the other away," and flow as "a stream without beginning or end [undermining] its banks and [picking] up speed in the middle" (Deleuze & Guattari, 1987, p. 25). These are pedagogies that, as Rotas and Springgay (2013, p. 283) write, "become an elastic membrane that move and vibrate and enable us to imagine learning taking place in unusual and discontinuous ways." These are pedagogies that embrace Guattari's notion of subjectification as a process of composition of various elements, at a particular historical/geographical/temporal moment, colliding in a highly particularized way.

The transversal movements that we illustrate in this final provocation are very different than the highly instrumentalized UNESCO transversal competencies in Tables 7.1 and 7.2. While the latter flatten and abstract living force, the former plug into and take charge of desires by "assuring their continuous connections and transversal tie-ins" (Deleuze & Guattari, 1987, p. 166). In other words, the transversal pedagogical encounters in the early childhood classroom are transgressive, resisting (at least temporarily) the neoliberal/globalist capture apparatuses. Flexibility takes a very different form in these two instances. While flexibility in the early childhood classroom is "responsive, relational, artistic and life-giving," flexibility in the UNESCO transversal competencies is externally driven with "start or end points of movement" (Rotas & Springgay, 2013, p. 285).

Toward a Vernacular of Velocities and Pedagogy of Transit

As we enter the emerging world of abstract appropriation and the efforts to absolute rule that is embodied by twenty-first-century global capitalism, we would argue that it becomes imperative to find a new politics. Such a politics cannot emerge without the capacity to engage and transform pedagogy. Education is, after all, what Althusser (2014), Gramsci (1992), and Freire (2000), among others, have noted as one of the most powerful, if not the most powerful engine of social production for global capitalism. It is our contention that the work of Guattari in his articulation of transversality as a revolutionary mode of subjectification has tremendous capacity for the transformation of all we have ever known about learning and becoming. To put transversality to work, however, will require both a new vernacular premised in speeds and slowness, rather than axioms and taxonomies, as well as the openings of points of affective transit. In short, it will require pedagogy rooted in the unconscious of Spinoza—that is to say, in a politics of immanent force and revolutionary capacity.

References

Alliez, E., & Goffey, A. (Eds.). (2011). *The Guattari effect*. London: Bloomsbury Publishing.

Althusser, L. (2014). *On the reproduction of capitalism: Ideology and ideological state apparatuses*. London: Verso Books.

Braidotti, R. (1994). *Nomadic subjects: Embodiment and sexual difference in contemporary feminist theory*. New York: Columbia University Press.

Cole, D. R. (2011a). *Educational life-forms: Deleuzian teaching and learning practice*. Rotterdam: Sense Publishers.

Cole, D. R. (2011b). The actions of affect in Deleuze—Others using language and the language that we make …. *Educational Philosophy and Theory, 43*(6), 549–561.

Cole, D. R., & Hager, P. (2010). Learning-practice: The ghosts in the education machine. *Education Inquiry, 1*(1), 21–40.

Deleuze, G. (1988). *Spinoza: Practical philosophy* (R. Hurley, Trans.). San Francisco: City Lights Books.

Deleuze, G. (1992). *Expressionism in philosophy: Spinoza* (M. Joughin, Trans.). New York: Zone Books.

Deleuze, G., & Guattari, F. (1977). *Anti-Oedipus: Capitalism and schizophrenia* (R. Hurley, M. Seem, & H. R. Lane, Trans.). Minneapolis: University of Minnesota Press.

Deleuze, G., & Guattari, F. (1987). *A thousand plateaus: Capitalism and schizophrenia*. Minneapolis, MN: University of Minnesota Press.

Foucault, M. (1979). *Discipline and punish: The birth of the prison*. New York: Vintage Books.

Freire, P. (2000). *Pedagogy of the oppressed*. London: Bloomsbury Publishing.

Gramsci, A. (1992). *Prison notebooks* (Vol. 2). New York: Columbia University Press.

Gregg, M., & Seigworth, G. (2010). An inventory of simmers. In M. Gregg et al. (Eds.), *The affect theory reader* (pp. 1–29). London & Durham: Duke University Press.

Guattari, F. (2005). *The three ecologies*. London: Bloomsbury Publishing.

Guattari, F. (2010). *The machinic unconscious: Essays in schizoanalysis* (T. Adkins, Trans.). New York: Semiotext (e).

Haraway, D. (2013). SF: Science fiction, speculative fabulation, string figures, so far. *ada: A Journal of New Media & Technology, 11*(3). http://adanewmedia.org/2013/11/issue3-haraway/.

Hardt, M., & Negri, A. (2001). *Empire*. Cambridge: Harvard University Press.

Hardt, M., & Negri, A. (2009). *Commonwealth*. Cambridge: Belknap Press of Harvard University Press.

Ingold, T. (2000). *The perception of the environment: Essays on livelihood, dwelling and skill*. London: Routledge.

Johnston, A. (2013). Jacques Lacan. In *Stanford encyclopedia of philosophy*. Recovered https://plato.stanford.edu/entries/lacan/.

Marx, K. (1993). *Grundrisse*. New York: Penguin.

Negri, A. (1996). Twenty theses on Marx: Interpretation of the class situation today. In S. Makdisi, C. Casarino, & R. E. Karl (Eds.), *Marxism beyond Marxism* (pp. 149–180). New York: Routledge.

Negri, A. (1999). *Insurgencies: Constituent power and the modern state* (Vol. 15). Minneapolis: University of Minnesota Press.

Pacini-Ketchabaw, V. (2017). *Making as a modality of weaving*. Located at: http://encounterswithmaterials.com/2017/04/14/making-as-a-modality-of-weaving/.

Pacini-Ketchabaw, V., Kind, S., & Kocher, L. (2017). *Encounters with materials in early childhood education*. New York: Routledge.

Rotas, N., & Springgay, S. (2013). 'You go to my head': Art, pedagogy and a politics to come. *Pedagogies, 8*(3), 278–290.

Sellar, S., & Cole, D. R. (2017). Accelerationism: A timely provocation for the critical sociology of education. *British Journal of Sociology of Education, 38*(1), 38–48.

Spinoza, B. (2000). *Ethics* (G. H. R. Parkinson, Trans.). New York: Oxford University Press.

Stengers, I. (2005). An ecology of practices. *Cultural Studies Review, 11*(1), 183–196.

Yoko, S. (Ed.). (2015). *Education Research Institutes Network (ERI-Net) regional study on regional synthesis report. transversal competencies in education policy & practice (phase I).* Retrieved http://unesdoc.unesco.org/images/0023/002319/231907E.pdf.

Hans Skott-Myhre is a professor in the Social Work and Human Services Department at Kennesaw State University. He is the author of Youth Subcultures as Creative Force: Creating New Spaces for Radical Youth Work, co-editor with Chris Richardson of Habitus of the Hood, co-editor with K. Gharabaghi and M. Krueger of With Children and Youth and with V. Pacini-Ketchabaw and K. S. Skott-Myhre co-editor of Youth work, Early Education and Psychology: Liminal Encounters. He has published multiple articles, reviews, and chapters.

Veronica Pacini-Ketchabaw is a professor of Early Childhood Education in the Faculty of Education at Western University in Ontario, Canada. Her current research, within the Common World Childhoods Research Collective, traces the common world relations of children with places, materials, and other species.

Luke Kalfleish is a Ph.D. candidate in Psychology at the University of West Georgia. His research interests include critical psychology, pedagogy, and Spinozist approaches to learning.

Part III
Transversal Movements Across International Educative Borders

Part III

Chapter 8
Transversality, Constraint and Desire in Australian and Iranian Classrooms

David R. Cole and Mehri Mirzaei Rafe

Abstract Félix Guattari's concepts were evolved in practical situations, often working with groups to change their situation. Transversality was one of his earliest conceptions (Guattari in psychoanalysis and transversality: texts and interviews 1955–1971. Semiotext(e), South Pasadena, 2015) and was designed to enhance communication between parties and to transform group dynamics. This chapter takes the concept of transversality as an educational thought, capable of dealing with aspects of globalization such as the loss of identity in a global capitalist situation and asks the questions:

(1) How can we enact transversality for educational contexts such as Australia and Iran, and thus to help us understand globalization?
(2) Further, what are the practical steps to perform transversality in education across international borders?
(3) What are the possible contradictions/paradoxes in the application of transversality to globalized educational contexts?

This chapter will look at the different contexts for education in Australia and Iran that have been chosen due to their relationships with capitalism. The key terms of analysis of these educational contexts for the chapter will be 'constraint' and 'desire' in both locations. The notion of transversality was invented by Guattari against the backdrop of and in Lacanian psychoanalysis, and the key differences between Lacanian psychoanalysis and Guattarian transversality will guide the unpacking of constraint and desire in Australian and Iranian teaching and learning contexts.

Keywords Transversality · Educational contexts in Australia and Iran Constraint · Desire

D. R. Cole (✉)
Western Sydney University, Penrith, Australia
e-mail: david.cole@westernsydney.edu.au

M. Mirzaei Rafe
University of Tehran, Tehran, Iran

D. R. Cole and J. P. N. Bradley (eds.), *Principles of Transversality in Globalization and Education*, https://doi.org/10.1007/978-981-13-0583-2_8

Introduction

This chapter is about globalization as it can be understood through an analysis of capitalist dynamics in Australia and Iran. Félix Guattari's assessment and predictions about capitalism in the 1970s and 1980s have largely come to pass; for example: 'Contemporary capitalism can be defined as *Integrated World Capitalism* because it has already settled all surfaces on the planet. No human activity can escape its grasp as it works to further overcode and control every mode of sociopolitical expression' (Guattari, 1981, p. 1). Guattari's argument was that the passage and intensification of Integrated World Capitalism (IWC) were making it increasingly difficult to think otherwise, or, indeed, to express another perspective from within its engulfing and suffocating apparatus (which is now everywhere). IWC is one of the main drivers for globalization in the ways that it is able to successfully integrate different parts of the economic system, and the development, for example, of digital social media since the 1990s has greatly enhanced the capacity of IWC to intervene in thinking, learning and in any communicative process, making escape from the eventuality of IWC, and all that this means, inextricable. This point works in unison with many other analyses of capitalism, such as that of Frederic Jameson (2003): '... [i]t is easier to imagine the end of the world than to imagine the end of capitalism' (p. 76). It is from this seemingly bleak starting point that this chapter begins. The concept that will be primarily put to work in an attempt to escape the contemporary iron cage of IWC is 'transversality', which is defined in mathematics as: 'a property of two intersecting submanifolds, where at every intersection point, their separate tangent spaces at that point together generate the tangent space of the ambient manifold at that point' (Hirsch, 1976, p. 5). In simpler terms, 'transversality' is not produced by verticality or horizontality, but forms its own dimension, which is always dynamic, intersectional, and by its very nature creates disturbances in one's perception of the dimensionality under investigation. A well-known example that one could refer to visualize this is the Boy's Surface (Fig. 8.1).

As one can see, the Boy's Surface cannot be described three-dimensionally without self-intersection. This means that the surface is productive of another dimension, understood in this chapter as 'transversality'. However, Guattari (2015) was less concerned about the precise mathematical understanding and definition of transversality, than he was to apply it to real institutional settings and to the treatment of patients suffering from mental diseases. As Guattari (2015) saw it, psychoanalysis exactly missed out on the intervening social and institutional forces that were largely at play in the patients' mental vicissitudes, and will be enacted here in globalized classrooms in Australia and Iran. Guattari (2015) imagined that these forces made their way into the interior minds of the patients and became embroiled with their subjectivities in an equal if not more powerful way than psychoanalytic factors. 'Treatment' was therefore in these terms a matter of freeing up and exploring the unconscious dimensions of the patients, and it constituted helping them to deal with exterior, invading forces, which in this chapter is primarily understood as the manifold aspects of contemporary globalization and all the ways in which they can merge with our consciousness

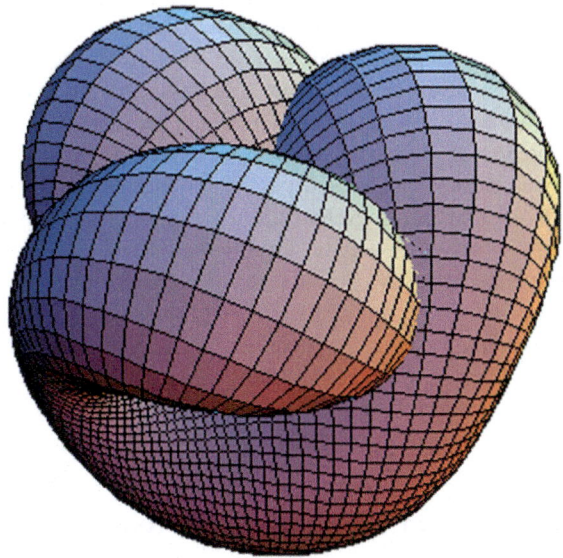

Fig. 8.1 A diagram of a manifold (Boy's Surface). Transversality lies in the intersecting planes of the figure. Figure used under Creative Commons licence 3.0, Unported (CC BY-SA 3.0). BoysSurfaceTopView.PNG

in terms of cognitive capitalism. Cognitive capitalism can be understood in the many, varied ways in which cognitive functions now play a critical part in the production of profit, for example, through social media. Guattari (2015) in this sense can be positioned as a liberatory thinker, who saw the predatory aspects of Integrated World Capitalism as causing mental disease, or 'pollution' as he termed it, seen, for example, in the connections between gambling, debt and capitalism and in the idiocy of the media that normalizes these connections (Guattari, 2000). In the context of this chapter, the literal 'treatment' of mental disease through the unfolding transversal dimension between the psyche and public life, though interesting, is not our major concern. Rather, the capacity for transversality to enable new thought in the educative contexts of Australia and Iran, and in relation to globalization, is key to understanding the intellectual work that is being done here. Australia and Iran have specifically been chosen for transversal treatment due to their differential relationships with capitalism. In this regard, the integrated and ubiquitous nature of contemporary globalization is forming a planetary scenario for mental disruption, with global inequities and environmental catastrophes looming as pressing reasons to seek new escape routes from the ways in which globalization is stopping us from thinking otherwise. The 'treatment' of transversality in the educative sphere constitutes the ways in which it can help us to free up learning and to create new dimensions for/of thought. These new dimensions happen when two or more planes collide (as in Fig. 8.1), transversality is created, and these collisions create further motion through the elongation of non-horizontal or non-vertical relations. In this chapter, the two planes of collision are figured through the desire and constraint of educational contexts in Australia and Iran. In contrast to, for example, a perhaps more straightforward, critical approach to the effects of globalization on education, transversality as a starting point does not provoke dialectics with contemporary capitalism, but works on its own terms, in its own ways, to create the possibility of singular expression in the current domain dominated by globalization. Transversality is on these terms certainly emancipatory and tends towards understanding globalization not simply as a homogenous, and homogenizing, power-driven movement of economics, trade and capital, but as a real, living, cognitive and affective process, having consequences across the human and non-human biosphere. In terms of its effects in education, transversality makes its complicated movement towards: '[t]he only acceptable finality of human activity [which] is the production of a subjectivity that is auto-enriching its relation to the world in a continuous fashion' (Guattari, 1995, p. 21).

Constraint and Desire in Globalized Classrooms

Guattari (2015) theorized transversality as a means to deal with specific mental problems at the La Borde Institute in France.[1] It is an attempt to comprehend the complex, often hidden and convoluted processes that may proceed as part of mental illnesses and their institutionalization. The job for this chapter is to connect this conception with globalized classrooms in Australia and Iran, which have been affected differently by recent developments in capitalism, e.g. the spread of social media and its related cognitivism. To do this, one may contrast transversality with a psychoanalytic framing of the problematic contained in and by globalized classrooms. The key term in the analysis here is *desire*. Desire in the context of a transversal reading has many nuances and meanings; it is creative, energetic, manifold and subtle. Transversality is an attempt to set desire free, in a parallel and similar way to the 'schizoanalysis' of *Anti-Oedipus*, which Guattari wrote with Gilles Deleuze (1984) and the rhizomatics of a *Thousand Plateaus* (Deleuze & Guattari, 1988), all of which are attempts at analysis outside of capitalist modes of working. Deleuze and Guattari (1984, 1988) argue that psychoanalysis, which has become co-opted by and in capitalism, gets desire wrong, exactly because it is constituted as a lack, which is henceforth exploited and reproduced by capitalism. For example:

> Desire, a function central to all human experience, is the desire for nothing nameable. And at the same time, this desire lies at the origin of every variety of animation. If being were only what it is, there wouldn't even be room to talk about it. Being comes into existence as an exact function of this lack. (Lacan, 1991, p. 224)

---

[1] Guattari worked intermittently at La Borde from 1955 until his death in 1992. Interestingly, Guattari was introduced by the founder of La Borde, Jean Oury, to his brother Fernand Oury. Fernand became heavily involved with the 'institutional pedagogy' movement, which was connected to the Modern School Movement, founded by Célestin Freinet (1896–1966). Guattari talks about his interest in alternative and emancipatory education in the book: *Molecular Revolution in Brazil* (Guattari & Rolnik, 2008)

In contrast, Deleuze and Guattari (1984) argue that desire is already coupled, circulating, material and real, seen, for example, in capitalism through their conception of: *desiring-machines*. In effect, capitalism does not simply limit desire, but locks it up in repetitive and mechanical processes such as exploitative work or, in the case of the chapter, globalized classrooms. For Lacan (1991), desire occupies an imaginary realm and is connected to the symbolic and the real through subjective mechanisms such as 'the other' and 'the phallic', which are both driven by lack. It is clear that Guattari (2015) especially borrowed from Lacan, who was a major figure from the 1950s to the 1980s (and beyond) and whose influence on Guattari can be seen throughout his work, for example, in his late *Schizoanalytic Cartographies* (Guattari, 2013), which refigures Lacan's triumvirate of the imaginary, symbolic and real as: existential territories (T), conscious universes (U), economies of flows (F) and machinic phyla (φ). Guattari's aim was to desubjectivize desire, to make it real and to allow it to function in group and world capitalist situations, wherein the complex dynamics of social and cultural mores drive consciousness and becoming. I have previously found Guattari's '4-zone' approach to the unconscious to be a fruitful one in terms of understanding the morphology of the identities of Sudanese families in Australia and young Muslims in Australia on Facebook (Cole, 2016). Here, the analysis of moving, interconnected desire intersects with globalized classrooms in Australia and Iran (see two sections below). Globalized classrooms have been subject to capitalism in different ways in Australia and Iran, which is the reason they have been chosen for transversal treatment, which unlike psychoanalysis operates to open up desire in both contexts and not reduce it to a lack or one-dimensional difference.

The analysis of transversality on desire is designed to free it up and to work against the confinement of desire in and as the self. However, one could ask how realistic a notion is the transversality of desire? Further, how can desire be absolutely free-flowing? Aren't we constantly coming up against the *constraints* in our desires, especially in the context of education where even the expression of desire can be censored? Constraint is therefore a necessary fulcrum of this chapter, not as a tendency towards equilibrium, but as a means to understand the processes of globalized classrooms, which are not only about free-flowing desire. Further, this is the point at which psychoanalysis intercedes and transversality leads off in the opposite direction. Psychoanalysis precisely 'treats' what it sees as the consequences of desires being thwarted as neuroses, paranoia, repressions and possible psychoses (Boag, 2006). For example, the famous Oedipus complex is perhaps the most obvious and determinant psychoanalytic mechanism in a society constituted by the nuclear, bourgeois family, with the taboo 'loves' and 'hatreds' for and of parents derived from primitive sexual drives, and consequently becoming part of the entangled, private fabric of such a (capitalist) society, based on tripartite sexual relationships. Psychoanalysis 'treats' the Oedipus complex in terms of analysis, by making the patient recount these desires for parents, their constraints, and explaining the consequences, e.g. as neurosis (Freud, 1913). In contrast, transversality, which does not tie sexuality up with mechanisms such as the Oedipus complex, leads outwards from its complex figuration, on an open, potentially global path, and away from the private sublimation of desire in familial units. Hence, sexuality is turned outwards, re-enters global vectors and can become part of the very flows of international capitalism (or the desires caused by and in capitalism), thereby mitigating against unwanted, embarrassed, self-regressive or guilty expression, and avoiding homogenizing control mechanisms such as patriarchialism, rigid bureaucracy or ruthless colonialism, as it will pass through the intersecting linkages of transversality and hence attempt to constitute a new, post-capitalist society, including different constraints, values, codes and hierarchy (and a subsequent new education).

However, transversality does not tend to a utopic 'sexual revolution', as it is only a mechanism for producing new dimensions (see Fig. 8.1). What it does is to continually produce new linkages, new figures, new thoughts and new ways to (re)conceptualize the world as maps and assemblages (Cole, 2015a), termed here through globalized classrooms in Australia and Iran that explore the dynamics of contemporary capitalism through open educational flows. The problem for empirical and cognitive science is that the evidence that transversality produces is necessarily emergent, unstable and, in short, a complex 'matter flow' that is never final and always in flux. So, how do we know that transversality can have recognizable, positive effects? Perhaps a repressed, oedipal society, based on capitalist exploitation and psychoanalytic analysis and with a concomitant education system, is better than a freed up, transversal one? It is the thesis of this chapter that this is not the case; however, we need to analyse concrete examples as planes of collision to begin to understand why, and in the context of this chapter, these transversal examples are constituted by globalized classrooms in Australia and Iran.

Australia

Australia is an incredibly geographically diverse country, with the majority of the population living near the coastline and in extensive cities such as Sydney, Melbourne and Brisbane. It is entirely connected to global and financial capitalism through various international mechanisms of exchange and trade deals, the legacy of being an important part of the British Empire, and all that this implies, such as the imprints of colonialization and racism. Australia is a democratic country with regular elections at local, state and federal level, and even though there is no restriction on possible political parties to represent diverse views, there is an established oscillation between large conservative and left-wing parties at the ballot boxes. In terms of education, recent good economic years that have largely depended on revenue from mining activities have delivered surpluses, which have funded an up-to-date education system, through a progressive tax regime. 'Quality, free education for all' and 'having a fair-go' are enshrined doctrines in Australia; however, inequality exists in and through the education system in Australia due to the existence of extremely expensive, elite private schools and differences in social–economic standing that have entrenched educational disadvantage in certain communities, for example, in remote Aboriginal Australian contexts (ACOSS, 2015).

In terms of transversality, desire and constraint, the relative freedom in Australia has encouraged alternative modes of education and the experimentation with educational contexts (Bambach, 1979). The freedom to do otherwise has led to educationalists exploring new modes of teaching and learning, and the avoidance of dualisms, such as those contained in the differences between direct instruction and constructivism (Cole, 2013). Rather, flexible and open models of pedagogy have enabled more children to learn well and more students to enter and study at university level. However, these positive push factors, which have performed a form of transversality, in that the Australian education system as a whole is not a top-down, authoritarian system, nor does it principally rely on local, lateral formations for its success, but has transversal means of support running through it, such as open-minded and experimental 'researcher–educators'[2], are to an extent constrained by the price that Australia has paid to be successful in the global capitalist marketplace. This price is seen, for example, at the exorbitant expense of housing in some areas, which has been pushed up due to international investment, concerned only with making a profit from the annual percentage increases in house prices and caring nothing about actually providing sustainable housing for Australians (Shrapnel, 2015). Again, the precise economic details which have produced this situation in Australia are not relevant to this chapter; however, what is of concern is the transversal relation between encouraging and supporting an open, free society, and the economic reality of this society, which is that unless one is an extraordinary entrepreneur, inherits wealth or has a very high paid job, of which there are few, one is consigned to live in debt and/or struggling to pay for the advantages and luxuries that are just at hand. Elsewhere, I have termed this situation in education as being called 'finance-subjectivity' (Cole, 2015b), which sits alongside all learning in highly developed, technological countries under the control of financial capitalism and await the next financial crisis due to overinvestment in unsustainable 'boom' sectors such as housing.

Access to digital media is ubiquitous in Australia. Even though such prolific access to the Internet and mobile devices to channel this access has become widespread, educators have sometimes struggled to adapt and cope with the influx of potentially new learning that this invasion of media constitutes. Good evidence for new learning is hard to find in this area (Newhouse, 2013), as the new learning that immersion in digital media implies also requires the wholesale reinvention of: (A) the curriculum as the digital curriculum; (B) the school buildings as mediated learning spaces; (C) pedagogy as digitally mediated pedagogy; and (D) cohorts as digitally connected study groups. All of these changes require investment, leadership and time, and even though there are examples of schools and universities which have made the switch to a new, digitally innovative experience in Australia (ibid.), many places inevitably lag behind and do not have the capacity to fully launch into the digital learning era. Added to this are global learning companies such as Pearson Inc., which attempts to sell courses and learning innovations to learning markets such as Australia, open to global capitalist intervention (Hogan, Sellar, & Lingard, 2015). In sum, the digital

---

[2]As can be seen through the large number of Australian publications that use progressive aspects of Deleuze and Guattari's (1984, 1988) ideas in their formulations. For example, (Cole, 2011).

learning situation in Australia can be explained through the concepts of transversality, desire and constraint, in that the prospect of digitally mediated education, which many young Australians experience from an early age through possessing Internet-connected digital devices, is not always realized in formal educative contexts. This is not a problem that can be simply solved through more capital investment in education, but is a signature aspect of globalization and its effects on learning, which is to produce capital differentials. Digital learning rushes into areas of paid for, desirable services, and lags behind in areas which are not subject to this push by the desires contained in and for capital, e.g. critical thinking, intense scholarship or reading and writing of a literary quality and standard (see Section 'Iran').

According to transversality, the psyches of young people in Australia are forming complicated machinic and imagistic relations with their digital devices, which remain as connected but moving circuits in their minds dependent on globalized messaging. Formal educative spaces are not entirely subject to such immersive circuitry and therefore form different circuits, such as 'teacher-student-student-textbook-whiteboard-teacher' (repeatedly/interchangeably). The point here is that globalized digital circuits are realized first for learning, and the adaptation and switching between different circuitries take cognitive load (Kalyuga, 2009). Students have to disconnect from the circuitries enabled by their globalized mobile devices, including the desires and constraints on thought that these circuits imply, before they can (re)connect with non-digitally mediated learning (e.g. critical thinking, deep scholarship and the reading and writing of the profound literature). There is a transversality to both realms (digital and non-digital), which is a dimension formed through the clashing of different modes of globalized planes in both dimensions and which this chapter suggests could have the greatest impact in terms of new learning (a new Australia–Iran learning dimension). One way to get to this impact and this new learning is to work transversally with another context that has been affected by the recent acceleration in globalization differently, such as Iran.

Iran

Iran is one of the cradles of modern civilization, with a coherent and strong Persian culture going back to perhaps 3000 BC and unified in 625 BC by the Iranian Medes. In contrast to Australian Aboriginal culture, which can claim multiple continuous oral cultures going back perhaps 40,000+ years, modern Australian society, which is largely a multicultural, immigrant nation, dates back to the British colonial settlement of the land previously occupied by the Aboriginal Australians in 1788. Thus, Iranian cultural identity has been very powerfully historically established and connected to the land that is called Iran, and does not have the dichotomies between Aboriginal and settler peoples that exist in modern-day Australia. Iran currently has approximately 3.4 times the population of Australia and 1/5th of the land mass. In terms of recent history, there was an Iranian Islamic coup in 1979, which has taken Iran away from ubiquitous, 'Western', secular and capitalist forces, understood under the rubric of 'globalization' in this book. It is in this area that the concepts of transversality, desire and constraint can do the most work as applied to education and to the contrasts and relays with Australian education as described above. The most salient points about the Iranian education system have been summarized by Paivandi (2012, p. 2) and lie in seven areas:

1. *The legislative framework of education*: Laws passed in Parliament, including the orientation law, and various legal rules concerning the goals and operation of the educational system have largely contributed to the transformation of education in Iran.
2. *The curriculum*: This includes the programmes, content of textbooks and school activities. The Ministry of Education has attempted to Islamize the content and curricula; textbooks have been rewritten several times to incorporate Islam.
3. *The organization and structure of the educational system*: Several reforms have been aimed at the structure of the educational system to make it more efficient. The last reform launched this year (2012) increased the duration of elementary school and reorganized high school.
4. *Teacher training*: Teachers have been a key component of the educational policy of the Islamic republic since 1979. Moreover, the state tries to exert total control over their training and recruitment.
5. *The social environment*: Educational institutions have become a place of political and ideological propaganda. The government has established several organizations (e.g. the paramilitary Basij) to dominate the social environment of schools and reinforce religious and political socialization.
6. *Enrolment*: The educational system of Iran has accomplished a significant increase in enrolment from primary school to university. There is indeed a growth in access to education, especially for girls, but regional disparities and social inequalities persist.
7. *Governance and organization*: Iran has historically been a centralized country. This trend has been reinforced since 1979, and the Ministry of National Education monopolizes authority over the educational system.

In short, the Islamic revolution of 1979 has attempted to establish an ideological homogenization of, in and through the education system, to ensure that Islam is consistently taught and upheld throughout the country. However, this type of homogenization is exactly where the forces of transversality, desire and constraint come into play. If anyone tells someone else that something is right and that a set of rules have to be followed, this immediately sets up the possibility of questioning that speech as an order or power imposition, and in acting other than the rules as stipulated (or wanting to act otherwise). In psychoanalytic terms, the repression of free speech, free organization and the attempted homogenization of thought under a sole Islamic banner through education sets up oscillatory anti-Islamic forces in the unconscious, driven by primary sexual repressions, seen for example, in the way Iranians have to dress, and that are reenforced through Iranian gender divisions, the treatment of men and women, and how power can be distributed between men and women in modern Iranian society (Shorish, 1988). In terms of transversality, the Iranian Islamic revolution in 1979 has set up a complex, interconnected dimension in the Iranian unconscious, which functions to express the counter-arguments and disagreements with the possible Islamic homogenizations of the mind as real. Transversality takes away the psychoanalytic reading of the situation and the particular Iran-isolated suggestion of sexual and gender-based repression and reinvents the desires and constraints of the Iranian population as interconnected machinery, which are plugging into and will henceforth plug into global forces as and when they are able through learning (globalized classrooms). The advantage of the transversal reading is that it takes account of the period that Iran has been out of the Integrated World Capitalist system *not as a lack*, but as a gathering of forces and energies, which have not been subject to, for example, the economic cycles of boom and bust in the West due to globalization, and the consequent psychic dismemberment that these oscillations have created (Guattari, 1995).

Restrictions in and because of the Islamic focus in the Iranian education system are balanced by the abilities in critical thinking, philosophical thought and the general emphasis on high-level intellectual, literary and literacy matters that the system currently successfully enables (Mohsenpour, 1988). The wholesale removal from the Integrated World Capitalist system has meant that the intensification of concomitant distractions, useless information, and the sensory and cognitive overload, which can be created and mediated by the globalized digital curriculum and which sits alongside an increase in predatory capitalist learning companies and the commercialization of learning and education, has largely not occurred in Iran. The transversal dimension of the Iranian education system precisely works in this space left vacant by the removal of Iran from globalization. Iranians have a highly developed sense of geopolitics and understanding of their place in the world, even if they disagree with the ideological orientation and the current political leadership (Paivandi, 2012). Identity resources are ready at hand in Iran, and even though minorities and women have been to an extent suppressed by the homogenized Islamification of Iran since 1979 (ibid.), there is no doubt that it is in many cases still easier for young people to 'know who they are', growing up in Iran than in, for example, Australia. In Australia, the transversal dimensions created by real and mediated digital life that are augmented by globalization can cause eddies and contradictions between who students 'think they are' and the mediated digital images that they increasingly live through (Newhouse, 2013), or between constraint and desire in representation and becoming in these realms. For example, access to ubiquitous social media can create identity questions for young people, as they can communicate online with numerous contacts as if it is real life, and these questions are not answered by coming from a powerful, combinatory, host culture. Transversality does not give us definite answers to these possible contradictions and rupture points in emerging identities, but allows us as educators and thinkers to follow them in all their complexity and not to get 'stuck' in their horizontality as locally determined or verticality as necessarily cultural, imposed and power-related. In Iran, this means experimenting with new modes and notions of Iranian identity and pedagogy; in Australia, this means looking seriously at the gaps and divisions that are being created by digital and real life in learning. In both cases, globalization serves as an underpinning for these transformations, as a virtually unstoppable, global machine that continues to usher in the future.

Conclusion(s)

The application of transversality, desire and constraint to globalized classrooms in Australia and Iran makes us aware of the pitfalls and speeds of the international interlinked situation. In terms of the three questions listed in the abstract of this chapter:

(1) Transversality is enacted locally through analysis and experimentation with contextual pedagogic and learning matters, as has been seen in this chapter in Australia and Iran. There is no one way 'to do' transversality, as it depends on the interactions between relevant clashing planes and the creation of a new dimension of thought out of and due to these intersections (see Fig. 8.1). In Australia, this often amounts to understanding how digital and real learning is intersecting with Australia's place in the world and how Australia copes with global events such as the GFC in 2008 or climate change. Globalization intersects with transversal becomings at all levels, as it is a mandated part of contemporary Australian experience and plays an increasingly important role in the development and education of the collective and individual. In places such as Australia, which are fully open to the forces of globalization, the highs and lows of being connected to a one-world situation have consequences beyond national, local or individual identity. With respect to, for example, climate change, transversality indicates a new, experimental and ever-changing dimension to be played with and indicates how humans relate to and are part of nature in/as contemporary globalization mutates and accelerates. This aspect of transversality was of uppermost importance to Guattari, as it intersects with ecology, as he states: 'Ecology in my sense questions the whole of subjectivity and capitalistic power formations, whose sweeping progress cannot be guaranteed to continue as it has …' (Guattari, 2000, p. 52). Fortunately, there are experimental, ecological educationalists in Australia, who understand the dimension of transversality and have begun activist work in the light of climate change and who represent a positive way forward, often in the face of ruthless, blunt and unyielding global economic rationalism. In Iran, the enaction of transversality has to work in the context of the wholesale Islamification of the education system. Clearly, working against the Iranian system in the unpredictable mode of experimentation described by transversality is potentially dangerous and would most likely clash against unidirectional authoritarianism that has been invested from the top-down by the ruling clerics. Luckily, transversality precisely works in a non-representational, unconscious sense and through the ways in which psyches may be connected discretely and globally, which is entirely possible in a digitally mediated situation. Iranians are and have been making such connections despite censorship, blockades and ideology, and it is in these connections that the future perhaps lies for Iranian transversality.

(2) Practical steps have already been taken in Australia to enact transversality internally and across international borders. Academics are free to travel from Australia to just about anywhere in the world if they have funding and the time,

and there is the beginning formation of a worldwide educational movement influenced by the work of Deleuze and Guattari (1984, 1988) and hence not merely horizontal or vertical. For Iran to join in with this movement requires scholars, activists and educators to work together and to make changes in the education system that allows for and encourages transversality and that plays with the constraints and desires of the population currently subjugated by the possible homogenizations of Islam. The most practical steps to do this would be to collaborate with others in the international Deleuze and Guattari movement that are already working with and through these ideas in education (Semetsky and Masny, 2013) and that can touch on everything from the unconscious to global movements in thought.

(3) One of the most positive aspects of applying transversality to globalized class-rooms is that it does not diminish or minimize the contradictions and paradoxes of the situation. Indeed, these are necessary parts of the evolution and robust determination of how and why to use transversality in the first place. However, rather than being driven by contradiction, as would be the case in the application of material dialectics to globalized classrooms, contradictions and paradoxes sit in the new dimension of transversality, not as problems, or as reasons to stop investigation and research, but as part of the mutant outgrowths and new forma-tions possible to tackle global matters, in the case of this chapter that deal with globalized classrooms in Australia and Iran and that will lead to pan-global, post-capitalist futures.

References

ACOSS (Australian Council of Social Services). (2015). Inequality in Australia: A nation divided [report]. Strawberry Hills, NSW: Australian Council of Social Services. Report at: http://www. acoss.org.au/wp-content/uploads/2015/06/Inequality_in_Australia_FINAL.pdf.

Bambach, J. D. (1979). Australia in the 1970's: A fertile context for educational experimentation and innovation. *Australian Journal of Teacher Education*, *4*(1). http://dx.doi.org/10.14221/ajte. 1979v4n1.3.

Boag, S. (2006). Freudian repression, the common view, and pathological science. *Review of General Psychology*, *10*(1), 74–86. https://doi.org/10.1037/1089-2680.10.1.74.

Cole, D. R. (2011). *Educational Life-forms: Deleuzian teaching and learning practice*. Rotterdam: Sense Publishers.

Cole, D. R. (2013). Deleuze and the subversion(s) of 'the real': Pragmatics in education. In D. Masny (Ed.), *Cartographies of becoming in education: A Deleuze-Guattari perspective* (pp. 53–73). Rotterdam: Sense Publishers.

Cole, D. R. (2015a). Strange assemblage. *Portal: Journal of Multidisciplinary International Studies*, *11*(2) (online): http://dx.doi.org/10.5130/portal.v11i2.3200.

Cole, D. R. (2015b). Finance-subjectivity: Thinking through the consequences of the Global Finan-cial Crisis in education. In M. A. Peters, T. Besley, & J. Paraskeva (Eds.), *The Global Financial Crisis and educational restructuring* (pp. 301–316). New York & London: Peter Lang.

Cole, D. R. (2016). Unearthing the forces of globalisation in educational research through Guattari's cartographic method. In D. R. Cole & C. Woodrow (Eds.), *Super dimensions in globalisation and education* (pp. 145–161). Singapore: Springer.

Deleuze, G., & Guattari, F. (1984). *Anti-Oedipus: Capitalism and schizophrenia* (R. Hurley, M. Steem, & H. R. Lane, Trans.). London: The Athlone Press.

Deleuze, G., & Guattari, F. (1988). *A thousand plateaus: Capitalism & schizophrenia II* (B. Massumi, Trans.). London: The Athlone Press.

Freud, S. (1913). *Interpretation of dreams* (A. A. Brill, Trans.) (3rd ed.). New York: Macmillan.

Guattari, F. (1981). *Integrated world capitalism and molecular revolution*. Presentation at the Conference on Information and/as New Spaces of Liberty (CINEL), Rio de Janeiro. Online at: https://adamkingsmith.files.wordpress.com/2016/10/integrated-world-capitalism-and-molecular-revolution.pdf.

Guattari, F. (1995). *Chaosmosis* (P. Bains & J. Pefanis, Trans.). Bloomington and Indianapolis: Indiana University Press.

Guattari, F. (2000). *The three ecologies* (I. Pindar & P. Sutton, Trans.). London: Athlone Press. Available online at: https://monoskop.org/images/4/44/Guattari_Felix_The_Three_Ecologies.pdf.

Guattari, F. (2013). *Schizoanalytic cartographies* (A. Goffey, Trans.). London: Bloomsbury.

Guattari, F. (2015). *Psychoanalysis and transversality: Texts and interviews 1955–1971*. (A. Hodges, Trans.). South Pasadena, CA: Semiotext(e).

Guattari, F., & Rolnik, S. (2008). *Molecular revolution in Brazil* (K. Clapshow & B. Holmes, Trans.). Los Angeles, CA: Semiotext(e).

Hirsch, M. (1976). *Differential topology*. Geneva: Springer-Verlag.

Hogan, A., Sellar, S., & Lingard, B. (2015). Commercialising comparison: Pearson puts the TLC in soft capitalism. *Journal of Education Policy, 31*(3), 243–258. https://doi.org/10.1080/02680939.2015.1112922.

Jameson, F. (2003). Future city. *New Left Review, 21,* 65–79. Available at: https://newleftreview.org/II/21/fredric-jameson-future-city.

Kalyuga, S. (2009). Knowledge elaboration: A cognitive load perspective. *Learning and Instruction, 19,* 402–410.

Lacan, J. (1991). *The seminar of Jacques Lacan: Book II the ego in Freud's theory and in the technique of psychoanalysis 1954–1955* (J.-A. Miller, Ed., S. Tomaselli, Trans.). New York: WW Norton & Co.

Mohsenpour, B. (1988). Philosophy of education in postrevolutionary Iran. *Comparative Education Review, 32*(1), 76–86.

Newhouse, C. P. (2013). Learning with portable digital devices in Australian schools: 20 years on! *The Australian Educational Researcher, 41*(4), 471–483.

Paivandi, S. (2012). The future of Iran: Educational reform education in the Islamic Republic of Iran and perspectives on democratic reforms [report]. Mayfair, London: The Legatum Institute.

Semetsky, I., & Masny, D. (Eds.). (2013). *Deleuze and education*. Edinburgh: Edinburgh University Press.

Shorish, M. (1988). The Islamic revolution and education in Iran. *Comparative Education Review, 32*(1), 58–75.

Shrapnel, B. I. S. (2015). Australian Housing Outlook 2015–2018—Report prepared for the QBE. Sydney: QBE Publication. Available at: https://www.qbe.com.au/.../j7031-australian-housing-outlook-report-20152018.pdf.

David R. Cole is an associate professor in education at Western Sydney University, Australia, and the leader of the globalization theme in the Centre for Educational Research. He has published 15 academic books and numerous (100+) journal articles, chapters, conference presentations and other public output. He has been involved with major educational research projects across Australia and internationally and is a world-leading expert in the application of the philosophy of Gilles Deleuze and Félix Guattari to education. His latest monograph is called *A Pedagogy of Cinema* (2016, Sense Publishers) with Joff P. N. Bradley.

Mehri Mirzaei Rafe is currently a doctoral student at the University of Tehran in the Philosophy of Education. She is also completing an internship at the University of Texas at Dallas in the Centre for Values in Medicine, Science and Technology.

Chapter 9
Transversal Resettlement Transitions: Young Refugees Navigating Resettlement in Greater Western Sydney

Mohamed Moustakim and Karin Mackay

Abstract Drawing conceptually on the work of Guattari (Psychoanalysis and transversality: texts and Interviews 1955–1971. Semiotext(e), South Pasadena, 2015), this chapter takes a transversal approach to mapping aspirational change in the stories of a group of young refugees who were at different stages in their 5 years of resettlement transitions after fleeing war-torn countries in North Africa, South Asia, and the Middle East, to seek refuge in Greater Western Sydney, Australia. Refugee resettlement entails a complex and multi-layered set of transitions that newly arrived refugees are required to make simultaneously and within a very short period of time. These transitions are often compounded by the hidden injuries of war, cultural dislocations and linguistic displacements, which present young refugees with formidable challenges of varying intensities that at the same time usher in endless new possibilities. Through transversality in an informal youth and community setting, young people, youth workers and researchers were able to circumvent vertical institutional hierarchies and go beyond horizontal arrangements of local services to carve out spaces where authentic dialogue "at different levels" and "in different meanings" could lead to meaningful change in group dynamics (Guattari in Psychoanalysis and transversality: texts and Interviews 1955–1971. Semiotext(e), South Pasadena, p. 113, 2015). In these intersecting spaces, representations of the past, present and future through painting, alongside mentoring and website design, helped young refugees map out their educational aspirations and make informed decisions about achieving the goals they had reasons to value, rather than succumb to institutional definitions of success.

Keywords Transversality · A/r/tography · Becoming · Informal education Mentoring

M. Moustakim (✉) · K. Mackay
Western Sydney University, Sydney, Australia
e-mail: m.moustakim@westernsydney.edu.au

© Springer Nature Singapore Pte Ltd. 2018
D. R. Cole and J. P. N. Bradley (eds.), *Principles of Transversality in Globalization and Education*, https://doi.org/10.1007/978-981-13-0583-2_9

Introduction

Australian Government funded refugee resettlement programs, particularly those that operate within formal institutions, have tended to employ strategies designed within narrowly focused objectives to engage young people in education, employment or training. Making successful transitions to Higher Education or to the labour market is an arduous task for most young people, including those born in Australia. However, the resettlement transitions that young refugees make are often compounded by the hidden injuries of war, cultural dislocations, linguistic displacements and increasingly naked xenophobia against migrants and refugees, exemplified in a recent Guardian article: *Pauline Hanson wears burqa in Australian Senate while calling for ban* (Murphy, 2017).

Resettlement is a complex set of material and social conditions, emerging from a conjunction of connected singularities or "critical thresholds" (Meiches, 2015) leading to the emergence of a multiplicity of assemblages (Deleuze and Guattari, 1988). For example, the tragic death of the two-year-old Syrian asylum seeker, Alan Kurdi, is a potent instance of a singularity that gave a human face to the refugee crisis (Kingsley and Timur, 2015). This example represented a critical moment in the global refugee crisis, a game changer that marked a shift to a more compassionate tenor in public and policy debates about the refugee crisis and gave rise to a consensus between some of the economically advanced Western nations to take on a fair share of the flow of asylum seekers. This in turn provoked a reaction from far-right political parties and their followers in major Western nations, such as France for example, where Marine Le Pen made it to the second round of the French presidential election on the 24th of April 2017. Nevertheless, the human flow of refugees continued to form assemblages of forced migrants around the world. Deleuze and Guattari (1988) describe an assemblage as any of a number of elements that are brought together into a single context and that can produce multiple effects. However, Bartlett and Vavrus (2014) emphasise the importance of conducting transversal analyses "across and through levels to explore how globalizing processes intersect and interconnect people and policies that come into focus at different scales" (p. 131). This mode of analysis helps unpick complex assemblages and affords new insights and nuanced understandings of refugee resettlement transitions in Western countries, such as Australia. For example, increased globalisation over the past seven decades has led to a surge in mostly unfettered flows of money, information, goods and services between countries and across continents. This has been accompanied by mass migration, with 250 million international migrants and 65 million refugees resettling in mostly Western countries (World Health Organisation, 2017). However, recent influxes of refugees fleeing war-torn countries in North Africa, the Middle East and South Asia marked "the final frontier of globalisation" (Zakaria, 2016). While the death of Alan Kurdi became a game changing moment in the management of the refugee crisis, it was nevertheless overshadowed by populist rhetoric, which exploited the anxieties expressed by segments of the host populations, who derived little benefit from globalisation and felt they were left behind. Notable examples of this reaction include

Brexit, the election of Donald Trump and the increasing popularity of One Nation in Australia, with Pauline Hanson at the helm. The terrorist attacks in France, Germany and America amplified the growing perception of a threat to Western nations from people whose values were considered alien, incongruent and threatening to their "way of life". Divisive rhetoric in public and policy debates about immigration in Western Nations, including Australia has become normalised. Hanson's proposal to ban refugees from Muslim countries from entering Australia gained traction, as evidenced by nearly half of the Australian public supporting such a ban in a survey conducted by Essential in 2016 (Murphy, 2016). The marginalising effects of such rhetoric on migrants and refugees who were already undergoing resettlement transitions in Australia are rarely adequately discussed in depth and with sensitivity. Consequently, there has never been a more urgent need to provide counter-narratives to negative portrayals of migrants and refugees in the media and in public and policy debates.

Against this backdrop, this chapter takes a transversal approach to mapping aspirational change in the stories of a group of young refugees during their initial five years of resettlement, with the support of a research project organised in collaboration between Western Sydney University and SydWest Multicultural Services[1] in Greater Western Sydney, Australia. Transversality has been described as

> a dimension that tries to overcome both the impasse of pure verticality and that of mere horizontality: it tends to be achieved when there is maximum communication among different levels, above all, in different meanings. It is this that an independent group is working towards. (Guattari, 2015, p. 113)

The Navigating Resettlement project was a year-long research project, which explored how young refugees navigated the complex physical, social and emotional journeys through a transversal research approach within an informal education setting. The primary focus was on dismantling hierarchical structures within the institution and reconfiguring interpersonal power relations between young people, researchers and youth workers. As such, the approach was highly congruent with the principles of informal education, which guided this research project, with its emphasis on the importance of young people's voluntary participation, empowerment, involvement in decision-making and commitment to social justice. The space in which the sessions were conducted brought together both structure and the unpredictable, which created movable living assemblages and potentiated possibilities for nomadic becomings. The aim of the project was to help young refugees make informed choices about their educational aspirations and life ambitions through creating a space where they could build on their strengths and develop confidence in confronting the myriad of challenges they faced. In line with the transversal approach, instead of facilitating a program that assumed that the young people had little relevant knowledge or experience to offer, we began with a general idea to design and

---

[1] SydWest Multicultural Services work with refugees and humanitarian entrants who have been in Australia for less than five years and are dealing with priority issues of settlement. They help refugees develop knowledge and the ability to access and navigate mainstream services and become independent.

develop a Website for young people by young people, through which stories of resettlement could be captured and used by future refugees as a reference point. As such, the program design did not assume an automatic deficit in young people's hopes and desires; instead, we were committed to hearing about their aspirations as they emerged and then explored these in discussions with them. We offered a variety of creative activities at a consistent time and place, focused on learning about the young people's lives and aspirations, to engender trust while remaining open and curious as to the direction the program might take.

The project unfolded through living assemblages to reveal hopeful and life-affirming aspirations as young people transitioned to independent living in Australia. Contrary to populist deficit discourses of refugees as threatening the social fabric of Australian society, the young people in this study evinced altruistic occupational narratives and life ambitions with transformative goals for other refugees and the wider Australian community, expressed in desires to become lawyers, doctors, humanitarian workers, teachers, and nurses, among others. These ambitions were rooted in the experiential singularities which gave rise to the new interconnected assemblages of which they became part. We argue that using a transversal approach to informal learning with young people made it possible to readily capture their emerging complex aspirations in a way that instrumentalist resettlement models cannot. We found that the transversal approach provided a space to explore and share aspirations and possibilities for their new lives in Australia, recognising the strengths they had gained through their past experiences, while acknowledging the challenges faced in their current circumstances.

Transversality of Resettlement Transitions

In this chapter, we draw on the concept of transversality put forward by Guattari (2015) to explore an alternative approach to refugee resettlement transitions in an informal education setting in Greater Western Sydney. We did this through involving all the research participants in the decision-making process from the outset. Genosko (2002) defines "[t]ransversality [as] the tool used to open up hitherto closed logics and hierarchies" (p. 78). To do this, Guattari argued, one has to begin with the group as "institutional group-subjects might be liberated from under repressive or stultifying forms of institutional organization" (p. 6). Transversality attempts to bypass the influence of vertical institutional structures and crosses boundaries of horizontal arrangements in organisations. It forms its own dimension that is "dynamic, intersectional, and by its very nature creates disturbances in one's perception of the dimensionality under investigation" (Cole & Mirzaei Rafe, 2018, this volume). In its earlier formulation, transversality was conceived as a device for reconfiguring power dynamics between therapists and mental health patients at La Borde psychiatric clinic in France where Guattari worked. The concept has since shifted to a broader philosophical approach with practical multidisciplinary applications (Genosko, 2002) but has maintained its primary focus on effecting change in asymmetrical power relations within rigid hierarchical institutional structures. There is no blueprint for "doing" transversality (Cole & Mirzaei Rafe, 2018), but its central mission is to foreground the "institutional object", a term used by Guattari to describe things that are normally in the background of institutions, such as the state and the organising systems, policies and principles reified in structural arrangements in institutions. In our research, we found that much of refugee resettlement transition interventions were guided by a set of funding criteria and institutional accountabilities that influence the orientation of young refugees' pathways into education and employment. For example, the organisation where this research was conducted was required to submit monthly returns to the funding body, with specific details of targets achieved against set objectives, including the number of young people enroled in education and training courses and those who were helped to gain employment during that particular month. These constraints also shape practices and relations between young refugees and the staff who work with them in resettlement institutions and constitute "what is real for these group subjects because they participate in its creation through negotiation and in the process develop new forms of subjectivity" (Genosko, 2002, p. 72).

Our aim was to circumvent hierarchical power relations in working arrangements through displacing authority in our relationships with young people in order to open up the "'potential space' of creativity and collectivity" (Genosko, 2002, p. 71). To achieve this, we mapped rather than traced, young refugees' aspirational change in ways that allowed us to unmap and remap (Clarke, 2005) their experiences of resettlement transitions, in the light of their individual and collective pasts, presents and futures. Deleuze and Guattari (1988) distinguish between mapping and tracing. They argue that mapping opens up in-between spaces to explore the unconscious, whereas tracing does little more than reproduce sameness. We were particularly interested in mapping the in-between "potential space" in our encounters with the participants. The concept of the "potential space" was first used by Winnicott (1971) to refer to what she called the "transitional object" in the mother–baby relationship, from dependence to independence. A space that can open up endless possibilities for growth and development, but used inappropriately, can lead to disastrous outcomes. For example, inconsistent parenting styles may lead to insecure attachment patterns between the infant and the caregiver (Ainsworth and Bowlby, 1991). Guattari took the idea of the potential space further to explore the in-between, "the middle" and "a non-localizable space" (Genosko, 2002, p. 75). Deleuze and Guattari distinguish between "smooth" and a "striated" spaces, as the two are characterised respectively by "nomadic and metric multiplicities" (1988, p. 555). We use the difference between smooth and striated spaces to distinguish between informal education and formal compulsory education. While compulsory education is guided by a national curriculum with standardised performance-based criteria, informal education is emergent and process oriented. It is based on voluntary participation, empowerment and active involvement in decision-making, with acute sensitivity to power relations. This is important because the multiplicity of subjectivities of the young people we worked with did not lend itself to a standardised intervention, but required the creation of a smooth nomadic space free from institutional constraints (Cole, 2016). We recognise that smooth spaces can exist within striated spaces and vice versa. We conducted our research in a non-government community organisation, which, while constrained by striated spaces through funding and accountability mechanisms, also provided endless possibilities for young people to make informed choices about their futures.

Living Assemblages and the A/r/tographic Imagination

We were guided by an A/r/tographic methodological approach (Irwin, 2004) as it offered a way to examine the assemblage of multiple identities, spaces, languages, cultural norms and ways of becoming that emerged transversally when working with young refugees in this research (see Fig. 9.1). These living assemblages became an important, emergent and relational space for all of us to learn about our own and others' aspirational desires. A/r/tography is a transversal approach consisting of expressive "movements in diverse directions instead of a single path, multiplying its own lines and establishing the plurality of unpredictable connections in the open-ended smooth space of its growth" (Semetsky, 2008, p. xv). It allowed us to inhabit the roles of Artist/researcher/teacher and were both part of the academy, but were also alienated and marginalised by academic institutional constraints. As Pryer (2004) points out "True liminars will continue to move away from the centre and challenge the dominant culture around them and choose to speak from the margins" (p. 199). A/r/tography, as conceptualised by Irwin (2004), is concerned with the knowings encountered when moving between the roles of artist, researcher and teacher. A/r/tographic research approaches have come to recognise that there may be many diverse and concurrently inhabited roles while conducting research (Irwin, 2004). It is a powerful tool as it validates embodied knowledge gained through praxis, process and lived experience, while also acknowledging the multiplicity of our being and becoming which is brought to consciousness in specific moments of knowing. Mackay (2011) refers to this process as "centring and decentring" (p. 123) where the physical or metaphorical movement between and within spaces opens up possibilities for the self so that alternate embodied perspectives can be seen and felt and where becoming something that was hitherto thought impossible became possible.

Similarly, Habermas sees art as having the power to "increase decentration of subjectivity" and littoral art as a form of communicative action, aimed at "decolonisation of the lifeworld" (Habermas as cited by Barber, 2013, p. 15). The liminal spaces encountered in the process of centring and decentring created making moments and sparks of imagining which created new ways of being, thinking and acting. The young woman seen in Fig. 9.1 had worked on the painting for several months, while engaging in conversations with others in the room about what the painting meant for her. It was in the doing, the making, thinking and moving, where the knowing of herself and others and the synergies between them were encountered and made known. A/r/tography provided a pedagogy that is non-dualistic in thinking and a way to recognise aspects of the self, which are often ignored in dominant approaches to teaching and learning in contemporary schools, such as the body, the spirit, the emotional, the intuitive, the non-rational and the sacred (Irwin, 2004). Irwin (2004)

Fig. 9.1 A/r/tography: imagining new ways of being, thinking and acting

asserts that these are vital elements to incorporate into educational praxis as they are still present in the "shadow self", a term originally used by Jung (1958, p. 11) to describe the unconscious aspects of the self.

The project sought to help create a Website for and by young refugees while capturing their stories of resettlement in Australia. It began with a series of creative activities aimed at learning about young refugees' educational aspirations through weekly Web design workshops and soon developed into a hive of activity ranging from a study support group to visits to the local university and painting on three doors representing the past, present and future. Data was captured through a wide range of methods, including dialogical focus groups, one-to-one conversations, creative painting and drawing activities as well as visual narrative using video recordings. While there was a reassuringly familiar weekly structure to the sessions, similar to striated space, in practice the sessions remained open, flexible and multifaceted smooth spaces, which eventually developed into unplanned living assemblages.

There were three main spaces in the room where young people could choose to move between, depending on their interests and desires, a triangulation between the creative space, the bank of computers and the homework support space. The creative space included three large reclaimed doors with depictions of young refugees' imagined past, present and futures, alongside a table scattered with colourful tubes of paint, various sizes of paper, collections of soft and rough brushes, messy plastic pallets with leftover dried up acrylic rainbow swirls of paint and an assortment of pencils and markers. Near the creative table was a rickety easel which interchangeably held large and small canvases for young refugees to work on. The creative space was a chaotic, smooth space with few boundaries (Deleuze and Guattari, 1988).

The three distinct but overlapping spaces, that can be seen in Fig. 9.2, became an assemblage of individuals engaged in learning and communicating within and between smooth and striated spaces. The striations being the structure, the regular timing, the consistency of the broad activities and the researchers and the workers who were familiar with the spaces. The smooth aspects being the choices that the young people made in which activities they participated in, with whom and when. The interactions they had and the stories they told created movable patterns of fluid living assemblages of multiple identities, subjectivities and becomings (Cole, 2013).

Of Nomads and Doorways: Traversing the Past, Present and the Future

> Waiting waiting, relieved hope my troubles are just beginning, mountains, horizons, get there can see the blue sky, Mirage desert see the oasis, approach it see nothing, journey. (Mackay)

Both artists and nomads work in liminal betwixt and between spaces which enable a transversal exploration of the boundaries of life trajectories as emergent becomings. Norton (1988) sees nomadic existence as being far away from the centres of power, and at the same time, out of reach of the law/government/power structures and in effect, this distance becomes a source of power, independence and freedom. Nomadism is about the careful consideration of fluid boundaries and limits and the recognition that these relationships and ways of thinking and being will need to be reworked in new contexts, times and places.

Like the nomadic way of thinking, we used littoral art projects, in that they were undertaken outside of the institution of formal schooling and were purposefully designed to open up communicative action through and by engaging in critical dialogue about important social issues. As shown in Fig. 9.3, young people were invited to map their aspirational desire through painting the past, present and future, in what became a kind of nomadic traversing (Pryer, 2004), both in the sessions and in the larger experiences of their lives. It was in the in-between spaces created by moving from one activity to the next, at the beginning or at the end of a session, or when

Fig. 9.2 Moving between spaces: living assemblages of multiple identities, subjectivities and becomings

a new person joined the group, that we learnt the most about their aspirations and desires. It was these informal unplanned momentary spaces that often revealed more than the structured activities. For example, as we walked out of a football stadium, where, as a group, we had watched a local soccer team play, a young man, Ahmed, who had recently arrived to Australia from Syria talked about his dilemma between pursuing his ambition to become a soccer player and what he had been told by his father was a more realistic and sensible career destination to become a teacher. Back in Syria, he was well known in his local village as a talented soccer player, but having moved to Australia, he felt lost and confused. He said:

> I don't know what to do. I have played for a professional scoccer team before and I know I am good at it, but my father tells me to finish my study and get a real job in Australia, like a teacher. I feel lost and not sure which way to head.

The feeling of loss and uncertainty expressed by Ahmed was common among most newly arrived young refugees who were forced to leave their home countries for Australia. In this transient space, they were not fully embedded there or here, they

Fig. 9.3 Mapping aspirational desire: painting the past, the present and the future

were both global refugees while needing to navigate local bureaucracies of going to school, learning a new language and new signs. In effect, they were everywhere and nowhere. They held memories of the past, while navigating the present and striving for hopeful futurity (Zipin, Sellar, Brennan, & Gale, 2013). The transversal research approach taken in this study allowed us to view these junctures as folds (Deleuze & Strauss, 1991), which at once collapsed space, time and place, past, present future, local, national global and yet simultaneously held all of these elements open for exploration. Three old wooden doors representing the past, present and future were brought into be painted on by the young refugees. Painting on the doors became a communicative action that made refugees' lifeworlds visible, as it became the mediating agent which allowed for a decolonization of the refugee transition experience possible (Barber, 2013). This was made possible through promoting communication "at different levels" and "in different meanings" (Guattarri, 2015, p. 113). Young people were encouraged to communicate in whichever language they wanted to use and there were no restrictions on what they could paint and on which door. The imagery of the doors was used to form "spaces of hope" and "transversal activism" (Barber, 2013, p. 103) for aspirational change. Transforming ordinary household items such as interior doors into canvases for painting the past, present and future enabled young people to shrink time and space into a moment of deep critical reflection and boundless imagination about their possible futures as innovators and producers, not merely passive recipients of refugee resettlement transition interventions. Expression through paintings was designed by the researchers to circumvent language barriers. Indeed this was an important part of our transversal research approach as we wanted to remove obstacles preventing young people from articulating their voice and expressing their agency and self-advocacy. Indeed, describing the marginalising and disempowering effects of not speaking English for newly arrived refugees in Australia, a 15-year-old young woman, Amina said:

> When you don't know the language, as my mum said, you might as well be deaf. I don't mean I was feeling deaf, I was feeling really, really dumb. I was feeling stupid and wondered what would happen in my future if I didn't learn the language.

Amina knew too well the consequences of her parents' illiteracy in the English language on her, her siblings and parents' extensive delay in seeking a family reunion visa in Australia. They had to stay behind in Pakistan for four years before they could join their mother and father in Greater Western Sydney. Amina said:

> after they (her parents) got the Permanent Residency, they couldn't apply for us, because the language was really difficult for them. If English is not your first language it is really hard to speak it and my parents couldn't speak it. So they couldn't apply for us for four years.

The images carefully crafted by the young people on the three doors condensed multiple meanings that they were subsequently able to describe using words and gestures when they were asked by the researchers to explain what the symbols meant to them. The use of mother tongue was encouraged, particularly for those who spoke little or no English. Acknowledging the linguistic, cultural and experiential assets they brought to the project was a key to building their confidence in making critical judgements and independent decisions for positive life choices. Not only did this enable full participation in the discussions, but the first language became a conduit to learning English. Most of the young people had basic knowledge of the English language and used it interchangeably with the language of their countries of origin to communicate with each other. They took it in turns to interview each other about what the paintings represented while filming the exchange using iPads. In the process, they were switching from one language to the other to describe and explain what their paintings symbolised. Their stories, captured through the paintings and subsequent dialogical one to one and group interviews, became a map of a living history of what had happened to prompt their flight out of the crisis. Their critical narrative accounts became a collective memoir of their experiences and represented a transversal and fluid rendering of their becomings (Cole, 2013). This allowed us to explore with them what lay behind their educational desires and to help them make informed choices about their imagined futures in Australia.

Mapping Desire and Aspirational Change

The Navigating Resettlement project adopted a transversal approach that considered how time, space and place collided and influenced individual and collective experiences of migration, while maintaining acute sensitivity to the singularities and effects that gave rise to them seeking refuge a thousand miles from home, such as war, alienation and loss (Cole, 2016). The informal youth and community work setting within which the Navigating Resettlement project took place made it possible to adopt a transversal reworking of power relations between the young people, the researchers and youth workers and allowed all these actors to open up spaces for meaningful dialogue. The A/r/tographic approach used in the research enabled us to ensure authentic communication was established "at all levels" and in "different meanings" (Guattari, 2015, p. 113). For example, rather than treating young refugees as a subjugated group to be investigated, we conducted a dialogical focus group, where both young people and adults talked about their desires and aspirations, their personal biographies and career journeys, highlighting the achievements and obstacles that some of us had faced along the way. We wanted to avoid instrumentalist models of employability and aspirational change as these have been shown to be of limited value (Smyth & McInerney, 2014). Instead we wanted to open up in-between spaces for them to explore and voice their imaginings of their futures, so that we could "follow their lead" guided by their emergent desires and hopeful becomings. In our respective, but overlapping roles as teachers, mentors and researchers, we resisted the "do as I do" and encouraged the young people to "do with us" (Deleuze, 1994, p. 23), as they were making sense of their experiences. The mentoring approach taken in this project encouraged young people to learn through doing with the mentors rather than expect them to emulate ideal role models, based on instrumentalist institutional ideologies, often couched in deficit representations of the other as being "at-risk" (Moustakim, 2015).

Through A/r/tography, we examined how young refugees' past, present and imagined futures influenced their experiences of becoming. The metaphor captured in the Navigating Resettlement project title has a remarkable resonance with the example of Deleuze's swimmer, quoted in Semetsky (2013) who "learns to swim through a becoming: herself in the water within intense bodily encounters with waves" (p. 82), as it speaks powerfully to the myriad of challenges of varying intensities that refugees encounter in new and unfamiliar surroundings in Australia. Like Deleuze's (1994) swimmer they learn to calibrate their thoughts, feelings and actions to the fluctuating material conditions of a new environment and, like nomads, through repetition, trial and error, embody experiential knowledge of the new terrain. For some young

Fig. 9.4 Navigating Resettlement: negotiating hopes, fears, desires and anxieties

people, experiences of alienation were compounded by uncertainty, particularly for those whose immigration status in Australia had not as yet been determined. One young man, Kumar, said:

> I am not sure what will happen to me. I am trying to work hard on my HSC exams and I have lots of dreams about the future, but the Immigration Department have yet to let me know where I stand. So, I am not sure. They could order me to go back to Sri Lanka, and all my dreams will be finished.

This young man depicted his hopes and desires, fears and anxieties in a digital collage where he represented two images of himself facing opposite directions, while perched on a precarious rowing boat at both ends, with dangers represented by sharks and crocodiles. Yet, a message in a bottle with his photograph appearing through the glass represented hope that his calls for help will be answered. The researchers noted a recurring theme of hope, against the odds, in all the young people's stories. They expressed high aspirations for the future, matched only by a strong desire, dedication and determination to succeed (Fig. 9.4).

In the interviews, focus groups and in their imaginings of the future, depicted in their spontaneously crafted paintings, young people described their ambitions to become doctors, lawyers, teachers, nurses and engineers. The motivations underlying these career aspirations were tied to their lived experiences. Throughout their forced migration experiences, they came into contact with professionals who rendered vital care and guidance, while some of them were stuck in the dark and motionless tunnel of the refugee camp, with not a speck of light in sight. The doctors and nurses healed both visible and hidden injuries of war and dislocation. The lawyers worked indefatigably to protect their human rights and to help them seek refuge somewhere safe. Their lived experiences became the raison d'etre for their high hopeful aspirations. They were not motivated by the extrinsic desires of lucrative occupations, but by the intrinsic value of helping others who will have the misfortune of walking in their shoes.

Their stories of aspirational change were consistent with Zipin et al.'s view of aspiration as emergent and "difficult to define or see, but grounded in the idea of the 'present-becoming-future'" (2013, p. 10). This is a departure from a conception of the "past-made-present" (ibid.) germane to dominant logics of aspiration. Viewing aspiration as the present becoming future frees oppressed individuals and communities from the shackles of the past, while opening up endless possibilities of becoming. As Appadurai noted "in strengthening the capacity to aspire, conceived as a cultural capacity, the poor could find the resources required to contest and alter the conditions of their own poverty" (2004, p. 59). This is not to say that the past was irrelevant to the young people we worked with and was to be ignored. On the contrary, as their critical reflective accounts of their experiences of forced migration and the lengthy and cumbersome processes involved in asylum seeking, the past constituted "lived-cultural intimations of potentially new futurity" (Zipin et al., 2013). Indeed, comments made by young people after the workshops suggest that for some of them, the encounters with the mentors helped crystallise their convictions about their career ambitions, for others they prompted rethinking original plans. A small number of young people were still uncertain about what they wanted to do in the future, except one young man who said: "I don't mind what I do. I just want to be happy".

Navigating Resettlement project harnessed young people's high aspirations through organising matched mentoring during two visits to Western Sydney University campus. Our aim during the first visit was to demystify university, so we organised a tour of the campus, including the library, lecture theatres, teaching rooms, sporting facilities, the café and in-between spaces where students normally socialise. A group of existing university students talked about their experiences of university life and their journeys into Higher Education. During the second visit to the university, we invited students and academics representing the breadth of career interests expressed by young people. The students and academics were drawn from a range of disciplines and included professors, researchers, lecturers, undergraduate and postgraduate students, who had agreed to act as mentors to the young people. They were encouraged to adopt a dialogical approach to mentoring by providing space for young people to ask them questions about their own career paths and experiences. The approach to mentoring taken in this project was based on a presupposition of equality (Ranciere, 1987). We did not position ourselves as possessing definitive "navigational maps" (Smyth & McInerney, 2014, p. 294) against which to trace young people's futures. We were keen to encourage young people to map, rather than trace, their educational aspirations transversally and for them to make their own decisions about what they deemed worthwhile rather than follow doxic logics of aspirations (Zipin et al., 2013).

Conclusion

For most young people, including those born in Australia, whether they are moving from Secondary school to Higher Education, employment or, increasingly, to unemployment, transitions can be fraught with challenges and uncertainties. However, for newly arrived young refugees to Australia, these challenges are compounded by the effects of forced migration, learning a new language and new ways of being and doing. The Navigating Resettlement research project has shown that during resettlement in Australia, young refugees have to negotiate multiple transitions simultaneously and within a very short period of time. We used transversality as a research methodology to develop nuanced understandings of the intersectional dimensions of refugee resettlement transitions that go beyond analyses of the impact of vertical and horizontal factors that influence the daily experiences of refugees. In mapping aspirational change in young people's stories of resettlement, our primary focus was on dismantling hierarchical structures within the institution and reconfiguring interpersonal power relations between youth workers, researchers and mentors. Opening up communications at different levels was as important as enabling young people to use different ways of meaning-making, such as painting, which was particularly helpful for young people who spoke little or no English. Transversality was highly congruent with the principles of informal education, which guided this research project, with its emphasis on treating young refugees as subjects who are able to make statements on issues that are important to them. This enabled us to understand the resettlement stories of young refugees and made it possible for us to explain our arrangement of the encounter space at SydWest Multicultural Services. Using A/r/tography helped us create smooth nomadic spaces where young people and adults could share their stories, hopes and desires, build on their strengths and develop confidence in confronting the myriad of challenges they faced. In future research with young refugees, we intend to examine the affective and unconscious dimensions of refugee resettlement in more depth, as we believe that this would provide new theoretical insights into the use of transversality as a research methodology for investigating refugee resettlement transitions.

References

Ainsworth, M. D. S., & Bowlby, J. (1991). An ethological approach to personality development. *American Psychologist, 46,* 331–341.

Appadurai, A. (2004). The capacity to aspire: Culture and the terms of recognition. In V. Rao & M. Walton (Eds.), *Culture and public action: A cross-disciplinary dialogue on development policy* (pp. 59–84). Palo Alto, CA: Stanford University Press.

Barber, B. (2013). *Littoral art and communicative action.* Champaign, IL: Common Ground Publishing.

Bartlett, L., & Vavrus, F. (2014). Transversing the vertical case study: A methodological approach to studies of educational policy as practice. *Anthropology & Education Quarterly, 45*(2), 131–147.

Clarke, E. (2005). *Situational analysis: Grounded theory after the postmodern turn*. Thousand Oaks, CA: SAGE.

Cole, D. R. (2013). Deleuze and narrative investigation. The multiple literacies of Sudanese families in Australia. *Literacy, 47*(1), 35–41.

Cole, D. R. (2016). Unearthing the forces of globalisation in educational research through Guattari's cartographic method. In D. R. Cole & C. Woodrow (Eds.), *Super dimensions in globalisation and education* (pp. 145–161). Singapore: Springer.

Cole, D. R., & Mirzaei Rafe, M. (2018). Transversality, constraint and desire in Australia and Iran. In D. R Cole & J. P. N. Bradley (Eds.), *Principles of transversality in globalisation and education* (this volume). Singapore: Springer.

Deleuze, G. (1994). *Difference and repetition*. (P. Patton, Trans.). London: Continuum.

Deleuze, G., & Guattari, F. (1988). *A thousand plateaus: Capitalism & schizophrenia II* (B. Massumi, Trans.). London: The Athlone Press.

Deleuze, G., & Strauss, J. (1991). The fold. *Yale French Studies,* (80):227.

Genosko, G. (2002). *Felix Guattari: An aberrant introduction*. London: Continuum.

Guattari, F. (2015). *Psychoanalysis and transversality: Texts and Interviews 1955–1971* (A. Hodges, Trans.). South Pasadena, CA: Semiotext(e).

Irwin, R. (2004). A/r/tography: A metonymic metissage. In R. L. Irwin & A. de Cosson (Eds.), *Aa/r/tography: Rendering self through arts-based living inquiry* (pp. 27–38). Vancouver: Pacific Educational Press.

Jung, C. G. (1958). *The undiscovered self*. New York: New American Library.

Kingsley, P., & Timur, S. (2015, December 31). Stories of 2015: How Alan Kurdi's death changed the world. Retrieved from http://www.theguardian.com/australia.

Mackay, K. (2011). Reclaiming the sacred: A festival experience as a response to globalisation. *Journal for the Study of Religion, 2,* 75–96.

Meiches, B. (2015). A political ecology of the camp. *Security Dialogue, 5,* 476–492.

Moustakim, M. (2015). Disaffected youth: intersections of class and ethnicity. In T. Ferfolja, C. Jones-Diaz, & J. Ulman (Eds.), *Understanding sociological theory for educational practices* (pp. 129–144). Cambridge: Cambridge University Press.

Murphy, K. (2016, September 21). Race discrimination commissioner criticises Pauline Hanson for stoking division. Retrieved from http://www.theguardian.com/australia.

Murphy, K. (2017, August 17). Pauline Hanson wears burqa in Australian Senate while calling for ban. Retrieved from http://www.theguardian.com/australia.

Pryer, A. (2004). Living with/in marginal spaces: Intellectual nomadism and artist/researcher/teacher praxis. In R. L. Irwin & A. de Cosson (Eds.), *A/r/tography: Rendering self through arts-based living inquiry* (pp. 27–38). Vancouver: Pacific Educational Press.

Ranciere, J. (1987). *The ignorant schoolmaster: Five lessons in intellectual emancipation* (K. Ross, Trans.). Stanford: Stanford University Press.

Semetsky, I. (2008). *Deleuze, education and becoming*. Rotterdam: Sense Publications.

Semetsky, I. (2013). *Edusemiotics—A Handbook*. Singapore: Springer.

Smyth, J., & McInerney, P. (2014). Ordinary kids' navigating geographies of educational opportunity in the context of an Australian 'place-based intervention. *Journal of Education Policy, 29,* 285–301.

Winnicott, D. (1971). *Playing and reality*. London: Tavistock Publications.

World Health Organisation. (2017). Refugee and migrant health. Retrieved from World Health Organisation website: http://www.who.int/migrants/en/.

Zakaria, F. (2016, November 6). Populism on the March: Why the west is in trouble. Retrieved from http://www.foreignaffairs.com/united-states.

Zipin, L., Sellar, S., Brennan, M., & Gale, T. (2013). Educating for futures in marginalized regions: A sociological framework for rethinking and researching aspirations. *Educational Philosophy and Theory, 47,* 227–246.

Mohamed Moustakim is a Senior Lecturer in Education at Western Sydney University. He worked as a teacher in Morocco in the early 80s and subsequently, as a Youth Worker in London for several years. Prior to joining Western Sydney University, he taught Youth and Community and Education Studies at a number of universities in the UK. Equity and diversity issues in education and alternative forms of schooling have been central to his teaching, and his research interests are specifically focused around identifying the barriers that prevent young people from marginalised groups from achieving the goals they have reason to value.

Karin Mackay is a lecturer and researcher in Culture and Society at Western Sydney University. She has a background in school-based primary and secondary education and currently works closely with schools through the Pre-service teacher placement program. She has worked for many years in community arts practice as an artist facilitator and engaging marginalised groups through stories and art. She is interested in research that uses embodied arts-based approaches for creative expression of silenced voices. She is interested in exploring informal, creative and critical approaches to community education that integrate the political, personal, spiritual, environmental and justice perspectives.

Chapter 10
Fugitive Pedagogy: Guattari's Ecosophy in the Mural Discourse of the Zapatistas

Mark LeVine and Bryan Reynolds

Abstract The Zapatista Army of National Liberation has been struggling for greater rights and autonomy for the indigenous Mayan peoples of Chiapas, Mexico for the last three decades. The iconography, semiotic system, and progressive myth-making the Zapatistas produce in the hundreds of murals adorning their communities disseminate a powerful anti-state and anti-capitalist ideology that mutually reinforces the Zapatista culture on which the functioning of their communities, economy, and overall sociopolitical campaign depend. We argue that their positive, forward-oriented and environmentally sensitive art, and the broader political, social and pedagogical discourses it represents, is strongly congruent with Guattari's intellectual focus and political orientation toward developing a transversal "ecosophy," an ethico-aesthetic perspective that can enable greater freedom from the heavy chains of both the Mexican government and the global neoliberal capitalist system in which Mexico is embedded.

Keywords Zapatistas · Ecosophy · Ecology · Autonomy · Pedagogy

Introduction

The Ejército Zapatista de Liberación Nacional (Zapatista Army of National Liberation, or EZLN), commonly known as the "Zapatistas," have been struggling for greater rights and autonomy for the indigenous Mayan peoples of Chiapas, Mexico for the last three decades. Formed in the mountains of the Mexican southeast, also known as the Lacandón jungle, in the 1980s by a group of urban Marxist revolutionaries who came together with rural Mayan peasants to create a radically new kind of revolutionary movement, the EZLN shocked the Mexican government,

M. LeVine (✉) · B. Reynolds
University of California, Irvine, USA
e-mail: mlevine@uci.edu

B. Reynolds
e-mail: bryan.reynolds@uci.edu

© Springer Nature Singapore Pte Ltd. 2018
D. R. Cole and J. P. N. Bradley (eds.), *Principles of Transversality in Globalization and Education*, https://doi.org/10.1007/978-981-13-0583-2_10

society, and world at large when they launched an insurgency on January 1, 1994, the day the North American Free Trade Agreement (NAFTA) formally came into effect. Through many ups and downs, victories and defeats, the movement remains one of the few indigenous anti-capitalist revolutionary movements of the post-Cold War era to not only rebel against its national government, but also continue to repel and hold off with significant success the forces and institutions of a powerful state and the global neoliberal order it represents and advances. As important, the Zapatistas have managed to imagine and create functioning autonomous institutions and networks for their communities continuing over the span of a generation that have inspired dissidents and activists across the world, making the public (yet masked) face of the movement, "Subcomandante Insurgente Marcos," the world's most famous revolutionary since Ché Guevara.

We have been studying the Zapatistas for a number of years, with a focus on how they use art and artistic production across their communities—from residential design, municipal buildings, and schools to public festivals—to further their values, aesthetics, and politics, consolidate and strengthen indigenous identities, and resist both the Mexican government and the colonizing mechanisms of global neoliberalism. Of crucial importance for our research is how the government acts as a political, cultural, and economic conductor for neoliberalism and how the political, economic, physical, and spatial discourses involved in state practices are confronted by indigenous counter-hegemonic discourses which are also informed by—and indeed, have defined—the imaginary of the "alter-globalization" movement that "*un otro mundo es possible*" (another world—that is, social, political and economic reality—is possible) (LeVine, 2005; Marcos, 2007; Reyes, 2015).

Through our fieldwork and documentary analysis, we have discovered that the iconography, semiotic system, and ultimately the progressive myth-making the Zapatistas produce in the numerous murals adorning their communities, especially their public buildings and schools, and various walls and billboards throughout the areas under their control in Chiapas, disseminate a powerful anti-state ideology that mutually reinforces the subjective territories and Zapatista official culture (the dominant, endorsed culture of Zapatistas) on which the efficient and generative operations of their communities, economy, and overall sociopolitical campaign depend. In a situation in which even well-meaning outsiders coming to Chiapas assume that "teaching belly dancing" constitutes "solidarity work" (Davies, 2009), the need for an indigenous-led, grounded education theory, curriculum, and praxis is impossible to downplay. And the process of creating this is exceptionally fraught when one considers that both the territory and the people of Chiapas reflect "significant 'bio-capital'" (Guattari, 2000), control and/or ownership over which the government, corporations such as Monsanto, mining, timber, and petroleum companies, and competing factions within the indigenous community as well, are all contending. It is in fact very hard to underestimate the financial and discursive, as well as the ideological power of the specific "bio-knowledge" possessed by the indigenous Mayans. Where Monsanto and the Mexican state want to reduce Mexico to essentially a monocrop producer of genetically modified, Monsanto licensed corn, the local population has a powerful interest in maintaining some 1,800 varieties of maize that have grown in

Mexico for thousands of years, each of which is finely attuned to the soils, climate and elevation of the region in which it is found. Moreover, with each variety of maize comes a detailed knowledge of the local ecology which maintains a proper balance between various flora and fauna in the ecosystem, all of which would be destroyed by the policies of the state and its corporate allies and sponsors. Finally, while the arrival of Mexican and global corporations that might have come in the era of high modernization, today they continue to penetrate the region in the guise of neoliberal ideologies and discourses which are themselves very fructive—they have their own allure and economy that are quite hard for people to resist until they are too wrapped into the system to be able to resist (LeVine, 2005; cf. Nail 2012). In this context, Zapatistas have to walk a very fine line in what they keep and what they get rid of from the traditional state education curriculum. The use of murals as defining visual motifs, especially in children's lives, provides crucial vehicles for disseminating a counter-capitalist ideology that is positive, forward-oriented, and life-affirming even as it remains grounded in tradition and the care of "our mother earth" (cf. Barmeyer, 2008).

Transforming Praxis and Epistemology

Both the philosophy and the praxis of the Zapatista movement share many assumptions and views with some of the most important aspects of Félix Guattari's *oeuvre*, individually and in his collaborations with Gilles Deleuze. On the one hand, this is not surprising and in fact has been noted by scholars such as Nail (2012) and Evans (2010), who have put Deleuze and Guattari into direct conversation with the Zapatista movement and the philosophy of Zapatismo. Moreover, Marcos, *née* Rafael Guillen Vicente, began his career as one of the leading intellectuals of a generation deeply influenced by French poststructural theory. In 1981, his thesis was awarded a National Medal of Excellence from President José López Portillo. Marcos' philosophical training, as Nick Henck details in his intellectual biography of Marcos (2014), included strong doses of both Louis Althusser and Michel Foucault and clearly, to some degree, demonstrated a familiarity with the other central figures in French poststructuralist Marxian philosophy from the same era. Marcos' academic research focused explicitly on the ideological underpinning of education in Mexico.

On the other hand, the Zapatista movement Marcos helped create and, to a significant extent, came singularly to represent was grounded in a philosophy that is quite literally rooted—better, rhizomed—in the soil of Chiapas. As we want to show through our readings of a number of murals located on the walls of the municipal and educational centers of two Zapatista-controlled zones, Oventik, in the northern Los Altos region and La Garrucha, in the Selva Tzeital region of southern Chiapas, the movement's grounding in both an environmentally sensitive relationship to the land and anti-capitalist—although not overtly Marxist—political philosophy is strongly congruent with Guattari's later intellectual focuses and political orientation toward developing a transversal "ecosophy," an ethico-aesthetic perspective that could enable human emancipation from the heavy chains of both the Mexican government and the global neoliberal capitalism Mexico supports. Indeed, the breaking of chains and imagining of other futures, both common themes in the murals, highlight the essentially positive vision pervading the movement across the Zapatista community's ranks, which is reflected in other art forms (literature, theater, poetry, and music) as well as in the murals (cf. Evans, 2010, p. 156).

In contrast to most other left-wing guerrilla insurgencies of the last hundred years, the EZLN has never sought to capture state power—indeed, as we explore below, it is far more resonant with the "anarchist/autonomist" project of Guattari and Deleuze than the various strands of Western Marxism that influenced the Mexican and broader Latin American left in the 1970s and 1980s. Rather, the Zapatistas seek to achieve political, economic, and cultural autonomy for the indigenous Mayans of Mexico, whose struggles are understood by Zapatistas and by most scholars studying them to be a microcosm of the broader struggles against neoliberal capitalism within Mexico and globally (cf. Cunninghame & Corona 1998; Levi, 2014; Esther, 2016). The Zapatistas do not seek to overthrow and replace the Mexican state. Instead, they embrace the symbols of Mexican nationalism as a component of their own ethnically focused ideology. It is common for murals depicting the red star flag of the EZLN to show the Mexican national flag along with or even above it. The Zapatistas have taken cognizance of the lessons offered by the struggles of other campaigns for freedom led by indigenous and oppressed populations in Mexico, Latin America and beyond, including Palestinians, African Americans, and Kurds, all of whom are represented in their murals. The ostensibly strange logic underlying Zapatista symbology and, through it, identity, that is, an indigenous-based rebel movement seeking both autonomy from and loyalty to a colonizing state, epitomize the impossibility of capturing, either in theory or practice, the Zapatista movement by any simple calculus. It requires an approach that explores fugitive elements of the subject matter under investigation as it contextualizes intersectionally (investigative-expansively), from substrata to efflorescence and avoids reductionism (dissective–cohesive modes) typical of analyses of left-wing revolutionary movements (cf. Nail, 2012, pp. 3–5).[1] As the Mexican critic Gustavo Esteva argues of the Zapatista-allied indigenous movement of Oaxaca (which borders Chiapas to the north), a truly revolutionary movement "owes its radicalism to its very nature: it is at ground level, close to the roots" (Esteva 2010, p. 986; Nail (2012, pp. 3–6) makes a similar point in arguing that Zapatismo and Deleuze and Guattari's philosophy both developed ideas of revolutionary praxis in the 1980s unsubordinated to state, party or vanguardism). In the case of the Zapatistas, as reflected in their murals, their roots are just as significantly apparent above ground as they are underground, hidden behind their ski masks and bandannas, and yet their aesthetic and symbology, and their attendant epistemology and praxis, are driven to

---

[1] For detailed explanation of fugitive explorations, as a methodological component of transversal poetics, as well as the dissective–cohesive and investigative–expansive modes of analysis; see Bryan Reynolds, *Transversal Subjects: From Montaigne to Deleuze after Derrida* and *Transversal Enterprises in the Drama of Shakespeare and his Contemporaries: Fugitive Explorations*.

experience and act in the world as close to ground level as possible. In consequence, the Zapatistas are a progressive culture of deep human–nature symbiosis.

The most important symbol of the movement is the snail (*caracol*), a seemingly lowly creature who nevertheless "advances, but slowly" (to cite one of the most important sayings in the Zapatista lexical universe)—to expect anything more when you are an indigenous movement up against five-hundred years of colonialism, genocide, and one of the world's most powerful states would be the height of stupidity and hubris. The snail's "antipathy" toward modern concepts of "faster is better," linearity, origins, and destinations is crucial to offering the indigenous Mayans of Chiapas the chance to create their own, more grounded histories and identities (Bahn 2009, p. 556) (Fig. 10.1).

The majority of images on the walls of Zapatista-controlled areas feature artwork that shows the indigenous people rooted into their land; an obvious allusion to the centuries of forced expropriation and exile from their land by the Spanish colonial forces and then the Mestizo elite. The leadership of the five "*juntas de buen gobierno*" (good governance councils), which are the equivalent of municipal or "county" authorities in the Zapatista-controlled regions, operate as a true collective leadership. Most adult members of the community, men and women equally, have to take a turn in the leadership role, and all "lead by obeying," seeking to "convince, not conquer." Their offices are adorned with murals, including the ones analyzed here that explicitly root the community in the earth, to reflect not only a "world that can fit many worlds" but a world—and indeed, a "philosophy"—where "the human being is a part of nature," as the murals commonly declare (all these phrases, in both Spanish and local Mayan languages, are on murals in the communities we have visited).

Such sentiments are not limited to Zapatista-inspired visual art, however. Marcos has also become a celebrated author of fiction, with fantastic stories drawn

Fig. 10.1 "Long Live the Struggle," wall mural in residential area of the autonomous municipality (*caricol*) of La Garrucha in southern Chiapas

from Mayan as well as European folktales and literature, all of which have strongly pedagogical aims (particularly his *Conversations with Durito*, 2005; Subomandante Marcos, 2001; cf. Henck, 2007; Gregory, 2000, p. 3)—to help readers understand the threats posed by neoliberalism and the successes, failures, hopes, and dreams of the indigenous peoples and their allies who are fighting to stop it (often like Don Quixote against his proverbial windmill). The Zapatistas have also routinely sponsored concerts, plays, and arts festivals (most recently under the rubric of "ComParte") that feature local and international participants, during which they commonly portray through theater the stories of their struggles and victories. Their artistic praxis forces a rethinking of the distinction emphasized by Deleuze and Guattari between art and philosophical thought, opening space for a transversal comingling of theory, practice, and critique that not only reveals links between aesthetics, ethics, and politics, but offer hope through the power and impact of their work that, *contra* Theodor Adorno, the power of contemporary capitalism is not so all-encompassing that the only method of critique left to the artist is to ostensibly withdraw completely from politics (cf. Ståhl, 2016; Abu-Manneh, 2015; Adorno, 1967a, b, 1991; LeVine, 2011). Here we define transversality as a dynamic state of metamorphosis goings beyond established parameters for subjectivity through which the scope of conceptual, emotional, and physical perception reconfigures. Zapatista art inspires transversal movement away from state-centric prescriptions for identity and subjectivity, and toward powerfully local and autonomous imaginaries.

Far from fleeing critical engagement with the "capitalist hydra" (EZLN 2016), Zapatista arts evoke a positive view of the future; there are very few negative or violent depictions or messages, as one sees in murals in the Occupied Palestinian Territories or other sites of intense oppression and conflict, such as Belfast. The positive attitude reflects an alternative philosophy of history that underlies rebellion against neoliberal globalization. To end the persistent deterritorialization and reterritorialization of neoliberal creative destruction, the Zapatistas answer with a powerful rhizomatic reinsertion, joyously, into the earth (cf. Bahn 2009, pp. 544–46). In a sense, both Guattari and the Zapatistas attempt to develop a "Marxism in a snail shell," that is, a powerful critique of capitalism that certainly owes much to Marx, yet without the fetishization of modernity and progress that has always haunted the Marxist project of liberation. Instead, advancing slowly but surely, or from the molecular outward, the goal was and is, as necessary, to encounter, assemble, create and ultimately, when the roots are deep enough, rebel (Marcos 2007). But how to move from the "encounter" to rebellion? For Zapatistas at all levels, as much as having a credible military deterrent against government attempts—either directly or through paramilitary groups—to seize back territory or otherwise destabilize the movement, the key is education. As with so many occupied and/or marginalized indigenous movements, education has long been at the frontlines of the struggles for rights, justice, democracy, and land for the Mayan inhabitants of Chiapas.

Like most other modernizing postcolonial states, the Mexican state for a very long time did all it could to discourage the use of local Mayan languages in the public sphere and in schools as well. As a result, local Mayans were forced to learn Spanish, while their rich indigenous languages were repressed. Even a few years ago, young students who spoke one of the Mayan languages in school were forced to kneel on metal bottle caps as punishment. Of course, given the scarce resources devoted to education in indigenous areas, this situation meant that young Mayans left school (if they were lucky, after six years of primary school) with very bad knowledge of either Spanish or their own languages. Beyond language, however, subjects like history, math, and science were taught in a way that highlighted and reinforced the marginalization of indigenous students, often through excluding their histories, or giving no or short shrift to local scientific knowledge when it came to agriculture, and so on (interviews conducted by LeVine and Reynolds in San Cristóbal de las Casas, Oventik, La Garrucha, Mexico, March 2017; cf. Davies 2009).

If the Zapatistas claim that "another world is possible" (*un otro mundo es possible*), then education is the *sine qua non* for realizing that dream. Indeed, among the most important functions of the local *caracoles*, or autonomous municipalities, has long been education, a task made more important as the government has offered education funding to previously deprived areas as part of its strategy to cleave support within Zapatista communities (Navarro-Smith, 2015). Whether at the level of theory and discourse, where Foucault's and Althusser's influence on Marcos is clear (Henck 2016), or at the level of grounded praxis with the numerous "*promotores*," or "education promoters" (as the usually young teachers are referred to) we have interviewed, it is widely understood by community leaders—who, it must be remembered, are drawn from community members on a regularly rotating basis—that an autonomous curriculum developed by indigenous teachers and the community is necessary to providing an environment in which young indigenous Chiapanecans can learn about their language, history, and traditional scientific and medical knowledge, the latter two being crucial in an environment in which mainstream medicine and agro-science are either out-of-reach or part of a broader government and/or corporate plans to control the community's bodies, land, and the fruits of its soil. Moreover, in a community striving for autonomy, in which the goal is precisely to remain as much as possible outside the control of the capitalist market, developing a local educational system in which students can acquire knowledge and skills that are not dependent on or suited only to the capitalist market (Cole, 2014), but instead "serve the community" (as most every interlocutor describes it)—whether medicine or math—is of fundamental importance.

Creating and implementing such a locally engrained, autonomous curriculum is not simply a matter of excising those parts of the standard curriculum that reflect racist or demeaning views toward indigenous peoples, or respecting traditional practices. As Marcos himself argued, there is a core epistemo-ethical difference between a rationalist–instrumentalist view of reason, knowledge, and science, and what Marcos describes as the "magical ideological tradition" of the indigenous population (quoted in Henck, 2016, p. 12), a belief we have seen shared by *promotores* in the field. At the heart of their attempts to reclaim their humanity, Zapatista epistemology, and its resulting pedagogy, in fact resonate with deep-seated positive anti-humanism—both because humanism's human–nature dualism and uncritical faith in scientific progress and growth have been so disastrous for both humans and nature (Bahn, 2009, p. 545), and because, in the wake of half a millennium of humanity-denying colonialism, any positive self-assertion can only arise outside the humanist epistemologies and ontologies that emerged and always travelled along with it.

The Ecosophy of Zapatista Art; or, Colorful Walls Make Stronger Communities

"Ecology," Guattari explains, "questions the whole subjectivity in capitalist power formations... We are talking about a reconstruction of social and individual practices which I shall classify under three complementary headings, all of which come under the ethico-aesthetic aegis of an ecosophy: social ecology, mental ecology, and environmental ecology" (Guattari, 2000, pp. 41–52). In our view, ecosophy as envisioned by Guattari and practiced by Zapatistas through their educational structures and artistic expressions reflects a transversal poetics in which subjective territory is deeply informed by a dual understanding of the term "subject": as a product of socializing processes that *subject* an individual to normalizing and authoritative modes of experience and comprehension particular to a society, culture, ideology, and aesthetic, and also as a condition of *subjectivity* and sentience forged from or in response to those processes.[2] Guattari describes processes of subjectification and the establishment of interiority in his terms:

> Rather than speak of the "subject," we should perhaps speak of *components of subjectification*, each working more or less on its own. This would lead us, necessarily, to re-examine the relation between concepts of the individual and subjectivity, and, above all, to make a clear distinction between the two. Vectors of subjectification do not necessarily pass through the individual, which in reality appears to be something like a "terminal" for processes that involve human groups, socioeconomic ensembles, data-processing machines, etc. Therefore, interiority establishes itself at the crossroads of multiple components, each relatively autonomous in relation to the other, and, if need be, in open conflict. (Guattari, 2000, p. 36)

Indicating the specifically embodied conceptual, emotional, and physical scope through which individuals perceive and experience, this multidimensional and processual space—Guattari's "terminal" or our "subjective territory"—is typically influenced, if not directly managed, by dominant sociopolitical conductors, such as familial, religious, juridical, media, and educational structures. These are the replicators, transmitters, and orchestrators of thoughts, meanings, and desires that interconnect a society's ideological, cultural, and affective framework. Sociopolitical conductors are authoritative agents, normally people in positions of power (parents, teachers, priests, community leaders), but also media sources (advertising, news agencies, textbooks, public murals) that work directly and discursively to *subjectify* individuals. They inculcate, entice, define, navigate, and regulate subjects. From the standpoint of the society they primarily serve, each modality of sociopolitical conduction endeavors to

---

[2]For more on the idea of a subject, according to transversal poetics; see Bryan Reynolds, *Transversal Subjects: From Montaigne to Deleuze after Derrida* and *Becoming Criminal: Transversal Performance and Cultural Dissidence in Early Modern England*.

avoid, repel, colonize, coopt, or destroy opposing discourses, subjective territories, and generators of transversal movement.[3]

Put differently, sociopolitical conductors work to organize and stratify articulatory spaces. These are material, impressionistic, and abstract spaces in which otherwise disparate matter, codes, ideas and affects cohere around an organizing principle virtually and actually, both diachronically and synchronically.[4] In contrast to machinations of state-oriented sociopolitical conductors, transversal power—in thought, affect, and action—is the force of uncontrollable, transformative movement beyond the limits of any subjective territory and is therefore especially dangerous to societal and government structures, and therefore the sociopolitical conductors that reciprocally support them. Hence, should sociopolitical conductors become dissident—like the one-time academic-turned revolutionary Subcomandante Marcos—to the societal and state structures from which they gained their authority, and/or become anarchically counter-hegemonic, they have the potential to influence the breakdown, transcendence, and even fugitive reconfiguration of a subjective territory, and with it the sociopolitical function it performs vis-à-vis the larger society, as transversal agents.

Marcos and his comrades were able to lead a population that had been subjugated and demoralized for centuries out of their prescribed subjective territory through transversal thought, alternative thinking that demands new ways of seeing, experiencing, analyzing, and talking about the ecosystem and broader worlds they inhabit.[5] If education is central to this process, we argue that the murals are central to the educative process. In the autonomous Zapatista communities where the majority of children study, hardly a wall exists that does not have some form of artwork related to the community and the Zapatista ecosophy along it. The murals are, from start

---

[3]For more on sociopolitical conductors and transversal movement; see Bryan Reynolds, *Performing Transversally: Reimagining Shakespeare and the Critical Future* and *Becoming Criminal: Transversal Performance and Cultural Dissidence in Early Modern England*.

[4]For example, consider the now very controversial articulatory space of Donald Trump, "Trump-space," which includes: 1) concrete changes to the environment, such as during his first one-hundred days in office, pre-production for the building of an eco-disastrous wall along the border between the USA and Mexico, prevention of random people from emigrating to the USA, deportation of people who have lived, worked, and raised families in the USA over decades, and killing people and destroying property and natural landscapes by dropping bombs on Yemen, Syria, and Afghanistan; 2) regular dissemination of questionable and unverifiable information coming from primarily the White House but also from other contingencies that together promote a consistent and therefore unifying impression of disingenuity and uncertainty; and 3) the grotesque fetishization of Trump through which his abstract value far exceeds any presidential or humanitarian qualities he might possess or has successfully demonstrated through quantifiable actions. Negotiating and channeling information streams, sociopolitical conductors, like White House Press Secretary Sean Spicer in the case of Trump-space, interface and infiltrate the spatiotemporal operations within articulatory spaces, such as those of news media, public intellectuals, and activists, as a means by which to identify, constrain, and appropriate sites of difference (contrasting information and perspectives), subjunctivity (hypothetical scenarios vis-à-vis uncertainty), and transversality (manifest indeterminate disarticulation and metamorphosis).

[5]On the genealogy of transversal thought in contemporary critical theory; see Gary Genosko, "Afterword: Subjects Matter," in Reynolds, *Transversal Subjects*, 262–71.

to finish, an exercise in community creation, identity, and solidarity—a focus on achieving unity through the radical acceptance of the "Other" that was also central to Deleuze and Guattari's later oeuvre (cf. Evans, 2010, particularly his discussion of fugitive subjects on pages 149–53, p. 156; Holloway, 2005). Most every mural is either developed and designed or approved by the community, with a "caravan" of local (and occasionally, foreign) artists either suggesting or realizing the mural to reflect a specific theme. While the style often verges between magical realism and surrealism, the implications are quite real. The Zapatista communities are represented as vibrant, rooted in history and territory, with women often in the lead, and historical leaders or inspirations, like Zapata or Ché, sharing space with women, children, and luxuriant trees—all representing the "way of the future," as the mural on the wall of the Caracol (municipal) building in La Garrucha puts it (Fig. 10.2):

As in this mural, it is common for the murals to feature numerous disembodied heads in *pasamontañas* hanging from trees or sprouting from stalks or stems, like flowers or pieces of fruit that symbolize the fecundity of both Zapatismo and the communities it has created. Any parent who has looked at their child's "history and social sciences" textbooks from kindergarten all the way to twelfth grade knows the importance of instilling notions of "civics" and "patriotism" at the heart of primary and secondary education. Similarly, Zapatista murals usually feature important phrases,

Fig. 10.2 "The way of the future," wall mural on municipal building of the La Garrucha autonomous municipality

in Spanish as well as the local Mayan language, often written into the coil of the *caracol* (which is often depicted as emanating from the mouths of the disembodied Zapatista heads). The imagery is at once profound and simple. Equally important, the murals are often painted low to the ground, to be at eye level with small children who will pass them regularly every day for most of their young lives, thereby constantly taking in the messages they convey. In an educational system largely bereft of textbooks or other official documents, such murals serve as history and civics texts, both teaching and reinforcing core Zapatista—that is, community—ideals.

At the same time, and crucially, the murals are never considered as finished works of art. As with life itself, they constantly change. They fade from the sun and rain and are destroyed if the building is taken apart to use the wood for something else. They can be painted over, expanded, or "revised," if the community decides the message is not precise enough or should be changed (e.g., the skin tone in a famous mural of Zapata in Oventik was darkened; a mural depicting a man was changed into one dominated by a woman's face, her thick hair rooting into the earth, quite literally). The power of the murals, and their sheer beauty and captivating appearance, helps account for the success and power of the Zapatista ongoing-revolution-in-the-making, one that has given them an unprecedented if often tenuous freedom from government control and allowed them to live autonomously, while at the same time capitalizing on the government that once oppressed them (Vargas-Santiago, 2015; cf. Nail 2012).

Minor Culture, Mural Discourse, Major Impact

Operating through this dynamic, the Zapatistas are a dissident but also "minor culture," substantiated by a "minor pedagogy," in terms similar to how Deleuze and Guattari describe "minor language." In *A Thousand Plateaus: Capitalism and Schizophrenia*, Deleuze and Guattari write:

> Minor languages are characterized not by overload and poverty in relation to a standard or major language, but by a sobriety and variation that are like a minor treatment of the standard language, a becoming-minor of the major language… Minor languages do not exist in themselves: they exist only in relation to a major language and are also investments of that language for the purpose of making it minor… They are not simply sublanguages, idiolects or dialects, but potential agents of the major language's entering into a becoming-minoritarian of all its dimensions and elements… (Deleuze and Guattari, 1987, pp. 104–6)

Deleuze and Guattari's idea of minor and major languages is based on their view of the minor and the major as sociopolitical factors, such as identities, operations, and systems, which are always seen as of position and not essence, as composites, and not individual or total expressions, as fluid processes and not stagnant or absolute states. Accordingly, the terms "majority" and "minority" refer, respectively, to qualitative identifications of powerfulness and powerlessness rather than quantitative identifications. Deleuze and Guattari write, "When we say majority, we are referring not to a greater relative quantity but to the determination of a state or standard in relation to which larger quantities, as well as the smallest, can be said to be minoritarian: white-man, adult-male, etc. Majority implies a state of domination, not the reverse" (1987, p. 291).

Unlike the majority, with its system of constancy and homogeneity, minorities are subsystems, fugitive to the majority, with potential for heterogeneity, multiplicity, and becomings. Deleuze and Guattari further explain:

> What defines a minority, then, is not the number but the relations internal to the number. A minority can be numerous, or even infinite; so can a majority. What distinguishes them is that in the case of a majority the... number constitutes a set that may be finite or infinite, but is always denumerable, whereas the minority is defined as a nondenumerable set... What characterizes the nondenumerable is... the *connection*, the "and" produced between elements, between sets, and which belongs to neither... What is proper to the minority is to assert a power of the nondenumerable, even if that minority is composed of a single member. That is the formula for multiplicities. (1987, p. 470)

The problem is not merely to distinguish between major and minor languages; rather, the problem is at the core "one of a becoming... not of reterritorializing oneself on a dialect or a patois but of deterritorializing the major language" (1987, p. 104).

Among the "minor" languages deployed by the Zapatistas to the effect described here are the murals, which reflect the kind of "nondenumerable" (Deleuze & Guattari, 1987) and multiple affective power that deterritorializes the power of the state, now kept away from Zapatista-controlled areas, to allow for the inscription in the minds of children as well as adults of a language and codes of liberation, of possibility, of worlds that "fit other worlds," as one well-known slogan puts it. Indeed, one of the most ubiquitous images in the murals is Zapatistas, represented by disembodied heads wearing *pasamontañas*, speaking *caracoles*, or snails, in confrontations with representatives of state power, such as the bulldozer attempting to uproot indigenous trees in a mural in Agua Clara (Fig. 10.3).

Similar to black Americans who, according to Guattari and Deleuze, "do not oppose Black to English, they transform the American English that is their own language into Black English" (Deleuze and Guattari, 1987, pp. 104–5), the Zapatistas similarly and quite literally "deterritorialize" (ibid., p. 116) and appropriate the language of the colonizer, Spanish, juxtapose it with their indigenous languages, and use them to frame the artwork of their murals, providing magical realist or even surrealist visions of the future that correspond to the inherently magical and surreal quality of the task of fighting, like a collective Don Quixote, against the windmills of capitalism (Vanden Berghe, 2009). In effect, such communities of black Americans escape the linguistic jurisdiction of the majority. In so doing, they are deterritorializing the major language from their conceptual space and progress their own fugitive minoritarian becomings of something other than what the state has prescribed.

What is more, the language acquired through the Zapatista education system provides them with exclusivity, privacy, and protection against many of the state's mechanisms of subjugation and surveillance. It provides them with their own emotional, intellectual, and political territory, their own communicative domain. Their mural pedagogy, in which they adapt standard modes of educational media to their own purposes and therefore take control over the establishment of subjective ter-

Fig. 10.3 Trees versus Bulldozers—Zapatistas speaking snails from the trees to the bulldozer attempting to uproot them

ritories within their own minor culture, works to make their culture official, but smartly, it is neither absolute or stagnate. The murals promote their political and pedagogical philosophy, and insistence on fluid, processual creation of identities, thereby acknowledging productively that subjectivity and thus identity are as changeable, unpredictable, and continuously transforming along with the natural world with which we live and coexist (Cole, 2017).

Walling in Zapatista-Space

Constantly in flux, or at least moving along existential planes with some degree of play, subjective territories dynamically interact with other subjective territories to which they respond. They hunker down, recoil, expand, or laminate together on nodals of convergence, such as a shared experience, belief or interest. Using an array of brilliantly designed motifs, each capitalizing on important cultural, historical, and ideological references that together present intermedial constellations with an immersive affects, the Zapatistas' murals significantly contribute to the inculcation and manufacturing of subjectivities that positively engender overlapping subjective territories for which the particular or predominant articulatory space they manifest, in this case "Zapatista-space," is steadily produced and reproduced. However, virtually and actually occupied and embodied by the population, Zapatista-space, the Zapatista identities which populate it, or rather the ongoing becomings-Zapatista of the locals, is reflected as well as inculcated and imbricated by the murals. The murals teach us that Zapatistas are organic, hybrid animal–vegetable–human, and efflorescing perpetually with effective duration to a cumulative magnitude that prevents alternative and opposing ideologies, the Mexican government, paramilitaries and other elite forces from gaining or regaining control over Zapatista-held territories, mental, and physical (Fig. 10.4).

Coextensive coefficients of the ecosystem in which Zapatistas subsist and flourish, Zapatistas live by a basic ethico-aesthetic code, which persists in line with Guattari's "ecosophical perspective," since it "does not totally exclude a definition of unifying objectives, such as the struggle against world hunger, an end to deforestation or to the blind proliferation of the nuclear industries; but it will no longer be a question of depending on the reductionist, stereo-typical order-words which only expropriate other more singular problematics and lead to the promotion of charismatic leaders" (Guattari, 2000, p. 34). Zapatistas value their community above themselves, above any individual or leader within their community they work hard and tirelessly, take care of each other, support other people in need, and protect the environment.

Fig. 10.4 "Caracol of Resistance." Wall mural in La Garrucha Autonomous Municipality featuring snail symbol and the phrase "Municipality of Resistance Towards a New Dawn", both Spanish and Tseltal

In this context, Zapatista education fosters not only the reterritorialization of identity and power within Zapatista-space (as both a territorial unit and discursive practice) and a constant becomings-Zapatista, but also a continuous becomings-ever "more other," as Marcos describes it, against the innumerable impossibilities for praxis presented by the realities of the capitalist system they face. This process increases the distance between the still somewhat magical world of the *caracol* so well reflected in the murals and the equally magical—fetishistic and reified—but far more damaging capitalist hydra and the vampiric lifeworlds it creates (Marcos 2016, p. 108).To be sure, the Zapatistas alignment with Guattari's ecosophy can be seen recently and directly in their production of "Fuck Trump" coffee, which they sold worldwide to raise money to support both victims of Donald Trump's policies and pro-immigrant resistance groups across the globe. Similarly, for Guattari, way back in 1989, Donald Trump was, not surprisingly, a primary example he offers for the types of opponents conscientious eco-responsible people are up against:

> Now more than ever, nature cannot be separated from culture; in order to comprehend the interaction between ecosystems, the mechanosphere and the social and individual Universes of reference, we must learn to think "transversally." Just as monstrous and mutant algae invade the lagoon of Venice, so our television screens are populated, saturated, by "degenerate" images and statements [*énoncés*]. In the field of social ecology, men like Donald Trump are permitted to proliferate freely, like another species of algae, taking over entire districts of New York and Atlantic City; he "redeveloped" by raising rents, thereby driving out tens of thousands of poor families, most of whom are condemned to homelessness, becoming the equivalent of the dead fish of environmental ecology. (Guattari, 2000, p. 43)

The Zapatistas' approach to combating capitalist ideology, what Guattari calls "monstrous and mutant algae," which is used to subvert and co-opt the subjectivities of indigenous Mayan peoples, testifies to the efficacy of transversal thought to which Guattari refers, thought that enables and affects expansions and reconfigurations of subjective territory, and can be seen diagrammatically expressed through the Zapatistas' murals.

It is our argument that the murals function as semiological assemblages of enunciation and education that, through their combination of verbiage, mythological referents derived from real-life personas (sometimes also legendary, like Subcomandante Marcos, Ché Guevara, Chairman Mao Zedong), and abstract or surrealist expressionist imagery, create networks of memory-making and legacy-building stories that become continuous. That is, they are coded as continuous in the process of (re)birth and becomings-Zapatista—epitomized, for instance, by the constant visual theme of Zapatista heads (represented by the ever-present *pasamontaña*) flowering on trees and plants ready to join the struggle against the Mexican state and capitalism (e.g., see Fig. 10.2). Zapatistas are always moving forward, no matter how slow—indeed, the slower the better, as indicated by the importance given to the *caracol*/snail, an ancient Mayan symbol that symbolizes for Zapatistas, as we have already discussed, the need to move slowly, deliberately, and well-rooted against the relentless hurricane of neoliberalism—the snail strategy at the heart of Guattari's molecular revolution.[6]

---

[6]See Guattari (1984) *Molecular Revolution: Psychiatry and Politics*. New York: Penguin.

The autonomous communities established by the Zapatistas throughout Chiapas, despite their diligent efforts to teach literacy as well as basic math, science, and history (focused, not surprisingly, on the histories of various indigenous and anti-colonial struggles in Mexico, Latin American, and globally during the last five-hundred years) remain broadly illiterate. Because of this, pedagogy remains, by necessity, disproportionately aural and visual compared with official pedagogy in Mexico. At the same time, fugitive to Mexico's official pedagogy, Zapatista education is openly ideological and teleological—it makes no claim to "objectivity" or neutrality—in that it is geared to realizing the goal of greater autonomy, freedom, and equality. As most every indigenous resident of a Zapatista community will tell you, the goal of education is to "serve the community" in the context of a long-term struggle against neoliberal capitalist globalization, and not advance the individual or prepare her or him for adult life within the capitalist system that oppresses and marginalizes them, or attempts to ferret them out in the interest of abolishing them (the focus on serving what are described as "community" needs and goals has, in societies across history and geography, been the rationalization and justification for various forms of hierarchization, oppression and exploitation, as well as trampling on individual choice. Working against such dynamics in this case—however imperfectly—is the truly rotating leadership and the explicit focus on placing the young, women and other traditionally subaltern members of the community in leadership positions.). One could in fact say, as has Marcos, that the Zapatista philosophy and praxis of education together emerged precisely out of the need for all activities, including schooling to "serve the community" by ensuring that such service encourages rather than frustrates the meeting of personal needs (Marcos, 2014, p. 81).

It is in this regard that the murals are particularly important to the larger health and functioning of the community. They are the language of cross-community communication, especially given that there are four indigenous Mayan languages spoken in the region (Spanish is the colonialist language, but not typically a first language), and thus they constitute semiotic assemblages of collective enunciation that enables and affects anti-state transversality as a means to expand subjective territory and think counter-hegemonically, in effect reinforcing the coherence among the indigenous populations of Chiapas. Zapatista ideology and culture as articulated through the murals reflects Guattari's ecosophic and ethico-aesthetic paradigms. That is, they are driven by environmental concerns and sensitivities and a deeply rooted knowledge of their ecosystems, inhabited by them for hundreds of generations. With uncanny accuracy, Guattari's call to action, however unknown to the Zapatistas, has been precisely implemented by them:

> A new ecosophy, at once applied and theoretical, ethico-political and aesthetic, would have to move away from the old forms of political, religious and associative commitment... There is at least a risk that there will be no more human history unless humanity undertakes a radical reconsideration of itself. We must ward off, by every means possible, the entropic rise of a dominant subjectivity. We need new social and aesthetic practices, new practices of the Self in relation to the other, to the foreign, the strange – a whole programme that seems far removed from current concerns. And yet, ultimately, we will only escape from the major crises of our era through the articulation of: a nascent subjectivity, a constantly mutating socius, and environment in the process of being reinvented. (Guattari, 2000, pp. 67-68)

Consistent with Guattari's ecosophy and call to action, the Zapatistas, as seen in the murals, generate a powerful indigenous environmental ethic and consciousness quite literally *avant* and *à l'extérieur-de-la-lettre*—that is, of the written word and all the discourses and disciplinarities that pass through it, creating a very specific Zapatista ecosophy. We can see this ethico-aesthetic in Fig. 10.1, a three meter long, one meter high ground-level mural in La Garrucha—past which all members of the community, especially children, pass many times a day on the way to the communal kitchen and bathrooms—that depicts the community stretching out into the distance, standing together under the banner "Viva la Lucha" (long live the struggle), holding hands while waving flags calling for "peace, education, land, democracy, information, justice" and similar goals, while *caracoles* and red EZLN stars adorn the sky.

Similarly, in Fig. 10.5, a double mural taking up an entire classroom wall in the *Caracol* of Oventik, we see a naked, brown-skinned woman, holding a heart in one hand and a multi-color ear of maize in the other, her hair thick green leaves, her arteries becoming roots, with "revolution" written in Spanish and several Mayan languages above her, while to her left is a giant star with the number "6" in the middle to represent the "Sixth Declaration of the Lacandón Jungle," the defining creed of the Zapatista movement, surrounded by the heads of women and men in *pasamontañas* and *paliacates* (handkerchiefs) like so many ears of maize.

The text at the top of the mural states: "That is why they say that the stars are born in the ground" (*por eso dicen que las estrellas se nacen en el suelo*). The power of these images is clear—particularly their empowerment of women (a constant central

Fig. 10.5 Classroom mural, Oventik autonomous municipality

theme in Zapatista discourse) and the focus on inherent links between humans and nature as vital to a proper balance between the two.

Although simultaneously heterogeneous in expression, we see the murals, and the entirety of Zapatista pedagogy as producing powerful singularities (individuals) as well out of the multiplicities of the group. As Guattari puts it, "One might object that large-scale struggles are not necessarily in sync with ecological praxis and the micropolitics of desire, but that is the point: It is important not to homogenize various levels of practice or to make connections between them under some transcendental supervision, but instead to engage them in processes of *heterogenesis*" (Guattari, 2000, p. 51). Zapatista pedagogy likewise opposes the dualistic separation of human and non-human/natural systems; when your lives depend on the ability to farm 1800 varieties of maize while fending off the Mexican state and the highly exploitative and (from an indigenous perspective, potentially) genocidal desires of corporations like Monsanto, who are forcing indigenous farmers to abandon native corn in favor of genetically modified monocultural corn whose seeds are owned and controlled by Monsanto itself, one cannot afford to have such a narrow, linear, quantifiable and commodifiable view.

The Zapatistas are the living embodiment of Guattari's desire that "Ecology must stop being associated with the image of a small nature-loving minority or with qualified specialists" (Guattari, 2000, p. 52), but rather with "literally reconstructing the modalities of 'group-being,' not only through 'communicational' interventions but through existential mutations driven by the motor of subjectivity" (Guattari, 2000, 34). According to Guattari, we must reach more broadly to question "the whole of subjectivity and capitalist power formations" in the interest of nonlinear, rhizomatic epistemological systems in which the "three scales" Guattari delineates—mind, society, and the environment—are holistically integrated. As Guattari puts it, "Here we are talking about a reconstruction of social and individual practices which I shall classify under three complementary headings, all of which come under the ethico-aesthetic aegis of an ecosophy: social ecology, mental ecology and environmental ecology" (Guattari, 2000, p. 41). The Zapatista ecosophical position, then, is like Guattari's: one of global resistance to Integrated World Capitalism (IWC), but in a more positive and praxis-focused manner than are similarly theorized notions of Michael Hardt and Antonio Negri, Manuel Castells or Fredric Jameson. Thus, in Fig. 10.4, from a structure near the *Caracol* building in La Garrucha, we see a giant *caracol* with the words, "The Caracol of Resistance [is] a New Dawn," written in Spanish and Tzotzil, winding out into a snail wearing a *pasamontaña*.

Through their consistent and widespread use of murals with iconography, branding, magical realist imagery, appropriations of symbols from other revolutionary groups, and so on, all representing progressively their ideology, the Zapatistas implement successfully a truly transversal mode of education that transcends literacy in any one language, as it moves across numerous semiotic systems, to generate inclusive and expansive subjective territories that mutually reinforce the official and mobile territory of Zapatista culture as well as the distinct Chiapas and Mayan cultures of which it is also a product. As we have already noted, Zapatista ecosophy, like Guattari's, "does not totally exclude definition of unifying objectives," of which creating another, alternative world that itself enables and "fits" many other worlds along with and inside it, is a chief objective. Like Guattari, to reiterate further, they believe that creating such a world will "no longer be a question of depending on reductionist, stereotypical order-words," as in Trumps campaign slogan, "Make America Great Again!," "which only expropriate other more singular problematics and lead to the promotion of charismatic leaders" (Guattari, 2000, p. 34).

Art Against the "Capitalist Hydra"

Speaking at an international *encuentro* in 2015 through his newly adopted identity of Galeano (in honor of one of the founders of the EZLN who had been brutally assassinated the year before), the Subcomandante formerly known as Marcos declared with respect to his new *nom de guerre*, that "when Zapatistas name the life of those who are missing, they come to exist in a different way" (cf. Alonso, 2015). His words reflected those on a mural on a school building in Oventik, painted in honor of the forty-three Mexican college students who disappeared and are assumed to have been brutally murdered in 2014. "You are now us" ("*Ahora eres nosotros*"), it declared, the phrase—which likely also references the martyred Galeano, written over a child's school desk placed next to a freshly dug grave. At this *encuentro,* Galeano (aka Marcos) emphasized the collective nature of Zapatista organization that must continue "without selling out, until the capitalist system is destroyed." He went on, discussing the hydra-like powers of present-day neoliberal globalized capitalism: "It's an economic crisis such as no other seen before because it has turned the most basic elements—water, air and light—into merchandise… and the traditions and customs of the corrupt political class have moved to organized crime, not the other way around" (Marcos/Galeano, 2014). The resonance with Guattari's belief that neoliberal capitalism is today "delocalized and deterritorialized… extending its influence over the whole social, economic and cultural life of the planet" is unmistakable (Guattari, 2000, p. 50). Against this new capitalism, resistance must continue in the form of "organized disobedience" against the state and its capitalist allies and sponsors, while ensuring that within Zapatista society the opposite dynamic, "leading by obeying" (*mandar obedeciendo*) continues to define how politics is engaged by the community. In this regard, a major task of education is precisely to teach each new generation of Zapatista children the "discipline" of resistance (the Foucauldian allusion is impossible to miss), for which "critical thought" serves as a strategic component by teaching the community how to act as "sentinels" who can see the "storm coming" before everyone else, and thus show others—in and outside the Zapatista communities—how to survive it.

The idea of critical thought, of the kind epitomized by thinkers like Guattari, Deleuze, Foucault, and of course Adorno and the Frankfurt School, as a sentinel points to the equally important, complementary yet distinct role of art, which is precisely to act as a portal showing the way to the other world the Zapatistas claim is possible—reached precisely by constantly becomings-"more other" (as Marcos stated above) till one is transversally outside the system, living both literally and epistemologically in another dimension (the *caracol* as the geographic space, Zapatismo as the discursive identity space), in some-other-where-but-not-here-space. Zapatistas see capitalism's present "destruction of nature," as former EZLN fighter turned economist Rosa Albina Garavito described it (Marcos/Galeano, 2014), as a unique threat not just to the ways of life of indigenous communities in Mexico, but to the life of the planet itself. In fact, this belief has always been at the core of Zapatista thinking, from that January 1994 when they launched their still ongoing "global war for humanity and against neoliberalism" (*lucha por la humanidad y contra el neoliberalismo*, cf. Baschet, 2008), which is why their declarations and *encuentros* have long referred to the global network of progressive anti-capitalist forces as the "intergalactic," to highlight how large and far-reaching (to other worlds) the coalition against hyper militarized neoliberal capitalism—that is, the hydra—must be to have a chance to succeed.

For Immanuel Wallerstein, creator of world systems theory and a long-time supporter of the Zapatista movement, the hydra represents a new phase in capitalism that is increasingly dangerous, as Galeano summarizes him, precisely because it is in "a structural crisis and cannot return to its previous stage" (quoted in Alonso, 2015). Wallerstein and Galeano both stress the unparalleled importance of creativity in evening the odds against so powerful a force, particularly creativity that cannot be commodified (and in so being, co-opted and denuded of power) and thus domesticated and controlled [as has happened to too many liberatory cultural forms and/or sub-/countercultures, from hippies to hiphop (cf. Frank, 1997)]. To "remain in symbolic resistance" is to invite certain defeat, which is why critical thought must always be geared toward praxis. What is the conduit that turns critical thought into engaged praxis—in Guattari's language, "collective praxes" (Guattari, 2000, p. 64); that which enables its sociopolitical conductivity? Put simply: Art.

Guattari's thought is resonant with the viewpoints and strategies described here. As he explains it, "Post-industrial capitalism, which I prefer to describe as *Integrated World Capitalism* (IWC), tends increasingly to decenter its sites of the power, moving away from structures producing goods and services toward structures producing signs, syntax and—in particular, through the control which it exercises over the media, advertising, opinion polls, etc.—subjectivity" (Guattari 2000, p. 47). For their part, fighting against this dynamic, the Zapatistas have constructed a counter-assemblage of signs, syntax, and practices aimed at undermining, traversing around, and transcending the divisive, hierarchical and oppressive dynamics of neoliberalism. As their murals emphasize, horizontalism, "leading by obeying" (*mandar obedeciendo*), dying in order to live (*morir para viver*), creating a "world where many words fit" (*un mundo donde quepan muchos mundos*), with the focus explicitly on a kind of anti-power—to propose rather than impose (*proponer y no imponer*), represent and not supplant (*representar y no suplantar*), convince and not conquer (*convencer y no vencer*, construct and not destroy (*construir y no destruir*), serve others and not oneself (*servir y no servirse*), and work from below rather than "seeking to rise" (*bajar y no subir*)—are all Zapatista mantras for success. Ultimately, the Zapatistas consider their ideology (*Zapatismo*) "not [as] a new political ideology, or a rehash of old ideologies. Zapatismo is nothing, it does not exist. It only serves as a bridge, to cross from one side, to the other… There are no universal recipes, lines, strategies, tactics, laws, rules, or slogans. There is only a desire—to build a better world, that is, a new world" (from an undated statement by the Clandestine Revolutionary Indigenous General Command of the EZLN).

Coda: Against Adorno—Toward a Critical Artistic Praxis

Allow us to end this discussion by returning to the mural in La Garrucha on the *Caracol* building (Fig. 10.2). It features a giant Pink *caracol* with the ever-present "Caracol of resistance toward a new dawn" curled into its conch. Along with it are ears of corn and the typical disembodied male and female Zapatista heads. Crossing through the middle of the shell are two machetes, while the entire *caracol* is surrounded by trees also filled/budded with disembodied female and male heads. The *caracol* stands on top of a green meadow, on one side of which is a stage with a band of Zapatista musicians performing and on the other side are other communal buildings. Underneath the scene, in Spanish and Tzotzil is written "the way of the future" (*El Camino del futuro*).

The scene represented in this mural represents precisely the world the Zapatistas hope to create. It is at peace, it is fecund, it is progressive, and there are no signs of capitalism in it. This mural for us symbolizes the power of art not just to imagine futures yet to be realized, but to help create them. Its example offers a damning yet positive critique of Adorno's belief that in late capitalist society not only praxis has disappeared but the only way art can critique an increasingly oppressive, massified, and reified society is by "turning in on itself" (Adorno, 1967a, b; Abu-Manneh, 2015). Adorno's loss of faith in the emancipatory potential of art as praxis leads him to imagine that only the most austere and difficult art could force people to think critically about their situation. To the extent his belief is accurate that revolution itself has become impossible today given the all-encompassing power of capital and unprecedented weakness and co-optation of the working class, his aesthetic judgment might well have merit.

But the Zapatistas are not trying to overthrow the state, nor are they depending on the working class to achieve their goals. Hence, they are not constrained by the limits on the sociopolitical conductivity of critical art that he observed (cf. Cole & Bradley, 2016). What is equally clear is that we still do not have a theory of political art in the service of a revolution at a snail's pace, which seeks to create other worlds within autonomous spaces that can then serve as models for other communities seeking to escape the clutches of the capitalist hydra. The Zapatistas have certainly gazed upon the horrors of capitalist modernity, but they would never agree that "there is no longer beauty or consolation except in the gaze falling on horror, withstanding it, and in unalleviated consciousness of negativity holding fast to the possibility of what is better" (cf. Adorno, 2005, p. 25). Another world, and with it, other futures, is possible, and the goal of their praxis, from art to education to activism, is to "advance, slowly, making mistakes" along the road to these futures.

References

Abu-Manneh, B. (2015). Tonalities of defeat and palestinian modernism. *Minnesota Review, 85,* 56–79.

Adorno, T. (1967a). Arnold Schoenburg, 1874–1951. In *Prisms* (pp. 147–72), (S. Weber & S. Weber, Trans.). Cambridge, MA: MIT Press.

Adorno, T. (1967b). Cultural criticism and society. In *Prisms* (pp. 17–34) (S. Weber & S. Weber, Trans.). Cambridge, MA: MIT Press.

Adorno, T. (1991). The position of the narrator in the contemporary novel. In *Notes to literature* (Vol. 2, pp. 30–36) (S. Weber, Trans.). New York: Columbia University Press.

Adorno, T. (2005). *Minima Moralia: Reflections on a damaged life.* London: Verso.

Alonso, J. (2015). Critical thought versus the capitalist hydra. Internationalist 360°, 1 August 2015, available at https://libya360.wordpress.com/2015/08/01/critical-thought-versus-the-capitalist-hydra-2/. Accessed April 21, 2017.

Bahn, J. (2009). Marxism in a snail shell: Making history in Chiapas. *Rethinking History, 13*(4), 541–60.

Barmeyer, N. (2008). Taking on the state: Resistance, education and other challenges facing the Zapatista autonomy project. *Identities, 15*(5), 506–27.

Baschet, J. (2008). La Lucha por la Humanidad y Contra el Neoliberalismo, Hoy. *CETRI,* 20 November 2008, available at http://www.cetri.be/La-lucha-por-la-humanidad-y-contra?lang=fr. Accessed April 20, 2017.

Cole, D. R. (2014). Inter-collapse ... educational Nomadology for a future generation. In M. Carlin & J. Wallin (Eds.), *Deleuze & Guattari, politics and education: For a people-yet-to-come* (pp. 77–95). London: Bloomsbury.

Cole, D.R. (2017). Individuation, vitalism and space in the overseas study tour. *Higher Education Research & Development.* Online pre-publication https://doi.org/10.1080/07294360.2017.1374356.

Cole, D. R., & Bradley, J. P. N. (2016). *A pedagogy of cinema.* Rotterdam: Sense Publishers.

Christlieb, P. F. (2014). *Justicia Autónoma Zapatista: Zona Selva Tzeltal.* Mexico City: Ediciones Autónom@s.

Cunninghame, P., & Corona, C. B. (1998, October). A rainbow at midnight: Zapatistas and Autonomy. *Capital & Class, 22*(3), 12–22.

Davies, T. (2009, August). Doing good solidarity. *Chiapas Update.*

Deleuze, G., & Guattari, F. (1987). *A thousand plateaus: Capitalism and schizophrenia* (B. Massumi, Trans.). Minneapolis: University of Minnesota Press.

Esteva, G. (2010). The Oaxaca commune and Mexico's coming insurrection. *Antipode, 42*(4), 978–93.

Esther, M. (2016). The Zapatista Struggle against global neoliberalism. Dorset Chiapas Solidarity, May 15, 2016, available at https://dorsetchiapassolidarity.wordpress.com/2016/05/15/the-zapatista-struggle-against-global-neoliberalism/. Accessed March 11, 2018.

Evans, B. (2010). Life resistance: Towards a different concept of the political. *Deleuze Studies, 4*(Supplement), 142–162.

EZLN (EjércitoZapatista de Liberación Nacional). (2016). *Critical thought in the face of the capitalist hydra I Contributions by the sixth commission of the EZLN.* Brisbane, AU: PaperBoat Press.

Frank, T. (1997). *The conquest of cool.* Chicago, IL: University of Chicago Press.

Genosko, G. (2009). Afterword: Subjects matter. In B. Reynolds (Ed.), *Transversal subjects from Montaigne to Deleuze after Derrida* (pp. 262–71). Houndmills, Basingstoke, UK: Palgrave Macmillan.

Gregory, S. (2000). John Berger & Subcomandante Marcos peasants, parables and politics. *Third Text, 14*, 3–9.

Guattari, F. (1984). *Guattari, Félix. Molecular revolution: Psychiatry and politics (*R. Sheed, Trans.). Harmondsworth: Penguin.

Guattari, F. (2000). *The three ecologies* (I. Pindar & P. Sutton, Trans.). London and New Brunswick: The Anthlone Press.

Henck, N. (2016). *Insurgent Marcos: The political-philosophical formation of the Zapatista subcommander*. Raleigh, NC: Contracorriente.

Holloway, J. (2005). *Change the world without taking power*. London, UK: Pluto Press.

Levi, G. (2014). Death of a Zapatista – Neoliberalism's Assault on Indigenous Autonomy. Znet.com, June 1 2014, available at https://zcomm.org/znetarticle/death-of-a-zapatista/. Accessed March 10, 2018.

LeVine, M. (2005). *Why they don't hate us: Lifting the veil on the axis of evil*. Oxford, UK: Oneworld Publications.

LeVine, M. (2011). New Hybridities of Arab Musical Intifadas. Jadaliyya, October 29, available at http://www.jadaliyya.com/Details/24562/The-New-Hybridities-of-Arab-Musical-Intifadas. Accessed May 30, 2018.

Marcos, S. I. (2001). *Questions and swords: Folktales of the Zapatista revolution*. El Paso, TX: Cinco Puntos Press.

Marcos, S. I. (2007). *Beyond resistance: Everything*. Durham, NC: PaperBoat Press.

Marcos, S. I. (2005). *Conversations with Durito: Stories of the Zapatistas and Neoliberalism*. Brooklyn, NY.

Marcos S. I. (as Galeano), (2014). Adiós Subcomandante Marcos, hola Subcomandante Insurgente Galeano. Available at http://www.contrasentido.mx/activismo/2014/adios-subcomandante-marcos-hola-subcomandante-insurgente-galeano. Accessed May 4, 2017.

Nail, T. (2012). *Returning to revolution: Deleuze, Guattari and Zapatismo*. Edinburgh, Scotland: Edinburgh University Press.

Navarro-Smith, A. (2015). Leadership transformation and the exercise of power: Political divisions in San Jerónimo Tulijá, Chiapas. *Identities: Global Studies in Culture and Power, 15*, 528–549.

Reyes, A. (2015). Zapatismo: Other geographies circa 'The end of the World'. *Environment and Planning D: Society and Space, 33*, 1–17.

Reynolds, B. (2002). *Becoming criminal: Transversal performance and cultural dissidence in early modern England*. Baltimore: Johns Hopkins University Press.

Reynolds, B. (2003). *Performing transversally: Reimagining Shakespeare and the critical future*. New York: Palgrave Macmillan.

Reynolds, B. (2006). *Transversal enterprises in the Drama of Shakespeare and his contemporaries: Fugitive explorations*. Houndmills, Basingstoke, UK: Palgrave Macmillan.

Reynolds, B. (2009). *Transversal subjects: From Montaigne to Deleuze after Derrida*. Houndmills, Basingstoke, UK: Palgrave Macmillan.

Ståhl, O. (2016). Kafka and Deleuze/Guattari: Towards a creative critical writing practice. *Theory, Culture & Society, 33*(7–8), 221–235.

Vanden Berghe, K. (2009). The Quixote in the stories of subcomandante marcos. In D. Reindert & T. Dhondt, (Eds.), *International Don Quixote*. Amsterdam, NL: Rodopi, pp. 53–69.

Vargas-Santiago, L. (2015). Zapatista muralism and the making of a community. In D. Taylor & L. Novak, (Eds.), *Dancing with the Zapatistas: Twenty years later*. Durham, NC: Duke University Press, ebook, no pages numbers, available at http://scalar.usc.edu/anvc/dancing-with-the-zapatistas/index. Accessed April 21, 2017.

Prof. Mark LeVine is Professor of history at UC Irvine and Distinguished Visiting Professor at the Center for Middle Eastern Studies at Lund University, Sweden, and a columnist at Al Jazeera, where he is extensively covered the Arab uprisings and the Israeli Occupation. He is the author and editor of a dozen books, including most recently *One Land, Two States: Israel and Palestine as Parallel States* (2014), and a forthcoming book on the next 50 years of the Occupation.

Bryan Reynolds is Claire Trevor Professor of Drama at the University of California, Irvine. He has held visiting professorships at Queen Mary University of London; University of Amsterdam; Utrecht University; University of Cologne; University College Utrecht; Goethe University Frankfurt; UCSD; American University of Beirut; University of Tsukuba; and University of Nairobi, Kenya. He is the author of *Intermedial Theater: Performance Philosophy, Transversal Poetics, and the Future of Affect* (forthcoming 2016); *Transversal Subjects: From Montaigne to Deleuze after Derrida*; *Transversal Enterprises in the Drama of Shakespeare and his Contemporaries: Fugitive Explorations*; *Performing Transversally: Reimagining Shakespeare and the Critical Future*; and *Becoming Criminal: Transversal Performance and Cultural Dissidence in Early Modern England*; and editor of five books, including *Performance Studies: Key Words, Concepts, and Theories*.

Part IV
Further Issues in Transversality, Education and Globalization

Chapter 11
Alice's Adventures: Reconfiguring Solidarity in Early Childhood Education and Care Through Data Events

Susan Naomi Nordstrom, Camilla Eline Andersen, Jayne Osgood, Ann-Hege Lorvik-Waterhouse, Ann Merete Otterstad and Maybritt Jensen

Abstract In this chapter, we textually enact Guattari's transversality by charting the affects and intensities of a curated tea party performed at an educational research conference through a series of data events. We embrace (k)not-knowing, complexity, chaos, and desiring nonsense as depicted by Lewis Carroll's *Adventures of Alice in Wonderland*. We experiment with Alice's cartographies, temporalities, geographies, and bodies to generate spaces for more-than/other-than-human child/hoods. In doing so, we embrace and embody curious transversals in an attempt to rupture understandings of how early childhood education and care might relate to solidarity in a globalized time.

Keywords Childhood · Solidarity · Data events · Affective movements

Raven Writing Desks (Connecting)

"Why is a raven like a writing-desk?" – The Mad Hatter. (Carroll, 1916, p. 24)

We begin again with the Hatter's riddle that initiated a conversation about meaning what one says, and the queerness of time, at a down-the-rabbit-hole tea party in *Alice's Adventures in Wonderland* by Lewis Carroll. We begin again with the 2016

S. N. Nordstrom (✉)
University of Memphis, Memphis, USA
e-mail: susan.nordstrom@gmail.com

C. E. Andersen
Norway Inland University of Applied Sciences, Hamar, Norway

J. Osgood
Middlesex University, London, England, UK

A.-H. Lorvik-Waterhouse
University of Southeast Norway, Notodden, Norway

A. M. Otterstad · M. Jensen
Oslo and Akershus University College of Applied Sciences, Oslo, Norway

© Springer Nature Singapore Pte Ltd. 2018
D. R. Cole and J. P. N. Bradley (eds.), *Principles of Transversality in Globalization and Education*, https://doi.org/10.1007/978-981-13-0583-2_11

Nordic Educational Research Association's (NERA) conference theme of social justice, equality, and solidarity in education. We begin again at a tea party other than the mad one in *Alice's Adventures in Wonderland* where Hatter, March hare, and Dormouse crowd together at one corner of a long table crying "No room! No room!" as Alice approached them (Carroll, 1916, pp. 24–25), performed at the conference by a collective of researchers (Otterstad et al., 2016). We begin again with the global refugee crisis in which Western countries cried out "No room! No room!" to refugees that figured prominently then, and still now, in the media. We begin again with data events from this other tea party that still perform on us one year later. We begin again with a conference call.

Rupturing Solidarity: Solidarities-to-Come

> Within educational systems, individuals are selected to different life paths and layers of society. While education traditionally has been assumed to provide opportunities for individuals and groups, the segregation of education appears to be a threat to the promotion of equality and social justice.
>
> In Nordic welfare systems, the solidarity of the middle classes has been one of the factors that enable equal public education. But how do social processes such as marginalization and diversification affect the role of educational solidarity as a facilitator of social mobility? How do these processes change the economic, cultural and social bases of social justice, equality and solidarity in the field of education? What potential does education have for promoting these values? The 44th NERA Congress invites participants to analyze the dimensions of solidarity in education and educational research today. (NERA, 2016)

Our response to this invitation from NERA was the curation of the Helsinki tea party performance and the collective generation of this chapter. In both, we engage in risky yet critical questioning of the notion of solidarity in Early Childhood Education and Care (ECEC). Through art-activist examinations of the Norwegian Early Childhood Framework, the English Early Years Foundation Stage Curriculum, and the United Nations Rights of the Child, we consider how the subject position of "child" is created and recreated within these imposed frameworks. The production of the subject position "child," however, does not exist solely within these frameworks. "Child" is the result of geopolitical space-time-matterings that generate different "childs" (not children). Consequently, there can be no singular "child". Much like Alice and her potions that physically change her body, "child" is in moments, in bodily movement. Such a conceptualization of child resists traditional notions of solidarity that are grounded in essentialist notions of child that create a human-centered or human-only sense of solidarity. In this chapter, we offer no definitive generation of "child" or of "solidarity." Instead, we deliberately engage in moments and movements with "child" and "solidarity" and examine the ethics of such work by delving into and textually enacting "transversality" (Guattari, 2015a, b).

We do this with Carroll's (1916) first Alice book as this story was designed to be productive in the in-between spaces. The Alice book helps us to gesture toward "an account of the entire universe, its terrors as well as its glories: the depth, the surface, and the volume or rolled surface" (Deleuze, 1997, p. 22). In particular, we think Alice with and alongside the refugee crisis. Localized responses to this crisis manifest very differently within given communities, but educational spaces—including early childhood centers, kindergartens, nurseries—are particularly entangled with globalization and the challenges it presents to nation-states in terms of what education should be and do. Early Childhood Education and Care sits in politicized tension in various contexts (Dryden-Peterson, 2016). Hence, justice, equality, and solidarity, despite figuring in many nation-state ECEC policies, need to be reconfigured accordingly. With Alice, a different solidarity (than the one we think is at work in normatively defined notions of early childhood) might emerge, what we call a "solidarities-to-come."

In this chapter, we offer several data events; strange representations of "our connectedness in the process of changing concepts as lookouts for movements, trying to displace our thinking as one molecule spins itself onto the next as part of ongoing entanglements" (Andersen & Otterstad, 2014, p. 100), of the performance that contingently situates solidarities-to-come. First, however, we theoretically set the stage of our Helsinki tea party and the chapter, as enactments of transversality. Following this, we move with the affective pulls of those data events, affective residues that linger in our tea cups like pernicious tea stains that refuse to leave the cup even after washing. We think of this as writing in event–riddles or data events, because we were never quite sure what happened at our tea party with approximately 20 conference attendees, much less how to make (non)sense of it. Each data event is out of sync, a watch that tells what year it is (Carroll, 1916). Consequently, we generate nonsensical responses to those events and the ethico-onto-epistemological response-abilities that inhabit us in order to create affective movements toward solidarities-to-come.

Artistic Reconfigurations

What/who/where/when is Alice? Within the performative symposium, we embraced (k)not- knowing, complex chaotic becomings and desiring, as depicted in the *Adventures of Alice in Wonderland*. By falling down the rabbit hole, as it were, we attempted to reconfigure solidarities within ECEC. By working with and through Alice's adventures, and entangling her cartographies with our worlds as early childhood researchers (from a variety of geopolitical locations), our desire by reconfiguring solidarities was to generate bodily spaces for more-than/other-than-human child/hoods (Fig. 11.1).

We curated a tea party symposium as an artistic event—an interactive performance creating space...place...time... for thinking with images, artworks, theories, poetry and cuddly toys. Inspired by the artists Annette Messager, Rune Guneriussen, Tim Burton, and Vladimir Clavijo-Telepnev, we arranged, rearranged, and returned to the same setups of the tea party differently (Barad, 2007). Working with art-based strategies inspired by the DADA movement (Bishop, 2012), we sought to explore and question solidarity. Feedback loops as creative strategies, disturbances, shifts, and obstacles were a part of the unfolding of our symposium (Fischer-Lichte, 2008). The

Fig. 11.1 Tea party table

DADA artists based their movement on planned irrational behavior, eccentricities, anarchy, and cynicism not unlike the nonsense world Alice falls into in the under-world. It is a loss of self. Rules change, heads are chopped off, and language does not mean the same anymore. Things and animals can talk, the constant question-ing and requestioning, riddles without solutions, a surreal world filled with shadows and despair but also playfulness, spectacles, humor, and absurdities. A collision that invites new entanglements between involves systems or even causes them to collapse. Something is out of control…. Something is lurking in the outskirts…

In many ways, the tea party symposium was a series of transversal acts. Guattari (2015b) wrote, "Transversality is a dimension that tries to overcome both the impasse of pure verticality and that of mere horizontality: it tends to be achieved when there is a maximum communication among different levels and, above all, in different meanings" (p. 113). We disrupted the traditional vertical and horizontal symposium through our event-based data performance approach. Bodies and knowledge are nor-mally distributed in a hierarchical or vertical fashion, in which a scholar(s) selected by the conference organizing committee speaks about her expertise in a particular discipline. Audience members, those wishing to gain knowledge in a particular disci-pline, are seated facing the speaker. They are supposed to be silent and taking notes. The tea party symposium, however, modified this structure by redefining people's roles in the symposium and, by extension, the knowledge generated. The modifications sought to reorient both person and structure so that people could no longer be "fixated on themselves [or] never see anything *but* themselves" (p. 113, emphasis in original).

The tea party symposium unfolded with several obstructions, such as limitations of time and physical space. The assigned tea party room was at the end of a Greco-Roman statue lined hallway on the fourth floor. Two statues at the back of the room served as a panopticon-like gaze over the four rows of pew-like desks that were bolted to the floor. As we stood on pew-like desks, moved what furniture could be moved and experimented with stationary furniture, we considered how such a space configured not only the performance itself but also that of solidarities-to-come by introducing non-human elements into the notion of solidarity.

We engaged in a reconfiguring of solidarity through artistic action. The installation of oversized and regular-sized playing cards was placed throughout the hallway as an invitation to the space. A mobile whiteboard was flipped horizontally and dressed with lace cloth and a miniature tea set to become a tea party table. A dress hung from the window. The curtains were drawn. A long collage of maps, several meters long and sewn together—towns, deserts, lines, borders, and rules—was created by Ann-Hege before the conference and rolled out to divide the room. In addition, there were soft and bony toys, tea cups, and other ephemera which acted as live installations. The audience was instructed to fill out identity cards prior to being rendered access, a registration card with nation, names, status, and pass number. The queen (Maybritt) organized the audience by giving everyone a playing card and determined where people would sit once they entered the rabbit hole. The judge (Susan) perched herself on a large piece of furniture that allowed her a panopticon-like gaze over the many bits of the Helsinki tea party. Some aspects of the symposium followed traditional scholarly expectations; for example, a formal introduction to the performance was provided and throughout narrations on our theoretical framework was offered. However, these were interwoven with unexpected ruptures including a film with media images from the refugee crisis of children and others, another film on World Refugee Day 2015 (https://www.youtube.com/watch?v=owMAlvYj0GE), thinking-doing dialogues, the sound recording of a child reading a scholarly text in Norwegian, the humming of an ancient Norwegian poem, and an animation of a clock with its hands spinning at high speed.

Working creatively with obstructions creates openings for intensities, uncertainties, and a lack of control (Christoffersen, 2011). Investigating the/our/their discomforts of solidarities with non-human objects, Carroll's (1916) nonsense was entangled in the becoming rules of the rabbit hole. People were exposed to shifts in the rules, for example where to sit, and to deliberate the inconsistency in how, and to whom, cups of tea were (not)served during the symposium. "The artists force new behavior patterns onto the audience, often plunge them into crises, thus denying the spectators the position of distanced, uninvolved observers" (Fischer-Lichte, 2008, p. 50). However, the audience by their acceptances or denials also co-created the rules and experimentations. Simply put, the audience and other events that happened during the performance questioned new/other moves of solidarity. The audience by their acceptances or denials were also co-creating the rules and experimentations with *coincidence* which foregrounded the questioning of new/other moves of solidarity (Damkjær, 2006; Deleuze, 1990).

Through films, our theatrical performance, and the physical arrangement of the room, we sought to articulate Deleuze's (1990) ideas about becoming, events, and paradox (here represented by the "heap" paradox). He wrote:

> The event is coextensive with becoming, and becoming is itself coextensive with language; the paradox is thus essentially a 'sorites,' that is a series of interrogative propositions which, following becoming, proceed through successive additions and retrenchments. Everything happens at the boundary between things and propositions. (p. 8)

We examined child refugees through art in order to manifest the idea that "there are bodies with their tensions, physical qualities, actions and passions, and the corresponding 'states of affairs' These states of affairs, actions, and passions are determined by the mixture of bodies" (Deleuze, 1990, p. 4). Our work with refugee children sought to realize how we are complicit in refugee politics that result in very real states of affairs that affect us all. For, as Deleuze wrote "all bodies are causes–causes in relation to each other and for each other" (op cit., p. 4). Through becomings, events, and paradox we created a space for ourselves and audience members to consider the important political-onto-epistemological response-abilities we have as researchers, educators, and activists to grapple with the complexities that (might and do) shape collective responses to the 'right way' to engage with solidarity, equality, and justice in ECEC.

Likewise, this chapter seeks to do similar work. We weave between the data events of the tea party symposium and how we are thinking through these events, events that still churn our bodies with possible thoughts. In so doing, we textually enact transversality in this chapter. We decenter authorial power by creating affective dimensions about ECEC and solidarity. To do this work, we share data events (A Helsinki Tea Party and Diesel Fumes Solidarity) and images (presented throughout the chapter) from the tea party symposium. Following each data event, we experiment with it so as to open continuous rethinking and new dialogues (Guattari, 2015b). Also, we draw mainly from feminist scholarship to decenter citational practices that uphold the patriarchy (Ahmed, 2017; Cole, 2011), possibly one of the most rigid vertical and horizontal organizing structures in academia. Guattari (2015a) in his description of transversality called for a politics of science "that is closer to the eco-systems of everyday life and yet with a grasp of the major stakes for the planet" (p. 134). Our politics of science is woman-centered, as we are all self-identifying women and feminists. Likewise, our grasps of the world around us are intimately linked with feminism and, by extension, feminist theorists. Our work with feminist theorists is very much situated in our individual research and in the communities in which we live. While we all inhabit the same world, we come from different countries, regions of those countries, and cities. Consequently, our work in this chapter brings about different creations as hybrid mixtures from these different locations. While Guattari (2015a) offered the following in terms of urban life and environmental, social, and mental ecologies, we think his words can be extended to our work in both the tea party symposium and this chapter about ECEC and solidarities-to-come. He wrote, "[e]nviornmental ecology, social ecology and mental ecology will never be able to result in major creations if they are only cultivated in one country, one neighborhood, indeed even just a continent of the well-off" (p. 134). Likewise, we believe that generative innovations in ECEC and solidarities-to-come must emerge from multiple places rather than singular locations with singular readings of feminism, such as we demonstrate here through the tea party. In this chapter, we stay with the trouble (Haraway, 2016) of our feminist globalized existence to create a different story about ECEC and solidarities-to-come.

> Alice: I wonder if I've been changed in the night. Let me think. Was I the same when I got up this morning? I almost think I can remember feeling a little different. But if I'm not the same, the next question is 'Who in the world am I?' Ah, that's the great puzzle!" (Carroll, 1916, p. 7)

A Helsinki Tea Party

Ann Merete looks out for Camilla—*I wonder if I/she thinks across and against solidarity with Alice - can you imagine how you/me can generate new thinking-connections of pastpresentpresence into new affective dimensions. And as such, I wonder - what might the Rabbit hole offer to avoid reproducing a stereotypical construction of solidarity – longing for a non-representative diffractive thinking including the materiality/ties of solidarities? Do you think this is not NON/SENSE and are there leakages and potentials to embrace the unknown and reconsider the not yet known solidarity to come?* Ingold (2000) *inspires walking, seeing and knowing as unfinished wayfaring processes, which may open for movements and to being affectively moved. My thinking needs to be/come experimental, curious, imaginative, responsible; reworking inspirations of solidarities.*

Camilla*: ... in my worldview together with WONDERland there is no ORDER to claim. Nothing can ever be trusted, not even when you are sleeping. The Rabbit hole is a time/place/space without limitations – nothing is ever impossible, and solidarity can continually become re-territorialized – as new potential set in motion* (Fig. 11.2).

Jayne, the Narrator*: ...to re-create, re-think and re-feel materials of solidarities beyond pedagogical systems that repeat structures and familiar categories and patterns - is by* Haraway (1997, p. 265) *articulated as; ... "models of solidarity and human unity and difference rooted in friendship, work, partially shared purposes, intractable collective pain, inescapable mortality, and persistent hope...."*

Ann Merete*:...living hers/ours/their theories is hard work – and reconfiguring solidarities in a geopolitically strange, unknown, unpredictable, chaotic world – in and with-wonderland/the underworld – raises questions about - trust? – rationalities? – care? – openness? – moral and affirmative and nomadic thinking...* (Braidotti, 2006; Roy, 2003). *When Alice is falling down the rabbit hole - other worldly worlds appear in time and space. Hybrids and queering creatures care and create solidarity to come. When the white rabbit and friends threw stones at the "huge Alice" -*

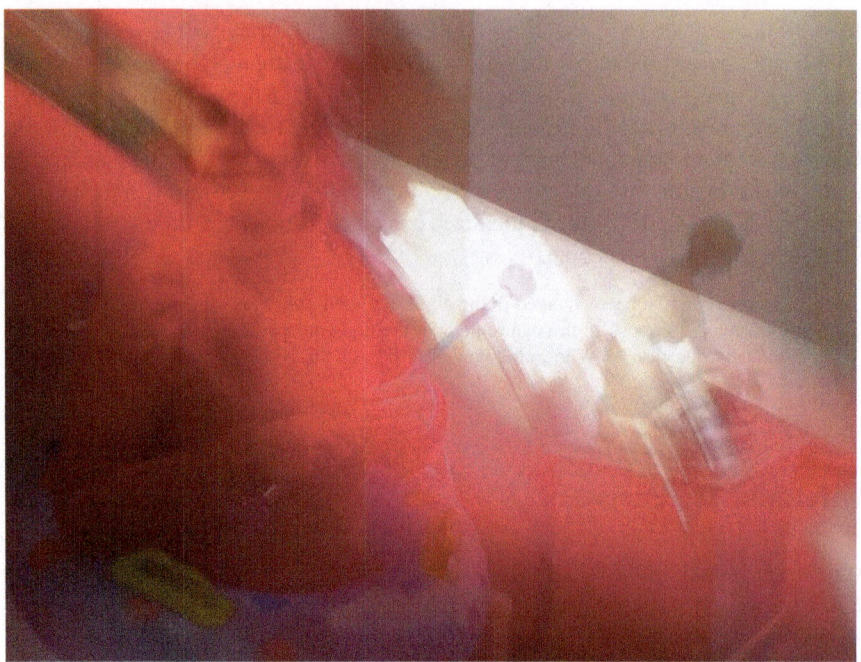

Fig. 11.2 Queen of Hearts: "... my logic is: "Cut off their heads..."

the stones transform and become rescue-cakes - the impossible happens again and again....

Maybritt, the Queen; ... *catch them and ... put them in prison!*

Ann Merete: *Politics of solidarity to come - is experimenting with location – embodiment- and partial perspectives - embracing more-than-human worlds. Such solidarity/worlds are connecting and sharing critical knowledges and webs of cyborg networks together – not as right or wrong – more as a manifest; be-ing-in-common-world-with* (Giugni, 2011). *Which also brings in what Karen Barad and Donna Haraway introduce as a living response-ability. This worldly-becoming-with reduces the possibilities to think of humans as singular, self-contained individual beings.*

Camilla: *A be-ing-in-common-with solidarities expands for multiple communities, fleeting, temporary manifestations* (Hird, 2009) *with/in multispecies –community, including all of those with whom our livelihood interrelate with and are interdependent on.*

Ann Merete: *Solidarity is about response-ability, about the possibilities of mutual response, which is not to deny, but to attend to power imbalances. Walking, seeing and knowing as unfinished wayfaring processes are entangling solidarity around families, children, borders, economy/capital, hesitation, desperation, silencing, death – are also circulating around what is valued as solidarity in the Norwegian Early Childhood Framework plan.*

The Kindergarten shall be based on fundamental values in the Christian and humanist heritage and tradition, such as respect for human dignity and nature, on intellectual freedom, charity, forgiveness, equality and solidarity, values that also appear in different religions and beliefs and are rooted in human rights. Respect for human dignity and nature, compassion, forgiveness and solidarity are values that appear in many different religions and beliefs and that are rooted in human rights (Ministry of Education and Research, 2011, p. 38)

Jayne, the Narrator: *She/they/we are not sure that these majoritarian words from the Norwegian Framework Plan have the potential to embrace the unknown and reconsider the not yet known solidarity to come.*

We suggest that the spatial arrangement of the room in which the performance took place became a model. As Haraway (2016) articulates:

A model is a work object; a model is not the same *kind* of thing as a metaphor or analogy. A model is worked and it does work. A model is like a miniature cosmos, in which a biologically curious Alice in Wonderland can have tea with the Red Queen and ask how this world works, even as she is worked by the complex-enough, simple-enough world. (p. 63)

The majoritarian desk-pews locked the guests at the risky tea party into place. Much like Alice who spent some time stuck in a room much too small for her body, guests' bodies shifted on the wooden pew desks. Different freedoms were sought in such small spaces. Simply put, we attempted to manifest and question the complex and simple ECEC frameworks, or worlds, that seek to stratify childhood becomings. In reconfiguring a risky model of ECEC, a cosmos, "tying together human and nonhuman ecologies, evolution, development, history affects, performances, technology, and more" (p. 63), the performance sought to articulate a messy becoming-with of solidarities-to-come.

Taking Risks with Alice, Mad Hatter Logic and Feminist New Materialist Thinking

The riddle "Why is a raven like a writing-desk?" posed by the Hatter in *Alice's Adventures in Wonderland* (Carroll, 1916, p. 24) has no answer. We also have no answer. Working with theories and philosophies that encourage praxis of "intellectual and worldly intervention" that "affects the material, habitual, every day and minute dimensions of living" (Bunz, Kaiser, & Thiele, 2017, p. 9) potentially frees us from the limitations of critique. Rather, we can embrace (k)not-knowing, wherein there are no clear answers or better solutions to the problems posed. But we can cling to a vision of critique as necessary and transformative. These perspectives are occupied with, "How to matter and not just want to matter?" (Haraway, 2016, p. 47). In this chapter, we have chosen to label these perspectives feminist new materialist thinking. In this performative text, and also in the tea party performance, we have worked with and through the ideas of Barad (2007), Braidotti (2009, 2012) Haraway (2008, 2016), Ahmed (2006), and van der Tuin (2015). Also, the work of Gilles Deleuze and Félix Guattari has been helpful. We hence draw from all these, and more, in our risky commitment to cut through habitual flows of life.

Hence, although primarily interested in feminist new materialist thinking, we "drink" and "eat" from various theoretical frameworks as these allow us, like cakes and drinks allowed Alice, to differ, to figure differently, "us" as critical researchers engaging with solidarity and hence avoiding the dangers of stratifying solidarity. These perspectives allow us to create risky riddles involving "child," solidarity, and ECEC. They "allow" us to approach solidarity in unconventional ways with Alice-inspired defying (nonsense) logic. They produce questions: "What do we need to do to bring the affirmative positivity of the future into play right now?" and "How to be responsible for all that lives?" (Braidotti, 2016). Questions that, just like the Mad Hatter's riddles, have no answer yet are generative for us as an "on-the-ground collective" (Haraway, 2016, p. 51) when we strive for more liveable worlds. Guattari (2015a) called for a rethinking of the politics of science "that is closer to the eco-systems of everyday life and yet with a grasp of the major stakes for the planet" (p. 134). By drinking and eating from a variety of theoretical frameworks that create different kinds of questions, we begin to develop our politics of science, one that is intimately linked to Guattari's vision. Desires find lines of flight through questions rather than answers. Risks are taken as these desires carry us to thinking and doing life differently in an effort to make a more just world. Thus, thinking with questions we have no intention of answering might be extremely powerful and co-productive of movement and transversal ethical lines.

These risky riddles insist we reconfigure our methodologies and rethink the relationship between theory and practice. It demands that we grapple with the inseparability of thinking-feeling-doing to move beyond simple representationalism. And we do this because it is part of processes of cultivating response-ability—it matters what ideas we use to think other ideas (Haraway, 2016). It offers a mode of enquiry that has deep and lasting affects and reshapes what we understand data might be, what research becomes, and the never-endingness of our "radical curiosity" (Haraway, 2016, p. 37). It demands a need for constant thoughtfulness about our decentered place in the world. As Haraway says (2016, p. 35): "It matters what thoughts think thoughts. It matters what knowledges know knowledges. It matters what relations relate relations. It matters what worlds world worlds. It matters what stories tell stories." In urging that we stay with the trouble, Haraway (2016) goes on to stress that the greatest danger we face is thoughtlessness; working within new materialist feminist frameworks insists heightened thoughtfulness: We become wayfarers, become entangled, track lines, cultivate response-ability, and recognize our place within the world. When there is no road map of enquiry, enquiry creates opportunities for reconfiguring precisely because we can experiment with new paths (Guattari, 2015a). Such a mode of enquiry is dynamic and creative, uncertain and surprising. It pushes us to think more and other—to break free from sedimented ways of knowing and being. By working to reconfigure established ideas, structures, practices, and policies in early childhood contexts that inform what we think we know, the familiar becomes strange and so offers generative possibilities to think about solidarity in early childhood in other ways.

We recognize that such work is risky. Risk, however, is a productive concept to practice our reconfiguring with. Buikema (2017), writing on risk and cultural critique, suggests that critical inquiry in a globalized and neoliberal world necessitates to "account for unforeseen and uncontrollable effects" and practice a willingness to "be risky" (p. 135). She goes on to claim that cultural critique is "a praxis of negotiation, response-ability and accountability" (p. 135). When we performed the Alice-inspired tea party engaging with solidarity at a time when "refugees in crisis" were on innumerable front pages, many unforeseen and uncontrollable things happened. Both during and after the performance, the attending delegates were invited (and even forced) to be part of the various scenes; e.g., to pass a border control, drink tea, move around, draw and speak. Without going into detail here, some of the responses adhered somehow to risk. As a collective, we were not prepared for this. Perhaps, we were prepared for the feeling of doing something risky, but not so much for a sense of scattered resistance toward being risky and the ethics of such work (which we develop in the following sections).

When thinking of risk together with the Nordic democratic values (e.g., solidarity, social justice, love of one's neighbor) that by law are working as the basis for pedagogical practices in Nordic ECEC, we wonder if our attempts at reconfiguring solidarity produced, for some, an embodied feeling that we were betraying the Nordic ECEC community, with its values and traditions that many think are currently under pressure. Hence to practice risky-ness is to also risk being accused of betraying one's community. However, we believe this is a risk worth taking as solidarity must be different, transnational, and less Eurocentric. There are, we suggest, many ways to "parry the risk of being perceived as a traitor of Western democratic practices" (Buikema, 2017, p. 140), and one might be to "horizontalize material-discursively produced inequalities" (van der Tuin, 2015, p. 7) and through this bring matter more intriguingly into the project of creating more liveable worlds for all that lives.

Diesel Fume Solidarity

"At any rate, I'll never go there again!" said Alice, as she picked her way through the wood. "It's the stupidest tea-party I ever was at in all my life!" Just as she said this, she noticed that one of the 26 trees had a door leading right into it. "That's very curious!" she thought. "I think I may as well go in at once." And in she went. (Carroll, 1916, pp. 25–26) (Fig. 11.3)

Susan, the Judge:
There is no essential past, no essential event or moment that can act as a unifying entity. Each event is unique for each of us. Each perspective is different. We perspective so differently.
How will we perspective this moment now that this event has passed through us? Is this event singular?
I think not.
It is plural.
It has passed and is passing through us differently.
Constituting us differently as we perspective it differently.
Even as we breathe the same air

Fig. 11.3 Diesel fume solidarity

we have nothing essential to hold onto.
Nothing essential from which we can define ourselves.
Another relation to further complicate our movements through space and time.
Has this cabinet of curiosity made us better or worse?
Probably both.
We cannot define ourselves against better or worse.
Perhaps we define ourselves through better and worse.
Always working for a better
solidarity-to-come, these curious women say.
Perhaps we seek out moments of solidarity to pass through us and make us think
so differently that we work toward something better.

Punctuated by the occasional roar of chainsaws and tractor engines, different conceptualizations of solidarity materialized, dissipated, and rubbed up against each other during the discussion following the performative tea party. Over 3000 Finnish farmers had materialized on the Presidential Square adjacent to the tea party, a University of Helsinki classroom. The farmers, many of whom traveled to Helsinki in their tractors, had arrived to protest the European Union's sanctions against Russia (McCann, 2016) and to call on the Finnish government to improve their livelihoods. For some conference attendees, this protest was the quintessential and unquestionable example of a globalized solidarity. Solidarity could be nothing else. How could others not be seduced by the diesel fumes of this solidarity that poured into the classroom? Fumes of an essentialized solidarity suffocated conversation. Like the plasticity of Alice, her ability to reorient and change with no predefined form as a final, the performance had no moral, no singular way of thinking about solidarity.

Alice Ethics

> Duchess: "I can't tell you just now what the moral of that is, but I shall remember it in a bit." "Perhaps it hasn't one," Alice ventured to remark. "Tut, tut, child!" said the Duchess. "Everything's got a moral, if only you can find it." (Carroll, 1916, p. 28)

Prior to the first Alice text (originally published in 1865), children's books tended to contain "highly moral stories in which horrid things happen to children who do not obey the very strict rules enforced upon them by adults" (Lovett, 2015, p. xii). In such texts, children are sinful beings to be righted by moral adults. The adults in the Alice texts, however, are unreliable, crazy even (Lovett, 2015). Rather than being silenced by educative moralizing adults, Alice criticizes the adults. She talks back. Hence, Alice texts appear to create an onto-epistemological ethics rather than a moralizing children's story. In Deleuzian thinking morality and ethics are two different things. The first is about judgments, and the latter is about creativity (Marks, 2005). There are no judgments to be made in *Alice's Adventures in Wonderland*. Rather, each event of the book creates different ways of knowing and being. Each event creates a different Alice so much so that she does not even know who she is anymore. The Alice text can be read as an ethics that maximizes, in creative ways, connections so that the possibilities of life can be expanded (Marks, 2005).

If we could just think one impossible thing, be creative with an aim to maximize connections, could habits of the earth that morality as something we already know or try to find does not disturb, become something else? Solidarities-to-come demand such an ethics. Such an ethics is a process of orienting and disorienting oneself in whichever assemblage one finds oneself. Ahmed (2006) wrote:

> The starting point for orientation is the point from which the world unfolds: the 'here' of the body and the 'where' of its dwelling. Orientations, then are about the intimacy of bodies and their dwelling places…Bodies may become orientated in this responsiveness to the world around them…In turn, given the histories of such responses, which accumulate as impressions on the skin, bodies do not dwell in spaces that are exterior but rather are shaped by their dwellings and take shape by dwelling. (p. 8)

Alice continuously orients herself in Wonderland. Each chapter moves with orientations and disorientations. Her body shape-shifts into other iterations of Alice. Each Alice brings about certain possibilities and delimits others. An alluring drink shrinks her and makes her impossible to be heard. Another drink enlarges her to the point where she is stuck within a space. Multiple Alices move through Wonderland. Similarly, multiple "childs" move through the world. However, the playfulness of Alice takes a serious turn for today's children. Potions are not so innocent, as is evidenced by recent chemical attacks in Syria. Polluted water and soil poison children. Global warming erases the most vulnerable of lands. These issues are environmental, social, political, and economic markers of the Anthropocene in which "like it or not, we are in the string figure game of caring for and with precarious worldings" (Haraway, 2016, p. 55).

Like Somerville (2016), we agree that "the question for educational research and praxis then becomes how to educate children of the Anthropocene in recognition of human entanglement in the fate of the planet" (p. 1162). We argue that a constant state of orienting and disorienting is warranted in the Anthropocene. As transversals of culture, politics, geographies, economic systems, and education situate children in the Anthropocene, we must be ethically-epistemologically-ontologically response-able to children of the Anthropocene. This work cannot be done with existing schemas (Guattari, 2015a, b). Guattari called for "'research into research', an experimentation with new paths for the constitution of collective assemblages of enunciation" (p. 135). The children's lives that are sometimes sacrificed for economic gains and political presents in the Anthropocene ask us researchers to experiment and to reconfigure childhood that is entangled, messy, risky, and response-able to humans, non-humans, and nature. This work will be full of riddles as we make "the conditions that must be created" (p. 135). This work will be full of fruitful failures (Guattari, 2015a, b). Just like Alice, we will experiment, create new conditions, and adjust to the solidarities-to-come.

Solidarities-to-Come

We attempted "to position research as 'astride' science, art, and social communication" (Guattari, 2015a, b, p. 135) in our performance. We created rhythms from philosophy, art, performance, and Early Childhood Education and Care. In discussing ecology, Guattari wrote that "environmental ecology, social ecology, and mental ecology will never be able to result in major creations if they are cultivated in one country, one neighborhood, indeed even if a continent of the well-off" (p. 134). From different cities and neighborhoods in Norway, to the UK, to the USA, we came together as wayfarers to create solidarities-to-come. While we acknowledge that we do come from well-off continents, ECEC looks different in each of our respective countries. Each country's, city's, and neighborhood's ECEC differs. For example, in Memphis, where Susan resides, there is no universal Early Childhood Education and Care. ECEC is reserved for those who can pay for private schooling. Federally funded programs such as Head Start exist for economically disadvantaged families, but are woefully underfunded. Simply put, Memphis, Early Childhood Education and Care is quite different from that of Oslo, Norway, or London, England (Fig. 11.4).

Different geopolitical locations and transversal disciplinary work created rhythms of solidarities-to-come as we responded to our everyday ecosystems in our Helsinki performance. Our everyday ecosystems, however, are always already linked to the global. In many ways, we sought to articulate in both the performance and this chapter "a collective awareness of the fact that the means of changing life and of creating a new style of activity, new values, are within reach, at least in our developed societies has not been gained" (Guattari, 2015a, p. 133). In both the performance and this chapter, we have sought to articulate a different collective assemblage of

Fig. 11.4 Solidarities-to-come

enunciation of both Early Childhood Education and Care and solidarities-to-come. This assemblage is at once global and local and is constantly arranging itself. As it moves with other assemblages, ethics is always in play as questions without answers proliferate. For example, in both designing the performance and writing this chapter, we have had to balance individual demands of time, politics of early career scholars, feminisms, art, research, and so on. We have moved hesitantly across space-time-matterings, listening to the questions, letting them give us pause as we do our ethical best with an ethics that always comes too late. These movements and pauses constitute a different awareness as we have worked together across the globe. As we practice solidarities-to-come in this chapter, we acknowledge that they are always works in progress and never perfect. Solidarities-to-come are verbs that undo our very way of knowing and being and create a different way of doing research and writing about Early Childhood Education.

Haraway (2016) wrote "Alone, in our separate kinds of expertise and experience, we know both too much and too little, and so we succumb to despair or to hope, and neither is a sensible attitude" (p. 4). Our Helsinki performance also included unanticipated bodily rhythms, the rhythms created by 3000 protesting farmers outside the university building. For some members of the audience, the diesel fumes that slowly entered the performance sought to stratify a creative ethical performance of a solidarity-to-come. However, these fumes and rhythms were always already multiple and co-present. There is no singular farmer. Each farmer is co-present with other materials and mortals. Likewise, there is no singular child, Early Childhood Education and Care, or solidarity. Our Helsinki performance and, by extension this chapter, manifests a becoming-with, a "material semiotics [that] is always situated, someplace and not noplace, entangled and worldy" (Haraway, 2016, p. 4). This work is rife with risky onto-ethico-epistemological response-abilities. Our response-abilities in this chapter aimed to loosen the systems of thought, create more lines of flight, and provide different fumes to smell.

down the rabbit hole
into the depth…
underground assemblages…
roots, darkness, breathing earth…
weightless in transit
…. connecting underworlds

WONDERLAND

nomads of transversality….
crossing non existing borders
wayfarers on waves without passports….
re-routing maps of desire….
haunting new territories…
… travelers, adventurers, conquerors, refugees…
trans-human…

backwards across lines of reality
cutting through memories…
escaping into surreal…

NO
MANS
LAND

never never land
haunting utopia…
dreaming of other futures…
entangling different pasts …

… rabbit hole presence

References

Ahmed, S. (2006). *Queer phenomenology: Orientations, objects, others*. London: Duke University Press.

Ahmed, S. (2017). *Living a feminist life*. Durham, NC: Duke University Press.

Andersen, C. E., & Otterstad, A. M. (2014). Researching the assemblage of cultural diversity in Norway challenging simplistic research approaches. *International Review of Qualitative Research, 7* (1), 93–110.

Barad, K. (2007). *Meeting the universe halfway: Quantum physics and the entanglement of matter and meaning*. London: Duke University Press.

Bishop, C. (2012). *Artificial hells. Participatory art and the politics of spectatorship*. London: Verso.

Buikema, R. (2017). Risk. In M. Bunz, B. M. Kaiser, & K. Thiele (Eds.), *Symptoms of the planetary condition: A critical vocabulary* (pp. 135–141). Lüneburg: Meson Press.

Bunz, M., Kaiser, B. M., & Thiele, K. (2017). Introduction: Symptoms of the planetary condition. In M. Bunz, B. M. Kaiser, & K. Thiele (Eds.), *Symptoms of the planetary condition: A critical vocabulary* (pp. 7–17). Lüneburg: Meson Press.

Braidotti, R. (2006). *Transpositions: On Nomadic Ethics*. Cambridge, UK: Polity.

Braidotti, R. (2009). Introduction. *Australian Feminist Studies, 24*(59), 3–9. https://doi.org/10.1080/08164640802645117.

Braidotti, R. (2012). *Nomadic theory: The portable Rosi Braidotti*. New York City, NY: Columbia University Press.

Braidotti, R. (2016, December 4.). *The philosopher's zone/Interviewer: J. Gelonesi*. The posthuman, RN, available at: http://www.abc.net.au/radionational/programs/philosopherszone/.

Carroll, L. (1916). *Alice's adventures in Wonderland*. New York, NY: Samuel Gabriel Sons & Company.

Christoffersen, E. E. (2011). Spilleregler og benspænd. In *Peripeti - tidsskrift for dramaturgiskestudier 16-2011*(135–141). Arhus: Århus University.

Cole, D. R. (2011). The actions of affect in Deleuze—Others using language and the language that we make …. *Educational Philosophy and Theory, 43*(6), 549–561.

Damkjær, C. (2006). Tilfældighed i bevægelse. In L. Engel, H. Rønholt, C. S. Nielsen, & H. Winter (Eds.), *Bevægelsens poetik - om den æstetiske dimension i bevægelse* (pp. 150–178). Copenhagen: Museum Tusculanums Forlag, University of Copenhagen.

Deleuze, G. (1990). *Logic of sense*. (M. Lester with C. Stivale, Trans.). New York, NY: Columbia University Press.

Deleuze, G. (1997). *Essays: Critical and clinical*. Minneapolis, MN: University of Minnesota.

Dryden-Peterson, S. (2016). Refugee education: The crossroads of globalization. *Educational Researcher, 45*(9), 473–482.

Fischer-Lichte, E. (2008). *The transformative Power of Performance: A new aesthetics*. New York: Routledge.

Giugni, M. (2011). Becoming worldly with the early years learning framework. *Contemporary Issues in Early Childhood, 12*(1), 11–27.

Guattari, F. (2015a). Transdisciplinarity must become tranversality (A. Goffey, Trans.). *Theory, Culture, & Society, 33*(5–6), 131–137. https://doi.org/10.1177/0263276415597045.

Guattari, F. (2015b). *Psychoanalysis and transversality: Texts and interviews 1955–1971* (A. Hodges, Trans.). Boston, MA: MIT Press.

Hird, M. (2009). *The origins of sociable life: Evolution after science studies*. Palgrave Macmillan.

Haraway, D. (1997). Modest_Witness@Second_Millenium. FemaleMan_Meets_OncoMouse. London, UK: Routledge.

Haraway, D. J. (2016). *Staying with the trouble: Making Kin in the Chthulucene*. London: Duke University Press.

Haraway, D. J. (2008). *When species meet*. Minneapolis: University of Minnesota Press.

Ingold, T. (2000). *The perception of the environment. Essays on livelihood, dwelling and skill*. London. Routledge.

Lovett, C. (2015). Introduction. In L. Carroll's (Ed.), *Alice's adventures in Wonderland and Through the looking-glass and what Alice found there* (pp. i–xv). New York City, NY: Penguin Books.

Marks, J. (2005). Ethics. In A. Parr (Ed.), *The Deleuze dictionary* (pp. 87–89). Edinburgh: Edinburgh University Press.

McCann, P. (2016). Finnish farmers stage protest outside government buildings. *The Irish Farmers Journal*. http://www.farmersjournal.ie/finnish-farmers-stage-protest-outside-government-buildings-203042. Accessed March 24, 2017.

Ministry of Education and Research. (2011/2017). (Kunnskapsdepartementet). *Norwegian early childhood framework plan*. Oslo: Ministry of Education.

Nordic Education Research Association. (2016). Call for papers. Available at http://blogs.helsinki.fi/nera-2016/. Accessed July 24, 2017.

Otterstad, A. M., Osgood, J. Andersen, C. E., Jensen, M., Lorvik-Waterhouse, A. H., & Nordstrom, S. (2016). *Reconfiguring early childhood solidarities symposium/performance*. NERA Conference, Helsinki, Finland.

Roy, K. (2003). *Teachers in Nomadic Spaces: Deleuze and curriculum*. Geneva: Peter Lang Inc.

Somerville, M. (2016). The post-human I: Encouraging "data" in new materialism. *International Journal of Qualitative Studies in Education, 29*(3), 1161–1172. https://doi.org/10.1080/09618398.2016.1201611.

van der Tuin, I. (2015). *Generational feminism: New materialist introduction to a generative approach*. London: Lexington Books.

Susan Naomi Nordstrom is Assistant Professor in Counseling, Educational Psychology and Research at University of Memphis, USA. Her research agenda includes post-methodology, ontology, and human and non-human relationships in a variety of settings.

Camilla Eline Andersen is Associate Professor in Early Childhood Education in the Faculty of Education and Natural Sciences, Norway Inland University of Applied Sciences, Norway. She is currently engaged in how to perform critique when installed in new material feminism and various philosophies of difference. In her later writings, she focuses on professionalism and race in early childhood installed in a Deleuzoguattarian philosophy of desire.

Jayne Osgood is Professor of Education (Early Years & Gender) at Middlesex University, London, England. Her present research methodologies and research practices are principally framed by feminist new materialism. She is developing transdisciplinary theoretical approaches that maintain a concern with issues of social justice and which critically engage with policy, curricular frameworks, and pedagogical approaches. Through her work, she seeks to reconfigure understandings of the workforce, families, and "the child" and "childhood" in early years contexts.

Ann-Hege Lorvik Waterhouse is a Ph.D. candidate at the University College of Southeast Norway, Norway. Her art-based research focuses on experimental artistic processes with a variety of materials and genres in visual arts in early childhood research.

Ann Merete Otterstad is Docent/Professor in Early Childhood Pedagogy and Cultural Diversity at the Institute of Early Childhood, Oslo and Akershus University College of Applied Sciences, Norway. Her concern is post-methodology, experimenting *in/with* post-human and affective theories in early childhood research and challenging what and when data are working.

Maybritt Jensen is Associate Professor in Scenic Art at the Institute of Early Childhood, Oslo and Akershus University College of Applied Sciences, Norway. Her arts-based research focuses practice-led research on performing art forms as circus and performance for very young children.

Chapter 12
The Ontological Plurality of Digital Voice: A Schizoanalysis of *Rate My Professors* and *Rate My Teachers*

Eve Mayes

Abstract Online evaluations (like *Rate My Professors* and *Rate My Teachers)* have been celebrated as forming wider publics and modes of accountability beyond the institution and critiqued as reinforcing consumeristic pedagogical relations. This chapter takes up the websites *Rate My Professors* and *Rate My Teachers* as empirical entry points to a conceptual discussion, after Félix Guattari, of the ontological plurality of digital voice, and its associated refrains and universes of reference. I turn attention from analysis of the *effects* of these digitized student evaluations to the *moment of their formation*—for example, when a student's finger clicks on a particular star rating. Refusing to separate human bodies from objects, environment and affects, inside from outside, 'real' from 'digital', I consider how emerging modes of online student evaluations of teaching shift individual and collective relations to 'expression' and subjectivity. This chapter also explores the transversal possibilities of de-subjectification offered in when the digital is understood as *intercesseur*: intersection/intercession.

Keywords Student evaluations of teaching · Student voice · Rate my professors
Guattari · Schizoanalysis

Student Evaluations of Teaching

Student evaluations of teaching (SET) in tertiary institutions have been used formatively to assess pedagogical progress, and summatively, as part of educators' performance review (Coladarci & Kornfield, 2007, p. 1). These evaluations have evolved from formal in-class evaluations on printed paper to online evaluations still administered and analysed by the institution. In recent years, online evaluations of tertiary educators and school teachers have shifted territories—beyond the institution, to sites like *Rate my Professors*, owned by MTV, "a subgroup of the multinational

E. Mayes (✉)
Deakin University, Geelong, VIC, Australia
e-mail: Eve.mayes@deakin.edu.au

© Springer Nature Singapore Pte Ltd. 2018   195
D. R. Cole and J. P. N. Bradley (eds.), *Principles of Transversality in Globalization and Education*, https://doi.org/10.1007/978-981-13-0583-2_12

media group Viacom" (Yoon, 2015, p. 112). In sites like *Rate My Professors* (http://www.ratemyprofessors.com), students can "rate" individual educators, their "level of difficulty", and, as an optional rating, "hot" or "um, no" in reference to "appearance". In the Australian version of *Rate My Teachers*, students select up to five stars in relation to the prompts: "easy", "helpful", "exam difficulty", "clarity", "textbook use", "knowledgeable" and an overall recommendation (from "nope" to "totally"). An open-ended text box invites students: "In your own words please describe your experience with [name of educator]". This "online rating phenomenon" has become a "globalized trend" (Villalta-Cerdas, McKeny, Gatlin, & Sandi-Urena, 2015, p. 182).

The extent to which students participate in sites like *Rate My Professors, Rate My Teachers,* and other comparable sites and the extent to which ratings on this site inform students' decisions about courses is debatable. Student statements about tertiary educators articulated on digital platforms may have, arguably, shifted from these particular websites to other online territories—for example, public Twitter feeds and private Facebook pages designed for particular university and course cohorts. It is not my purpose here to map these various de- and re-territorializations, nor to write about the most current manifestation of (what I will term) *digital voice* about tertiary teaching[1]. Rather, *Rate My Professors* and *Rate My Teachers* are employed as empirical entry points to a conceptual discussion, after Félix Guattari, of the ontological plurality of digital voice. Sites like *Rate My Professors* and *Rate My Teachers* are analysed as mutations of the disciplinary mechanisms of the corporate university in the control society (Deleuze, 1992). I consider, too, other transversal approaches to institutional analysis.

Online evaluations (like *Rate My Professors)* have been asserted to strengthen the "participatory agency" of student evaluation in a wider public beyond the university (Yoon, 2015, p. 110). Declarations of a "return to the freedom and flow of the Greek agora" (Hearn, 2010, p. 421) suggest that more pedagogical ethical practices can be engendered through transparent, open evaluation (Arvidsson & Piertesen, 2013). However, concerns have been raised about student evaluations of teaching, both in their conventional institutional administration, and in the mutations of these evaluations to websites beyond the control of the institution.

A trajectory of literature on university-administered student evaluations of teaching (SET) with technicist concerns works with statistical analyses, mapping the relationships between evaluation indices, and recommending ways to enhance evaluation validity and reliability and minimize bias (Marsh & Roche, 1997; Uttl, White, & Gonzalez, 2017). The content and construct validity of university-administered SET are called into question for the effects of variables including gender, physical attractiveness, grading leniency, and workload on student ratings (e.g., Onwuegbuzie et al., 2007). Coladarci and Kornfield's assessment exemplifies the logics of such technicist approaches to SET: "when instruments are properly constructed and the resulting data thoughtfully considered, SET can be an important source of information for both improving teaching and informing personnel decisions" (2007, pp. 1–2).

---

[1]While it is beyond the scope of this chapter, further work is needed that maps the reach of these sites, and how they conspire with data mining industries.

Like university-administered student evaluations of teaching (SET), sites like *Rate My Professors* have also been subject to studies of their validity and bias. A common concern raised is the influence of attractiveness ("hotness"), grading lenience, gender, race and sexuality on student evaluations, with a range of studies exploring their effects on the 'validity' of rating results (e.g., Clayson, 2014; Davison & Price, 2009; Freng & Webber, 2009; Legg & Wilson, 2012; Subtirelu, 2015). It is argued that reading previous reviews shapes students' subsequent perceptions of educators (Lewandowski, Higgins, & Nardone, 2012), and that these evaluations impact on educators' "self-efficacy" (Boswell, 2016). Those defending the validity of sites like *Rate My Professors* note the close correlation of these ratings with university-administered SET (e.g. Kindred & Mohammed, 2005).

Critical scholars have approached university-administered SET and sites like *Rate My Professors* and *Rate My Teachers* with an eye to what these evaluations produce, and the shifts in institutional culture that these evaluations suggest. They have raised concerns about how summative student evaluations, and sites like *Rate My Professors* and *Rate My Teachers* have reconstituted pedagogical relations and undermined democratic education. Mockler and Groundwater-Smith (2015) analyse documents relating to student evaluation of teaching and learning in ten Australian universities for their implied conditions of speaking, listening, skills, attitudes and dispositions, systems, and organizational culture. They conclude that these documents reconstitute students as "clients as opposed to being learners" and as "consumers of an educational product" (pp. 93–94). By extension, sites like *Rate My Professors* and *Rate My Teachers* could be deemed even more problematic, profiting from advertising alongside student ratings. Gonzales and Núñez (2014) describe the institutional drive to become a "world class" university in a "competitive transnational market", including the display of positive student evaluation statistics, as indications of the emergence of the "ranking regime" (p. 2), and raise concerns about how these practices (re)shape the work of those who work for these institutions. Ritter (2008) argues that, of more importance than the "measurable accuracy" of *Rate My Professors,* is how the website "reflects the increasingly convergent interests of consumer culture and academic culture, shaping the ways that pedagogy is valued and assessed by students within the public domain" (p. 259). These contemporary critiques can be brought into productive conversation with Deleuze's *Postscript on the Society of Control* (1992), to explore the transmutation of the (corporate) university from an enclosed site of monitoring and linear progression through time-space, to a state of "perpetual metastability" (p. 5). In societies of control, individuals are opposed "against one another" (p. 5); the "operation of markets" becomes "the instrument of social control" (p. 6); the corporation (university) emphasizes "supposedly necessary reforms" (p. 4), "perpetual training" and "continuous control" (p. 5).

Such critical approaches do not assume that there might be a more 'reliable', 'valid' or 'unbiased' mode of evaluating tertiary teaching and learning; rather, they examine the subjectivities and regimes that are *generated* alongside the formation of student evaluations of teaching. Ritter (2008) describes the cultural phenomena of online evaluations as a "public, polyvocal enterprise encompassing ideologies that are often internally competing" (p. 260). Fielding (2011) argues that students have become "data sources" for "high performance learning organization"; "student voice" has become a way to foreground individual choice, and reinforces broader patterns of consumer citizenship (pp. 10–11). These critiques have directly contrasted "marketi[zed]" and "commodif[ied] versions of 'student voice'" (in these modes of SET) with "genuine attempts to create and embed democratic processes" and relationships through the radical reconfiguration of human bodies in institutions (Mockler & Groundwater-Smith, 2015, p. 93).

This chapter's analysis of *Rate My Professors* and *Rate My Teachers* extends this critical work, but turns attention from the *effects* of these digitized student evaluations to the *moment of their formation*—for example, when the student's finger clicks on a particular star rating. Working with Guattari's schizoanalysis, which was developed as an extension of transversality, I examine the ontology of *digital voice*—how it forms and its existential vectors. I seek to unwind an implicit assumption in much previous work on SET that there are atomized subjects (student, and teacher, for example), separated from objects (a paper survey, or a digital survey completed on an electronic device). I also critically question the assumptions that evaluations composed by students either correspond with a 'reality' of the pedagogical relation or not, and that SET formed digitally are necessarily less democratic than the face-to-face encounter.

Schizoanalysis

Guattari's (and Deleuze's) schizoanalysis is concerned with dismantling the "'ontological iron curtain between being and things'" (Pierre Levy, cited by Guattari, 1995b, p. 8) wherein things and beings are seen as separate. Such an approach enables analysis of the multiplicitous forces at work in online SET sites in producing particular subjectivities, such as the economics of capitalism, with implications for analysing pedagogical relations. Guattari rejects a view of subjectivity "in which each person is shut inside a monad and is then forced to construct a means of 'communication'" (Guattari, 1995b, p. 12)—frustrated students, for example, who must find a way to 'express' themselves to their tertiary educator. The individual is, instead:

> [...] something like a 'terminal' for processes that involve human groups, socio-economic ensembles, data processing machines etc. Interiority establishes itself at the crossroads of multiple components, each relatively autonomous in relation to the other, and, if needs be, in open conflict. (Guattari, 2000, p. 758)

The *I*, then, that speaks and is addressed, or that is addressed and types a response, is an *event* existing each moment at the intersection of a range of processes (Guattari, 1995a, b). What is produced in the moment of verbal (or typed) articulation are collective *agencements* of enunciation (Deleuze & Guattari, 1980/1987, pp. 80–85)—arrangements that exceed the human 'expressive' agency of saying how I feel and meaning what I say. *Agencement*, the French word frequently translated as *assemblage*, is a noun and a verb; *agencements* are simultaneously "arrangement[s]" and the act of "arranging" of heterogeneous corporeal and incorporeal, actual and virtual, elements (translators' note 30, in Guattari, 2000, p. 82).

Entwined with this rejection of the atomized subject, Guattari (and Deleuze) contest the psychoanalytic conception of the Oedipal subject who intrinsically *lacks*—associated with their critique of followers of Freud and Lacan (see Bryant, 2006). According to a reductionistic mode of analysis, the student *lacks* skills, knowledge, pedagogical satisfaction, or writes a negative evaluation because of particular felt deficits in instruction. In turn, the educator must satisfy the desire of the Oedipal student subject who *lacks* skills, knowledge, and pedagogical satisfaction. For Guattari (and Deleuze), in contrast, desire precedes the social production of *lack*; desire is affirmative and productive, connecting flows and generating differences (Cole & Bradley, 2014). Desire "is always assembled" (Deleuze & Guattari, 1980/1987, p. 229), investing in social relations and immanent conditions. This approach does not deny *lack* in pedagogical relations and educational institutions—*lack,* rather, is "created, planned and organized in and through social production" (Deleuze & Guattari, 1983, p. 28). A schizoanalytic approach examines the *agencements* that produce particular e/affects: how desire becomes reconstituted as *lack,* as well as the other lines of possibility simultaneously at work.

Schizoanalysis studies the machinic systems at work in the production of utterances (verbal or typed) and the subjectivities that these systems produce (Guattari, 1989/2013). Guattari's close attention to technological machines is useful for the study of *digital voice*. He moves beyond a "machine as anathema" approach that worries that "technology is leading us to a situation of inhumanity and of rupture with any kind of ethical project" (1995b, p. 8). The technological machine is connected "with other machinic systems which are not themselves technological"; there are also linguistic, social, economic, aesthetic, biological, music, logic, cosmic and eco-systemic 'machines' (Guattari, 1995b, p. 9). For Guattari, the atomized subject becomes a multiplicity in arrangement with these machinic systems. Guattari's interest in technological machines is not (only) in their representational content—for example, their transmission of a student's inner thoughts about an educator. The interest in machines is in their entangled relations with emerging modes of *subjectification*[2]—that is, how technological machines become imbricated in processes of capturing and stratifying subjects.

Attending to the machinic enables an analysis of the composition of *digital voice*—in its machinic processes of subjectification—beyond the atomized subject separate from computer, and beyond a normative pre-evaluation of the corrupting influence of the technological machine. Refusing to separate human bodies from

---

[2]I spell this word as *subjectification* after the spelling used in translations of Guattari and Deleuze and Guattari's work cited in this chapter. I acknowledge, however, a distinction between *subjectification*: "a thoroughly stratified or captured position", and *subjectivication*: "subjective operations which, although operating within social machines, use the processes of these social machines to form lines of escape from them" (Murphie, 2001, p. 1315). For Murphie, both concepts "involve one's implication in contemporary social machines" and both are "pragmatic" (Murphie, 2001, p. 1315). Both processes may be at work in manifestations of *digital voice*, as I argue below.

objects, environment and affects, inside from outside, 'real' from 'digital', I explore how emerging modes of online student evaluations of teaching shift individual and collective relations to expression and subjectivity, and proliferate combinations of subjectivities in relation to education and the educator: *client-learner-consumer-student-friend*. These shifts may be connected to and may open up universes of reference (see below); they may engender subjectifications that are liberating and/or potentially damaging.

Digital Voice: A Concept

Voice is what is spoken from collective *agencements* of enunciation—bodies, affects, discourses, environments, matter, objects, histories, visions—rather than the 'expression' of an individual human subject (Deleuze & Guattari, 1980/1987, pp. 80–85). In *Schizoanalytic Cartographies* (1989/2013), Guattari uses the word *voix/voie* for voice/pathway—with the French allowing a "homophonic link between path and enunciation" (p. 3). To combine *voice* with *digital*—to form the concept of *digital voice*—is to productively entwine the 'subjective' and 'material' (which were never separated), and to conjoin the utterance with the path(s) of its formation. Guattari borrows from Pierre Levy the conception of the machinic as "interface", a 'hypertext'" (1995b, p. 8). The "word-processing machine", Guattari argues after Pierre Levy, "completely changes one's relationship to expression"—its "interfaces [...] compose and singularize this new universe of reference: writing, the alphabet, printing, computing, the laser printer, Linotype, database, image bank, telecommunications" (Guattari, 1995b, p. 11).

Digital voice, then, is constituted in the interfaces of body, subjectivity, machine, website, among other elements—as curser is moved to a star rating, finger taps mousepad, score enters system, stars illuminate. To explore the constitution of *digital voice* is to explore its ambivalences; accelerations and mutations may not always be in the direction of emancipation nor devastation alone. Guattari and Deleuze's concept of the refrain becomes helpful in these explorations of the movements of star ratings, affects, histories, desires, and futures.

In thinking about *digital voice* as forming in star ratings on sites like *Rate My Professors* and *Rate My Teachers,* I consider the refrains (*ritournelles*) that order entwined existential and digital territories. There are digital paths *I* habitually traverse each morning—through email accounts, social media sites, and their hyperlinked lines of drift—before I re-open a Word document from the previous day. These are "ways of doing things, the little gestures, [...] the embodied patterns, that make up our existence" (Walkerdine, 2013, p. 760). These paths are ritualized, part of my existential (re)orientation to the world, to feeling 'held' again in it each morning. Through these territories (made and re-made each day), there are *refrains*—rhythms that temporarily create order from chaos (Deleuze & Guattari, 1980/1987). Like the lullaby sung by the child when the child feels afraid, the refrain generates a temporary feeling of security (Deleuze & Guattari, 1980/1987, p. 299). Refrains, for Deleuze and Guattari, are not only musical, but can be sensory, discursive, or semiotic, for instance, Proust's refrain of dipping a biscuit in tea and its associated comforting memories, a familiar word spoken, or the friendly face emerging that brings with it a sense of equilibrium (Guattari, 2000, p. 31). These refrains have an "existential function" (Guattari, 1995b, p. 10). Refrains develop "into territorial motifs and landscapes", even as alterations are introduced as refrains move (Deleuze & Guattari, 1980/1987, p. 323).

It is not the case, however, that individuals devise their own refrains; Guattari argues that we become "'captured'" by [our] environment, [...] by the refrains that go round and round in [our] heads" (Guattari, 2008, cited by Pindar & Sutton, 2008, p. 5). The star rating is a refrain that has emerged and moved with and by the proliferation of digitized evaluations—these are evaluations not only of educators, but also of Ebay buyers and sellers, hotels, AirBnb places, Uber drivers, Amazon products, and so on *("was this answer helpful?")*. The refrain of the star rating affects the movements we make—*I* pause when booking accommodation online if I cannot find previous star ratings for the host or hotel. The star rating, alongside the price tag, constitute my feelings of security in my consumer choice of where to stay. The star rating is a refrain in my consumer subjectivity, built on the "founding myth of capitalist subjectivity": "'I am the master of myself and of the universe'" (Guattari, 1989/2013, p. 26). After (or during) an unpleasant experience of a service, the capacity to complete a star rating offers the promise of having done a public service for future potential consumers. The star rating as refrain offers to protect the potential consumer from a potentially disagreeable encounter, "intoxicat[ing]" and "anaesthetiz[ing]" with "a collective feeling of pseudo-eternity" (Guattari, 2000, p. 34).

Beyond the semiotics of the star, the questions asked on sites like *Rate My Professors* and *Rate My Teachers* serve as a grid that curtails the relations that are possible. In *Dialogues,* Deleuze and Parnet lampoon the imperative to "'explain oneself'" in the conventional interview, conversation or dialogue, where the interviewee must respond to questions that they have not invented (Deleuze & Parnet, 2006/1977, p. 1). We might think, here, of the pre-formulated SET or *Rate My Professors* question to be answered by the student. The question becomes a "grille [...] such that everything which does not pass through the grille cannot be materially understood" (Deleuze & Parnet, 2006/1977, p. 20). The student, for example, is compelled to rate the educator's "exam difficulty" and "textbook use"—but the educator may not have set an exam, nor used a textbook, and "difficulty" may be the goal of the pedagogical exchange. Deleuze and Parnet find "particularly stupid" the question, "'What are you becoming?'" (or *'How has this course changed you?'*) since, "as someone becomes, what he is becoming changes as much as he does himself" (Deleuze & Parnet, 2006/1977, p. 2). The aim in the face of such questions, then, becomes to "get out" (Deleuze & Parnet, 2006/1977, p. 1)—to avoid completing a student evaluation, or to avoid reading student evaluation responses.

We might, then, analyse how the star rating as a refrain, and the question as a grille, have become part of processes of ordering educational territories, and the universes of reference that accompany sites like *Rate My Professors* or *Rate*

My Teachers. Guattari, in his essay, *On Machines,* describes the *"universes of reference"* that develop around a machinic system, by which he means "ontological heterogeneous universes, which are marked by historic turning points, a factor of irreversibility and singularity" (Guattari, 1995b, p. 9). *Rate My Professor* and *Rate My Teacher* are semiotically connected to institutional geographical and pedagogical territories, institutional evaluations, histories of pedagogical relations—that have formed in relation to particular associations between bodies, machines, subjects, worlds. Guattari notes the connections between shifts in learning language for children and shifts in the universes of reference of a word-processor:

> [C]hildren who are learning language from a word-processor are no longer within the same types of universes of references as before, neither from a cognitive point of view (of how there may be another organization of memory, or rather memories…), nor in the order of affective dimensions and social and ethical relationships. (1995b, p. 11).

Likewise, it might be argued that tertiary and secondary students engage with *Rate My Professors* and *Rate My Teachers* within different universes of reference to those previously associated with pedagogical evaluative practices. Below, I suggest some of the universes of reference associated with online SET.

Clicking on the name of my university on *Rate My Teachers*, I am asked: *"In your own words please describe* [University name]. *What do you want the world to know?"* It is promised that my digital utterance will be amplified—"the world" will come to "know" what this particular institution is like. This could be described as a *universe of reputation,* as an extension to previous work on the "digital 'reputation' economy" (Hearn, 2010) and the "digital reputation society" (Yoon, 2015). The evaluator becomes, in the production of an evaluation, a "'prosumer' of data related to the reputation of others", to be consumed by others (Yoon, 2015, p. 109). In the simultaneous production of a rank or list (for example, of educators at an educational institution), the student (and the educator) locates their self in this universe of reference. The educator (and student) is to study these lists according to the logics of the society of control: "the brashest rivalry [is] a healthy form of emulation, an excellent motivational force that opposes individuals against one another and runs through each, dividing each within" (Deleuze, 1992, p. 5). To produce a rating, and read a rating, is to "simultaneously individuate and fit ourselves into the logic of the market; we find our 'selves' in the list" (Hearn, 2010, p. 429). In these universes of "academic consumerism" (Gregory, 2011, p. 169), these ratings and reports become folded in with self-constructed accounts of the entrepreneurial educator subject (who includes student evaluation data in their performance review). These ratings and reports become entwined with normative evaluations of future pay scales. They become threaded into promotional statements used to market the educational institution as capable of satisfying the desire of the Oedipal student subject who *lacks* pedagogical satisfaction.

A simultaneous dulling and activation is at work in such processes, that may be paralleled and distinguished from Guattari's discussion of the television. In *Chaosmosis,* Guattari describes the work of the television: when watching television, "I exist at the intersection", of "perceptual fascination" that almost hypnotises, captivated with the "narrative content" while laterally aware "of surrounding events (water boiling on the stove, a child's cry, the television…)", and occupied by "a world of phantasms" in "daydreams" (1995a, pp. 16–17). Guattari continues: "My feeling of personal identity is thus pulled in different directions"—the "refrain that fixes me in front of the screen" rules in this instance (1995a, p. 17). An online evaluation of teaching may seem, in contrast to the television, to enable the evaluator to actively construct their own narrative, to activate their own pedagogical daydreams, to articulate their own institutional fascinations. Yet, the vocabulary and signs for constructing an account of pedagogical relations are circumscribed to the categories and linguistic prompts of the website *("easy", "helpful", "textbook use"*…). These star ratings and linguistic categories become a refrain of tedious repetition—students may be invited to complete multiple student evaluations of teaching each semester, filling these in (amidst the cacophony of other star rating systems) automatically, without thought[3]. Guattari argues that "[c]apitalistic subjectivity" forms through the "controlling and neutralizing [of] the maximum number of existential refrains" (2000, p. 34). In SET, and sites like *Rate My Professors* and *Rate My Teachers,* the number of existential refrains (to describe the educator, the student, and their immanent relation) are circumscribed, curtailed to enable maximum efficiency in institutional analysis (for SET) and data mining (for sites like *Rate My Professors*). While decentred flows of power, where the student can discipline the educator, offer "a multiplication of the anthropological angles" on questions of pedagogical quality and effectiveness, these may be accompanied by "a growth of particularisms and racisms" (Guattari, 1989/2013, p. 1). These machinic processes of subjectification may reinforce a seemingly inevitable cycle of hierarchies and antagonisms, and narrow what is understood to be teaching, learning, and pedagogy: what is formed in the interfaces between students, educators, matter, signs, worlds.

Transversal Possibilities

Creative interventions, or "new weapons" (Deleuze, 1992, p. 4), are necessary in order to disrupt these refrains and their universes of reference. To consider alternative possibilities relating to pedagogical evaluation, this final section takes up Guattari's interest in transversal institutional experiments in clinical practice. In his political activism and clinical practice at the La Borde clinic (see Dosse, 2007/2010; Genosko, 2002, 2003), Guattari jumbled and re-worked conventional clinical hierarchies, "seek[ing] something that runs counter to the 'normal' order of things": transversal relations and "dissident vectors" where "other intensities […] form new existential configurations" (Guattari, 2000, p. 30). I extend this work to consider the openings potentialized by greater attention to pedagogical *agencements* beyond the humanistic student/educator relation alone.

---

[3] Acknowledgement and thanks to one of the anonymous reviewers for suggesting this point.

Guattari's *transversality* exceeds both "pure verticality [reified hierarchies] or simple horizontality [flattened 'democracy']" (Genosko, 2009, p. 51), by introducing "specific and tangible" "variations in relationships that disrupt, rework but also productively inhabit hierarchies" (Ringrose, 2015, p. 399). The aim, in Guattari's clinical practice at La Borde, was to experiment with *agencements*, to see what might happen differently with a slight tweak, with an introduction of something new—towards new existential and institutional configurations. In experiments like "cook for a day", where a patient with psychosis was repositioned in another role (cook), shifts were effected not only in human relations, but also in relations of food matter, people, machines and space. Such creative productions of new relations were oriented towards the future (to what might be) rather than the past. Rather than returning to analyses of individual or collective past (Oedipal) causes of present problems, these interventions are aimed to create forward looking movements—directed towards virtual futures where the new is fashioned (Cole, 2014).

Guattari's clinical creative experiments might be juxtaposed with contemporary pedagogical work that reworks pedagogical relations in educational institutions. Fielding, a long-term advocate for "radical collegiality" in education (1999), has described work that seeks to reconfigure student/educator relations as a "transformative 'transversal' approach" (2001, p. 124). Cook-Sather, Bovill and Felten (2014) have written about their recent interventions in tertiary settings that seek to "draw on students' insights not only through collecting their responses to our courses but also through working with them to study and design teaching and learning together" (p. 1). They do not dismiss course rating processes, but rather frame them as a potential "starting point for expanding into a more collaborative, sustainable student-faculty partnership orientation towards assessment" of particular units or courses (p. 188). They describe a re-positioning of "both students and faculty as learners as well as teachers" (p. 7) as "radical—even counter-cultural" (p. 1), contrasting this work to the "student-as-consumer model that has become increasingly prevalent in higher education" (p. 7). These are "partnerships" that require students and educators to step "out of traditional roles" (p. 9) and to work processually (p. 195), for example, to co-design a unit or course, dialogue about the progress of a course, and collaboratively evaluate the course. We might compare this work to the La Borde interventions; the co-production of curriculum and relations is oriented forwards (to what might be) rather than only backwards (to the past semester). These interventions are, potentially, cautious combinations of capacities that open up curricula and pedagogy towards new refrains and universes of reference beyond the consumeristic student/teacher binary.

Collective (Digital) Assemblages of Enunciation?

However, interventions like La Borde's "cook for a day" and the interventions discussed by Cook-Sather, Bovill and Felten (2014) are arguably institutionally-initiated, engineered by teams of clinicians, counsellors, or educators, with the patient or student perhaps less aware initially of the institutional experiment that is about to transpire. In analyses of contemporary institutional evaluative interventions, there may also be an anthropocentric focus on student/educator subjectivities and human relations—a logic that, if we meet face-to-face, the relation will necessarily be more life-affirming. A profound ecosophical shift is needed in order to shift contemporary consumeristic styles of thought: experimentation with and analysis of the interconnections of environmental (and digital) ecologies, social ecologies, and mental ecologies (Guattari, 1996, p. 264).

Established categories (such as 'evaluation', 'teaching' and 'learning') need to be displaced through reworking material, digital and social arrangements. Guattari writes:

> What I am precisely concerned with is a displacement of the analytic problematic, making it drift from systems of *statements* and preformed subjective *structures* toward *Assemblages of enunciation* able to forge new coordinates for reading and to 'bring into existence' new representations and propositions. (Guattari, 1989/2013, p. 17, emphasis his).

Yet, how might we move beyond questions of how to improve the technical validity of SET, or how to impede the mutations of sites like *Rate My Professors*? Further creative experimentation is needed institutionally, and beyond institutions, in an attempt to displace the present analytic problematic. Further interrogation is needed of what environmental, digital, social and corporeal conditions enable and generate the invention of "new coordinates" that "'bring into existence'" novel pedagogical relationalities and evaluative practices (Guattari, 1989/2013, p. 17). To suggest the potentiality of attending to moments of micropolitical, transversal movement, I turn to a contemporary example. In this example, we glimpse an affirmative re-constitution of pedagogical relations—even as this moment is quickly recaptured.

In a recent study where I invited tertiary educators to construct a narrative of *"something that you did as part of your tertiary teaching to explore, challenge, disrupt or experiment with the ideas of 'evaluation' and 'feedback'"* (see Mayes, under review), one educator ('Scott', a pseudonym) gave an account of using the video recording function on his university's online learning platform:

> I trialled with [students], initially not providing students a choice: "Right, you're going to receive audio feedback [on their assignment work]. Within that audio feedback somewhere, I will subsume your grade, so you have to listen to it." [...] I tried that and, you know, students seemed to respond well to that. [...] [T]he first years all would say, "Oh, really enjoyed that". It was about how it was novel; it was different, it was about an engagement with me. [...] The novelty of it was good, the fact that it was immediate, and I emailed it to them. So, they clicked on it, and they listen[ed] to it immediately. [...]
>
> [T]his is just one person's comment: that, "I didn't get a very good grade but I like that you were supportive in your feedback" – there's an emotional, there's a tonal, you know, you can talk about, "look, I get a sense of what you're saying here but [...] – I think you should articulate it this way" or "hey this is the section where you really need to develop your own...." There's a supportive voice through that, that perhaps isn't necessarily available or perceived in a written feedback, I don't know. [...] That was the sense I got from that individual's verbal feedback [to me]. [...] [J]ust looking at words – they could be written by anyone, but if they're hearing my voice and they've got that connection with me that there's a more of a supportive tone. That's the feeling I sort of got with that individual's comments

– that even though they hadn't done particularly well, they didn't feel like all hope is lost. [...] It was "Oh okay [Scott] sort of understands - Okay, yeah I still feel supported through this stuff."

The digital video recording function serves as an *intercesseur*—a French word that is often translated as 'mediator', but that may be better translated as "intersection/intercession" (Stivale, 2008, p. 41). It is not so much that Scott recording his verbal voice allows the 'tone' to be transmitted without alteration to the student, who can then more 'accurately' interpret the intention of Scott's feedback. Rather, the pathway of formation—an utterance spoken in Scott's office and captured and transmuted with digital video recording apparatus, moving and played back by the student in another place and time—produces what Scott names a "supportive voice". This *digital voice* is different from the initial utterance—with an emergent pathway of formation, transmutation, and reception.

Stivale (2003; 2008) has eloquently described the pedagogical work forming between Claire Parnet, Deleuze's former student, and Deleuze, in the co-authored book *Dialogues II* and the documentary *L'Abécédaire de Gilles Deleuze, avec Claire Parnet [Gilles Deleuze's ABC Primer, with Claire Parnet]* (Boutang, 1996). According to Stivale, it is in the "interchange between teacher-student as well as the assemblage to which their exchange gives voice" that "hierarchical rapport" is "reverse[d] and scramble[d]"— "that is, of just who is teaching and learning" (Stivale, 2003, p. 33). Thought congeals between the two of them—Claire Parnet is an *intercesseur* to thought—in arrangement with a growing list of other *intercesseurs:* "AND Félix, AND Fanny, AND you [Deleuze], AND all of those whom we speak, AND me [Parnet]" (Deleuze & Parnet, 2006/1977, p. 26).

To extend Stivale's discussion of pedagogical *intercesseurs,* working with Scott's account of the video recording of his voice, it is not only human bodies who serve as *intercesseurs* in the production of thought. The digital camera and microphone participate in the generation of a video recording of Scott's 'feedback.' The speakers or earphones, that play this recording when the student taps the ▶ icon, contribute to the co-production of pedagogical thought between Scott, the student and others—as an interface or extension. New refrains—classroom refrains repeated but shifted to another territory—may be in formation as *digital voice* moves along these pathways. Universes of reference are also at work: "historic turning points" circulating around the work of which Scott's (recorded) voice speaks—past classroom conversations mingle with Scott's (recorded) discussion of the student's work in its singularity.

Simultaneous subjectifications and de-subjectifications may be at work in these movements of *digital voice.* As the student 'sees' Scott's face on the video recording, the evaluator is re-humanized: the evaluator that the student sees at this digital interface is (understood to be) Scott—the educator whom the student has worked with for a semester (at least). Yet, this encounter is removed from the embodied pedagogical relation in the classroom—each is de-subjectified from the spatial and corporeal proximity of the face-to-face encounter. "[A] supportive voice" congeals between words and things, humans and machines, past and present and future. There are de-subjectifying movements "outside the two" that flow "in another direction" (Deleuze

& Parnet, 2006/1977, p. 5) from the hyper-visibility of the evaluated educator subject even as, paradoxically, Scott's face is hyper-visible in its digitally mediated form.

The potentiality of this encounter, at the digital interface, should not be overstated. Indeed, there were correlative conservative movements at work in Scott's later attempt to continue experimenting with the potentiality of *digital voice*. Scott continued to give an account to me of his attempt to introduce this video-feedback processes with his second-year undergraduate students, giving them "a choice: whether they want a written or audio [feedback]". Unlike his first-year students, these second-year students "all wanted [feedback] written", not in video-recorded form. Scott's working theory was that these students "perhaps are already conditioned that 'at university this is the process, you do this, you receive it, this written feedback or this rubric or we access it online, and that's what I'm comfortable doing'", while the first years "hadn't had that experience yet, [and so were] more open to it". The stabilizing refrain is compelling; we cling to what is familiar and safe.

For Scott, these second-year students' responses made him wonder whether there is the need for "a bigger conversation that goes to our diet of assessment that we offer students and the diet of feedback [they receive]".

Conclusion

In this chapter, I have offered ways of thinking about the interfaces and intersections/intercessions of the digital in pedagogical evaluative practices. I have crafted a concept of *digital voice*—that entwines the 'subjective' and 'material', and conjoins the utterance with the path(s) of its formation (*voix/voie*). Exploring an empirical example, I have suggested that, while *digital voice* is ambivalent, it offers possibilities for affirmative modes of transversal pedagogical practice. In the video recording of Scott's verbal feedback, there is a moment of radical potential—where something other than the antagonisms of evaluation (of both student and educator) seems to be in formation. Affirmative movements towards different pedagogical relations materialize—even as these are quickly redirected (and, indeed, such uses of video recording of educators' feedback may be soon be swiftly captured and mandated to educators by institutions).

The educator, the student and the technological machine are not set apart, but work together in processes that may generate particular forms of subjectification (Cole, 2007). To pluralize analysis of the intersections and intercessions of being, words and things renders the digital neither destructive, nor necessarily liberating. Whether or not the digital is anathema or emancipating (or both simultaneously) depends on *what happens in the moment where the utterance forms and where it moves*. Each component in the collective *agencement* of enunciation (thoughts, affects, machines, matter) dynamically participates in how and where this moment will turn. Therefore, experimentation is necessary with collective *agencements* of enunciation. What is formed in the moment when a pedagogical evaluation is formed must be understood in relation to its paths (*voix/voie*)—the path(s) of its formation and what the evaluation *does* as it travels. The pedagogical task (and the pedagogical potential) becomes, then, to attune to what is happening in particular assemblages—and to note how particular institutional processes may be deployed to form lines of escape from present repetitious patterns of subjectification.

Acknowledgements I thank the two anonymous reviewers, the editors, as well as Be Parnell, Monique Dagleish and Julian Sefton-Green for their thoughtful and constructive feedback on an earlier draft of this chapter. The detailed and affirmative tone of the feedback of these readers is particularly appreciated. An earlier version was presented at the 2017 *Gender and Education* conference at Middlesex University in a symposium chaired by Genine Hook and Melissa Wolfe: *Affective Relationality as Response-ability.* I thank Genine, Melissa, Christine Gowlett (co-presenter), Yvette Taylor (discussant) and the attendees of this symposium for their engagement and for generative conversations around the issues raised in this paper. These voices are entwined with this chapter's authorial 'I'.

References

Arvidsson, A., & Piertesen, N. (2013). *The ethical economy: Rebuilding value after the crisis*. New York: Columbia University Press.

Boswell, S. S. (2016). Ratemyprofessors is hogwash (but I care): Effects of Ratemyprofessors and university-administered teaching evaluations on professors. *Computers in Human Behavior, 56*, 155–162. https://doi.org/10.1016/j.chb.2015.11.045.

Boutang, P.-A. (Writer). (1996). L'Abécédaire de Gilles Deleuze, avec Claire Parnet [Gilles Deleuze's ABC Primer, with Claire Parnet]. Paris: La Femis & Sodaperaga Productions.

Bryant, L. R. (2006). Lacan and Deleuze: A Pet Peeve. Retrieved from https://larvalsubjects. wordpress.com/2006/05/22/lacan-and-deleuze-a-pet-peeve/.

Clayson, D. E. (2014). What does ratemyprofessors.com actually rate? *Assessment & Evaluation in Higher Education, 39*(6), 678–698. https://doi.org/10.1080/02602938.2013.861384.

Coladarci, T., & Kornfield, I. (2007). RateMyProfessors.com versus formal in-class student evaluations of teaching. *Practical Assessment, Research & Evaluation, 12*(6), 1–15.

Cole, D. R. (2007). Virtual terrorism and the internet e-learning options. *E-Learning, 4*(2), 116–127.

Cole, D. R. (2014). Inter-collapse … Educational Nomadology for a Future Generation. In M. Carlin & J. Wallin (Eds.), *Deleuze & Guattari, politics and education: For a people-yet-to-come* (pp. 77–95). London: Bloomsbury.

Cole, D. R., & Bradley, J. P. N. (2014). Japanese English learners on the edge of 'chaosmos': Félix Guattari and 'becoming-otaku'. *Linguistic and Philosophical Investigations, 13*, 83–95.

Cook-Sather, A., Bovill, C., & Felten, P. (2014). *Engaging students as partners in learning and teaching: A guide for faculty*. New York: Jossey-Bass.

Davison, E., & Price, J. (2009). How do we rate? An evaluation of online student evaluations. *Assessment & Evaluation in Higher Education, 34*(1), 51–65. https://doi.org/10.1080/02602930801895695.

Deleuze, G. (1992). Postscript on the societies of control. *October, 59*, 3–7.

Deleuze, G., & Guattari, F. (1980/1987). *A thousand plateaus: Capitalism and schizophrenia* (B. Massumi, Trans.). Minneapolis: University of Minnesota Press.

Deleuze, G., & Guattari, F. (1983). *Anti-Oedipus: Capitalism and schizophrenia* (R. Hurley, M. Seem, & H. R. Lane, Trans.). Minnesota: University of Minnesota Press.

Deleuze, G., & Parnet, C. (2006/1977). *Dialogues II* (H. Tomlinson & B. Habberjam, Trans.). London: Continuum.

Dosse, F. (2007/2010). *Gilles Deleuze & Félix Guattari: Intersecting lives* (D. Glassman, Trans.). New York: Columbia University Press.

Fielding, M. (1999). Radical collegiality: Affirming teaching as an inclusive professional practice. *Australian Educational Researcher, 26*(2), 1–34. https://doi.org/10.1007/BF03219692.

Fielding, M. (2001). Students as radical agents of change. *Journal of Educational Change, 2,* 123–141. https://doi.org/10.1023/A:1017949213447.

Fielding, M. (2011). Student voice and the possibility of radical democratic education: Re-narrating forgotten histories, developing alternative futures. In G. Czerniawski & W. Kidd (Eds.), *The student voice handbook: Bridging the academic/practitioner divide* (pp. 3–17). Bingley, UK: Emerald Group Publishing Limited.

Freng, S., & Webber, D. (2009). Turning up the heat on online teaching evaluations: Does "hotness" matter? *Teaching of Psychology, 36*(3), 189–193. https://doi.org/10.1080/00986280902959739.

Genosko, G. (2002). *Félix Guattari: An aberrant introduction.* London: Continuum.

Genosko, G. (2003). Félix Guattari. *Angelaki: Journal of the Theoretical Humanities, 8*(1), 129–140. https://doi.org/10.1080/09697250301196.

Genosko, G. (2009). *Félix Guattari: A critical introduction.* Northhampton: Pluto Press.

Gonzales, L. D., & Núñez, A.-M. (2014). Ranking regimes and the production of knowledge in academia: (Re)shaping faculty work? *2014, 22.* https://doi.org/10.14507/epaa.v22n31.2014.

Gregory, K. M. (2011). How undergraduates perceive their professors: A corpus analysis of Rate My Professor. *Journal of Educational Technology Systems, 40*(2), 169–193. https://doi.org/10.2190/ET.40.2.g.

Guattari, F. (1989/2013). *Schizoanalytic cartographies* (A. Goffey, Trans.). London: Bloomsbury.

Guattari, F. (1995a). *Chaosmosis: An ethico-aesthetic paradigm.* Bloomington: Indiana University Press.

Guattari, F. (1995b). On machines. *Complexity,* 8–12.

Guattari, F. (1996). Remaking social practices. In G. Genosko (Ed.), *The Guattari reader* (pp. 262–273). Oxford: Blackwell.

Guattari, F. (2000). *The three ecologies* (I. Pindar & P. Sutton, Trans.). London: The Athlone Press.

Hearn, A. (2010). Structuring feeling: Web 2.0, online ranking and rating, and the digital 'reputation' economy. *Ephemera: Theory and politics in organization, 10*(3/4), 421–438.

Kindred, J., & Mohammed, S. N. (2005). "He will crush you like an academic ninja!": Exploring teacher ratings on Ratemyprofessors.com. *Journal of Computer-Mediated Communication, 10*(3). https://doi.org/10.1111/j.1083-6101.2005.tb00257.x.

Legg, A. M., & Wilson, J. H. (2012). RateMyProfessors.com offers biased evaluations. *Assessment & Evaluation in Higher Education, 37*(1), 89–97. https://doi.org/10.1080/02602938.2010.507299.

Lewandowski, G. W., Higgins, E., & Nardone, N. N. (2012). Just a harmless website?: An experimental examination of RateMyProfessors.com's effect on student evaluations. *Assessment & Evaluation in Higher Education, 37*(8), 987–1002. https://doi.org/10.1080/02602938.2011.594497.

Marsh, H. W., & Roche, L. A. (1997). Making students' evaluations of teaching effectiveness effective: The critical issues of validity, bias, and utility. *American Psychologist, 52*(11), 1187–1197. https://doi.org/10.1037/0003-066X.52.11.1187.

Mayes, E. (under review). Alternatives to end-of-semester student evaluations of teaching: Narrative accounts of tertiary educators committed to inclusive pedagogies. *Teaching in Higher Education.*

Mockler, N., & Groundwater-Smith, S. (2015). *Engaging with student voice in research, education and community: Beyond legitimation and guardianship.* Dordrecht: Springer.

Murphie, A. (2001). Computers are not theatre: The machine in the ghost in Gilles Deleuze and Félix Guattari's thought. In G. Genosko (Ed.), *Deleuze and Guattari: Critical assessments of leading philosophers* (Vol. III, pp. 1299–1331). London: Routledge.

Onwuegbuzie, A. J., Witcher, A. E., Collins, K. M. T., Filer, J. D., Wiedmaier, C. D., & Moore, C. W. (2007). Students' perceptions of characteristics of effective college teachers: A validity study of a teaching evaluation form using a mixed-methods analysis. *American Educational Research Journal, 44*(1), 113–160.

Pindar, I., & Sutton, P. (2008). Translators' introduction. In F. Guattari (Ed.), *The three ecologies* (pp. 1–11). London: Contimuum.

Ringrose, J. (2015). Schizo-feminist educational research cartographies. *Deleuze Studies, 9*(3), 393–409. https://doi.org/10.3366/dls.2015.0194.

Ritter, K. (2008). E-valuating learning: "Rate My Professors" and public rhetorics of pedagogy. *Rhetoric Review, 27*(3), 259–280. https://doi.org/10.1080/07350190802126177.

Stivale, C. J. (2003). Deleuze/ Parnet in *Dialogues*: The folds of post-identity. *The Journal of the Midwest Modern Language Association, 36*(1), 25–37. https://doi.org/10.2307/1315396.

Stivale, C. J. (2008). *Gilles Deleuze's ABCs: The folds of friendship*. Baltimore, MD.: Johns Hopkins University Press.

Subtirelu, N. C. (2015). "She does have an accent but…": Race and language ideology in students' evaluations of mathematics instructors on RateMyProfessors.com. *Language in Society, 44*(1), 35–62. https://doi.org/10.1017/S0047404514000736.

Uttl, B., White, C. A., & Gonzalez, D. W. (2017). Meta-analysis of faculty's teaching effectiveness: Student evaluation of teaching ratings and student learning are not related. *Studies in Educational Evaluation, 54,* 22–42. https://doi.org/10.1016/j.stueduc.2016.08.007.

Villalta-Cerdas, A., McKeny, P., Gatlin, T., & Sandi-Urena, S. (2015). Evaluation of instruction: Students' patterns of use and contribution to RateMyProfessors.com. *Assessment & Evaluation in Higher Education, 40*(2), 181–198. https://doi.org/10.1080/02602938.2014.896862.

Walkerdine, V. (2013). Using the work of Félix Guattari to understand space, place, social justice, and education. *Qualitative Inquiry, 19*(10), 756–764. https://doi.org/10.1177/1077800413502934.

Yoon, K. (2015). Affordances and negotiations of the digital reputation society: A case study of RateMyProfessors.com. *Continuum, 29*(1), 109–120. https://doi.org/10.1080/10304312.2014.968525.

Dr. Eve Mayes is a lecturer in Pedagogy and Curriculum at Deakin University. She completed her PhD, *The lines of the voice: An ethnography of the ambivalent affects of student voice*, at the University of Sydney. Her research explores the social (re-)production of educational inequalities using the conceptual tools of Deleuze, Guattari and others. Eve was formerly an English and ESL teacher in government comprehensive schools in NSW.

Chapter 13
Schizoanalysis, Counselling Praxis and a Sandbox Dirge

Jeff Smith and Scott Kouri

Abstract Counselling offices provide passages within, outside, and between the institutions that code and re-direct affect and human behavior. Those without access to capital and other forms of privilege, who wish to make their way from outside to the center of social life, are obliged to learn the codes of psychological deficiency and accompanying forms of labor (i.e., self-help, mindfulness, and expert intervention) that are required to achieve mental health. In an age of affective labor, we argue counselling in education provides potential sites for new forms of what Guattari (Chaosmosis: An ethico-aesthetic paradigm. Indiana University Press, Indianapolis, 1995) calls "subjectivation." Rather than maintaining the counsellor/client subject binary, subjectivation refers to an open process comprised of unknown fluxes, clinical experiments, and temporal subjectivities. If we flood the networks of capital and counselling with our own unconscious flows, opportunities for a schizoanalytic of counsellors become possible. In the following chapter, schizoanalysis enacts the transversality of this book, and we explore our struggles as counsellors, through the writing and analysis of clinical examples.

Keywords Counselling · Pedagogy · Schizoanalysis · Affect

Introduction

The counselling office connects pedagogical machines to analytic machines and exemplifies a site of production for neoliberal subjectivity and globalization. For example, students enter this passage in the name of care and behavioral health, usually for misbehavior at school. If the counsellor fails to curtail the given behaviors within the school context, the student may find themselves outside of it, with a referral

J. Smith (✉)
Brandon University, Brandon, Canada
e-mail: smithresponding@gmail.com

S. Kouri
Camosun College Counselling Services, Victoria, Canada

© Springer Nature Singapore Pte Ltd. 2018   211
D. R. Cole and J. P. N. Bradley (eds.), *Principles of Transversality in Globalization and Education*, https://doi.org/10.1007/978-981-13-0583-2_13

to a community therapist and/or alternative educational institution. The community therapist who struggles to facilitate change may refer to a psychiatrist (if they have access to such a sought-after resource). When medication and expert knowledge fail, and a "fall through the cracks" occurs, the emergency mental health team and other institutions of containment are called upon by friends, family, and other professionals for the person existing outside the system. Students that find themselves on the outside would need to work the counselling passage to get back in. The transition from outside (i.e., street person, addict, ex-con, etc.) to in require order words drawn from the community counselling context (i.e., day program, group therapy, community support worker, youth, and family counsellor), vocational or forensic counsellor, and/or school counsellor. Each passage requires certain permissions and documentations to move on. The majoritarian Western mental health trend dictates which psychological codes and interactions are to occur between experts and nonexperts to produce a corrective counselling encounter. These codes are required for the passage of both counsellor and client, through idiosyncratic human conduct, which is perpetuated by the client as the center of globalized, neoliberal social life where one functions (at least in public places) according to the normative modes of human existence. This particular counselling dyad operates as a subjugated group. Deleuze and Guattari (2000) developed the concepts of subject group and subjugated group to differentiate between encounters that increase the revolutionary potential inherent in groups that remain open to unconscious flows and those subjugated encounters that adhere to routinized interactions. In an age of affective labor, where work can be constituted by the relations that one performs, we argue counselling in education provides potential sites for new forms of subjectivation (Guattari, 1995). Subjectivation is a term that Foucault proposed that should replace "subject," as it infers a multiply constituted process in flux, as opposed to a static transcendental subject. If we flood the networks of capital and counselling with our own unconscious flows, opportunities for a "schizoanalytic education" of the counsellor as a subject group become possible due to the transversal connections that become apparent.

As counsellors who have worked in public school systems, postsecondary institutions, and with individuals outside the educational system, we, in this piece, transversally map the desire that has hijacked our attention since the days that we, as adolescents, sat in our own school counsellor's offices. Mainstream counsellor training typically fails to account for the risks inherent in the subjugation of desire. This subjugation occurs through pedagogy that endorses the distribution of some and the delimitation of other affects, thoughts, and behaviors. Here, we are also considering counselling as a form of pedagogy and psychoeducation that instructs young people in particular deployments of affect and thought (Cole, 2011). As such, counselling practice parallels the pedagogy of the classroom and helps produce an individual subject. Much of counselling is directed toward exploring people's values and interests (which are founded in preconscious investment), and we are attempting to theorize an unconscious desire that comes before the production of the human subject. Some of us have doubled down on our privilege and returned to the original castrating office in an attempt to recoup what has not yet been lost and based on the pretense of mastering our wayward unconscious processes. In this context, we perform illusory observations of the objectified other (i.e., our clients, ourselves, our colleagues) and attempt to tame and direct the unconscious processes that are thought to be causing disruptions to daily living.. We are working in a realm of code that tends toward subjugated group formation.

Guattari (1995) writes that

> Psychoanalytic treatment confronts us with a multiplicity of cartographies: that of the analyst and analysand, and of the family, the neighborhood, etc. It is the interaction of these cartographies that will provide regimes to the different assemblages of subjectivation. None of them, whether fantasmatic, delirious or theoretical, can be said to express an objective knowledge of the psyche. All of them are important insofar as they support a certain context, a certain framework, an existential armature of the subjective situation. Our question here is not simply of a speculative order, but is posed in very practical ways: how appropriate are concepts of the Unconscious, offered to us on the psychoanalytic "market," to actual conditions of the production of subjectivity? (p. 11)

In this paper, we explore schizoanalysis as a possibility for transversing the capital-pedagogical-clinical machine, through a direct encounter between bodies. In this encounter, desire drives bodies into new configurations, producing desire for the sake of desire itself. This writing project is an attempt to schizoanalyze our affective labor as counsellors. It is not a mapping of the systems of control from an objective position, but rather an exploration of our own desiring machines. By putting ourselves under analysis and laying our "forever-going training" alongside the interminable education of students in educational institutions, we deconstruct the horizontal hierarchy of helper and helpee. By returning to the scene of our own production, we transversally map a way out for ourselves and others. The unconscious processes and desires that flow through our own bodies as counsellors interacting with others are schizoanalyzed throughout this paper as an analytic writing practice, a process that we have articulated elsewhere (Kouri & Smith, 2016).

The names and situations of these clinical encounters have been scrambled, to obscure the opportunity for representational identification. In this way, we protect the privacy and dignity of those we seek to support in our work, thereby maintaining the basic human right to privacy and in keeping with standard ethics practice, all patients have been advised that these encounters could be used for research purposes. Our adherence to a particular social justice ethic, as a coding of desire, provides a site for analysis in which the social investment is explored to determine what, when, where and why we would apply such an ethic, and whether it would be appropriate to engage in schizoanalysis. It is useful to differentiate between a preconscious ethics (Deleuze & Guattari, 2000) (i.e., equal access to education for all and the use of socially just forms of counselling to address violence and oppression) and unconscious processes (i.e., "I felt like a wolf when they howled back at me on that intense night in Santorini"). While we work most often in the preconscious realm in our work, in our writing, and in our clinical work, we schizoanalyze to see where desire takes us. As this is a risky experiment, we don't impose it upon our clients without their consent and instead utilize it most regularly only in our writing and supervisory processes.

Schizoanalysis 5[1]

Alex is late or possibly absent again this morning, and his foster parent has not been returning my calls this week. This is the third session he's missed of the five appointments booked thus far. The bell rings for the next block to start, and I pick up the receiver to call first block Bill: "Is Alex there by chance?", "Nope" says Bill, "I haven't seen him this week." I open up my case notes from the last session he attended and reflect upon the conversation. He shared that he spends time next to a boiler in the basement of the school sometimes. He says it is one of the only places he can relax, not just at school but anywhere, and pleaded that I not tell anyone. My response, a string of questions, rightly provoked his suspicion, and our conversation grew unproductively. He wouldn't say how he gets in there. He didn't mention the custodian. He denied there being any safety concerns. He knows it's against the rules. He isn't using any illicit substances while he is there. He hasn't been experiencing any further suicidal ideation.

I haven't shared the coordinates of Alex's hideout with anyone else, as it would breach our agreement for confidentiality, although I could likely make a case from an occupational health and safety perspective. If I were to talk, the vice principal would act swiftly, likely implicating the youth, myself and custodian in some sort of bureaucratic process likely contributing to the end of the custodian's job, if not this young man's school life. Ultimately, my choice to protect this territory was induced by the affect that overcame me when Alex shared about his experience in this space and how it provides the sort of calm that is hard to come by. His face relaxed when he described how the heat warms his tired bones and how his ears have become attuned to the frequencies of water coursing through the pipes. I asked him what that space does for him and he said: "Well, I don't feel like I fit into the machine up here," and he gestured to the door and beyond, "...down there, in the heat, I am beyond the machine," and he went on to describe how he has been able to complete most of his assignments by the light of his headlamp. He states it's the only place he can think. I recall a conversation I had a long time ago with the custodian about how he prefers to eat lunch in the boiler room over the staff room, because it affords him time to think. I suspect that he and this young man have developed a mentoring relationship. Something I've completely failed to do. I happen to like the custodian a great deal; however, I fear that the sentiment is not mutual. In his company, I feel a sense of unworthiness as seeing beyond the dominant staff narrative that he is a strange recluse, I've come to realize that his depth of character far surpasses that of my colleagues and myself. He is rumored to be a doctor of philosophy, but speaks in "koans" when asked direct questions about his identity and personal history. If there is anything that bothers me about this man, it's not that he is eccentric, but rather that he is doing a better job than I am with Alex. The neoliberalism and globalization that lives in my nerves gets knotted up about this. About my role. About failure. The custodian sees through all of the same bullsh*t that Alex is looking past. It's not that I don't see it, but that I choose to be it. This thought propels me into a reactive decision,

---

[1] See Kouri & Smith (2016) for Schizoanalyses One Through Four.

I'm going to go down to this f*cking boiler room. Without any further thought, I go straight out my door and down the hall toward an unused part of the school, where the stairwell to the boiler room exists. I can hear the cacophony of sounds down there, which I find frightening. My heart is racing because "what if someone sees me here" or "what if the custodian comes out just now" or "what if the goddamn door is unlocked." I turn the handle, but it doesn't budge. I feel the sudden urge to take a sh*t. I make my way back toward my structured life of offices, classrooms, and staff bathrooms. I let out a fart that is louder than I had planned and speed up my walk while reaching into my pocket for the iPhone. Check the time. Check the e-mail. Check the Facebook. Now I'm at a door for which I can turn the handle. I enter the stench of civilization: urinal deodorant overcome by a generous spray of Febreeze. I sit down and check the time. Check the Twitter. Check the news.

Affective Therapeutic Labor

Global capitalism increasingly tends toward the affective, targeting our relationships, communication, and emotions as training grounds for labor (Hardt & Negri, 2005). Paranoid concepts and practices about mental health that intervene in the unconscious are now dispersed throughout the social landscape as profitable tools. For example, discourses that circulate about a mental health crisis among Indigenous Youth are accompanied by "best practice" trainings that emphasize focus on the individualized negative thoughts and feelings of these young people. The practice of focusing on the minds of Indigenous People has been referred to as psycholonization (Todd & Wade, 1994) and fails to provide adequate therapeutic analysis of the colonial context and ancillary effects on psychological functioning. Interventions implemented by professionals and laypeople alike transform the socius into an ever-proliferating field of mental health. Counsellors, as normalizing agents in educational settings, commit to evidence-based forms of practice that are meant to stabilize the identities of students like Alex. Subtle and explicit forms of revolt, idiosyncratic thought, and expressive singularity are targets for re-coding and territorialization by subjugated groups. The counsellor's job is often construed as facilitating the formation of healthy neurological function and attachment, however overcoding desire with dominant values and communication patterns, runs the risk of decreasing unique forms of thinking and attaching to other living beings and objects. Even the most humanistic values are funneled via affective labor, and into the abstract value of the dollar sign (Cole, 2012). Health, happiness, a good life, and networking have become the important soft skills of a mentally stable person's marketing profile. Therapeutic practice and education are overinvested in establishing a normative baseline of mental functioning for a timely entry or return to work and/or school.

Counselling in education exemplifies many of the contradictions of contemporary capitalism and colonialism. Clinical work increasingly individualizes suffering, perpetuating the illusion of separateness, and leaving unchallenged the values of competition, autonomy, and ownership that underlie isolation and cultural dislocation. The trauma and pain that inhere within systems of racialized and gendered violence and poverty are remapped onto an individual psyche and/or neurological network. For example, a young person contemplates suicide after being removed from her family home by social services, is diagnosed with depression and prescribed SSRI medication for her mood. When asked about her suicidality, she states she would rather be dead than spend another night in a foster home. By locating the problem in the young person's neurology, the mental health system fails to account for the real reasons this young woman is preparing to die, which includes a history of being abused by foster parents. Where the body was previously absent in counselling, neuroscience could now be seen as the foundation of a new science and economics that capitalize on the body's reactions to exploitation and alienation. Anxiety, depression, addictive behaviors, suicidality, and a host of other "disorders" may be viewed as potentially jeopardizing people's inclusion in the labor market and property ownership. Coding people's suffering as individual pathology and calculating it through "loss of work" or "economic drain" metrics opens new markets for pharmaceutical companies and evidence-based therapeutic approaches. Owners, investors, managers, and officials exploit workers and citizens to the point of psychological distress and contribute to the mental health market where consumers seek "healing" and/or normalizing interventions such as pharmacology and cognitive therapy. Experiences of distress, disenfranchisement, alienation, and systemic oppression are coded as individual neurobiological or cognitive problems, remnants of attachment or early life trauma, or loss of personal meaning.

Alternatively, critical and socially oriented thinkers have attempted to recontextualize mental illness as cultural and spiritual dislocation (Alexander, 2008) or as an embodied resistance to entering and perpetuating an unjust and unfulfilling social life that exploits them and others (Reynolds, 2010). Furthermore, in an age where white supremacy and xenophobia are on the rise, anxiety and fear must be looked at as possible reactions by majoritarian subjects as they encounter limits to attaining positions within society that they feel entitled to. Counsellors who code inequity and disconnection primarily as mental disorder fuel their own and big pharma's interests. Their persistent attempts to adjust people to the capitalist system that exploits them and their clients are akin to what Deleuze and Guattari (2000), following Reich, describe as "desiring our own oppression."

Hardt and Negri (2005) argue that in this new age of Empire, affective labor and immaterial production become targets for capitalist profiteering. Affective labor—once the domain of the "specialists of the unconscious" (Guattari, 1979)—is increasingly marketed as being central to the education of managers, service providers, and interface programmers. The language of psychology is no longer the sole domain of the mental health professional. Hardt and Negri (2005) write, "When our ideas and our affects, or emotions, are put to work, for instance, and when they thus become subject in a new way to the command of the boss, we often experience new and intense forms of violation or alienation" (p. 66). In such a context, students and worker's creative abilities, their capacities for relationship, communication, and emotion, and their ability to generate and navigate code are the new targets of capital (Skott-Myhre, 2015). The basics of subjectivity and social life—relationships, love, and communication—are now contractual elements in a pay-for-service machine where unions and careers are undermined and citizens have little to no protection.

Affective labor directly produces cooperation, communication, knowledge, and social relatedness and, as such, is biopolitical. Whereas previous forms of labor produced *the means* of social relatedness through an economic image of the factory, the current tendency is toward the production of networks of cooperation, partnership, and communication. At the level of subjectivity, however, affective labor opens the body's capacities to capital. Students in dominant Western nations such as Canada and the USA must leave school with the right social skills, cultural values, attitudes, and ways of speaking (Cole, 2013). This tendency is particularly inflected at the intersection of new demands on students to subjectivize in sellable ways. The general tendency toward selling emotional and communication ability has been beta tested in counsellor subjectivity for at least fifty years. Counsellors have, over time, moved toward a relational and interpersonal paradigm where warmth, alignment, rapport, and disclosure have come to replace Freud's (1914) rules of abstinence or Jung's idiosyncratic approach. Rather than confronting the unconscious elements within each of us, we seek cooperation for our mutual financial gain. The world of work becomes more like a counselling office, while the counselling office becomes a sales floor.

Schizoanalysis 6: The Tracker

After my long and unproductive day at the school, I have to get to my invoices. The school doesn't pay me enough to satisfy the ravenous requirements of the city, so I peddle affects on the side. Private affective sales compensate for the fledgling unionized educational context. Yes, it's tracking day, invoice time, and I need to send my bills to my clients. March 31st. I have two hours left to have the bills out on time. I need to be organized, so nobody gets away without paying. I have a bill template that I prepare for each client. I look for a signature font, and I like brush script. I like brush script because it looks like cursive. I open a folder called "March" within a folder called "billing 2017" within a folder called "billing" within a folder called "private counsellor." These files constrain the private dancer in me, keep her in order, and keep that cash rolling in. I have to check e-mails to see how much I agreed to with each person. This goes against the better judgement of my analyst, who recommends I never discount because I need to believe I'm worth a certain amount. The idea is that you treat people differently if you give them a different rate; i.e., talk is cheap when the rate is low. Anyway, back to my tracking, I have to go back into their e-mails sometimes to remember their last names because I don't do an intake. I run a primitive system, but I'm learning. I've got one dude who didn't pay his bill, I continue to harass him every month for the past 6 months in hopes of recouping my loss there. He's a f*cking bully, I don't care as much about the money with him, it's more about wasting my f*cking time, it was bullsh*t therapy, he came because he was suspended from work for blowing up at his boss. He wanted me to report his attendance to his employer, but he was bullsh*tting that he was going to make any changes. I tried motivational interviewing him. When all else fails, we can always blame the client. Repetition. He's been fired from a job in the past, as a garbage man, for assaulting a cyclist during one of his routes. I send off his invoice again. How much could I buy an automated system for? This is taking far too long… It kills my affects, so I'll have to rig something else to do this for me. I didn't even finish my tracking, now I feel like I have to get up in the morning and do it again. Repetition.

Schizoanalysis 6.2: Tracking the Tracker

I've been documenting the movements of the tracker. The objective observer, a human becoming machine, always attempts the last word. Even if the other person tries to work something more dignified in on their behalf, the objective observer can spring back to overpower the resistance. Like the psychiatrist throttles the worldview of the freshly diagnosed, reterritorializing their every move, the objective observer enunciates with finality. The transversal writer writes back though. We go back and forth. We do street analysis (Kouri & Smith, 2016). William Basinski erupts on the computer speaker as the tracker pummels the keys in response to the objective observer. They go back and forth erecting and tearing down barriers, seeking passage within the order words. Finally, the files topple over giving way to free verse poetry and circular dancing. A fire on the beach. A nonviolent celebration of the anima. A breath heaves from beneath the glutinous belly of patriarchy and its endless filing.

Subject-Supposed-to-Have

Today's subjects are increasingly at the disposal of capital, work, data mining, and marketing. Life within affective global capitalism, however, circumvents *and* opens possibilities for clinicians to relate to a generation of students as they are initiated into a form of work unknown in history. A transversal mapping of counselling in education explores how the same networks that disseminate contemporary notions of disorder, failure, and repair are also channels for an alternative schizoanalytic education and practice. The inability of young people to arrive at the consolidated identity that is structured and signified by job security, home ownership, and marriage marks them as lacking and deficient. Deleuze (1992) foreshadowed the difficulties that the subject would have in arriving in a digitalized information society, one he called a society of control. Rather than the docile and disciplined body required for industrial capitalism that Foucault (1975) theorized, Deleuze pointed out that where code and signs reign, a new flexible subject would be required. While psychology begins to take into account the shifting economic and social factors in North America, via narrative therapy and other postmodern approaches that attend to discourse and intersectional politics, it lacks a critique of the normative majoritarian subject of late capitalism, our colonized relations to land and resources, and the whiteness and oedipalized familialism that underpins it. Guattari, along with Deleuze (2000), critiqued the familialism that informs current forms of psychotherapy as a magical disavowal of social reality and the real fluxes of desire, arguing that only under specific conditions could both desire and oppression be territorialized on the heterosexual "mommy-daddy-me" triangle. Colonialism depoliticizes social life by reterritorializing responsibility and relationship on the nuclear family. The nuclear family, birthed alongside capitalism and colonialism in seventeenth century Europe, becomes the ideal of kinship relationality and the most viable economic and reproductive unit. Family therapy and other systemic orientations have developed out of this colonial frame and retain familialism by locating disorder within the nuclear family unit. Clinical problems are often attributed to the behavior of young people, and a great deal of time is spent working through "anxiety" related to parenting "at risk" children with psychiatric disorders. There has been a recent resurgence in Christian, conservative, and nationalistic social discourse which frames youth and adolescence as particularly at risk. This risk discourse is coupled with a power designated to counsellors to send young people to institutions for their own safety without their consent. Some young people report spending eight to fourteen hours waiting to be decertified by a psychiatrist so they can go home and rest, while others are refused the institutional support they seek due to being deemed "low risk" for suicide.

It is important to explore the material consequences of Western familialism and the ways that the white family displaces, literally and metaphorically, kinship systems and cultures through colonial expansion. The vanquishing of North American lands to make way for industry, colonial expansion, and resource extraction emerged with white supremacy and entitlement. Today, slick commercial marketing, instant communication on social media, and neocolonial relations to land and property constitute the landscape of dominant contemporary subjectivizing processes that counsellors encounter regularly. Today's white, straight, and heteronormatively emerging adults compete for dwindling resources with peoples historically excluded from recognizable positions within the social system. Advances in identity politics provide racialized people with access to goods and social positions that many white people took for granted historically, leading to the emergence of fear and entitlement, anxiety and depression of subjugated groups of young white people. When colonialism remains invisible, white people end up feeling that it is their land and resources that are being encroached upon by an imaginary colonialism 2.0. Indigenous and racialized people, immigrants and migrants/temporary and foreign workers, sexual minorities, and foreign property owners all threaten the entitlements that structure the subject-supposed-to-have. The subject who is supposed to have land, bodies, money, and opportunity at their disposal has pressed colonial desire into the deepest recesses of his mind, feeling victimized and justifying further menace to others and the planet.

Schizoanalysis 7: Colonial Desire

I'm back at my private office after another deadening day at the institution. I'm working with a man (let's call him Mr. One) who is constantly checking his phone screen for a reply from his realtor. He's decided to purchase a property closer to the city center rather than the more rural area he was exploring when we had our session last month. His levels of anxiety have heightened with the increase in cost, and we talk at length about self-soothing strategies that work for him. He is hip to mindfulness. Reads Shambala. He is a thoughtful neoliberal. He displays his awareness by stating that he wants everything other people have and is worried about missing out on the opportunity to ever get into the market if prices continue to rise. This mapping of property ownership onto the larger neoliberal and globalized ontology of lack is a common problem for us middle-class white settlers in the unceded First Nation territories.

The intersection between land and lack reminds me of another client (why not call him Mr. Two?) who has been lamenting a financial situation that prevented him from getting into the market and, he speculates, led to the separation from his long-term partner. He relies on some loosely organized political theory from his bachelor's degree to defend against his deferred desire for companionship. But… back to Mr. One who is talking some nonsense about creating a leasehold for himself and then donating the land to a First Nation in 100 years, once it's been well picked over by a generation or two of land occupiers. This slight settler move to innocence, a way to live a little less guilty on occupied territory, will allow him to keep one foot in the social justice world, while he jams his other leg into the bear trap of the mortgage broker.

Mr. Two talks about how he has been escaping into the music of his youth, with a particular obsession with King Diamond, and getting lost in the overly simplistic narratives of good and evil. He often talks about saving his money for the next economic downturn, at which point he'll finally be able to "enter the market." Both Mr. One and Two complain about foreigners buying investment properties and driving up the price of real estate. They also talk about how it was easier for their parents' generation to get into the market because "back then, it wasn't about a market, it was about a home." According to Mr. Two, the foreign investors are coupling their efforts with an influx of drugs flowing through the darkweb, "f*cking up wacky little white hip hop screenagers who are self-medicating on Xanax and occasionally falling into fentanyl overdose." "Naloxone please"! He bellows and punctuates with a sinister cackle. I cast my artificial smile to the floor, concealing bared teeth more so, in response to this antisocial and conspiratorial gallows humor. For the second time in a month, I constrain my urge to slap some sense into this aging white fellow, as he represents, for me, a thoughtlessness that continues to dog me in my own interactions in other social contexts, regarding other issues. We sit quietly for a few seconds, as the shadow threatens to swallow the light within and between us, before I ask a few questions to facilitate therapeutic process as a form of damage control.

In North America, large swaths of majoritarian subjects are cathecting their loss of entitlement as hate, scapegoating, and racism toward people more oppressed than them, rather than seeking a more egalitarian system for all. Media, political parties, and multinational corporations perpetuate xenophobic, colonial, and racist discourses to maintain their power at the expense of life itself. Any understanding of the limitations and possibilities of counselling in education must thoroughly deal with the guilt, appropriations, and accompanying well-documented moves to innocence (Tuck & Yang, 2012). Counsellors who adopt social justice terminology and perform discourses of ally ship while retaining individualized mental health discourses in their clinical work risk maintaining privilege based on a damage-centered view of the other (Tuck, 2009).

Disposability

Neoliberal, globalized life produces particular forms of subjectivity and socius. Empire exercises necropolitical powers over life and death by determining both the feasibility of liveable forms of life and the precarity or disposability of bodies. The expendability of specific subjects, bodies, or groups in Empire is undertaken through not only economic disenfranchisement, but also the perpetuation of unending war, the blurring of police and military functions, and the criminalization of resistance. The constancy of environmental collapse discourse, the modulation of security and insecurity, and presidential warnings of enemies distant, within, and at our borders, produces differential exposure to the threat or actuality of death.

Historically and continuous into the present, the capital-colonial system has benefitted from the liquidation of hundreds of thousands of Indigenous and racialized people, as a precursor for nation building in North America and elsewhere. Not only has capitalism required what Marx (1908/2013) refers to as primitive accumulation via the appropriation of Indigenous lands and slave labor, industrial capitalism required disposable bodies to work in conditions which guaranteed death (Richardson & Reynolds, 2012). In our contemporary world, racial and gender differences continue to structure precarity and vulnerability to violence (Butler, 2004). At the same time, the middle class is disappearing, creating increased concern for those who are used to a modest amount of privilege and safety. This loss of privilege, coupled with cultural dislocation, accompanies ongoing racist and colonial violence, in the desperate search for a safe position within society, yet also opens opportunities for a broader ethics of solidarity. In terms of mental health, our practice with white middle-class young people often demonstrates how a deferred arrival into a system of privilege and safety manifests as internalized anxiety and depression. On the one hand, our ethics of solidarity and justice seeking push us toward practices which seek to contextualize young people's suffering and invite them into critical conversations about their lives and the lives of others. On the other hand, we wonder about the possibilities of creative modes of less specified encounters in therapy as a productive force (Skott-Myhre, 2014). While being responsive to oppression in our conversations, we also seek a transversal ethics that invites us to produce the future together without guarantee or safeguards.

Schizoanalysis 8

Mr. Two arrives to session with his guitar, to perform an acoustic rendition of Abigail, a song that he once used in a political theory class to analyze the force of capital. I am intrigued and lean back in my chair. Mr. Two tunes his guitar by ear and then launches into the song with little warning:

> "Abigail, I know You're in control of her brain, Abigail
> And I know that You're the one that's speaking through her, Abigail
> Miriam can You hear me"
> "I am alive inside Your Wife
> Miriam's dead, I am her head."

He stops the performance at this point, and, while strumming quietly in the background, he explains that Abigail represents the force of capital that drove his ex-wife from their ten-year marriage. He breaks back into song, his voice louder and hoarser this time:

> "Abigail, don't You think I know what you've done, Abigail
> I'll get a priest, he will know how to get her soul back"

Back into the monologue: "you see, you're the priest (he gestures toward me with a dismissive wave) but you weren't much help were you"? I shuffle awkwardly in my presider's chair. "And my ex, who is Miriam for our purposes, tried to warn us through her unrealized suicide note that there was no straight-forward way for our little triad to save her soul." He invokes desperation with the next verse, his voice becoming more frantic:

> "Oh Jonathan, this is Miriam, our time is out
> Remember the stairs, it's the only way"
> "Abigail, nothing I can do but give in, Abigail"
> "Jonathan, I agree…Yes I do"
> "I am alive inside Your Wife
> Miriam's dead, I am her head, soon I'll be free!"

And with the final verse ending he launches into a wild guitar solo that seems to undo his semi-cogent analysis with a vitriol of picking and aggressive string bending, that pulls the instrument out of tune. He finishes with a motif that sounds like a child's sandbox dirge. A refrain that seeks to soothe the fear of "ghosts, priests, and therapists." We sit in contemplative silence for a few seconds, and then, I leap in with a few questions about his song analysis, going straight for the conscious aspects of his narrative. This ongoing and habitual failure to work productively with the unconscious is congruent with the kinds of training I've received. My invitation leads to a repetition, and he talks about his ex-wife's suicide attempt and that he had to let her go so she could survive, and how she found comfort in a home with a permanent address and well-heeled fellow. "Now I'm back out on the roam" he trails off with a bluesy inflection, another single white majoritarian nomad playing with a minor key.

Conclusion

Counselling in education has been a nebula for the production of remedial subjectivity for half a century. Individuals and groups who resist or subsist outside of contemporary capital and its colonial codes are rendered invisible or expendable. Intensities, expressions, and singularities of thought are often overlooked in counselling and education, all too often recoded, curtailed, or commodified through normalizing therapy. Counselling in education, by adopting the brain-centric and cognitive-rationalist theories of mainstream psychology and psychiatry, has contributed to increased psychologization of people within capitalism and colonialism. The simultaneous marginalization of creative therapeutic labor occurring outside the evidence-base, which is upheld as an important professional ethic, motivates unsuspecting helpers to maintain the rule of hierarchy and normalization, contributing to forms of control and exploitation. Yet as a system with roots in the unconscious, counselling provides revolutionary opportunities to reconfigure relations to one another, the unconscious, and the living world. New relational, communicative, affective, and subjectivizing practices, developed in proximity to the unconscious, can be dispersed as tools for creative collaboration to expand counselling's radical and emancipatory margins. Our gambit has been to argue that the relational and unconscious processes at the heart of counselling in education provide creative opportunities for resistance to the subsumption of life to capital and begins by experimenting with our own affects and desires. A schizoanalysis of counselling praxis and education shows the immanent relations between self and other and problematizes the myth that we can stand outside and evaluate objectively. Instead, we aspire to free desire in our relationships, express our idiosyncrasies, and love those we meet along the way.

References

Alexander, B. K. (2008). *The globalisation of addiction: A study in poverty of the spirit*. Oxford: Oxford University Press.

Butler, J. (2004). *Precarious life: The powers of mourning and violence*. New York: Verso.

Cole, D. R. (2011). The actions of affect in Deleuze—Others using language and the language that we make …. *Educational Philosophy and Theory, 43*(6), 549–561.

Cole, D. R. (Ed.). (2012). *Surviving economic crises through education*. Geneva: Peter Lang.

Cole, D. R. (2013). Affective literacies: Deleuze, discipline and power. In I. Semetsky & D. Masny (Eds.), *Deleuze and Education* (pp. 94–112). Edinburgh: Edinburgh University.

Deleuze, G. (1992). Postscript on the Societies of Control. *October*, *59*, 3–7.

Deleuze, G., & Guattari, F. (2000). *Anti-Oedipus: Capitalism and schizophrenia* (R. Hurley, M. Seem, & H. R. Lane, Trans.). Minneapolis, MN: University of Minnesota Press (Original work published 1972).

Foucault, M. (1975). *Discipline and Punish: the birth of the prison. New York*: Random House.

Freud, S. (1914). *Psychopathology of everyday life*. London: Unwin.

Guattari, F. (1979). *The machinic unconscious: Essays in Schizoanalysis*, (T. Adkins, Trans.). Los Angeles, CA: Semiotext(e).

Guattari, F. (1995). *Chaosmosis: An ethico-aesthetic paradigm* (P. Bains & J. Pefanis, Trans.). Indianapolis, IN: Indiana University Press.

Hardt, M., & Negri, A. (2005). *Multitude: War and democracy in the age of empire*. New York: Penguin Press.

Kouri, S., & Smith, J. (2016). Street analysis: How we come together and apart in localized youth work peer supervision. In H. Skott-Myhre, V. Pacini-Ketchabaw, & K. Skott-Myhre (Eds.), *Youth work, early education, and psychology: Liminal encounters* (pp. 35–49). New York: Palgrave Macmillan.

Marx, K. (2013). *Capital*. Ware, Hertfordshire: Wordsworth (Originally published 1908).

Reynolds, V. (2010). *Doing justice as a path to sustainability in community work*. Retrieved from http://www.taosinstitute.net/Websites/taos/Images/PhDProgramsCompletedDissertations/ReynoldsPhDDissertationFeb2210.pdf.

Richardson, C., & Reynolds, V. (2012). "Here we are amazingly alive": Holding ourselves together with an ethic of social justice in community work. *International Journal of Child, Youth and Family Studies, 1*, 1–19.

Skott-Myhre, H. (2014). Schizoanalysis: Seizing desire as the first act of revolutionary psychotherapy. *Psychotherapy and Politics International, 12*(3), 189–195.

Skott-Myhre, H. (2015). Deleuzian perspectives: Schizoanalysis and the politics of desire. In I. Parker (Ed.), *Handbook of critical psychology* (pp. 306–314). London, UK: Routledge.

Todd, N., & Wade, A. (1994). *Domination, deficiency, and psychotherapy. Part I*. The Calgary Participator: Fall.

Tuck, E. (2009). Suspending damage: A letter to communities. *Harvard Educational Review, 79*(3), 409.

Tuck, E., & Yang, K. W. (2012). Decolonization is not a metaphor. *Decolonization: Indigeneity, 1*(1), 1–40.

Jeff Smith is a certified clinical counsellor and accredited music therapist in private practice and a sessional instructor at Brandon University. He has seventeen years of clinical experience in diverse settings (emergency shelters, youth clinic, street outreach, forensic psychiatric hospital, HIV/AIDS day center and long-term care, conservatory of music, jiu jitsu martial arts club, and nature-based outdoor settings). His research interests include language exchanges in therapeutic settings, music improvisation, and songwriting. He has authored and co-authored articles about practicing music therapy with underhoused and underemployed youth and adults, use of response-based language in counselling, wonder as ontology in child and youth care work, ontology of love in social work, and alternative consultation and supervision practices.

Scott Kouri is a Ph.D. student at the School of Child and Youth Care, University of Victoria, and counsellor in private practice and at Camosun College. He works as a depth psychotherapist focusing on Empire as a context for therapy. Foregrounding affective, political, and experimental writing, he has co-authored numerous papers including: Risking Attachments in Teaching

Child and Youth Care in Twenty-first Century Settler Colonial, Environmental and Biotechnological Worlds; Street Analysis: How we come together and apart in peer youth-work supervision; and Catastrophe: A transversal mapping of colonialism and settler subjectivity.

Chapter 14
Afterword: Zhibo, Existential Territory, Inter-Media-Mundia

Joff P. N. Bradley and David R. Cole

> *To describe urban life, at the end of the millennium, to appreciate what it tends towards, implies a choice of values relative to the social good, to the position of the imaginary in relation to the media, to the relation between the natural, the cosmic and the artificial, the machinic.* (Guattari, Osborne, Sandford, Alliez, 2015, p. 131)

> *An ecology of the virtual is just as pressing as ecologies of the visible world.* (Guattari, 1995, p. 91)

> *Oh, dear. We've become a race of Peeping Toms. What people ought to do is get outside their own house and look in for a change.*

> Stella, (Thelma Ritter), Jeffries' nurse, in Hitchcock's *Rear Window.*

Abstract In undertaking transversal research into the problems of contemporary Japanese urban life, we shall critically examine the production of subjectivities pertaining to live streaming. This is undertaken to conceptualize the changing nature of subjectivity and social relations in contemporary transnational and transcultural capitalism. We shall look to Félix Guattari's semiotic theory to interpret the era of Integrated World Capitalism (IWC). For Guattari, the production of subjectivity is pivotal to explaining the functioning of contemporary capitalism. As he claimed in

This article is a modified version of: Joff P. N. Bradley. Zhibo, Existential Territory, Inter-Media-Mundia: A Guattarian Analysis. *China Media Research* 2017; 13(4): 77–89.

J. P. N. Bradley (✉)
Teikyo University, Tokyo, Japan
e-mail: joff@main.teikyo-u.ac.jp

D. R. Cole
Western Sydney University, Sydney, Australia

his lifetime, subjectivity has become the number one objective of contemporary, capitalist society. Contra the trend to exploit subjectivity for monetary gain, Guattari's goal is to identify mutant nuclei of subjectification which may engender a change in the order of things. His work is applied to new communication technologies like live streaming (Zhibo) to account for the existential breakdowns and breakthroughs which may ensue for individuals who use these technologies. Bradley has designated this as the *Zerrissenheit* or torn-to-pieces-hood of subjectivity (Bradley in Tamkang Review, 44(2): 37–62, 2014).

Keywords Live streaming · Media landscape · Existentialism · Transversality Future learning

Vignette

> We are not in the world, we become with the world; we become by contemplating it. Everything is vision, becoming. We become universes. Becoming animal, plant, molecular, becoming zero. (Deleuze & Guattari, 1994, p. 169)

It is early evening on Boxing Day 2016, my undergraduates and I are meeting in Shinjuku in Tokyo for our yearly seminar Bonenkai ("forget the year" party). Via the Line application, and after what seems like hundreds of messages over the previous weeks, we have agreed to meet at the east exit. I get to Shinjuku in good time because I know how busy the station is but absentmindedly I follow my normal work pattern and path and proceed to the wrong exit. Outside, enshrouded by a vortex of people, I wait awhile but nobody comes. Then predictably an avalanche of truncated messages ensue; constant beeps, pings and vibrations—a system of communication which operates through a textual and oral mix of broken English and Japanese, the interspersing of emoticons and photographs of local landmarks to direct me to where I am supposed to be. I give up and someone resolves to come and find me among the throng. Subject R comes around the corner but something is different about her person. For one, I discern she is chatting away loudly in Chinese. Upon closer examination I notice that she is loaded with battery packs and technological prostheses; chief among them and positioned at the end of the arms-length retractable pole which she is carrying is an I-Phone and protruding below her face is a professional-looking microphone (Fig. 14.1). She beckons me in to this strange world, her world, and explains that her fan club is with her this evening on *Douyu*. I peer into her phone—scrolling questions and comments set in colored kanji flood the screen—"O! nice teacher!", "Can you say something in Japanese?" "Where are you from?" "Did you like China?" "Do you know David Beckham?" Subject R obliges and translates the questions back into Japanese and English and along the way to the rendezvous point with the other students explains further about her job. I am stunned, as 10,000 fans are watching in on this live stream from afar. I am at a loss. My theoretical orientation is down. My cultural coordinates - the pollution of distances (Virilio), スキゾキッズ (schizo kids; Asada, 1984), 島宇宙 (shimauchu-ka, island universes or nebularization; Miyadai,

Fig. 14.1 Subject R broadcasting herself while walking through Tokyo (All images are used with permission)

2007—interior and annexed milieus—those spaces were young people communicate with a small circle of friends and with small networks to the exclusion of anybody else), *vacuoles de non-communication* (Deleuze, 1995)—all gone. This soon deepens my pessimism regarding the potential of technologically mediated "universes of reference." Yet in this breakdown of my conceptual order, an epiphany appears. I remember the interview 'Postmodernism and Ethical Abdication' in which Guattari says to Nicholas Zurbrugg (Genosko, 1996, p. 115):

> The future which lies ahead is much more likely to be that of Bangladesh, Mexico, or Tokyo, where millions of inhabitants cluster together. In this respect, it is necessary to reinvent the body, to reinvent the mind and to reinvent language. Perhaps the new telematic, informational, and audio-visual technologies can help us to progress in this direction.

I look again and see Subject R is totally at ease with this new media and spatial ecology. She is one with a world infused with kinetic images of buildings "traversed from top to bottom by parallel neon bars" as Guattari says in *Tokyo Proud* (Genosko & Hetrick, 2015, p. 13). Perhaps for some like Miyadai Shinji this is another depressing instance of an "island universe"—essentially signifying the end of communication—but I resist this conclusion and adopt a pharmacological view of the "mega-network of miniaturized equipment" (Guattari, 2016, pp. 47–48)—seeing live streaming as both poison and cure. Subject R's job has compelled me to rethink my stance toward the communication practices found in the ephemeral fads and trends of viral semio-capitalism.

Theoretical Constellation

Interpreted through an account of a possible fourth (media) ecology (Ueno, 2016;
Zhang, 2015)—an extension of Guattari's notion of the three ecologies (social,
environmental, and psychical), this chapter seeks to account for the passage from
Asada's schizo kids - marginal, wild, minor - and theory of escape (tōsōron, 逃走論)
to マルチ・キッズ [multi-kids] (Yaginuma, 2010). In the 1980s, Asada described
schizo kids as young people leading nomadic lives who refuse to follow traditional
ways of life. The escape from Japanese civilization necessitated, Asada claimed, (now
read as a kind of orthodox Nietzschean, accelerationist reading of Deleuze and Guattari's *Anti-Oedipus*), a paradigm shift from the paranoiac to the schizophrenic type.
The Japanese word "toso" usually means "escape," but it was also used as a homonym
to suggest "struggle." To escape means to struggle. Under Asada's "gay science"
of struggle and escape, youth traversed Japan's world of "infantile capitalism" (see
Asada in Miyoshi, & Harootunian, 1989, p. 275)[1] and indulged in the economy
as a childlike game. Clearly, Asada wished to accelerate this trend, writing in *Tōsōron*:
行先なんて知ったことか。とにかく、逃げろや逃げろ、どこまでも、だ。(Do
you know where to? Just escape! Escape! To wherever.) The schizo lifestyle was
defined as contemporary, irresponsible, and postmodern—postmodern because
the lifestyle was constructed without deciding anyone fixed position or identity.
Capitalism in Japan functioned smoothly despite its infantile characteristics—it
passed through the three stages of elderly capitalism, adult capitalism, and infantile
capitalism. For Miyadai, small groups or "island-universes" adopt exclusive values,
lifestyles, and beliefs to the exclusion of others. Intimacy leads to indifference to
people outside their tribe, communication network or islands. We may perhaps also
understand the live streaming phenomenon in terms of Karatani Kojin's "counter-
act" theory which relies on the strategy of "exiting and transcending" (*choshutsuteki
na taiko*), "super-capitalism" (*cho-shihonshugi*) or what he names the trinity of
"capital, nation and state." A counter-act or resistance is less to do with direct
confrontation and more to do with "withdrawal," "disappearance," "desertion,"
"exodus," or "flight." A counter-act therefore seeks change through exhaustion with
the system: this can be differentiated from the kind of hyper-consumption "for any
absurd purpose" of which Baudrillard describes. Karatani invokes a twin-pronged
counter-strategy of "immanent" (*naizaiteki*) and "exscendent" (*choshutsuteki*)
in relation to Japanese capitalism. The term "exscendent" here is a neologism

---

[1]In reality, however, Japan did not at all mature. Far from it. It seems to be growing progressively
more infantile. Yet Japanese capitalism appears to be functioning all the more smoothly and effectively. Is the formation of the adult subject in fact really necessary and indispensable to capitalism,
if not to modernization? The answer, I think, is "no." What is indispensable is, rather, the process
of relative competition; it does not matter whether the relationship becomes internalized or remains
external. Clearly, the latter is the case with Japan. Thus, in Japan, there are neither tradition-oriented
old people adhering to transcendental values nor inner-oriented adults who have internalized their
values; instead, the nearly purely relative (or relativistic) competition exhibited by other-oriented
children provides the powerful driving force for capitalism. Let's call this infantile capitalism. This
is a remarkable spectacle, and, in many senses, deeply interesting.

suggesting "exiting and transcendent" (Cassegard, 2007, 2008; Cazdyn, 2012, p. 58). We may also read live streaming through the notion of interbeing-in-the-world, following the interological turn in media ecology (Zhang & McLuhan, 2016).

As can be seen from the previous remarks, this chapter is primarily concerned with addressing the mental-media ecologies and woes impacting upon youth. It thus makes technology the fourth component in the triadic ecology. In particular, and from a transdisciplinary, interological, and transversal point of view (Zhang, 2015), we shall address the issue of existential territory in the *non-places* (Augé, 2008) of the world. To this end, the chapter looks at a singular experience of space and time, or more concretely expressed, at the "world" or milieu of a female Chinese student learning English in a Japanese university, whose "presence" is always elsewhere, mediated and dominated by transnational and transcultural media and flows. Through examining her work as a popular live streamer, recording day to day life in Tokyo via mobile phone technology to tens of thousands of followers in China, we shall consider the meaning of alienation, presence, language and, importantly, the belonging of a subject who is living a form of *inter-media-mundia or interworldliness*. The point to be made is that global flows of money and minaturization act as a shield to effectively ward off difference and the experience of the other—yet they also rip the self further away from "deconnected" and "emptied" space, from a relation to the *hic et nunc*. Media thus acts as a machine of hyper-alienation from the immediate milieu. As the Chinese student jumps from one metropole to another Shanghai-Tokyo-Shanghai - suffering existential stress in the meantime—she rejects the unknown to instead reterritorialize on an established network and imagined community "back home." In this way, technology acts as an imagined land of security and sanctuary (Conley, 2012).

Douyu

My student uses the live streaming phone app Douyu, which has considerable popularity in China. Although the live streaming phone app market has more than 200 rivals in China such as Ingkee, the principle is the same: streamers distribute live video and simultaneously interact with viewers. Ingkee says that 50 million users have already downloaded their app. Douyu claims its own figure is more than 120 million. It is estimated that Weibo users created 10 million live broadcasts from April to June 2016—a 100+ increase over the first three months of the year. Weibo claims to have 282 million monthly active users and draws in revenue from video ads and taking a cut of virtual gifts.[2] Douyu claims that average daily active users total around 15 million people and has around 200 million active users monthly. In 2016, China's live-stream market revenue totaled 15 billion yuan. The figure is forecasted to rise

---

[2] New mobile applications like Douyu are not limited to China. Live streaming or self-broadcasting is a viral commodity in Southeast Asia also. For example, Indonesian youth use Bigo Live, released in March 2016, to explore their personal life.

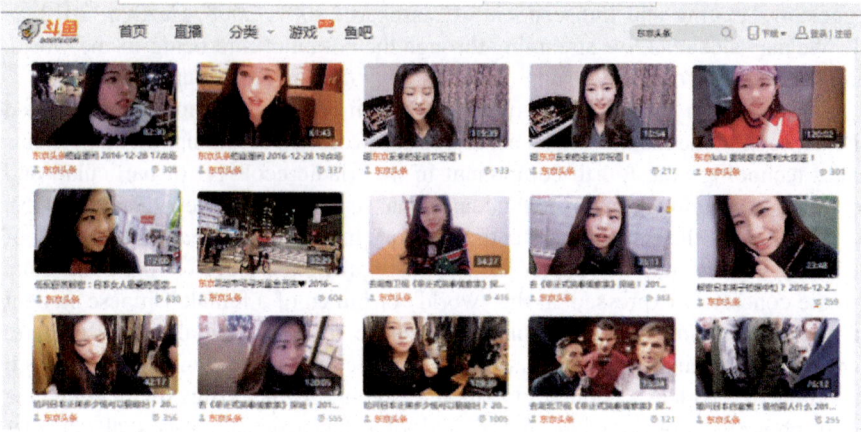

Fig. 14.2 Images from Subject R's live streaming feed

to 60 billion yuan by 2020. Although live broadcasting is not exclusive to China, for example, in the USA, there are live streaming services such as Meerkat and Twitter's Periscope, and Facebook Live, there is something distinctive about the phenomena in China (Fig. 14.2).

The research shows that in recent years billions of yuan have been invested in China's live-streaming websites. The craze really started to take off in 2014. Why? Because there is an audience for live streaming. Under neo-liberal economic policy, we are all encouraged to be self-entrepreneurs. To sell and market what we have—brains, good looks, skills, youth. From the safety of their own homes, people pay to watch others. Voyeurs look at the world through someone else's eyes.[3] What is fascinating about live streaming is how the host and audience interact. Viewers, sometimes in the tens of thousands at any one time, can send instant messages which are streamed across the screen in real time. We might ask why people wish to watch others so obsessively and pay for the privilege. Is it mere boredom or loneliness? The other side of this is that hosts may feel this sense of boredom and loneliness as well, but something else is happening also on an existential register which needs to be accounted for.

The most popular streams are video game focused or those which follow the daily lives of female hosts or "Stream Queens." Viewers can buy virtual gifts such as images of flowers or bottles of beer for their favorite hostesses who receive a portion of the revenue stream, with the site getting a significant cut.[4]

Soon after she became a student, Subject R gave her part-time job to participate in the virtual world of live streaming. For Subject R the app can pay much more than her dead-end part-time job did. It is clearly a moneymaker. What is remarkable about Subject R's work is that instead of staying in front of her screen at home for

---

[3] http://www.wired.co.uk/article/live-streaming-entertainment.

[4] http://www.shanghaidaily.com/business/it/Douyus-funding-to-boost-livestreaming/shdaily.shtml.

six or seven hours a day (data input clerk), she gets out and about, interfacing with the architecture of the city, interacting simultaneously with its people in the here and now and virtually with fans elsewhere. Subject R says the work can be grueling, in walking around the city, constantly interacting with fans and interviewing people, but again she enjoys the attention and the difference.

From a Guattarian point of view, her comportment to the world is a kind of involution—*interbeing*, rhizomatic, always intermezzo. Her life is schizzed by a transversal or translocal processes characterized by immediate political geographic relations (I am a foreign student expected to be at school, etc), but also by those affects directed at the body (walking for hours a day), capital flows across the earth (a percentage in the takings from virtual gifts), ideological investments in a social field, (a Chinese in Tokyo discussing Chinese culture and politics), and thought itself (who am I, what am I doing here?). The geography of Shinjuku is there physically but it is also mediated, part of a mental assemblage and ecology. Her iPhone and the interactions with it construct a mental landscape. In some ways, the enthusiasm for transhumant live streaming or flaneurship is of course comparable to the euphoria for GPS-led Pokémon Go, which has done much to further blur the distinction between the real and mediated gaming environments. Her contraption of microphone-extension pole-iPhone does more than set up a simple sound circuit. Instead of communing with a mobile phone, she engages with the cityscape—perpendicular and oblique—albeit an urban media escape equipped with instant messages and constant questions and suggestions. It is not simply the case that the live streamer is alone in another world—suffering a form of autism—because she is also connected with thousands of followers.

Live Streaming

Live streaming can be understood as a model of new capitalist subjectivities. One performs a service for others in exchange for virtual gifts. Always on call, online, live streamers stream in immaterial universes and are implicated in the production of subjectivities across nation, culture and language. Their way of working, being and living constitutes a statement about interology and interbeing (Zhang, 2015). These immaterial universes are transcultural and transnational. Across the screens of the live streamer flow a-signifying signs of emotion—hearts, fruit, emoticons. Live streaming represents the creation of new worlds of reference, existential territories, and collective assemblages of enunciation. The live streamer traverses concrete locations and territories and is transient in virtual spaces of consumption, spaces of temporariness and transience, devoid of social relation. She could be anywhere in the world, positioned in an anonymous space, "without solidarity, without tomorrow, without commitment, without common interests, a game society" (Lévinas & Aronowicz 1990, p. 111). In these spaces, affects are not solely of one's own making. They are impersonal, nonhuman, unnatural. The immanent affects of face-voice-screen-text-screen-voice-face-voice-relay operate to and through the live streamer. The immediate milieu is mediated through the microphone-pole-phone arrangement engendering an existential constellation of nonhuman affects. The streamer's communication with fans and with people in the local milieu is part of an existential group nucleus. The live streamer, or what we may call through the Chinese and Japanese language-inflected neologism 直播-族 (*Zhibo-zoku*), traverses an *intermonde* or *interkingdom*.

Her place in the local milieu is one of an unnatural participation. In this sense, Guattari's speculative cartography is able to account for the invention of spaces between existential territories and incorporated universes of values. In this respect, ecosophy is applicable to the phenomenon of live streaming. It is a philosophy of the virtual ecology of the immediate info-sphere which can grasp the relay between subjectivities, environments, and the myriad production of subjectivities. The task ahead is to draw the cartography or "inter-monadic transversality" (Guattari, 1995, p. 117) of the live streamer.

Four Functors

Overseeing the concrete live streaming machine, one could state that there is an abstract machine of transversality—which is functioning across nations, cultures, classes, and ages. We can explain the abstract machine's operations through Guattari's four functors schematic. The machinic assemblage of the live streamer can be understood through the four functors - the economy of fluxes (actual real), machinic phyla (actual possible), incorporeal universes (virtual possible), and existential territories (virtual real). Regarding the functor of flux (libido, signifier, capital, labor), the live streamer is embroiled within material streams of fleeting eyes and feet, traffic signals, train lines, station announcements, chat bots, streaming video data, electric signals, translanguaging, interpretation, translation, neon signs, phonetic tones, battery life, work-day-student-life-commuting-time, libidos, desires, financial remuneration. The second functor in relation to machinic phyla creates an objective deterritorialization as live streamers are part of a machinic phylum of smart phone machines and apps, more powerful processors, more RAM, interactive screens, more miniturization, game networks, chat lines, VPN escape routes, extraction of rare earth materials, slave labor factories in China, brought on by rapacious competition from Twitter, Facebook, and the hundreds of competitors on the mainland and in Hong Kong. Live steaming is and will mutate into something else, better platforms, aggressive monetarization strategies, amateur pornography, voyeurism, exhibitionism, self-obsession, psychical illnesses—mental pollution.

What connects incorporeal universes to existential territories is a subjective deter-ritorialization. In terms of the first, live streaming sites are incorporeal universes in themselves. People sit at their desks, watch on the train, sing and dance, chat about mundane matters—there is a constant traversing of the virtual possible with new content, new utopias, or inaugural assemblages. The connection with existential territories where streamers and their fans form a shared and intimate world, albeit a virtual one, offers the potential to ward off the psychical excesses of Integrated World Capitalism. There, incorporeal universes are singular, viral, frantic, lawless;

they quickly come into being and pass away and in doing so—bring about a change in existential comportment to the world and impact on the psycho-sphere of its users. The existential territories of individuals operate in a multi-dimensional and transversal milieu—they engineer repetition and refrains. "I am doing a live broadcast for fans in China—may I interview you?" This refrain uttered hundred times a day by the live streamer. The refrain takes place in the territories of Shinjuku, Shibuya, or Harajuku—in restaurants, train stations, on the street. The milieu is heterogeneous. The streamer interfaces with her fans *via* the screen, *via* Chinese kanji, and Asian multiliteracies (the meaning and knowledge of gift giving in China and Japan)—she speaks to machines hundreds and sometimes thousands of miles away, via microphone, via telephone signals, via data packets, via a-signifying semiotics, via buffered signals.

Integrated World Capitalism

In a brief bout of optimism, Guattari believed that new miniaturalized technologies could be directed away from negative ends via molecular, transversal reorganization to more positive, life-affirming goals. From the democratic chaos of live streaming, one could imagine him saying that one must isolate the "multitude of vectors of resingularization, of attractors of social creativity in search of actualization" (Guattari, 1995, p. 117). The question arises: Is there a possibility of individual and/or collective re-singularization in live streaming? At first glance, it seems difficult to see how live streaming is consistent with this radical aspect of Guattari's thought. Indeed, for Virilio, for his part, no group or community can divert the negative impacts of technology regarding exchange, displacement, and communication. For him, the challenge to technology's subjection of the earth must emerge at the wider political and philosophical level. He designates the negative impact of technologies as the catastrophe of the pollution of distances and claims it will not be lonely individuals who reconfigure technology's subjection. Like most of us, such people suffer from dromospheric pollution, the contamination of "time distances" and the compression of "depth of field" (Virilio, 1997, p. 40). Virilio writes (1995, p. 35): "With acceleration there is no more here and there, only the mental confusion of near and far, present and future, real and unreal—a mix of history, stories, and the hallucinatory utopia of communication technologies." To colonize the psyche is the "great catastrophe" (Virilio) and "drama of globalization"—leading to the pollution of distances. For Virilio, the ecological catastrophe is accompanied by the catastrophe of the pollution of the distances, that is to say "the reduction of the world to nothing" (Virilio & Guattari, 1995, *my trans*). Virilio's remarks are consistent with Heidegger, who claims in the essay 'The Thing' in 1950 that the domination of the televisual by the machinery of communication will lead to "the abolition of every possible remoteness" (Heidegger, 1971, p. 163). Virilio insists that the ramifications of the concept of one world time has deflated the sphere of the world before our very eyes. Meanwhile, for Berardi, and with applicability to *Zhibo*, phenomena such as depression and panic are psychopathologies that traverse the social mind as well as the unconsciousness, and are connected to informational overload and competitive stress under globalization.

So from Miyadai's "island universes" of disconnection, indifference, and monadic transversality to Berardi's "islands of slowness," from connection as control to conjunction as creativity and meaning-making, should or can we imagine "lines of escape from the spreading universe of unhappiness, in terms of islands of slowness, of convivial corporeality?" (Berardi, 2014, p. 92). Berardi warns that accelerated processes of info-technology multiplied by "semiocapitalist exploitation" (2014, p. 201) suggest that information cannot be easily translated into "cosmos, mental order… and sympathy" (2014, p. 201).

Fourth Ecology

The fan is not a person but a nickname, a polyphonic sound, an emoticon, part of the metaphysics or ecology of image, an ecology of technologies or media, in other words, part of the "world picture" (Fry, 2012), a component in an "aeonic economy." This sense of the "ecology of the image" can be fittingly described as a *fourth ecology*. How can the *fourth ecology* better interpret the phenomena of live streaming? The relationship is virtual—gifts, messages, requests, words of enthusiasm. The streamer transverses the local milieu, through refrains on her phone, and refrains at the station. Her transversality is a crossing. a going across, a form of walking, travel, sailing, running, flying. To cross or traverse means to move from A to B, as in to cross the road from one side to another. In other words, transversality could be figured as a journeying. Her agency is machinic, balletic, kinetic, surrounded by phatic and haptic images, wall images, building images, advertisements, train signs, interfaced by nonhuman objects and machines—communication by swishing, swirling, prodding, probing—a sweeping, transversal movement… "a stream without beginning or end" (Deleuze & Guattari, 1987, p. 25). To understand this vehicular comportment we can use the concept of *transversality*. Contending that a fourth media ecology complements Guattari's three ecologies thesis, Ueno (2016) argues that this fourth ecology is crucial to understanding the contemporary moment's relation to ecosophy. It is essential to understand how the fourth ecology of the image is affecting, and redefining the environmental, social, and psychical ecologies. Concurring with this stance, we can extract the following observations: Live streaming is an example of collusion with transnational flows of immaterial labor and info-semio-capitalism. It expresses the delirium and delusion of technology. On this point Ueno says (Thouny & Yoshimoto, 2017, p. 143): "Info-semio-capitalism in the current era of globalization and neoliberalism forces us not only to participate in the production of signs, symbols, and knowledges in our cognitive labor but also to engage in the very production of subjectivity." The demand to extend and refine the three ecologies thesis has also been taken up by other writers. Zhang is one of them who argues (Zhang, 2016, p. 345):

The picture, however, is incomplete if we do not explicitly recognize and take into consideration a fourth ecology, namely, the ecology of technologies or media, which bears significantly upon the three ecologies examined by Guattari… It is time for us to make a strategic shift of perspective and envision the world in terms of the ecology of machinic assemblages, which encompasses all four dimensions, namely, the environmental, the technological, the social, and the mental.

Affirmation of Machinic Animism and *Cine-Trance*

The live streamer engages in a form of machinic animism, a "strange ecology" which interfaces with the local milieu, with virtual ecologies, a huge array of semiotic registers. Live streaming produces a virtuality of the world, an inter-world. It reconfigures what Guattari describes in *Psychoanalysis and Transversality* (2015, p. 112) as the "coefficient of transversality"—a way of altering perception. It allows the users to see the world from a new perspective. In this way, my epiphany with Subject R allowed me to consider my own intellectual blindness to the new possibilities offered by these technologies. The concept of transversality allowed me to see the world afresh. It removed my "intellectual blinkers." We can therefore heuristically decode the recent phenomena of live streaming through the concept of transversality and bring out the ramifications for other relevant media ecologies. Describing the concept as a tool to prise open "closed logics and hierarchies" (2002, p. 78), Genosko outlines the potential of transversal thinking (2002, p. 55) (Fig. 14.3):

> [T]ransversality belongs to the processual subject's engendering of an existential territory and self-transportation beyond it. The key concepts involved are: mobility (traversing domains, levels, dimensions, the ability to carry and be carried beyond); creativity (productivity, adven-

Fig. 14.3 Info image of Subject R

turousness, aspiration, laying down lines of flight); self-engendering (autoproduction, self-positing subjectivity), territories from which one can really take off into new universes of reference.

Live streaming is thus part of a transversal and transcultural continuum. Through the live stream, a processual and collective subjectivity creates an existential territory. But more than this, live streaming takes its user beyond the immediate milieu, the *hic et nunc*: There is a "self-transportation beyond it" to possible new universes of reference as Genosko says. The live streamer who in engineering impersonal sensations and affects operates in a virtual atmosphere of ontological and aesthetic *chaosmosis*: there is a becoming machine-part of a transversal assemblage or construct—transcending the natural/technological dichotomy. The body without organs of the live streamer is traversed by inhuman perceptions and affects - "nonhuman becomings of man"... "nonhuman landscapes of nature" (Deleuze & Guattari, 1994, p. 169). The dogmatic insistence upon the nature/culture, nature/technology divide is undermined when we see transversal interactions between ecosystems, the mechanosphere and social and individual universes of reference (Guattari, 2000, p. 29). In this instance, one could say that *transversality* disrupts the binaries that organize the world of work and reason. As Deleuze and Guattari declare in *Anti-Oedipus* (1983, p. 2):

> There is no such thing as either man or nature now, only a process that produces the one within the other and couples the machines together. Producing machines, desiring machines everywhere, schizophrenic machines, all of species of life: the self and the non-self, outside and inside, no longer have any meaning whatsoever.

Live streamers mutate into the screens and terminals around them and in their hands. The video camera also transforms those to whom it is pointed. Live streamers enjoin their local milieu, in a form of *cine-trance,* a form of psycho-geography, a tactile synesthesia—being one "with" the medium. A package of data—from screen and walls to the retinas of Chinese viewers, from screen and walls to the retinas of the live streamer, from micro portable screen to the walls and screens of Tokyo. Fans too are part of a video game, part simulation, part simulacrum. The fans are actively directing the interaction of the streamer—requesting, cajoling, seducing—not merely vegetating but actively engaged in consuming, questioning: theirs is a desire to remote control the live streamer. The live streamer is a virtual girlfriend, or akin to a character in *Final Fantasy*. The live streamer's work is an act of traversing, a flâneur and voyeur in the Sprawl. Traversing Shibuya crossing, crossing between cultures, translating languages and cultures, the live streamer interacts with hyper phatic and haptic surfaces, not only surfaces in the local milieu but those further afield, surfaces mediated by Chinese and Japanese characters, Western alphabets, mixed semiotics, different economic regimes. While this may well prove to be another mode of attention-grabbing, it also allows for a more interactive relation with the local milieu. A Zhibo streamer's interactions with her fans thus contest any straightforward reading of traditional modes of attention-grabbing.

In this strange state of transformation—akin to Jean Rouch's cine-trance aesthetic—the live streamer is a "mechanical eye accompanied by an electronic ear" (Rouch & Feld, 2003, p. 39). The *cine-trance* of the live streamer creates an interbeing amid the rapid flow of images, leaking and passing into others, mixed with Kanji, advertising refrains, images of bodies, producing a hypnosis, a neuro-state induced through the lens of the camera, involving the live streamer, her object of attention, and her fan base. The cine-trance of the live streamer grants access to the *intermundia*—that is to say, participating in interactive events that are perhaps visible only to "children, madmen, and primitives" (Deleuze & Guattari, 1983, p. 264). Elsewhere, Guattari will say that looking at the world through different collective practices—the eyes of children, the elderly, the disabled—will help break with the standard, mass-mediatized gaze (Guattari, Osborne, Sandford, & Alliez, 2015, p. 134).

In terms of Subject R's interactions, hers is a life in the cracks, an in-betweenness of becoming-Japanese and the struggle to ward off reterritorializing on an essential Chinese identity. Her generation embraces live streaming as a new form of machinic eros. The live streamer's mobile body pans across the surface of objects, interactive advertising, a self-surveillance camera to rival universal, face-recognition surveillance cameras, and the technologies of the Tokyo Metropolitan police. Optimistically put, the new technology which ushers in the world of live streaming is a mode of deterritorialization. It produces new intensities and the in-betweens of multiplicities. It is the job of media ecologists to chart the ramifications of this fanatical fadism.

In interfacing with millions of others faces, metropole hopping, traversing spaces occupied by millions of eyes, feet, sounds, words, in movement, not thinking as such, new material and semiotics practices flourish—new patterns of interality emerge. The movement of images takes over thinking. The movement thinks through the screen. Ideas are created in the mutual intertwining of micro-interalities (微細間性) with the neon-*Umwelt* or neon-world. Ideas and thoughts are directing rather than stemming from the isolated direction of the subject. The subject is decentered as impersonal intensities and affects compel the movement of thought in this relation to the neon-*Umwelt*. Thought comes from the outside of a current milieu: it is a force that moves through *personal enunciation* rather than being enshrined within it. The live streamer thus gives herself over to other forces, to the nonhuman, to the technological. This position is also described albeit with a cautionary note in 'From Chaos to the Brain,' the title of the conclusion of *What is Philosophy*? (Deleuze & Guattari, 1994, p. 201) which invokes the notion of "a little order" as protection from the chaos:

> Nothing is more distressing than a thought that escapes itself, than ideas that fly off, that disappear hardly formed, already eroded by forgetfulness or precipitated into others that we no longer master. These are infinite variabilities the appearing and disappearing of which coincide. They are infinite speeds that blend into the immobility of the colorless and silent nothingness they traverse, without nature or thought. This is the instant of which we do not know whether it is too long or too short for time. We receive sudden jolts that beat like arteries. We constantly lose our ideas.

From *Umwelt to Unwelt, from Excrescent to Exscendent*

If we regard live streaming as the extraction of surplus value from loneliness, we can perhaps consider it better through Jean-Luc Nancy's stance regarding the destruction of the world and the dominance of the unworld or vile world. From milieu to unworld, there is a underside to this process, where technological mediation can lead to the loss of collective memory. Similarly, Begag (Conley, 2012) draws attention to North Africans living in an interworld between Paris and their lives back home. The comportment of immigrants to the world is elsewhere, unreferenced by the local milieu, by the experience of immediate space and time as they are effectively communing elsewhere. While this is important for the sense of ethnic identity, for Begag, if they do not care to learn the local language, be with local people, embrace local culture and ethnic difference, there is a risk they will become content to be merely indifferent. Despite their migration, they are immobile. In this sense, televised images of an imagined community back home stall the process of becoming-other. This is what Virilio determines as the pollution of distances. The refrain turns out badly—exhausts itself. This is the refrain which resists becoming-otherwise, which reterritorializes on the familiar, the safe, the striated order of formalized rules and obligations. This is the refrain which dare not embark on the unknown. There emerges a strong sense of resistance to becoming-other. Immigrants, retaining a fixed way of doing things from their homeland, construct a simulacra of what they have left behind. Toward off existential anxiety, desire here turns to nostalgia and withdraws, to the fictional spaces of cable TV programs imported from home. Soap operas act as a reterritorializing literature. Desire turns to rot. Foreign students like Subject R may at times follow this model—a fixed way of life, a simulacra of the homeland.

Desire for live streaming is not only about the desire for the block of expensive micro technology held in the hand, nor is it simply about desire for fans, money, or mere narcissism. Why? Because as Deleuze says, one always desires through an *ensemble*. Desire is not desire for *objet petit-a* as such; it is never a teleology. One does not desire the totality of the *ensemble* or aggregate either transcendent to it either. I do not desire Shinjuku in itself, nor the attention-grabbing signification, nor the immersion in neon, crowds, and noise. Contra Lyotard, neither do I enjoy—perversely—soaking up the alienation, loneliness, boredom and indifference. Live-streaming desire forms from within an aggregate and this desire flows within an arrangement of desire… walking, make-up, English-Japanese-Chinese, architecture, street signs, sound refrains, train jingles, flows of virtual gifts. The live streamer is an assemblage of foreign student, Chinese woman, fashionable, confident girl. Moreover, the engineering of new subjectivities is thus always an activity of meta-modeling (Guattari, 2013, p. 17). In this respect, the task of schizoanalysis is to understand what happens when one inheres in the screens of live streaming or animation. It is to understand both how one can become quickly captured or hypnotized by the "perceptual fascination" of live streaming, and to understand the role of the unconscious in desiring this hypnotic state. It is a question of appreciating how the subjectivity is torn to bits as a consequence. How does the live streamer retain a sense of self as components of subjectification sweep past? What is the nature of the refrain that fixes the live streamer in front of the screen and what is the nature of the desire that desires this mental pollution, a desire, in other words, which desires its own repression. Here we learn from Guattari in his essay "Transdisciplinarity Must Become Transversality" who asserts that the standard, mass-mediatized gaze of Integrated World Capitalism "corrupts our intellect and our sensibility" (Guattari, Osborne, Sandford, & Alliez, 1995, p. 134). But equally, we also deploy his concepts to look for potential moments of resingularization. Schizoanalysis and transversality are thus the theoretical coordinates for understanding the politics of media ecological enslavement, the imperatives of social control, and "the normalization of collective labor power" (Guattari, 2011, p. 89). So as to grapple with the production of IWC as a modelization of "behavior, sensibility, perception, memory, social relations, sexual relations, imaginary phantoms, etc" (Guattari & Rolnik, 2008, p. 39), we must therefore construct/deconstruct global processes through and with the notion of transversality understood as a "tool box of modelization" (Guattari, 1996, p. 192).

Conclusion

Semio-capitalism covets movements of immaterial expression and labor, capturing the tendencies and qualities of these movements of immanent machinic expression, to channel them toward the extraction of surplus value of life, in order to monetarize all that lives. In this respect, semio-capitalism is a vampire preying upon the isolation and loneliness of youth. There is no space, individual, or group exempt from complicity with this aggressive form of semio-capitalism. The question as always is how to inflect the relation. As the live streamer traverses smooth spaces of hyperconsumption in a kind of homeless, isolated drift, with her nomadic subjectivity always in transit, never at home, a homelessness in the body, her embodiment glides across boundaries, bodies, cultures, languages, and gender positions. Here as ask: Aided by virtual technologies, how can this transcultural aspect lead to the reinvention of the other forms of alterity? What Guattari's schizoanalysis aims to do is to metamodel a different way of being and living today. Through an experimental collage of models, and by creating singular maps of psychical life, Guattari is aiming to create the basis for a new kind of politics, a new way of doing things, a new kind of ecology and sensibility which questions the whole of subjectivity and capitalistic power formations. Guattari is thus the consummate media ecologist striving for a philosophy of *dissensus* which turns orthodox formations and enunciations inside-out—engineering a fourth dimension beyond distinct models of ecology, socius, and mental life. From Guattari's ethico-aesthetic paradigm, to understand the functions and interrelations of power and technology, we must understand the way power inheres in modes of subjectivation, that is to say, the way in which one is constituted *qua* subjectivity. The critique of Integrated World Capitalism then is premised on the role of technology and the way it produces new ethico-political formations. I began this paper with the quote by Jeffries' nurse Stella in Hitchcock's *Rear Window.* Why?

Because live streaming seems to challenge her observation. We can reformulate the point as follows: Voyeurism abounds in the *unworld* of capitalism but people are essentially always outside their own house or milieu, always transhumant rather than immobile or invalidated. What we need to do perhaps is look *out* for a change—less loneliness, less indifference, less *hikikomori* syndrome, or hermetic lifestyle—and more becoming-other. From vacuoles of solitude and silence to conjunctive concatenation and finally the settling of scores.

References

Augé, M. (2008). *Non-places: Introduction to an anthropology of supermodernity*. London: Verso.
Asada, A. (1984). Tōsōron: Sukizo, kizzu no bōken. [*On escape: Adventures of the Schizo Kids*]. Tō kyō: Chikuma Shobō.
Berardi, F. (2014). *And: Phenomenology of the end*. Finland: Aalto University publication.
Bradley, J. P. N. (2014, June 1). The Zerrissenheit of subjectivity. *Tamkang Review, 44*(2), 37–62.
Cassegard, C. (2007). Exteriority and transcritique: Karatani Kojin and the impact of the 90's. *Japanese Studies, 27*(1), 1–18.
Cassegard, C. (2008). From withdrawal to resistance. The rhetoric of exit in Yoshimoto Takaaki and Karatani Kojin. *Asia-Pacific Journal: Japan Focus, 6*(3), 33–41.
Cazdyn, E. M. (2012). *The already dead: The new time of politics, culture, and illness*. Durham: Duke University Press.
Conley, V. A. (2012). *Spatial ecologies: Urban sites, state and world-space in French cultural theory*. Liverpool: Liverpool University Press.
Deleuze, G. (1995). *Negotiations: 1972–1990*. New York: Columbia University Press.
Deleuze, G., & Guattari, F. (1983). *Anti-Oedipus: Capitalism and schizophrenia*. Minneapolis, MN: University of Minnesota Press.
Deleuze, G., & Guattari, F. (1987). *A thousand plateaus: Capitalism and schizophrenia*. Minneapolis, MN: University of Minnesota Press.
Deleuze, G., Guattari, F., Tomlinson, H., & Burchell, G. (1994). *What is philosophy?*. New York: Columbia University Press.
Fry, T. (2012). *Becoming human by design*. London: Berg.
Genosko, G. (1996). *The Guattari reader*. Oxford, UK: Blackwell Publishers.
Genosko, G. (2002). *Félix Guattari: An aberrant introduction*. London and New York: Continuum.
Genosko, G., & Hetrick, J. (2015). *Machinic eros: Writings on Japan*. Minneapolis: University of Minnesota Press.
Guattari, F. (1995). *Chaosmosis: An ethico-aesthetic paradigm*. Bloomington, IN: Indiana University Press.
Guattari, F. (1996). *Chaosophy*. New York: Semiotext(e).
Guattari, F. (2000). *The three ecologies*. London: Athlone Press.
Guattari, F. (2011). *The machinic unconscious: Essays in schizoanalysis*. Cambridge, MA: Semiotext(e).
Guattari, F. (2013). *Schizoanalytic cartographies*. London: Bloomsbury.
Guattari, F. (2015). *Psychoanalysis and transversality: Texts and interviews 1955–1971*. New York: Semiotext(e).
Guattari, F. (2016). *Lines of flight: For another world of possibilities*. London: Bloomsbury.
Guattari, F., Osborne, P., Sandford, S., & Alliez, É. (2015, September). Transdisciplinarity must become transversality. *Theory, Culture & Society, 32*, 131–137.
Guattari, F., & Rolnik, S. (2008). *Molecular revolution in Brazil*. Los Angeles, CA: Semiotext(e).
Heidegger, M. (1971). *Poetry, language, thought*. New York: Harper & Row.

Lévinas, E., & Aronowicz, A. (1990). *Judaism and revolution. Nine Talmudic readings*. Blooming-ton, IN: Indiana University Press.

Miyadai, S. (2007, January 1). Shimauchu ni setsuna ni mureru tokumei nokanojotachi. ['Island universes' and the swarming of anonymous girls]. Passingtime/Tbs. *Institute of Media, 68*, 2–7.

Miyoshi, M., & In Harootunian, H. D. (1989). *Postmodernism and Japan*. Durham, NC: Duke University Press.

Rouch, J., & Feld, S. (2003). *Ciné-ethnography*. Minneapolis: University of Minnesota Press.

Thouny, C., & Yoshimoto, M. (2017). *Planetary atmospheres and urban society After Fukushima*. Singapore: Springer.

Ueno, T. (2016). Yottsu no ekorojī: Ferikkusu gatari no shikō. [*Four ecologies: The thought of Félix Guattari*]. Tō kyō: Kawadeshobō shinsha.

Virilio, P. (1995). *The art of the motor*. Minneapolis, MN: University of Minnesota Press.

Virilio, P. (1997). *Open sky*. London: Verso.

Virilio, P., & Guattari, F. (1995). *Entretien Paul Virilio sur Félix Guattari (31 Janvier 1994)*. Paris: Gautiell.

Yaginuma, R. (2010). *Posutomodan no jiyū kanri kyōiku: Sukizo kizzu kara maruchi kizzu e*. Yoko-hama: Shunpūsha.

Zhang, P. (2015). Prologue to interology: In lieu of a preface. *China Media Research, 11*(2), 57–67.

Zhang, P. (2016). The four ecologies, post-evolution, and singularity. *Explorations in Media Ecol-ogy. 15*(3+4), 343–354.

Zhang, P., & McLuhan, E. (2016, January 1). The interological turn in media ecology. *Canadian Journal of Communication, 41*(1), 207–225.

Dr. Joff P. N. Bradley is Associate Professor in the Faculty of Language Studies at Teikyo Uni-versity, Tokyo, Japan. He is currently researching the teaching of critical thinking and philosophy through film in the Japanese university. With David R. Cole, he is co-author of *A Pedagogy of Cinema* (2016) and co-editor of both *Educational Philosophy and New French Thought* (2017), and with Dr Tony See, co-editor of *Deleuze and Buddhism* (2016).

David R Cole is an Associate Professor in Education at Western Sydney University, Australia, and the leader of the Globalisation theme in the Centre for Educational Research. He has pub-lished fifteen academic books, and numerous (100+) journal articles, book chapters, conference presentations, and other public output. He has been involved with thirteen major educational research projects across Australia and internationally and is a world-leading expert in the applica-tion of the philosophy of Gilles Deleuze and Félix Guattari to education. David's latest monograph is called: *A Pedagogy of Cinema* (2016, Sense Publishers) with Joff P. N. Bradley.

Index

A

Adorno, 154, 167, 169
Agamben, 76
Alice, 12, 175–178, 181, 183–185, 187, 188
Animist, 5
Anthropocentric, 205
Anti-colonial, 164
Arendt, 76
Asia, 71, 74, 102, 131, 132, 231
Assemblages, 41, 44, 79, 85, 87, 88, 92, 93,
    107, 111, 122, 132–134, 136, 138, 163,
    164, 188, 190, 205, 208, 213, 233, 234,
    237
Asylum, 132, 144
Australia, 11, 117–124, 126–128, 131–134,
    137, 139, 141–143, 145
Australian, 11, 117, 122–125, 127, 132–134,
    196, 197

B

Baudrillard, 230
Bauman, 55
Berardi, 236
Blinkers, 68, 78
Body, 7, 43, 54, 79, 89, 92, 98, 100, 103,
    105–108, 135, 136, 176, 183, 187, 200,
    216–218, 229, 233, 238, 239, 241
Bradley, 9, 10, 13, 227, 228
Brazil, 1, 86, 120
Buddhism, 73
Burqa, 132

C

Capitalism, 2–4, 6, 7, 9–13, 21, 22, 24, 68, 75,
    83, 84, 86, 94, 97–102, 104, 112,
    117–123, 152, 154, 159, 160, 163,
    166–169, 198, 215, 218, 219, 221, 223,
    227, 229, 230, 235, 236, 241, 242
Chaosmosis, 22, 33, 37, 44, 84, 89, 92–94,
    202, 238
Chiapas, 11, 149–154, 164, 166
Childhood, 10, 12, 13, 83, 84, 86, 93, 98, 109,
    112, 175–177, 182–184, 188, 190
China, 13, 35, 227, 228, 231, 232, 234, 235
Coefficient, 22, 26, 78, 237
Cole, 2, 4, 11, 13, 33, 48
Communist, 89
Community, 2, 5, 11, 34, 35, 39, 54, 70, 85, 87,
    103, 131, 134, 136, 142, 150, 152, 153,
    155–159, 162, 164, 165, 167, 182, 185,
    212, 231, 235, 240
Computerization, 41
Control, 9, 19, 22–24, 27, 28, 33, 44, 54, 57,
    85, 99, 102–105, 108, 111, 118, 122,
    123, 125, 150, 155, 159, 160, 162, 168,
    178, 179, 185, 196, 197, 202, 213, 218,
    220, 222, 223, 236, 238, 241
Corporate, 20–22, 28, 52, 54, 91, 98, 151, 155,
    196, 197
Cosmos, 76, 86, 183, 236
Counselling, 12, 13, 211–213, 215–218, 221,
    223
Cyborg, 182

© Springer Nature Singapore Pte Ltd. 2018
D. R. Cole and J. P. N. Bradley (eds.), *Principles of Transversality in Globalization
and Education*, https://doi.org/10.1007/978-981-13-0583-2

D
Daoism, 73
Database, 200
Deleuze, 1, 3, 7, 9, 22, 24, 28, 33, 47–53, 56,
        57, 59, 60, 68, 70, 72, 74, 75, 77, 84, 87,
        89, 90, 94, 98–101, 105–109, 120, 121,
        123, 128, 132, 135, 142, 151, 152, 154,
        156, 158–160, 167, 180, 183, 197–201,
        206, 212, 216, 218, 219, 229, 230, 236,
        238–240
Deligny, 87
Derrida, 78, 152, 156
Desire, 11, 50, 58, 70, 78, 93, 99, 103, 104,
        107, 108, 117, 120, 121, 123–127, 138,
        143, 166, 169, 177, 190, 199, 202, 212,
        213, 215, 219, 220, 223, 240, 241
Deterritorialization, 21, 41, 77, 78, 88, 154,
        234, 239
Dialectic, 103
Digital, 6, 12, 13, 32, 55, 118, 123, 124, 126,
        127, 143, 195, 196, 198–200, 202,
        205–207
Douyu, 231

E
Ecology, 7, 34, 77, 79, 80, 87, 89, 110, 127,
        151, 156, 163, 166, 181, 188, 227,
        229–231, 233, 234, 236, 237, 241
Ecosophy, 22, 37, 45, 70, 74, 79, 80, 85, 149,
        151, 156, 157, 163–166, 234, 236
Education, 1–6, 8–14, 21, 22, 24, 25, 28, 34,
        47–60, 67, 68, 71, 75, 78, 80, 83–85,
        87–94, 97, 98, 100–103, 112, 117,
        120–128, 132–135, 144, 145, 150, 151,
        154, 155, 157, 158, 160, 163–167, 170,
        175–177, 183, 188, 190, 197, 200, 204,
        211–213, 215, 216, 218, 221, 223
E-learning, 13, 123, 124, 205
English, 6, 51, 53, 91, 141, 145, 160, 176, 228,
        231, 240
Excellence, 47, 48, 51, 53, 54, 57, 60, 71, 151
Existential, 41, 70, 80, 84, 92, 121, 161, 166,
        198, 200, 201, 203, 204, 213, 227, 228,
        231–235, 238, 240

F
Facebook, 20, 121, 196, 215, 232, 234
Feminism, 12, 91, 180, 181
Folktales, 154
Foucault, 19, 23, 25, 71, 74, 75, 100, 104, 105,
        151, 155, 167, 212, 218
Freinet, 5, 20, 84, 86, 87, 120
Freud, 48, 99, 199, 217

G
Gan, 10, 83, 85, 95
Genosko, 134, 157, 229, 237, 238
Geophilosophy, 67–70, 73–78
Glissant, 71–73
Globalization, 1–12, 53, 68–70, 74–76, 78, 80,
        100, 117–120, 124–127, 150, 154, 164,
        177, 211, 214, 235, 236
Google, 20
Grundrisse, 99
Guattari, 1–13, 19–27, 32, 33, 37, 41, 44,
        47–49, 57, 58, 60, 68–70, 72, 74, 75,
        77–80, 83–94, 97–103, 106, 109, 112,
        117–121, 123, 127, 128, 131, 132, 134,
        135, 149, 151, 152, 154, 156, 158–160,
        162–168, 175, 176, 178, 180, 183, 184,
        188, 195, 196, 198–205, 211–213, 216,
        219, 227–230, 234–239, 241

H
Habermas, 136
Haraway, 110, 181–184, 190
Hardt, 98, 103, 104, 166, 216
Hegel, 71
Helsinki, 176, 177, 179, 180, 186, 188, 190
Heterogenesis, 37, 44, 166
Hiphop, 168
Holocene, 92
Homelessness, 163, 241
Husserl, 48

I
Illiteracy, 141
Ingkee, 231
Interbeing, 72–74, 77, 79, 231, 233, 239
International, 6, 11, 38, 39, 91, 117, 122, 123,
        127, 128, 132, 154, 167
Iran, 11, 117–122, 124–128
IWC, 4, 6, 75, 118, 166, 168, 227, 241

J
Jameson, 118, 166
Japan, 1, 13, 74, 84, 85, 91, 230, 235
Jung, 10, 69–74, 77, 79, 137, 217

K
Kafka, 87
Kindergarten, 158, 183
Kress, 6

L
La Borde, 5, 9, 20, 23, 27, 84, 87, 90–92, 120,
        134, 203, 204

Lacan, 99, 101, 121, 199
Latour, 5
Lazzarato, 56, 57, 87
Live streaming, 227–240
Lyotard, 240

M

Machinic, 5, 7, 13, 56, 73, 79, 84–86, 91–93,
    99, 121, 124, 199, 200, 202, 203, 227,
    234, 236, 237, 239, 241
Marazzi, 3
Marcos, 150, 151, 153–155, 157, 163, 164,
    167, 168
Marxism, 152, 154
Masny, 21, 128
Mayans, 11, 150, 152–155
Mechanosphere, 49, 163, 238
Metaphysics, 7, 52, 89, 236
Mexico, 1, 11, 149–152, 155, 157, 164, 168,
    229
Micropolitics, 166
Microsoft, 20
Minoritarian, 159, 160
Mondialization, 69, 76
Mundia, 77, 227, 231
Murals, 11, 149–154, 156–166, 168

N

Nancy, 76, 240
Negri, 98, 100, 103–105, 166, 216
Neoliberal, 10–13, 22, 32, 42, 45, 59, 77, 97,
    98, 101, 104, 106, 112, 149–152, 154,
    164, 167, 168, 185, 211, 212, 220, 221
Neoliberalism, 10, 21, 150, 154, 163, 168, 214,
    236
Nietzsche, 230
Nomadism, 138
Normapathy, 93
Norway, 188

O

Oedipus, 120, 121, 230, 238
Online, 11–13, 55, 101, 111, 126, 195–198,
    200–203, 205, 207, 233
Oslo, 188
Oury, 5, 20, 84, 85, 91, 93, 120
Outcomes, 9, 19, 20, 28, 51, 52, 56, 135

P

Pharmacology, 216
Phenomenology, 10, 68, 70, 73, 79
Philosophy, 3, 6, 10, 12, 31–34, 36, 37, 40–45,
    48, 50, 52, 59, 67–74, 77–79, 83, 87,
    151–154, 161, 164, 188, 214, 234, 239,
    241
Photograph, 143
Plastic, 138
Poetry, 10, 85, 86, 89, 91, 152, 177, 218
Posthuman, 32
Postmodernism, 229
Poststructural, 12, 151
Proust, 49, 50, 58, 87, 201
Psychoanalysis, 48, 57, 89, 92, 98, 117, 118,
    120, 121, 237
Psychology, 84, 87, 216, 218, 223
Psychotherapy, 219

Q

Quadrillage, 23–25
Qualitative, 159

R

Race, 68, 197, 227
Rate my professors, 195–198, 201, 203, 205
Reich, 216
Resingularization, 44, 78, 235, 241
Rhizomatic, 32, 72, 73, 78, 154, 166, 233

S

Sartre, 48, 68, 73, 90, 99
Scapegoating, 221
Schizoanalysis, 12, 13, 69, 70, 75, 77, 78, 90,
    92, 120, 198, 199, 211, 213, 223, 240,
    241
Schizophrenic, 84, 230, 238
Semetsky, 142
Semio, 84, 229, 236, 241
Semio-capitalism, 84, 229, 236, 241
Semiotics, 5–7, 84, 190, 201, 235, 238, 239
Sensation, 33, 93
Sexuality, 121, 197
Shamanistic, 92, 93
Situationist, 38, 39
SOAS, 67–75, 77–80
Social, 1–8, 10, 20–24, 26–28, 31, 35, 42, 44,
    47–49, 51, 53, 56, 57, 69, 70, 75, 77, 79,
    80, 85, 88–90, 95, 98–104, 108, 109,
    112, 118–122, 125, 126, 132–134, 138,
    149, 150, 156, 158, 163, 164, 166, 167,
    176, 180, 181, 185, 188, 197, 199, 200,
    202, 205, 211–213, 215–221, 227, 230,
    233, 235–238, 241
Speciesism, 71
Spinoza, 7, 37, 52, 98, 105–108, 112
Stiegler, 80
Streaming, 13, 227–240, 242
Stream queen, 232

Stupidity, 80, 91, 93–95, 153
Subjectification, 21, 41, 100–106, 109, 112,
    156, 195, 199, 203, 207, 208, 228, 241
Subjectivity, 4, 13, 21, 26, 44, 48, 78, 79, 87,
    88, 92–94, 100, 101, 104, 106, 107,
    120, 123, 127, 135, 136, 154, 156, 161,
    164, 166, 168, 195, 198, 200, 201, 203,
    211, 213, 216, 217, 221, 223, 227, 228,
    236, 238, 240, 241
Supercomplexity, 52
Superdiversity, 51
Sydney, 11, 122, 131, 133, 134, 141, 144
Syria, 139, 157, 188

T
Tanigawa, 10, 83, 85, 86, 89–94
Tarde, 5
Tehran, 130
Television, 94, 163, 202, 203
Texas, 130
Textbook, 124, 196, 201, 203
Tokyo, 228, 229, 231, 233, 238, 239
Transdisciplinarity, 21, 241
Transversality, 1–5, 7–13, 19–23, 25–28, 33,
    34, 40, 44, 47–53, 57, 58, 60, 67–80, 85,
    88, 97–99, 101–104, 108, 109, 112,
    117–128, 131, 133–135, 145, 154, 157,
    164, 175–178, 180, 190, 198, 204, 211,
    234, 236–238, 241

U
Unconscious, 2, 6, 10, 13, 69, 70, 75, 78,
    85–87, 92, 98–102, 106–109, 112, 118,
    121, 125–128, 135, 137, 145, 211–213,
    215–217, 223, 240
Undergraduate, 34, 144, 207

University, 1, 8, 9, 12, 13, 20–23, 25–28,
    31–34, 36, 37, 39–45, 52–54, 56, 67,
    70, 77, 78, 123, 125, 133, 137, 144, 186,
    190, 196, 197, 202, 205, 207, 231
Utopia, 69, 191, 235

V
Virilio, 228, 235, 240
Virtual, 23, 37, 41, 50, 78, 87, 89, 91, 100,
    199, 204, 227, 231–238, 240, 241

W
Waterhouse, 12
Whiteboard, 124, 179
World, 2, 4–6, 8, 13, 20, 28, 32, 33, 40, 43,
    50–54, 57–59, 68–72, 74–80, 83, 84,
    92, 93, 102, 105, 108, 110, 112,
    118–122, 126, 127, 132, 150, 153, 155,
    161–163, 166–169, 178–185, 187, 197,
    200, 202, 203, 217, 220, 221, 223,
    227–229, 231–241
Worldings, 188
Worldlessness, 76
Worldmaking, 75
Worldy, 190

X
Xenophobia, 132, 216

Z
Zapatista, 11, 149–155, 157–160, 162–169
Zerrissenheit, 228
Zhibo, 13, 227, 228, 234, 236, 238
Zigzag, 77